Poetry

D

Poetry

The Ultimate Guide

Richard Bradford

First published 2010 by
PALGRAVE MACMILLAN

Palgrave Macmillan in the UK is an imprint of Macmillan Publishers Limited,
registered in England, company number 785998, of Houndmills, Basingstoke,
Hampshire RG21 6XS.

Palgrave Macmillan in the US is a division of St Martin's Press LLC,
175 Fifth Avenue, New York, NY 10010.

Palgrave Macmillan is the global academic imprint of the above companies
and has companies and representatives throughout the world.

Palgrave® and Macmillan® are registered trademarks in the United States,
the United Kingdom, Europe and other countries

ISBN 978–1–4039–9460–8 hardback
ISBN 978–1–4039–9461–5 paperback

This book is printed on paper suitable for recycling and made from fully
managed and sustained forest sources. Logging, pulping and manufacturing
processes are expected to conform to the environmental regulations of the
country of origin.

A catalogue record for this book is available from the British Library.

A catalog record for this book is available from the Library of Congress.

10 9   8   7   6   5   4   3   2   1
19 18 17 16 15 14 13 12 11 10

Printed and bound in Great Britain by
CPI Antony Rowe, Chippenham and Eastbourne

For
Amy Burns,
Helen Theresa Burns and Gerard Burns

Contents

Acknowledgements   viii
Introduction   **xi**

PART I   WHAT IS POETRY?   **1**
1   The Basics   3
2   A Definition of Poetry: The Double Pattern   25

PART II   HISTORY: THE RENAISSANCE TO POSTMODERNISM   **47**
3   The Renaissance   49
4   The Restoration and the 18th Century   67
5   Romanticism   78
6   Victorian Poetry   92
7   Modernism and After   102

PART III CRITICISM AND CONTEXTS   **123**
8   New Criticism   125
9   Formalism and Structuralism   133
10   The Role of the Reader and Poststructuralism   140
11   History, New Historicism and Cultural Materialism   150
12   Psychoanalysis   158
13   Deconstruction   167
14   Gender   182
15   Nation, Race and Place   204
16   Evaluation   228

Epilogue – Why Do We Write and Read Poetry?   255
Bibliography   262
Index   267

Acknowledgements

I wish to thank the University of Ulster for appointing me as a permanent Research Professor, a position that has allowed me to complete this book alongside work on several other publications. Kate Haines and Felicity Noble of Palgrave Macmillan have been patient and helpful, and Maggie Lythgoe has done scrupulous and intelligent work as a copy-editor.

Without the help of Dr Amy Burns the book could not have been written.

The editor and publishers wish to thank the following for permission to reproduce copyright material:

Aitken Alexander Associates Ltd and John Murray (Publishers) for an extract from 'The Village Inn' © John Betjeman by permission of The Estate of John Betjeman, from *Collected Poems*, by John Betjeman © 1955, 1958, 1962, 1964, 1968, 1970, 1979, 1981, 1982, 2001. Reproduced by permission of John Murray (Publishers); Anvil Press Poetry Ltd for an extract from 'Lambchops' Ally' taken from *Human Rites: Selected Poems 1970–1982* by E.A. Markham. Published by Anvil Press Poetry in 1984; Astra for an extract from her poem 'Coming Out Celibate'; Bloodaxe Books for an extract from 'Against Coupling' by Fleur Adcock, *Poems 1960–2000*, Bloodaxe Books (2000); Carcanet Press Ltd for an extract from 'Sherdi' by Sujata Bhatt, from *Point No Point*, Carcanet (1997); Carcanet Press Ltd for an extract from 'Barnsley and District' by Donald Davie, from *Collected Poems*, Carcanet (1990); Carcanet Press Ltd and New Directions Publishing Corp. for 'This Is Just To Say' by William Carlos Williams, from *The Collected Poems: Volume I, 1909–1939*, copyright ©1938 by New Directions Publishing Corp. Reprinted by permission of New Directions Publishing Corp.; The Estate of Andrew Crozier for an extract from 'Coup de Main' by Andrew Crozier, from *Printed Circuit*, Street Editions, Cambridge (1974), by kind permission of Jean Crozier; David Dabydeen for an extract from his poem 'Slave Song', from *Slave Song*, Dangaroo (1984); Faber and Faber Ltd for an extract from 'The Come-on' from *Selected Poems 1964–1983* by Douglas Dunn, Faber and Faber (1986); Faber and Faber Ltd and Farrar, Straus and Giroux for an extract from 'Broagh' from *Selected Poems 1966–1987* by Seamus Heaney, Faber and Faber (2002), 'Broagh' from *Opened Ground: Selected Poems 1966–1996* by Seamus Heaney. Copyright © 1998 by Seamus Heaney. Reprinted by permission of Farrar, Straus and Giroux, LLC; Faber and Faber Ltd and Farrar, Straus and Giroux for an extract from *Omeros* by Derek Walcott. Copyright © 1990 by Derek Walcott. Reprinted by permission of Farrar, Straus and Giroux, LLC; Faber and Faber Ltd and Farrar, Straus and Giroux and The Society of Authors as the Literary Representative of the Estate of Philip Larkin for extracts from 'An Arundel Tomb', 'As

Bad as a Mile' and 'Mr Bleaney' from *Collected Poems* by Philip Larkin, edited by Anthony Thwaite, Faber and Faber (2003). Copyright © 1988, 2003 by the Estate of Philip Larkin. Reprinted by permission of Farrar, Straus and Giroux, LLC; Farrar, Straus and Giroux for an extract from 'A Country Club Romance' from *In a Green Night* by Derek Walcott. Copyright © 1990 by Derek Walcott. Reprinted by permission of Farrar, Straus and Giroux, LLC; Flinders University, School of Humanities, for an extract from 'In Introduction' by Kamala Das, from Vincent O'Sullivan, Kamala Das and S.C. Harrex (eds) *Kamala Das: A Selection, with Essays on Her Work,* Centre for Research in the New Literatures In English (1986); The Gallery Press for an extract from 'A Disused Shed in Co. Wexford' by Derek Mahon, from *Collected Poems* (1999) by kind permission of the author and The Gallery Press, www.gallerypress.com; David Godwin Associates for extracts from 'A Martian Sends a Postcard Home' and 'Professor Klaeber's Nasty Dream' by Craig Raine, copyright © Craig Raine, 1979, from *A Martian Sends a Postcard Home*, Oxford University Press (1979); Tony Harrison for an extract from his poem *V*, from *Selected Poems*, Penguin (1987) and *Collected Poems*, Penguin (2007); David Higham Associates Ltd and New Directions Publishing Corporation for an extract from 'When, Like a Running Grave' by Dylan Thomas, from *The Poems of Dylan Thomas*, copyright ©1939 by New Directions Publishing Corp. Reprinted by permission of New Directions Publishing Corp. Rosemary Hobsbaum for an extract from 'A Lesson in Love' by Philip Hobsbaum, © Rosemary Hobsbaum, c/o WATCH copyright project, from *Coming Out Fighting*, Pan Macmillan (1969); Linton Kwesi Johnson for extracts from his poems 'One Love', from *Dread Beat and Blood*, Bogle L'Ouverture (1975) and 'Inglan Is a Bitch', from *Tings an Times: Selected Poems*, Bloodaxe Books (1991); Tom Leonard for his poem *Unrelated Incidents No 3*, © Tom Leonard from *Outside the Narrative* (Poems 1965–2009) Etruscan Press/WordPower 2009; Liveright Publishing Corporation and W.W. Norton & Company Ltd for "I(a". Copyright © 1958, 1986, 1991 by the Trustees for the E.E. Cummings Trust, from *Complete Poems: 1904–1962* by E.E. Cummings, edited by George J. Firmage. Used by permission of Liveright Publishing Corporation. "I(a" is reprinted from *Complete Poems 1904–1962*, by E.E. Cummings, edited by George J. Firmage, by permission of W.W. Norton & Company. Copyright © 1991 by the Trustees for the E.E. Cummings Trust and George James Firmage; Mzwakhe Mbuli for an extract from his poem 'Ignorant'; PFD for an extract from 'From Lucy: England a University' by James Berry from *Hot Earth, Cold Earth* (© James Berry, 1995) reproduced by permission of PFD (www.pfd.co.uk); The Random House Group Ltd and United Agents for extracts from 'White Balloon' from *New and Collected Poems* by Dannie Abse, published by Hutchinson. Reprinted by permission of The Random House Group Ltd. Reprinted by permission of United Agents on behalf of Dannie Abse © Dannie Abse 2009; University of California Press and University of Connecticut, literary executor for the Estate of Charles Olson, for an extract from 'Maximus to Gloucester, Letter 27' by Charles Olson, from *The Maximus Poems*, Copyright © 1985, The Regents of the University of California, University of California Press (1985). Works by Charles Olson published during his lifetime are copyright © the Estate of Charles Olson. Used with permission; Wesleyan University Press for Agha Shahid Ali, 'Postcard from Kashmir' from *The Half-Inch Himalayas* © 1987 by Agha Shahid Ali. Reprinted with permission of Wesleyan University Press, www.wesleyan.edu/wespress.

Every effort has been made to trace all the copyright holders, but if any have been inadvertently overlooked the publishers will be pleased to make the necessary arrangements at the first opportunity.

Introduction

The title of this book might seem somewhat presumptuous but its contents justify the claim. It is the first ever single-volume account of English verse to include a comprehensive definition of poetry per se, a detailed history of its various permutations from Shakespeare to the present day, a lengthy survey of 20th- and 21st-century critical approaches to poetry, an introduction to poetry and gender, an examination of how race and nationality inform poetic writing and, finally, a chapter that deals with the elusive, controversial issue of evaluation – in short, how do we distinguish between good, acceptable and abysmal verse?

Part I is concerned primarily with the double pattern, the unique, definitive feature of verse. It opens with Chapter 1 'The Basics', which includes a guide to the various techniques and devices of which poems are comprised, and a brief introductory survey of the predominant critical approaches to verse that will be covered in more detail in Part III. Chapter 2 is a survey of five poems drawn from various periods of post-16th-century literary history. Each differs considerably from the others but all incorporate the factor that is unique to poetry, the double pattern. This chapter is the foundation for the rest of the book: it provides a comprehensive definition of poetry.

The subject of Part II, entitled 'History: The Renaissance to Postmodernism', is self-evident. It comprises Chapters 3–7, which cover the predominant autonomous periods of English poetry since the Renaissance. It documents the ebb and flow of technique, custom and experiment and offers tentative explanations for the major transitions in the history of English verse. The double pattern is shown to be both an index to these permutations and the enduring feature of verse, the factor that transcends change and mutation.

In Part III, Chapters 8–13 tour the different critical schools whose adherents have, since the end of the 19th century, scrutinized the essential characteristics of poetry, examined its relationship with other discourses and questioned its status as an autonomous genre. I have not attempted to present these critical ideas as all-embracing interpretive packages, because to narrow one's perspective to a 'Formalist reading' or 'psychoanalytical interpretation' of a given poem is to favour the theory at the expense of the poem. Poems are unlimited in their range of topics and their means of addressing them and to force such works into a specific analytical framework blinds one to key aspects of their diversity and unpredictability. Instead, I have emphasized the dynamic relationship between given interpretive and theoretical schools and poems that variously indulge or undermine the presuppositions of the former.

Chapters 14 and 15, respectively 'Gender' and 'Nation, Race and Place', involve issues far too protean, indeed divisive, to be treated simply as critical approaches. As a consequence, I have attempted succinct accounts of how critics, poets, theorists and less easily classifiable figures have involved themselves in what amounts to a centuries-old seminar on how poetry reflects and engages with our gender, where we come from and our cultural, national and racial legacies.

Chapter 16, 'Evaluation', is by its nature the most controversial. It brings together issues and questions raised in all previous chapters and concentrates on something that everyone who has ever read a poem experiences but which is rarely if ever addressed in academia and is taken for granted by those who review poetry in the press: by what criteria do we judge the quality of a poem and the competence of a poet?

The subtitle to the Epilogue is self-explanatory. Poetry is as old as recorded language, and it endures: why? My answer is relatively brief and it is designed to point up the continuities and recurring curiosities of the rest of this book. Poetry is essentially about language and since language makes us what we are, the poem will last as long as us.

PART I

WHAT IS POETRY?

1

The Basics

Poetry is unlimited in its range of subjects. The speaker of the poem can be old, young, male, female, mad, bad or mysteriously unidentifiable. The poem can be addressed to a fictive acquaintance, a friend, an enemy, a lover, a wife, a husband, God, or you, the reader. It can use all types of diction and idiom: local dialect, neo-Latinate syntax, formal or informal diction, grammatical, ungrammatical, hesitant or purposive modes of speech. Poetry can be, say or involve anything, but it will always be informed and influenced by another factor, the factor that identifies it as poetry.

John Donne's 'The Flea' involves its male speaker in an attempt to persuade his female listener that sex with him will not be as disagreeable or shameful as she thinks. What is the difference between this and the kind of exchange that we might overhear in the pub? The intention, content and context of the public house seducer might be the same as those of Donne's speaker; they might even share a talent for elaborate and persuasive metaphor and a taste for informal, familiar idioms. It is unlikely, however, that the man in the pub will have marshalled his language into an iambic pattern and gathered his sentences into three identical and incredibly complex stanzas. This is the double pattern. At one level we treat a poem much as we would any other unit of language; we read through the words to attain a basic sense of their meaning, collecting as we go evidence on the context and intention of the statement and on its writer or speaker. The poem, however, employs devices and effects that hinder and complicate this process.

In all non-poetic genres and classes of language, priority is placed upon the delivery of the message, but, uniquely, poetry is concerned as much with the processes and material of language as it is with its use as an efficient medium of exchange. Some might argue that fiction too is preoccupied with the peculiarities and arbitrariness of language, given that every novel is premised upon the creation of a world or state of mind that are falsifications of reality. But while novels do not pretend that the events they record or individuals they represent are aesthetic – as might a historical survey or a biography – they are nonetheless predatory in their borrowings from the fabric of linguistic discourses that make up the world. Letters in fiction, conversations between characters, events and scenes reported by narrators have a great deal in common with their counterparts outside the novel. The novelist trims and manipulates according to the broader demands of their work, but success is judged by the extent to which the finished product is believable and compelling. Even with such experimental devices as James Joyce's stream of consciousness in *Ulysses*, mimesis is still the governing principle. Joyce was attempting for the first time to offer a linguistic representation of our prelinguistic condition – hence his general abandonment of punctuation and coherent syntactic structure; he was not writing about language, but using language as a means of representation.

Poems, from the seemingly transparent to the most dense, elliptical or impenetrable, are governed by a preoccupation both with what language can do and what language is. Read any poem. Choose one at random from a compendious anthology that covers everything from Chaucer to Concrete Poetry and even if the piece that appears before you on the page seems, at least at first, incomprehensible, you will within a few lines detect a hint of companionability. The words might not seem to make a great deal of sense but they are nevertheless words, which you will recognize as part of your waking routine, from reading the newspaper, saying hello to the dog, or paying due allegiance to the deity of your choice. You could, in the poem, be puzzled by the manner in which these units of meaning are put together but they are in themselves familiar. This is your first encounter with the double pattern. There is a sense of recognition, of becoming attuned to language as you customarily encounter it, as something that makes sense, but there is also an awareness that perversely, deliberately the poet is not quite allowing language to make sense. Medbh McGuckian begins stanza two of 'Venus and the Rain' with

> On one occasion, I rang like a bell
> For a whole month, promising the torn edges
> The birth of a new ocean (as all of us
> Who have hollow bodies tend to do at times): ...

As individual units of syntax, the phrases and subclauses are comprehensible enough but when we attempt to place a frame around their general meaning, paraphrase them, we become confused. What 'occasion' might this be, we wonder, and how can anyone ring 'like a bell' let alone do so 'For a whole month'? Can a 'new ocean' (what became of the old one?) be promised to 'torn edges'? And why is she dividing up her sentence into lines, units which seem arbitrarily related to the already perplexing cascade of nuances. We can at a single reading of the poem steal the impression of a shifting peripheral presence which will rise to the surface, slip away or be displaced by other seemingly incongruous images. In doing so we are approaching the poem as we might any other linguistic text or statement, in the expectation that it will discharge a coherent unit of meaning, a message. Poems, being assembled from the same units of language as everything else, invite us to do this yet at the same time they thwart our expectations. They do so by creating an interplay between words and phrases that no longer pays adherence to the general rules of clarity and coherence. The words of a poem operate at one level according to an internalized fabric of interactions: some, such as the stanza, rhyme, sound pattern and regular metre, are traditional though entirely arbitrary features of verse, while others testify to a particular poet's decision to detach their poem unilaterally from the rules of normal discourse. At another level, we are invited, often feel obliged, to make sense of the poem to bring it into line with all other texts and statements whose founding principle is clarity and transparency. It is the tension between these two spheres of structure and meaning – the arbitrary network of devices and linguistic interactions that grant the poem a sense of autonomy, and the poem's link with the world of non-poetic discourses, secured by their shared raw material, language – that constitutes the double pattern. We will examine the double pattern in detail in Chapter 2, but for the time being let us concentrate on the nature of these uniquely poetic features.

Metre and rhyme indicate a stylistic difference between traditional poetry and other forms of language. Even those poets who reject rhyme and metre retain in free verse the unit that is the distinctive feature of poems: the poetic line. But the deployment and recognition of poetic form complicates rather than answers the question of why poetry is different. Surely the use of poetic form cannot fully explain the character of a genre as old as language, used in all languages and commanding, among many, a neo-religious respect?

Metre, rhyme and the use of the poetic line involve the organization of the material of language – sound, emphasis, rhythm – in a way that is impractical and arbitrary. In conversation, rhyme is a peculiarity, even an embarrassment; when we write letters to the local council, it is unlikely that we will divide up our language into free verse lines. The conventions and habits that prompt us to avoid such usages are based upon the precondition that ordinary language is concerned with the clear and efficient delivery of a message. Rhyme and the free verse line will interfere with the delivery of the message and draw attention to the medium through which it is delivered. Language becomes self-referential and the double pattern is brought into operation. Metre, rhyme and free verse are the most obvious cases of poetic self-reference. There are many others.

Craig Raine begins the final stanza of 'An Enquiry into Two Inches of Ivory' with

> Day begins.
> The milkman delivers
> penguins with their chinking atonal fuss.

The visual and acoustic similarity between the white-bodied objects being gathered into a cosy group by the milkman and our memories, probably from television, of penguins huddling together and emitting random 'atonal' noises may not previously have occurred to us. Raine uses language to create an interface between prelinguistic images and ideas that have no logical or rational connection. The relations between the images and references of the poem effectively overrule our habitual modes of thinking. Such metaphoric uses are by no means forbidden in ordinary language. You could indeed point out to your neighbour that the milk bottles remind you of penguins, but, assuming that neither of you had recently consumed anything illegal, the conversation and your respective frames of reference would soon return to the prevailing context of the milk bottles as part of your familiar daily fabric of events and objects. Poems, rather than defer to the terms and conditions of the familiar world, tend to create their own worlds, in which connections and associations are formed in the mind of the poet. Raine begins his poem with the image of a vacuum cleaner, which

> grazes
> over the carpet, lowing,
> its udder a swollen wobble ...

Light switches become barn owls, light bulbs 'electric pears', wall phones wear spectacles and clothes 'queue up' in the wardrobe. The poem appropriates ordinary and familiar images and creates relationships between them that are disorderly, subversive of our conventional expectations of how language mediates the world.

Not all verse is as voraciously, self-consciously metaphorical as Raine's, but the creation of a world with its own internalized relations, which echo but do not replicate the world outside the text, is an endemic feature of poetry.

We have so far considered two characteristics of poetry: poetic form and metaphor. What they have in common is the ability to focus upon the nature and power of language itself rather than its practical, utilitarian function. Metre and sound pattern obstruct and complicate the production of meaning by foregrounding the material of language at the expense of transparency and clarity. Metaphor involves language in the appropriation and juxtaposition of ideas and objects that in the rational world language would classify, catalogue and distinguish. Poetry reverses the pragmatic, functional role of language. Language is generally used to refer to, specify, indicate, mediate or articulate things, feelings and ideas. Poetry draws words and their meanings into concentrated spheres where their expected distinctions and relationships will be variously unsettled, complicated or re-examined: the double pattern.

This definition of poetry can be tested against the two other literary genres that use language to create their own self-referring worlds: the novel and drama. The best way to distinguish between poetry, the novel and drama is to compare a localized extract of the text with its entirety.

It is possible to locate sections of novels and plays which, in their own right, involve no obvious literary features. Sections of first- and third-person narrative could easily have come from a biography, an autobiography or a journal. Passages where narrative is integrated with dialogue or reported speech could belong to a magazine article on an evening in the local pub. Passages of dialogue from modern plays could have been recorded verbatim in a real front room, on a bus, in a courtroom.

The literariness of such passages, their difference from the real world, becomes apparent only when we recognize that their integration with the broader structural patterns of the text outweighs their correspondences with the world outside the text. As we read on we might find that the apparently objective third-person narrator has an exclusive and comprehensive knowledge of the thoughts and activities of the main characters that in non-fiction would be implausible or impossible; or that the realistic dialogue between two characters actually functions as part of the patently unreal structure of a dramatic text which organizes, rather than reflects, the spatial and temporal actions of the characters.

Choose an extract from a poem and you will find that literariness, its patent and self-conscious difference from non-poetic discourse, will be far more localized and concentrated. The most obvious instance of this will be the interference of poetic form – from dense sound patterns to the line endings of free verse – in the routine production of meaning. Poems, such as John Milton's *Paradise Lost* or Alexander Pope's *The Rape of the Lock*, can, like novels and plays, involve dialogue, extended narratives and narrators. But in poems each of these broader structural elements is informed by localized poetic devices. Milton's narrative account, the speeches and dialogic exchanges of God, Satan, Adam and Eve are pervaded by the metrical and syntactic conventions of blank verse. Pope's account, the narrative of the card game and Belinda's utterances are organized by the tight symmetry of the heroic couplet. Shorter lyric poems such as Keats's odes, Shakespeare's sonnets or the two-line economies of the modern Imagists might seem to have little in common with narrative verse, but all these subgenres share a unifying characteristic: poetic language will constantly unsettle or intensify its familiar non-poetic function and form.

In what follows I will offer a more detailed account of the devices employed by poems to create their own networks of form and meaning – key features of the intrinsically poetic aspect of the double pattern.

Prosody and poetic form

The poetic line draws upon the same linguistic raw material as the sentence but deploys and uses this in a different way. Our awareness of the grammatical rules that govern the way words are formed into larger units of meaning is based upon our ability to recognize the difference between individual words. Words are made up of sound and stress, identified respectively by the phoneme and the syllable. The function of sound and stress in non-poetic language is practical and utilitarian: before we understand the operative relations between nouns, verbs, adjectives and connectives, we need to be able to relate the sound and structure of a word to its meaning.

Traditional poetry uses stress and sound not only as markers and indicators of meaning but also as a way of measuring and foregrounding the principal structural characteristic of the poem, the line. In most poems written before the 20th century, the line is constructed from a combination of two or more of the following elements:

1 A specified and predictable number of *syllables*: the most commonly used example of this is the 10-syllable line, the pentameter.
2 A *metrical pattern* consisting of the relation between the stress or emphasis of adjacent syllables: the most frequently used metrical pattern in English involves the iambic foot, where an emphatic syllable follows a less emphatic one, with occasional variations, or 'stress reversals'.
3 *Rhyme:* the repetition of the phonemic sound of a single syllable at the end of a line.
4 *Assonance and alliteration*: the repetition of clusters of similar vowel or consonant sounds within individual lines and across sequences of lines.

The persistent and predictable deployment of two or more of these features is what allows us to recognize the traditional line as an organizing feature of most pre-20th-century poems.

Metre

The 'iambic pentameter', consisting of 10 syllables, with the even syllables stressed more emphatically than the odd, is the most frequently used line in English poetry. It is the governing principle of Shakespeare's blank verse; of non-dramatic blank verse poems, including Milton's *Paradise Lost* and William Wordsworth's *The Prelude*; and of the heroic couplet, the structural centrepiece of most of the poems of John Dryden and Pope.

A shorter version is the octosyllabic line or 'tetrameter', examples of which can be found in many of the couplet poems of Jonathan Swift, in Matthew Arnold's 'Stanzas from the Grade Chartreuse', and in Alfred Tennyson's *In Memoriam*. The iambic pentameter consists of five metrical feet, while the tetrameter has four. The following are examples of these, with ´ indicating the most emphatic and ¯ indicating the less emphatic syllables:

> Iambic pentameter (from Milton's *Paradise Lost*):
> Sūch pleás | ūre tóok | thē Sérp | ēnt tó | bēhóld

> Iambic tetrameter (from Swift's 'Cassinus and Peter'):
> Twō cóll | ēge Sóphs | ōf Cámb | rīdge grówth

These are examples of stress syllabic metre, in which a consistent balance is maintained between the number of syllables of a line and its stress pattern. Alternative stress syllabic lines include seven-syllable tetrameters (as in William Blake's 'The Tyger'), which comprise three iambic feet and a single stressed syllable:

Tý´ | gēr Tý´ | gēr, búr | nīng bŕight.

Lines such as this, with an odd number of syllables, can also be scanned as trochaic (that is, stress/unstress: ´ ¯):

Tý´gēr | Tý´gēr | búrnīng | bŕight.

The trochaic foot more frequently features as a substitute or variation in a line of iambic feet. This occurs in the first foot of Shakespeare's line:

Nów īs | thē wín | tēr óf | oūr dís | cōntént

Stress syllabic lines consisting of three-syllable feet are generally associated with comic poetry and song. The three-syllable foot, the 'anapaest', creates a rhythmic pattern that deviates from the modulation of ordinary speech far more than its two-syllable counterpart; as in Goldsmith's couplet, consisting of anapaestic (¯ ¯ ´) feet:

Hēre líes | Dāvīd Gár | rīck, dēscríbe | hím whō cán
Añ abrīdǵe | mēnt ōf áll | thāt īs pleás | ānt īn mán.

Some poems vary the syllabic length of a line, while maintaining the same number of emphatic or stressed syllables in each. This is called 'pure stress metre'. An early example of pure stress metre is Samuel Taylor Coleridge's 'Christabel' and a more recent one occurs in T.S. Eliot's *Ash Wednesday*, in which the differing length of each line is anchored to a repeated pattern of two major stresses:

Lády of sílences
Cálm and distreśsed
Tórn and most whóle
Róse of mémory

The internal structure of the poetic line is only one element of its function as the organizing principle of poetry.

Rhyme and the stanza

Rhyme binds lines together into larger structural units. The smallest of these is the couplet, rhyming aa bb cc (for example the majority of poems by Dryden, Pope and Swift). More complex rhyme schemes enable the poet to create stanzas, the simplest of these being the quatrain, rhyming a b a b. (The octosyllabic quatrain is used by Donne in 'The Ecstasy' and its pentameter version in Thomas Gray's 'Elegy Written in a Country Churchyard'.)

The stanza can play a number of roles in the broader structure of the poem. Narrative poems, which tell a story, often use the stanza as a way of emphasizing a particular event or observation while tying this into the broader narrative (for example Spenser's *The Faerie Queene*, Keats's *The Eve of St. Agnes* and Byron's *Don Juan*). In *In Memoriam*, Tennyson uses the so-called 'envelope stanza' (a b b a). This couplet within a couplet provides a formal counterpoint to the tragic or emotional focus of each stanza.

Shorter lyric poems, which focus upon a particular sensation, feeling or single event, often use the stanza as a counterpoint to improvisation and spontaneity. Donne's 'The Relic' consists of three very complicated stanzas:

	When my grave is broke up again	a
8 syllables	Some second guest to entertain,	a
	(For graves have learned that women-head	b
	To be to more than one a bed)	b
6 syllables	{And he that digs it, spies	c
10 syllables	{A bracelet of bright hair about the bone,	d
6 syllables	{Will he not let 'us alone,	d
	And think that there a loving couple lies,	c
10 syllables	Who thought that this device might be some way	e
	To make their souls, at the last busy day,	e
	Meet at this grave, and make a little stay?	e

On the one hand, the complex permutations of line length and rhyme scheme create the impression of flexibility and improvisation, as if the metrical structure of the poem is responding to and following the varied emphases of speech. But this stanzaic structure is repeated, with admirable precision, three times; and as we read the poem in its entirety, we find that the flexibility of the syntax is matched by the insistent inflexibility of the stanza.

The sonnet

The sonnet resembles the stanza in that it consists of an integrated unit of metre and rhyme: the Shakespearian sonnet consists of three iambic pentameter quatrains followed by an iambic pentameter couplet, while its Petrarchan counterpart rhymes abba abba cdc dcd. It differs from the stanza in that the sonnet is a complete poem. Most sonnets will emphasize a particular event or theme and tie this into the symmetries, repetitions and parallels of its metrical and rhyming structure.

The ode

The most flexible and variable stanzaic forms will be found in the ode. Wordsworth's 'Ode on Intimations of Immortality' consists of eleven sections. Each of these involves a pattern of metre and rhyme just as complex and varied as Donne's stanza in 'The Relic', except that in the Immortality Ode the same pattern is never repeated. The open, flexible structure of the ode is well suited to its use, particularly by the Romantic poets, as a medium for personal reflection; it rarely tells a particular story, and it eschews logical and systematic argument in favour of an apparently random sequence of questions, hypotheses and comparisons.

Blank verse

A form that offers a similar degree of freedom from formal regularity is blank verse, consisting of unrhymed iambic pentameters. Prior to Milton's *Paradise Lost* (1667), blank verse was regarded a mixture of poetry and prose. It was thought appropriate only for drama, in which language could be recognizably poetic (that is, metrical) while maintaining realistic elements of dialogue and ordinary speech (without rhyme). *Paradise Lost* offered blank verse as an alternative to the use of the stanza or the couplet in longer narrative or descriptive poems.

Milton's blank verse creates a subtle tension between the iambic pattern of each line and the broader flow across lines of descriptive or impassioned speech. A similar balance between discursive or reflective language and the metrical undertow of the blank verse line will be found in the 18th-century tradition of landscape poems (for example Thomson's *The Seasons* and Cowper's *The Task*) and in Wordworth's 'Tintern Abbey' and *The Prelude*. The most flexible examples of blank verse, where it becomes difficult to distinguish between prose rhythm and metre, can be found in the poems of Robert Browning, particularly *Ring and the Book*:

> So
> Did I stand question and make answer, still
> With the same result of smiling disbelief,
> Polite impossibility of faith.

Free verse

Before the 20th century, poems that involved neither rhyme nor the metrical pattern of blank verse were rare. Smart's *Jubilate Agno* and Whitman's *Leaves of Grass* replaced traditional metre with patterns redolent of biblical phrasing and intonation, and Blake in his later visionary poems (1789–1815) devised a very individual form of free verse. It was not until the 20th century that free verse became an established part of the formal repertoire of English poetry.

Free verse (from the French *vers libre*) is only free in the sense that it does not conform to traditional patterns of metre and rhyme (see T.S. Eliot's 1917 essay 'Reflections on "Verse Libre"'). The poetic line is maintained as a structural counterpoint to syntax, but is not definable in abstract metrical terms.

Free verse can be divided into three basic categories:

1 Poetry that continues and extends the least restrictive elements of traditional poetry, particularly those of the ode and blank verse. T.S. Eliot's 'The Love Song of J. Alfred Prufrock' is a monologue with an unpredictable rhyme scheme and a rhythmic structure that invokes traditional metre but refuses to maintain a regular beat or pattern. A similar effect is achieved in Auden's 'Musée des Beaux Arts'. In *The Four Quartets*, Eliot often uses an unrhymed form that resembles blank verse but which frequently deviates from a regular iambic pattern (see, for example, Part I of 'Little Gidding').

2 Poems in which the line structure reflects the apparent spontaneity of ordinary speech. Line divisions will often be used as an imitation of the process through which we transform thoughts, impressions and experiences into language. Easthope (1983) calls this form 'intonational metre'. A typical example of this is Lawrence's 'Snake':

> A snake came to my water trough
> On a hot, hot day, and I in pyjamas for the heat,
> To drink there.

3 Poems in which the unmetrical line variously obstructs, deviates from or interferes with the movement of syntax. In Pound's 'In a Station of the Metro', the two lines function as an alternative to the continuities of grammar:

> The apparition of these faces in the crowd;
> Petals on a wet, black bough.

The space between the lines could be filled by a variety of imagined connecting phrases: 'are like', 'are unlike', 'remind me of', 'are as lonely as'. Individual lines offer specific images or impressions: the reader makes connections between them.

In William Carlos Williams' 'Spring and All', the line structure orchestrates the syntax and creates a complex network of hesitations and progressions (examples can be found in Bradford, 1994). The most extreme example of how the free verse line can appropriate and disrupt the structural functions of syntax will be found in the poems of E.E. Cummings, where the linear movement of language is effectively broken down into visual units.

Recognizing and naming the formal structures of poetry raises more complex questions. Most specifically: how do we account for the ways in which verse form variously creates and distorts meaning? We can note how an iambic pentameter organizes language, but how does it alter our understanding of it? Does the fact that words rhyme indicate some special relationship between their meanings? Pope begins his 'Epistle to Dr. Arbuthnot' with the couplet:

Shut, shut the door good John, fatigued I said
Tye up the knocker, say I'm sick I'm dead!

The semantic contrast between 'said' (living speech) and 'dead' (terminal silence) is itself underpinned by the metrical symmetry of the two lines. This is a case of poetic form supporting the wit and irony of its words. Less certain relationships between form and meaning occur in the dense sound patterns of Gerard Manley Hopkins' and Dylan Thomas's verse: to note and explain every interface between form and meaning in these would require a computer, not a human reader. We will consider examples of how to deal with poetic form in Chapter 2, but for the moment consider a conundrum. Criticizing poetry, either in an essay or in conversation, involves a form of translation. We discuss poems in the way we discuss everything else. Our language is prosaic: we refer methodically to items, facts, devices, effects, apparent meanings. Criticism is normative; it reduces the oddities of poetic structure to the pragmatics of ordinary discourse. The conundrum is: when we 'make sense' of a poem, do we dispossess it of its principal intention – to oblige us to re-examine the means by which we make sense?

Metaphor

Metaphor is derived from the Greek verb 'to carry over'. When words are used metaphorically, one field of reference is carried over or transferred into another. Wordsworth (in 'Resolution and Independence') states that 'The sky rejoices in the morning's birth'. He carries over two very human attributes to the non-human phenomena of the sky and the morning: the ability to rejoice and to give birth. Richards (1936) devised a formula that enables us to specify the process of carrying over. The 'tenor' of the metaphor is its principal subject, the topic addressed: in Wordsworth's line the activities of rejoicing and giving birth. The 'vehicle' is the anologue carried over to the subject from a different frame of reference: in Wordsworth's line the activities of rejoicing and giving birth.

Metaphor is often referred to as a poetic device but it is not exclusive to poetry. Metaphors will be found in newspaper articles on economics: 'The war (vehicle) against inflation (tenor)'; in ordinary conversation, 'At yesterday's meeting (tenor) I broke the ice (vehicle)'; in novels, 'He cowered in the shadow (vehicle) of the thought (tenor)' (Joyce's *A Portrait of the Artist as a Young Man*); in advertisements, 'This car is as good on paper (vehicle) as it is on the road (tenor)'.

The principal difference between Wordsworth's metaphor and its non-poetic counterparts is its integration with the iambic pentameter:

Thē ský | rējói | cēs iń | thē mórn | īng's bírth.

We could retain the metaphor and lose the metre: turn it into the kind of unmetrical sentence that might open a short story or a novel:

I watched the sky rejoice in the birth of the morning.

One thing lost is the way in which the pentameter organizes and emphasizes the tenor and vehicle of the metaphor: 'ský | rējói | cēs' and 'mórn | īng's bíṛth.' In order properly to consider differences between poetic and non-poetic uses of metaphor, we should add a third element to tenor and vehicle: the 'ground' of the metaphor. The ground is essentially the context and motivation of the metaphor. For the journalist, the ground of the metaphor is the general topic of economics and inflation and the particular point they are attempting to make about these issues. For the conversationalist, the ground is the awareness, shared with the addressee, of yesterday's meeting and their role in it. For the advertiser, the ground involves the rest of the advertisement, giving details of the make, price and performance of the car, and the general context in which cars are discussed and sold. In non-poetic uses of metaphor, the ground or context stabilizes the relation between tenor and vehicle. The metaphor will involve a self-conscious departure from the orderly relation between the use of language and the prelinguistic world of facts and detail. It would be regarded as bizarre and mildly disturbing if the conversationalist were to allow the original metaphor to dominate the rest of their discourse: 'I sank through the broken ice into the cold water of the boardroom. There we all were: fishes swimming through a dark, hostile world …'.

In poems, however, this relation between ground, tenor and vehicle is often reversed. It is the language of the poem, as much as the reader's a priori knowledge, which creates its perceived situations and context. It constructs its own ground, and metaphor becomes less a departure from contextual terms and conditions and more a device that appropriates and even establishes them. Donne's 'The Ecstasy' begins with the stanza:

> Where, like a pillow on a bed,
> A pregnant bank swelled up, to rest
> The violet's reclining head,
> Sat we two, one another's best;

The tenor is the garden in which 'we two' are situated; the vehicle involves a combination of images denoting intimacy and sexuality: 'pillow', 'bed', 'pregnant', 'swelled up', 'the violet's (flower, denoting female) reclining head'. This opening instance of the carrying over of rural horticultural images into the spheres of human sexuality becomes the predominant theme of the entire poem, underpinning more adventurous speculations on the nature of the soul. Again, the dynamics of contrasting and associating verbal images has unsettled the stabilizing function of ground or context.

Donne is part of the Metaphysical School of poetic writing whose taste for extended metaphor is a principal characteristic of their verse, but the practice of creating tensions and associations between the words and images of the poem at the expense of an external context transcends particular schools, fashions and historical groupings.

In Keats's 'Ode to a Nightingale', the image of the actual bird becomes a springboard for a complex sequence of associations and resonances: song, poetry, immortality, age, youth, death. The sense of there being a particular place and time in which Keats saw the bird and heard its song is gradually replaced by the dynamics of Keats's associative faculties: the relation between the vehicles unsettles the relation between vehicle, tenor and ground.

A classic case of vehicle undermining tenor occurs in T.S. Eliot's 'The Love Song of J. Alfred Prufrock' (lines 15–22). This begins with the tenor (the city fog) being carried over into the vehicle of an unspecified animal which 'rubs it back upon the window-panes', 'rubs its nuzzle on the window-panes' and 'licked its tongue into the corners of the evening'. By the end of the passage, the actual vision of city streets that inspired the comparison has been overtaken by the physical presence of this strange beast, which 'seeing that it was a soft October night, Curled once about the house, and feel asleep'.

Metaphor is the most economical, adventurous and concentrated example of the general principle of 'carrying over'. Samuel Johnson defined metaphor in his *Dictionary of the English Language* (1755) as 'a simile compressed in a word'. Donne's metaphor (from 'The Relic') 'a bracelet of bright hair about the bone' would, as a simile, be something like: 'the brightness of the hair about the bone reminds me of the difference between life and death'. Simile postulates the comparison: X is like Y. Metaphor synthesizes the comparison: X is Y. Metonymy is logical metaphor, in which the comparison is founded upon an actual, verifiable relation between objects or impressions: 'crown' is used instead of 'king', 'queen' or 'royalty'. Allegory involves an extended parallel between a narrative and a subtext that the allegory variously reflects or exaggerates. Edmund Spenser's *The Faerie Queene* is a medieval fantasy with allegorical parallels in the actual world of the Elizabethan court.

Simile, metonymy and allegory establish a balanced relationship between the use of language and conventional perceptions of reality, and occur as frequently in non-poetic discourse as in poetry. Metaphor involves language in an unbalancing of perceptions of reality and is more closely allied to the experimental character of poetry.

Hawkes (1972) provides a brief, accessible guide to metaphor, and Bradford (1997) offers a detailed account of metaphor and other figurative devices.

Syntax, diction and vocabulary

The terms 'poetic diction' and 'poetic syntax' should be treated with caution. Any word, clause, phrase, grammatical habit or locution used in non-poetic language can be used in poetry. But at the same time their presence within the poem will subtly alter their familiar non-poetic function.

The metrical structure of a poem can accommodate the apparent hesitations and spontaneities of ordinary speech, but at the same time fix them as parts of a carefully structured artefact. Consider what happens when syntax crosses the space between two poetic lines, an effect known as 'enjambment'. A classic example of this opens Milton's *Paradise Lost*:

> Of Man's first disobedience, and the fruit
> Of that forbidden tree, whose mortal taste

The implied pause at the line ending might suggest, on Milton's part, a slight moment of indecision: is he thinking of the figurative 'fruit' (the result and consequences) of man's disobedience, or the literal fruit of the act of disobedience? He chooses the latter.

The placing of the word might also be interpreted as the complete opposite of fleeting indecision. The tension between the actuality of the fruit and the uncertain consequences of eating it is a fundamental theme of the poem, and Milton encodes this tension within the form of the poem even before its narrative begins.

In non-poetic language, the progress of syntax can be influenced by a number of external factors: an act or verbal interruption by someone else, the uncertainty of the speaker or the fraught circumstances of the speech act. In poetry, apparent hesitations or disturbances of syntax are a function of the carefully planned, integrated structure of the text.

The ability of poetry to absorb and recontextualize the devices and registers of non-poetic language is evident also in its use of diction, vocabulary and phrasing. The social or local associations of particular words or locutionary habits can be carried into a poem but their familiar context will be transformed by their new structural framework. In Tony Harrison's *V*, the poet converses in a Leeds cemetery with an imagined skinhead whose hobbies include the spraying of graffiti onto gravestones:

> 'Listen cunt!' I said, 'Before you start your jeering
> The reason why I want this in a book
> 's to give ungrateful cunts like you a hearing!'
> *A book, yer stupid cunts not worth a fuck.*

The diction and idiom of both speakers is working class and northern, but this specific, locative resonance is itself contained within a separate language, with its own conventions: each regional idiomatic flourish is confidently, almost elegantly, reconciled to the demands of the iambic pentameter and the quatrain. The realistic crudity of the language is juxtaposed with the controlled irony of Harrison's formal design: the skinhead's real presence is appropriated to the unreal structure of the poem, involving the internal and external rhymes, 'book' and 'fuck'. In a broader context, the language of working-class Leeds is integrated with the same stanzaic structure used by Gray in his 'Elegy Written in a Country Churchyard', in which the poet similarly appropriates the voice of a 'hoary headed swain'. Gray's and Harrison's language and experience are centuries and worlds apart but they are brought into contact by the ahistorical forms and structures of poetry.

This tendency for poetry to represent and at the same time colonize the habits of non-poetic discourse is a paradox that has taxed poets and critics – most famously in Wordsworth's Preface to *Lyrical Ballads*. Wordsworth rails against the stultifying poeticization of ordinary language, of how the conventions and style of 18th-century verse had dispossessed poetry of the 'real language of men'. But while he advocates a new kind of poetic writing, he concedes that poetry must announce its difference in a way that will 'entirely separate the composition from the vulgarity and meanness of ordinary life'. In short, although poetry should be about 'ordinary life', it must by its very nature be separate from it.

D.H. Lawrence's poems in the Nottinghamshire dialect, Robert Burns' and Hugh MacDiarmid's use of Scots idiom, grammar and diction emphasize region and very often class, but no matter where the words come from or what social or political affiliations they carry, they are always appropriated and acted upon by the internal structures of poetry.

Wordsworth's desire to separate poetry from the 'vulgarity and meanness of ordinary life' sounds suspiciously elitist and exclusive, and there is evidence of this in the work of a number of our most celebrated poets. In Part II of *The Waste Land*, Eliot represents the speech patterns and, so he assumes, the concerns of working-class women:

> Now Albert's coming back, make yourself a bit smart,
> He'll want to know what you done with that money he gave you
> To get yourself some teeth. (lines 142–4)

We will be expected to note the difference between this passage and the sophisticated command of metre and multicultural references of the poem's principal voice, Tiresias. With whom would we associate T.S. Eliot? Tiresias or the women?

The sense of poetry as carrying particular social and political allegiances (principally male, white, English, middle class, educated) has prompted acts of stylistic revolution. William Carlos Williams, in the free verse collections of *Spring and All* and *Paterson*, effectively discards those conventions of rhyme and metre that restrict his use of ordinary American phrasing and vocabulary. Linton Kwesi Johnson makes the structure of his poems respond to the character of his language:

> But love is
> jus a word;
> give it MEANIN
> thru HACKSHAN.

MEANIN and HACKSHAN are words appropriated from 'standard' English by West Indians, and the fact that Johnson has used poetry to emphasize their ownership is significant. The unusual concentrations and foregroundings of poetry can unsettle just as much as they can underpin the allegiances and ideologies of diction and vocabulary.

Groom (1955) provides a survey of post-Renaissance poetic diction. Davie (1955) is good on the dynamics of poetic syntax. Jakobson (1960) offers the most complex linguistic survey of poetic syntax; see Bradford (1994) on this. For an account of how diction, idiom and vocabulary function as indices to issues such as race and nationality, see Chapter 15.

Who's speaking?

Much of what we know of the speaker of a poem is provided by the poem itself. The information that enables us to construct a mental picture of the speaker is known as the poem's 'deictic' features (from the Greek, 'pointing' or 'showing'). In Donne's 'The Flea', the deictic features tell us that the speaker is male, that his listener is female, that the speech act is in the present tense and improvised, and that their situation casts doubt upon 17th-century standards of health and cleanliness: the active presence of the flea does not seem particularly unusual or distressing. Renaissance lyric poetry is particularly prone to constructing such detailed dramatic contexts. The Romantic or the free verse lyric tends to tell us more about the effect of an experience or object upon the speaker than it does about their personal history, tastes or habits. A typical example is Wordsworth's sonnet 'Upon Westminster Bridge', where the words of the speaker construct an emotionally charged record of his vision of the city, but tell us little of who he is.

We can, of course, draw parallels between the speaker (the poetic persona), and what we know of the life, the historical, social, even psychological condition of the poet. This can be a speculative activity (did Coleridge's known habit of taking opium play a part in the bizarre, unstructured character of 'Kubla Khan'?), or it can be founded upon straightforward indications that it is the poet who is speaking: Tennyson's *In Memoriam* and Yeats's 'Easter 1916' are about real events experienced by each poet.

The shifting relation between our knowledge of the poem and the poet informs poetry criticism. The most extreme case of contextual biographical interpretation is probably Lowes' *The Road to Xanadu* (1927), in which he traces every theme, image, virtually every word of 'Kubla Khan' back to Coleridge's known reading and interests. The antithesis of this method is Jakobson's model of the poetic persona as a construction of the poem's own internalized system of images and stylistic devices.

The relation between the persona, the perceived context of the poem and the actual context in which it was written is particularly important for feminist criticism. My own references to the 'he' of Wordsworth's 'Westminster Bridge' is

based only in part upon my knowledge that Wordsworth wrote it. An anonymous poem written in 1802 is far more likely to reflect the perceptions and
experiences of a man than a woman, not simply because there have been more
male than female poets, but, more importantly, because male habits, affiliations
and roles are encoded in the apparently asexual conventions of traditional
poetic writing. Consider a random selection of 16th- or 17th-century poems.
Those that address or enact the issues of love or sexuality will be fashioned from
the deictics of the male perspective, and those that are more concerned with
God or philosophy will postulate an experience of scholarship, debate and a
mastery of current learning that is compatible with contemporary conventions
of how women should think, act and speak. Anne Finch wrote in 1714:

> Alas! A woman that attempts the pen
> Such an intruder on the rights of men
> ...
> To write, or read, or think, or to enquire
> Wou'd cloud our beauty, and exaust our time,
> And interrupt the Conquests of our prime;

There is a self-conscious tension in these lines between Finch's awareness of her
perceived role and the fact that the conventions and stylistic features of her
discourse (particularly the heroic couplet) are traditionally associated with the
male voice.

It could be argued that the position of women in poetic writing is strength-
ened when habit and convention are overturned by revolutionary themes and
techniques that have no established gender associations. Modernism proved to
be a focal point for a variety of women poets whose creative energy was no
longer frustrated by the monolith of male-dominated, traditional writing:
Gertrude Stein, Amy Lowell, Harriet Monroe, Hilda Doolittle, Marianne Moore.
See Chapter 14 for a detailed account of how gender stereotypes are variously
reinforced and undermined by the speaking presence of the poem.

Poetry and criticism

Poetry criticism is as old as poetry. Aristotle and Plato considered the value and
function of poetry. They differed on this; Plato saw it as a dangerous perversion
of the correct relation between language and reality, while Aristotle regarded its
inventive, figurative character as a healthy contribution to the discipline of
argument and debate. Criticism of English poetry began effectively in the 16th
and 17th centuries and its practitioners inherited two principal concerns from
their classical forebears. On the one hand, writers such as George Puttenham
(*The Arte of English Poesie*, 1589) and Samuel Daniel (*A Defence of Rhyme*, 1603)
were concerned with adapting the rules and conventions of classical rhetoric to

the English language and to the new conditions of poetic writing (they were particularly interested in metre and rhyme). On the other, the debate begun by Aristotle and Plato was continued: Philip Sidney's *The Defence of Poesie* (1595) involves itself with the status and influence of poetry within the turbulent contemporary discourses on politics and religion.

From the 17th century to the end of the 19th century, writings about poetry maintained the Renaissance emphasis upon its structure and function. Pope's *An Essay on Criticism* (1711) is a survey, in poetic form, of contemporary discussions of the classical origins of English poetry, of how poetry should treat the natural and political world and the style, diction, metre and proper subjects of poetic writing. Samuel Johnson's *The Lives of the Poets* (1779–81) involves short studies of English poets since the Renaissance, in which Johnson comments on their stylistic qualities, influence and general relevance to cultural life. Johnson's sense of English poetry as indigenous tradition, responsive to its own historical conditions, would become a keynote of Romantic criticism. In his Preface to *Lyrical Ballads*, Wordsworth engages with what he regards as the failure of the established English poetic tradition to offer new and challenging perspectives on the condition of modern man; and the urge to revitalize poetry, to evolve original and provocative modes of writing, is a characteristic of the critical work of Coleridge, Shelley, Keats and Blake.

Most pre-20th-century poetry criticism is involved with the activity of writing poetry and with the relation between poetry and its political, social and intellectual conditions. These concerns have been maintained through the 20th century, particularly by poet/critics such as Pound, Eliot, Auden and Heaney, but they have been supplemented by the emergence of poetry criticism as an academic discipline. The theoretical principles and the potential social benefits of teaching and studying English poetry in schools and universities were first mooted by the Victorian writer Matthew Arnold, but it was not until the 1920s and 30s that academic poetry criticism began to evolve the methodology and practices of an analytical discourse. Sidney, Pope and Wordsworth had discussed the respective qualities and styles of poets, and the purpose, relevance and future of poetry. The new, educationally affiliated critics involved themselves in the activities of dissecting and reassembling existing poems; naming and analysing their stylistic properties not for the purpose of writing verse but rather with the objective of showing how it works and contemplating its unique and perverse production of meaning.

The earliest and the most influential groups of academics were the New Critics and the Formalists. Both begin with the premise that poetry, by definition, creates effects and levels of meaning that non-poetic discourse will deliberately avoid. In their book *Understanding Poetry* (1938), the New Critics Cleanth Brooks and Robert Penn Warren discuss the procedures through which poetic writing is created:

[The poet] cannot assemble them [an episode, a metaphor, a phrase, a metrical device] in a merely arbitrary fashion; they must bear some relation to each other. So he develops his sense of the whole, the anticipation of the finished poem, as he work with the poem, and moves from one part to another. Then as a sense of the whole develops, it modifies the process by which the poet selects and relates the parts, the words, images, rhythms, local ideas, events etc … It is an infinitely complicated process of establishing interrelations. (pp. 526–7)

Brooks and Penn Warren present the poem as a separate linguistic and experiential universe. Their putative poet has not completely abandoned involvement with or reference to the world outside the text, but each of 'his' moves and strategies is governed principally by the interactive relation between the parts of the poem.

This model of how poems are created is reflected in the new critical procedures of analysis and interpretation. In *The Well Wrought Urn* ([1947]1968), Brooks is concerned with the use and effect of poetic paradox, but, as he explains, his objective is not simply to disclose a catalogue of oppositions, incompatible images and contradictions; rather, to treat paradox in poems as an element that permeates and unifies the broader fabric of the text. In his analysis of Donne's 'The Canonization' (Brooks takes his title from the poem's image of the urn, which seems variously to connote life, death, art and immortality), Brooks forages through the local stylistic effects of the poem and concludes that its metaphors, images and referential themes draw upon the all-embracing, paradoxical relation between transient pleasures of temporal love and the transcendent nature of the spirit. In Brooks' view, the poem's reluctance to resolve or settle this grand paradox, but rather to build it into an all-inconclusive structural theme, is a testament to its quality; poem's enact and intensify the problems of the human condition, they do not solve them.

Brooks' general principle, that our ultimate critical objective is to show how the parts of the poem contribute to its complex entirety, underpins William Empson's *Seven Types of Ambiguity* ([1930]1961) and W.K. Wimsatt's essays on metre, diction and rhetoric in *The Verbal Icon* (1954). This critical activity is given the general name of 'close reading', and its archetypal Formalist version can be found in the much-discussed essay by Jakobson and Jones on Shakespeare's Sonnet 129 (see Pomorska and Rudy, 1987). Their method is analogous to the anatomist's or the pathologist's treatment of the human body. They list every semantic and syntactic operation of individual words and supplement this with an equally exhaustive survey of every feature of the text's deployment of metre, assonance, alliteration, rhyme and grammatical parallelism. Their objective is not to disclose a new dimension of the poem's meaning; rather to show how forms such as the sonnet create a continuous, multidimensional interface between structure and effect and, as a consequence, resist paraphrase and summary.

Since the 1960s, the New Critical and Formalist treatment of poetry has been subjected to a number of antagonistic, rejectionist rereadings. The New Critics have been accused of detaching the study of poetry from the real experience of social, political and ideological division that informs our lives. Terry Eagleton (1983, pp. 48–9) argues that the New Critics' emphasis upon the poem as 'a self-sufficient object' effectively 'disentangl[es] it from any social or historical context'; that their taste for showing how '"tensions", "paradoxes" and "ambivalences"' are 'resolved and integrated by its solid structure' was underpinned by their political ideal of a 'new organic society' redolent of Fascism.

A more sustained assault upon the validity of New Critical practice has come from theorists who promote a reader-centred model of interpretation. The premise for this shift in focus was established with Roland Barthes' well-known article 'The Death of the Author' (1968), which reflects contemporaneous conjectures that the text – the poem included – and the reader are the exclusive sources of meaning. Later theorists argue that the educational, cultural and social circumstances that influence our perceptions of poetry are principally responsible for what we claim to 'find' in it. Jonathan Culler (1975, Ch. 8) re-examines the 'formal patterns' (metaphor, metre, poetic diction, genre and so on) that provide critics with the methodology for their analysis of poems. He does not dispute the fact that these features exist as constituent parts of the text in question, but he claims that their apparent relation to each other and their resultant effect are due as much to the critic's own expectations of structure and signification as they are to the particular and unique operations of poems. For an amusing and more detailed version of Culler's exercise, see Stanley Fish's 'How To Recognise a Poem When You See One' (1980), discussed in Chapter 10, in which Fish convinces his undergraduate class that a random list of surnames on a blackboard is a Modernist religious lyric. Their interpretations are slick, sophisticated, informed and very depressing – depressing in the sense that robotic analysis has replaced evaluation. To correct this imbalance, the closing chapter of this book is concerned exclusively with the controversial issue of evaluation.

The distinction between the ideas of Culler and those of the New Critics underpins a large number of recent critical debates. The New Critics base their work on the precondition that poems are structurally and functionally different from other types of discourse and that consequently they create effects and meanings that do not occur in the non-poetic circulation of ideas and references. Culler and Fish shift our attention towards the context and circumstances in which the poem is understood and argue that poetic structure and function are variable elements, dependent upon such factors as the educational competence of the reader. This premise re-emerges in feminist criticism of poetry. The reading of poems that are written primarily by men and which reflect the activities, concerns and desires of men (at least 80 per cent of all pre-20th-century verse) will inevitably be affected by the reader's own experience as either a man or a woman: whatever is apparently intrinsic to the poem (the New Critical emphasis) cannot remain immune from such a fundamental difference in the reader's sense of identity (see Chapter 14).

Marxist literary theories have been concerned far more with fiction than poetry. This, at least by implication, reinforces the New Critical notion of poetic difference. Novels are more mimetic than poems; they draw more freely upon their own social and political contexts and consequently serve better the Marxist view that literature can only be properly understood within a larger framework of social reality. The patent oddities of poetic writing are frequently regarded by Marxists as a token of the privileges of middle-class or aristocratic culture: games played with language by those who dominate the social and political uses of language (see Caudwell, 1937). Christopher Hill's Marxist reading of *Paradise Lost* (1977) is concerned more with its relation to the social, religious and ideological conflicts of 17th-century England than with its effects and qualities as a poem per se. Over the past three decades, the study of the historical and political context of literature has been dominated by the post-Marxist schools known as 'New Historicism' and 'Cultural Materialism', whose relevance for poetry will be examined in Chapter 11.

Sigmund Freud (1900) compared the bizarre, surrealistic collages of the dream with its linguistic counterpart in 'a poetical phrase of the greatest beauty and significance'. Most psychoanalytic critics, including Jacques Lacan, regard poetry as variously subversive and symptomatic of the arbitrary relation between language and the unconscious. Perhaps our attraction for the unusual and sometimes disturbing effects of poetic language allows us a conscious glimpse of our rarely articulated desires, fears and fantasies (see Chapter 12).

Deconstruction, like most recent theories of criticism, draws upon ideas and practices evolved outside literary studies. If deconstruction can be said to have a premise or founding principle, it is that our perceptions of reality are sustained by our ability to postulate them in language. When we deconstruct a text, we show how its apparent affirmation of order or truth is constantly unsettled by its necessary dependence upon the falsifications of language. This radical branch of philosophy found a welcoming home in the literary critical academy of the late 1960s, particularly in the work of poetry critics who were tiring of the well-rehearsed practices of New Criticism. The attraction was obvious: poetry deliberately and constantly unsettles the accepted relations between language and reality; it appropriates familiar images and ideas and (as the Formalists put it) defamiliarizes them. The problem that had taxed the New Critics was of how to return the perverse, irrational discourse of poetry to the world in which language is supposed to disclose truths and make sense. Deconstruction provided not so much a solution as an escape from the problem. Deconstructionists argue that our attempts to distil an unrefined and immutable truth from *any* kind of linguistic text is a contradiction in terms since language creates rather than mediates truth. Poems are self-deconstructive. Their use of ambiguity, irony, paradox and metaphors that are endless and self-sustaining involves a disclosure of the fact that language mediates nothing; rather, it thickens and complicates levels of signification. Therefore, poetry critics should not concern themselves with resolving the paradoxes and contradictions of poetic discourse; they should follow, even celebrate, the limitless aporias (from the Greek – a track without end) of poetry. Culler (1983, pp. 204–5) performs a deconstructive reading of that New Critical classic 'The Canonization':

> [The] self referential element in Donne's poem does not produce or induce a closure in which the poem harmoniously is the thing it describes ... Self reference does not close it in upon itself but leads to a proliferation of representations, a series of invocations and urns, including Brooks's *The Well Wrought Urn* ... [which] are at once within the poem and outside it and can always be continued and has no end.

Chapter 8 studies the New Critical and Formalist methods, while deconstruction is covered in detail in Chapter 13.

2

A Definition of Poetry: The Double Pattern

Poetry is the most versatile, ambidextrous and omnipotent of all types of speech or writing, yet, paradoxically, it is the only one which is unified by a single exclusive feature, that which enables us to identify it and which separates it from every other kind of linguistic expression. This element is the keystone of my definition of poetry and it is called 'the double pattern'.

As an example of the double pattern in operation, consider John Donne's poem 'The Flea':

> Mark but this flea, and mark in this,
> How little that which thou deny'st me is;
> It sucked me first, and now sucks thee,
> And in this flea, our two bloods mingled be;
> Thou know'st that this cannot be said
> A sin, nor shame nor loss of maidenhead,
>   Yet this enjoys before it woo,
>   And pampered swells with one blood made of two,
>   And this, alas, is more than we would do.
>
> Oh stay, three lives in one flea spare,
> Where we almost, yea more than married are:
> This flea is you and I, and this
> Our marriage bed, and marriage temple is;
> Though parents grudge, and you, we're met,
> And cloistered in these living walls of jet.
>   Though use make thee apt to kill me,
>   Let not to that, self murder added be,
>   And sacrilege, three sins in killing three.
>
> Cruel and sudden, hast thou since
> Purpled thy nail, in blood of innocence?
> Wherein could this flea guilty be,
> Except in that drop which it sucked from thee?
> Yet thou triumph'st and say'st that thou
> Find'st not thyself, nor me the weaker now;

> 'Tis true, then learn how false, fears be;
> Just so much honour, when thou yield'st to me,
> Will waste, as this flea's death took life from thee.

Before tackling the mechanisms of the poem, let us begin with some straightforward observations.

We cannot see the speaker but we know he is a man because from the evidence in the text it is clear that he is addressing a woman and that his intention is to persuade her to have sex with him. During this exercise, he employs an impressive range of rhetorical figures and devices, principally the predominant metaphor of the fleabite, which, at various points throughout the poem, is refashioned to represent the sexual act. In the opening stanza he argues that her apparent reluctance to have sex with him is unfounded. Sex, he contends, is no more distressing or immoral than an insect bite. Moreover, just as the flea has 'enjoyed' biting both of them, so, he implies, might they delight in a comparable mixing of fluids. The flea, he observes, swells and feels pampered by its harmless and pleasurable act – so why should not they?

Between the first and the second stanza something happens. We cannot see it but we can infer from his words that the woman has rejected his argument. She has indeed attempted to swat the flea, to destroy the active feature – in technical terms, the vehicle – of his metaphor. She fails, at least in her first attempt, and he pleads for restraint: 'Oh stay' (the 17th-century informal version of 'Oh stop!'), he begs, don't kill it. The man is thinking and speaking in response to the unforeseeable, he is improvising. Now he readjusts his metaphor to suit new circumstances, and in doing so, he begins to contradict himself. In the first stanza he stated that the fleabite, like sex, involved no great moral consequences. Now he alters his approach and argues that it is of major significance for both of them. The mingling of their blood in the insect is compared with the physical and spiritual union of marriage, and the flea is promoted to the status of a religious icon: it is a temple, a church, whose 'living walls' sanctify their union. The metaphor seems almost to have acquired a hungry momentum of its own. The man even begins to speak to her as if they were already married. 'Though use make thee apt to kill me', he concedes, meaning that the routines of coexistence might well breed bitterness, the destruction of that symbol of their potential union, the flea, would amount to the violation of some higher covenant involving them and it: 'And sacrilege, three sins in killing three'.

His grand hyperbole, inspired as it is, appears to have left the woman unconvinced, since between stanza two and stanza three, she succeeds in dispatching the insect. 'Cruel and sudden, hast thou since/Purpled thy nail, in blood of innocence?', he observes, no doubt marshalling his mental resources for yet another twist upon the original metaphor. He begins with a mild rebuke and next returns to his initial presentation of the flea as a harmless, innocent, agent of pleasure. Then, still thinking and speaking on the spot, he refashions this image to renew his strategy of seduction. Neither of them, he informs her, is the 'weaker now' and this is a measure of the 'false fears' behind her reluctance to accept his argument and his advances.

One could argue that in 'The Flea', Donne has conducted an exercise in mimesis. We have no record of how people spoke to each other in the early 17th century but evidence suggests that it would not be entirely implausible for an educated intelligent individual to marshal his thoughts into extended metaphors – if characters in contemporaneous drama in any way resembled members of the audience, then flamboyant figurative language was something of a fashion statement. Significantly, Donne informs the piece with a special claim upon credulity and believability by creating a dialogue, albeit with one party remaining silent. He contends, she responds and he makes further use of his sophistication – by degrees suave and suspect – to offer yet another version of his original proposition. Exchange the early 17th-century informal idiom and vocabulary for its early 21st-century counterpart and play down the figurative excesses and religious imagery and it could be an exchange overheard last week in a restaurant, albeit one with a somewhat unappealing tolerance of insects. 'The Flea' seems at one level a wonderfully plausible, authentic rendering of actuality, yet at another we are made aware that both of its characters are patently unreal, they do not exist and could never have existed.

It is unlikely although not entirely unthinkable that a person could be so flamboyantly inventive for so long – the hearer, four centuries ago and today, would more likely feel impatient than impressed – but it is impossible to conceive of him doing so while fitting his speech into three identical stanzas, each rhyming aa bb cc ddd; three couplets and a triplet. The meticulous baroque design is further complicated by the fact that each couplet comprises first an eight-syllable, octosyllabic line, followed by a ten-syllable pentameter line, with the triplet made up of an octosyllable and two pentameters. Moreover, each line is iambic, in that, with very slight exceptions, every even syllable is stressed more emphatically than the two syllables that precede and follow it, a stress pattern usually represented as follows:

Ō stáy, thrēe líves īn óne flēa spáre

Iambic metre, the most frequently employed system in traditional English verse, admits of some variation and flexibility, in the sense that the five even syllables do not in speech receive an equal emphasis and nor do the five odd syllables. However, the relative relationship of lower-to-higher-to-lower is maintained throughout the line.

What we encounter in every component part of 'The Flea', from individual syllables to complex rhyme schemes and a perpetual metaphor, is a tension between immediacy – it is in the present tense and the speaker appears continually to adjust his words to unforeseeable circumstances – and a structure so self-evidently arbitrary and complex that it completely undermines any claim upon spontaneity and authenticity.

This is the double pattern in action. One half of the double pattern is made up of devices, effects, habits and frames of reference that poetry shares with all other linguistic discourses; as I have indicated, 'The Flea' could, just, be a record of a conversation overheard in a bar. The other half of the pattern pulls against this: it announces the text as a poem by marshalling aspects of language into patterns that serve no purpose elsewhere in language yet which play a role in the way the poem is structured and, most significantly, in how it discharges meaning.

Donne's poem is a fine example of the double pattern at work because within it the tension between the two halves is continually, often minutely, foregrounded. Consider line five of stanza two:

> Though parents grudge, and you, we're met

In one respect, this is an example of stylistic realism, a man forced into a grammatical informality while attempting to keep his words ahead of events. A more considered version would be:

> Though you and your parents grudge, we're met

But the 'and you' phrase in Donne's line is unfeigned, as though the man is struggling to gather his syntax while his thoughts and ideas are racing ahead. At the same time, however, the apparently improvised line conforms perfectly to the arbitrary structure of iambic metre:

> Thōugh párēnts grúdge, ānd yóu, wē're mét

The line announces itself as at once spontaneous and systematically contrived. This could indeed be said of the entire poem, with the metaphor seeming heedlessly adaptable to whatever is required of it while admitting of such tortuous layerings of rhetoric and imagery as to defy any credible sense of spontaneity. The complexity of each stanza seems to betoken a desire by Donne to test himself, to see if he has the skill to sustain at least the impression of immediacy while fitting his words into a determinedly difficult abstract design, repeated three times. He even sews into the texture of the poem a secondary sound pattern, which, on a brief reading, beguiles like a distantly heard snatch of music but, on closer attention, involves an exercise in brainwashing via internal rhyme. The flea, the bite, the man and the woman are drawn into a chain of semantic and phonetic associations: 'this flea', 'in this', 'me is', 'Me', 'thee', 'be', 'This flea', 'and this', 'temple is', 'kill me', 'added be', 'killing three', 'guilty be', 'from thee', 'fears be', 'to me', 'from thee'. Critics have for centuries debated the effect of repetitive sound patterns – predominantly, rhyme, assonance and alliteration – on our standard cognitive mechanisms. No firm conclusions have been reached but by consensus it is accepted that they interfere with our ability to make sense of language. They create a layer of echoes that runs as a counter-current to the conventional relationship between phonetics and semantics, sound and meaning. One might argue that Donne's dense fabric of internal and external rhymes creates a beguiling musical accompaniment to the speaker's sophistry, something that might plausibly be a reflection of his personal manner, indeed his temperament. However, this impression of guileless charm is undermined by evidence of planning and calculation. Continually, the swirling sound patterns return us to the five predominant themes of his argument: 'this flea', 'is', 'thee', 'be', 'me'. We cannot be certain if this would have some subliminal effect upon the listener, an almost hypnotic counterpart to the twisted logic of the argument, but the effort that went in to organizing this effect testifies to the fact that it was pre-planned and not spontaneous.

There is a portrait of Henry VIII by Holbein (c. 1536, now housed in the Thyssen-Bornemisza Collection, Madrid) that is famed for its ability to beguile, often unnerve, onlookers. Practically everyone who sees it is stunned by its unusual authenticity. It is not that Holbein has captured something exclusive to the notorious monarch, more that the face in the frame appears to acquire a mobility; from different perspectives, his expression appears to alter and his eyes, infamously, seem capable of following you around the room. The effect is powerful and because of this transient. We quickly withdraw from our state of transfixed credulity and remind ourselves that what we are looking at is an assembly of paint and canvas put into operation by an immensely talented craftsman.

The experience is peculiar and magnetic. We almost simultaneously apprehend a flicker of pure reality alongside a complex act of representation. Our struggle to reconcile a sense of unmediated perception and our admiration for the processes that make this available are comparable to our encounter with Donne's 'The Flea'. At one level, the poem is engagingly transparent; we feel that we are listening to an encounter between two living human beings and we become sufficiently persuaded and intrigued to form opinions about what sort of man he is – his background, the reason for his showy ostentatious manner – and to wonder about his silent addressee; is she impressed, anxious, fearful, bored? At the same time, Donne embeds these two individuals so deeply in a network of sound patterns and figurative devices that they become functions of language; not figures who use and respond to words but creations of words.

In Art and its Objects (1980, p. 213), Richard Wollheim evolved a general theory on the nature and effects of the visual arts, which he called the 'twofold thesis', using Holbein's portrait of Henry VIII as a paradigmatic example of this:

> If I look at a representation as a representation, then it is not just permitted, but required of me, that I attend simultaneously to object and medium. So if I look at Holbein's portrait, the standards of correctness require me to see Henry VIII there; but additionally I must – not only may but must – be visually aware of an unrestricted range of features of Holbein's panel if my perception of the representation is to be appropriate.

There are obvious parallels between Wollheim's twofold thesis and the double pattern, in the sense that in both the poem and the painting we are aware almost simultaneously of the object and the medium that makes the object available. There is, however, a significant difference. The medium of the visual arts is a metalanguage, a representational system in its own right with generic habits and conventions, comprising material such as paint, stone, canvas and wood. The medium of poetry is words, the same words that we use throughout our conscious existence. Poetry does not reinvent language, it can only use what is already available. What it does is to create unusual relationships between words, relationships that persist for the duration of a single statement, the poem. In the visual arts, the relationship between the medium and the object, and by object we effectively mean reality, is infinitely flexible. Up to the mid-19th century, virtually all art was representational, in the sense that the perceiver did not need to understand the history or conventions of painting to recognize the thing in the picture. Since then, however, artists have pioneered a variety of unprecedented techniques that explore the very nature of perception and exist-ence. Often their paintings do not attempt simply to imitate physical objects but rather employ shapes, colours and juxtapositions in order to raise questions regarding our relationship with what we complacently term 'reality'. So while Holbein was a traditional representational painter, Wollheim's twofold thesis is relevant also to pictures by figures such as Jackson Pollock, many of whose best-known works involve blocks of colour divided by geometric designs. Pollock's object might not be immediately recognizable to the perceiver but, as Wollheim states, our recognition of the fact that his painting exists in the same extended generic field as Holbein's causes us to engage in a process of interpretation, a contemplation of its object, albeit one that is an abstract fabric of ideas rather than a human being.

The fact that the compositional and interpretative conventions of painting can accommodate the radical differences between Holbein and Pollock illus-trates the dissimilarity between the twofold thesis and the double pattern and, in turn, the uniqueness of poetry both as a literary genre and a means of expres-sion and representation.

It would be impossible for a poet to create the equivalent of a Pollock painting for the simple reason that the only source for a poet's medium, his raw material, is language. Certainly one could, if so inclined, create something that in formal terms resembles a poem but is so purposively incoherent, sometimes ungram-matical, as to disrupt any clear sense of what it means – and, as we will see, poems that come close to this formula have been produced by esteemed practi-tioners of the genre. However, even though the relationship between the constituent parts of the piece creates a sense of opacity and confusion, the fact that poetry draws exclusively upon language for its components means that verse can never obtain a level of abstraction or incomprehensibility comparable with Pollock. Its fundamental indivisible building blocks are words and however haphazardly one assembles a string of individual words, they will interact to create broader strands of meaning, albeit sometimes unorthodox and semi-coherent. Painting can make worlds of its own, revise and refresh its own conventions of design and signification. But poetry is tied to the medium that does not merely reconstruct perceived reality, it is part of perceived, and lived, reality. We, as human beings, can neither think nor function without language; language is inseparable from our existential condition. Poetry appropriates and refashions aspects of language according to its own conventions. These conventions are seemingly arbitrary and purposeless, given that in all non-poetic uses of language, the abstract regulations that allow us to assemble and decode messages serve a self-evident purpose: the organizational principles of the medium – predominantly grammar – are designed to occasion the most efficient and unambivalent delivery of the message. Poetic devices, such as the stanza, rhyme schemes, alliterative and assonated patterns, metrical form and the persistent use of metaphor, make no obvious contribution to the principles of clarity and precision that underpin virtually all uses of language. The occurrence of rhyme in ordinary speech is usually accidental. It is a cause of embarrassment and is guarded against because the repetition of sound will draw the listener's attention away from the logic of the statement. Similarly, if someone held a conversation, delivered an address or wrote an article while adhering to a strictly iambic pattern, most witnesses would pay less attention to the message and more to the curiosity of the spectacle. Metaphor does, of course, feature frequently in ordinary language but tacit customs are maintained to regulate its effects. Were you to reply to your GP's enquiry on how you felt with the declaration that you were 'lonely as a cloud that floats on high o'er vales and hills', the GP would, with some justification, regard this either as a facetious gesture or evidence of a burgeoning nervous breakdown. More significantly, metaphor in everyday language is, by habit, the exception to the predominating literal, transparent mood of the rest of the text. It is used with indulgent caution to underscore a particular point but it never becomes a persistent, extended feature of the text. Donne maintains and refashions his metaphor of the fleabite for the entirety of the poem, and in verse – particularly during Donne's period of the Renaissance – such exercises in figurative endurance are as much the custom as the exception.

Donne's poem is a useful exemplar for the workings of the double pattern, since it involves an unremitting tension between those aspects of language that feature both within and outside poetry and those that are licensed for persistent systematic use in verse. However, the operations of the double pattern in poems by other authors from different periods are by degrees far less conspicuous, self-conscious and consistent. It will be the purpose of the remainder of this chapter to examine poems that differ greatly in character and manner and to show that, despite such variations, the double pattern persists as their defining characteristic.

For poems that have least in common with Donne's, we should go to the early 20th century, to the work of those who advocated and practised the aesthetics of Modernism. Modernist poetry developed into a number of distinct, sometimes antithetical, subgenres but its originating tenets focused upon a desire to unshackle the writer and the poem from what were seen as the restraints of conventional writing, specifically, traditional metre and rhyme schemes and the characteristic accessories of orotund diction and portentous metaphor. Free verse, or *vers libre*, was born and one of its most celebrated practitioners was the US poet William Carlos Williams. The following is Williams' 'Spring and All':

> By the road to the contagious hospital
> under the surge of the blue
> mottled clouds driven from the
> northeast – a cold wind. Beyond, the
> waste of broad, muddy fields
> brown with dried weeds, standing and fallen
>
> patches of standing water
> the scattering of tall trees
>
> All along the road the reddish
> purplish, forked, upstanding, twiggy
> stuff of bushes and small trees
> with dead, brown leaves under them
> leafless vines –
>
> Lifeless in appearance, sluggish,
> dazed spring approaches –

This poem has, it seems, purged itself of every device and technique that we customarily associate with poetic writing. There are no metaphors and the closest Williams comes to a figurative gesture is in the phrase 'dazed spring'. The adverb 'dazed' is usually associated with a living creature rather than a season, but we are likely to encounter many similar usages in informal speech: 'the dead of night', 'lazy days', 'happy places' are, strictly speaking, rhetorical figures of speech but they are taken for granted by most as the routines of verbal exchange.

The only apparent concession to conventional verse is the use of poetic lines but these do not attend to any abstract formal structure; there is nothing that resembles metre and there are no sound patterns or rhymes. The lines seem improvised, random, the kind of sequence that one might find in a notebook. Indeed, the syntax itself is casual, sometimes haphazard and heedless. There is a verb phrase at the beginning of the poem – the speaker seems to have picked out a thought in mid-sentence – and we are left to wonder what exactly is 'By the road to the …'. One might assume that he means 'I am standing by the road' or 'I was looking down the road' but neither of these oblique possibilities is thereafter confirmed or reinforced. The sentence structure of the poem as a whole is paratactic (using a style in which clauses are joined without using conjunctions); unfocused, apparently improvised and composed guilelessly at the moment of inspiration or perception. Prior to Modernism, this effect was never encountered in literary writing and rarely if ever in any other species of formal discourse, being found only in the rambling hesitations of casual speech or in the letters and notebooks of the ill-educated. The overall impression is of an attempt to preserve for posterity the moment at which prelinguistic perception becomes language. The passage

> All along the road the reddish
> purplish, forked, upstanding, twiggy
> stuff of bushes and small trees

seems a record of the speaker attempting to match what he sees with a satisfactory description, trying out various words from his mental lexicon in the hope of coming upon the right one. The 'reddish/purplish, forked, upstanding, twiggy/stuff', he states, hoping that eventually he'll find the phrase he is searching for.

In this respect, there are parallels with 'The Flea'. Both speakers are busily adjusting their verbal output in accordance with unfolding circumstances, in one case the responses of the listener and in the other the cumulative impression of a passive scene. At the same time, while Donne's poem involves a persistent counterpoint between artifice and improvisation, Williams' poem attempts to rid itself completely of the former. It is as though Holbein's Henry VIII has stepped off the wall and become as real as his onlookers, no longer a composite of paint, canvas and self-evident painterly devices.

It is difficult to imagine how an equivalent to Williams' poem could be executed in the visual arts, given that a distinction between object and medium, the twofold thesis, is a basic requirement for works of painting and sculpture. There is, of course, the well-known anecdote concerning artist Tracey Emin's 'installation', comprising an unmade bed, randomly distributed items of clothing and half-empty bottles of alcohol. Legend has it that the gallery cleaners were unable to distinguish between object and medium, given that the debris from the launch party seemed to merge into Ms Emin's artefact, and went on to clear up the entire room.

If there are indeed parallels between 'Spring and All' and Emin's bed, a significant question is raised regarding craftsmanship and technique. Irrespective of any alleged cultural or ideological subtext that might attach to Ms Emin's piece, it is self-evidently the case that as an artwork in its own right, it required of its producer no effort, skill or intellectual engagement. Even if we had no interest in art or the general state of contemporary culture, any of us could produce something which, as a medium, was possessed of comparable qualities. Since Williams appears to have achieved a similar level of transparency, a transcendence of the devices and conventions of verse, has he too produced a 'poem' that

makes no claims to be a meticulously crafted work of art, that is, in truth, something that any one of us, given the inclination, might jot down?

To address this question, we must consider the fact that Williams, while
rejecting the traditional poetic line, that is, the unit that pays heed to some
abstract notion of a given length or metrical structure, does not abjure the line
as a de facto token of poetic design. Williams' lines do not conform to any
predictable or consistent pattern but they exist, tangibly, as supplements to the
standard building blocks of words, clauses and sentences. As a consequence, he
has invoked the tension between the two aspects of the double pattern, a gesture
that both pays allegiance to the defining characteristics of poetry and places
before an author a fundamental test of skill. Consider lines two–five:

> under the surge of the blue
> mottled clouds driven from the
> northeast – a cold wind. Beyond, the
> waste of broad, muddy fields

Is there any logic or apparent purpose in Williams breaking up the already
casual sentences into arbitrary structures? Intriguingly, the line ending at 'blue'
could have been a complete, conclusive statement. Metonymy (logical metaphor) is found frequently in ordinary speech: 'wheels' has long served as a
colloquial substitute for car, as has 'the crown' for the royal family. It would not
involve a strenuous imaginative effort for Williams' speaker to settle upon 'the
blue' as an alternative to sky. Suddenly, however, we swing around the line
ending to find that 'blue' has been returned to its traditional adjectival role.
Why, we wonder, does he leave 'the' dangling at the end of the subsequent two
lines? Is he mocking the decorum of traditional versification where custom
would discourage such ungainly constructions? Perhaps, but when we consider
the manner of the poem as a whole, we begin to discern an intent at once more
radical and commendable. In Modernist prose, the technique that comes closest
to eroding the distinction between the impersonal formalities of expression and
the inchoate jumble of thought and impression is stream of consciousness, best
known in Joyce's *Ulysses*, and involving what appears to be language imitating
the randomness of mental activity. Williams seems to be evolving a uniquely
poetic counterpart to this. In grammar, there is no device that accommodates
the pauses and hesitations that are an inevitable feature of unrehearsed speech,
but the curious, unclassifiable gap between 'the' and 'northeast' seems to imitate
the moment that it takes for the speaker to synchronize his perception of the
cloud with his intuitive sense of the compass. Similarly, 'Beyond, the' suspends
the syntactic movement, briefly, while the speaker's mind searches for a means
of describing a featureless landscape.

'Enjambment' is the formal description of what happens when a poetic line
cuts between two closely related units of grammar. In traditional verse, it is
indulged by critics and used by poets with a certain amount of caution, given

that it undermines the ordinance that coherence is paramount. The standard defence for it is that it sets up a pseudo-musical counterpoint between syntax and metre, but since Williams has abandoned all concessions to the latter, he seems to be both invoking and rewriting the regulations of conventional verse. The

> small trees
> with dead brown leaves under them
> leafless vines

is in appearance guilelessly unplanned – it seems as unostentatious as a snatch of conversation – but in fact it incorporates two very different levels of meaning. The small trees could well be perceived as having 'dead brown leaves under them', with the pause allowing the perceiver to gather his thoughts into a more succinct, almost tragic summary: 'leafless vines'. Alternatively, the relaxed demotic manner of the poem might encourage one to close the gap at the line ending and read 'under them leafless vines' as an unbroken, albeit ungrammatical, sequence.

There is no evidence, either within the poem or implied by its apparent context, that enables us to reach a conclusion on which of these interpretations is correct. That Williams sews into the same sequence of words two simultaneously present but distinct trajectories of sense testifies to the fact that despite the considerable differences between the two poems, 'Spring and All' and 'The Flea' belong within the same corpus of texts and that their creators are attuned to a single, uniquely poetic feature of composition, the double pattern. Williams rejects the traditional orthodoxies of metre and rhyme schemes and figurative devices, yet still makes use of the tactile materiality of language to create a contrapuntal relation between the progress of his syntax and a fabric of pauses and hesitations. He employs features of language that have no designated function outside poetry to create multiple layers of sense.

Donne's and Williams' poems belong at opposing ends of the broad spectrum of texts that incorporate the double pattern as their generic keynote. At Donne's end, we encounter verse that involves a thickening and foregrounding of purely conventional poetic devices to the extent that univocal single registers of meaning are at every level disrupted or supplemented. At the other end, Williams' conventional, self-evidently poetic devices and conventions are used sparingly, yet the fact that they are present at all, sometimes in unprecedented unorthodox manifestations, is sufficient to create a conspicuous relationship between the two halves of the double pattern.

The following is an extract from a poem that belongs at roughly the halfway point between Donne and Williams on the spectrum of the double pattern. It is from Alexander Pope's *An Essay on Criticism: Part I* (lines 9–18):

> 'Tis with our judgements as our watches, none
> Go just alike, yet each believes his own.

> In poets as true genius is but rare,
> True taste as seldom is the critic's share
> Both must alike from Heaven derive their light,
> Those born to judge, as well as those to write.
> Let such teach others who themselves excel,
> And censure freely who have written well
> Authors are partial to their wit, 'tis true,
> But are not critics to their judgement too?

The subject of the poem is literary criticism, the means by which we should properly judge and evaluate literature, and in a broader sense it addresses the general issues of taste and aesthetics. It deals with a complex variety of questions: How do we tell good from bad art? What controls and motivates our decisions in these matters? What defines genuinely good taste?

It is written in heroic couplets (sequences of iambic pentameters rhyming aa, bb, cc), the most frequently used metrical form of all poems written between the late 17th and the mid-18th century. The opening couplet contains a simile: our evaluative faculties are like our watches. Our watches might keep different times and our tastes might be subject to our temperament, yet each of us believes what our watch tells us, just as we trust that our judgements are correct.

This couplet establishes a working formula for the rest of the passage, and indeed one that predominates throughout the poem. It particularizes two ideas, objects or principles, compares or contrasts them, and distils from this an apparently well-founded conclusion.

The next couplet deals with two archetypes, the poet and the critic. The former, it contends, will rarely be a true genius, just as the latter will infrequently be in possession of flawless taste. The parallels between the rhythmic pattern of each line and the semantic contrast between the rhyme words 'rare' and 'share' provide a supplement to the rhetorical symmetry of the argument.

Couplet three again focuses on the poet and the critic, emphasizing the shared characteristics and again using the structure of the couplet as a support mechanism for the proposition. 'Heaven' and 'judge', whose semantic relationship requires no explanation, are placed at a central point in each line, immediately prior to the caesura (pause/break in a line of verse), which draws special attention to them, a framing device not available in non-poetic language. This two-word interplay of emphasis and meaning becomes, with the rhyme words 'light' and 'write', a four-part interaction. In four syllables ('Heaven' would have been pronounced 'Heav'n), key thematic points of the 20-syllable thesis are picked out and emphasized. The unquestioned qualities of enlightenment ('light') that derive from religious commitment ('Heaven') are comparable to the ideals of judgement ('judge') necessary both for literary writers and commentators, those who 'write'.

Comparable operations occur in virtually every other couplet in this lengthy poem. The intrinsically poetic dimension of the double pattern, predominantly metre and rhyme, becomes the scaffolding for the broader thesis of the poem, which Pope builds from a systematic sequence of syllogisms rehearsed in every couplet and with each offering a slight adjustment or shift upon its predecessor.

Pope's poem differs from Donne's and Williams' in a number of ways. In terms of its objective and purpose, it has more in common with a prose essay (as indicated in its title) or the modern newspaper article than with what we customarily deem to be the characteristic dispensation of poetic writing. Correspondingly, it creates a mutually productive symmetry between the two dimensions of the double pattern. The examples of counterpoint and contrast between each dimension evidenced, albeit in varying degrees, in Donne's and Williams' poems is here exchanged for a programme of cooperation. The formal structure assists in the promotion of the logic of the argument, with the two lines of each couplet providing a formal parallel for the operation of its corresponding two-part syntactic and rhetorical unit.

Consider the following:

> Authors are partial to their wit, 'tis true
> But are not critics to their judgements too?
> Both must alike from Heaven derive their light,
> Those born to judge, as well as those to write.
> 'Tis with our judgements as our watches, none
> Go just alike, but each believes his own.
> Let such teach others who themselves excel,
> And censure freely who have written well.
> In poets as true genius is rare,
> True taste as seldom is the critic's share.

I have rearranged the five couplets virtually at random, yet the passage retains an apparent sense of continuity and inherent logic. My experiment emphasizes how successfully the two halves of the double pattern cooperate and create a system of mutual support in each couplet. Each unit in the broader argument is virtually self-contained. Attempt this with stanzas, or lines, from any poems other than those written in couplet form during the Restoration and 18th century, or even redistribute the order of sentences in a prose passage, and chaos and incoherence will be the result.

The period when the so-called 'Augustan couplet' was the predominant feature of all verse was the only one in the history of poetry when the collective will of poets and the broader cultural establishment maintained that the principal criteria for acceptable poetic writing were clarity, precision and coherence, in pursuit of a specified programme of description or prescriptive logic. As a consequence, the two parts of the double pattern, features shared by verse and prose and features specific to the former, were caused to operate in a manner that did not create a split focus, a bifurcation of meaning, for the reader. Logic,

parallelism and discernment were the watchwords of 18th-century poetic sensibility. It is intriguing, therefore, that while poems by Pope and his peers differ so
radically from those of Donne and Williams, the factor that underpins, secures
this difference is also that which unites the verse of all three within the same
commonwealth of texts, the double pattern.

T.S. Eliot's 'The Love Song of J. Alfred Prufrock' is routinely cited as a landmark in the early history of Modernism but, as the following extract shows, it
differs considerably from Williams' piece, also thought to exemplify the early
20th-century avant-garde:

> And the afternoon, the evening, sleeps so peacefully!
> Smoothed by long fingers,
> Asleep … tired … or it malingers,
> Stretched on the floor, here beside you and me.
> Should I, after tea and cakes and ices,
> Have the strength to force the moment to its crisis?
> But though I have wept and fasted, wept and prayed,
> Though I have seen my head (grown slightly bald)
> > brought in upon a platter,
> I am no prophet – and here's no great matter;
> I have seen the moment of my greatness flicker,
> And I have seen the eternal Footman hold my coat, and snicker,
> And in short, I was afraid. (lines 75–87)

The only similarity between Eliot's and Williams' poems is that their speakers
are monologists. There is certainly no putative listener, no counterpart to
Donne's disgruntled woman, and the haphazard improvised manner of their
address indicates that neither speaker intends to offer his meditations to a
public audience comparable to that of Pope's.

Eliot's speaker, like Williams', improvises listlessly but seems less able to focus
upon a specific topic. Discontinuity is his dictum and the governing principle of
his address appears to be some private idiosyncratic fabric of memories and
associations. He begins with a metaphor, turning the evening into a living creature, but the discipline and system of counter-logic that informs most figurative
language, even in poetry, seems to escape him. He loses control of his invention.
How, we wonder, can the embodied 'evening' have 'fingers' and by what means
has it entered the room to recline on the floor between the speaker and the
mysterious someone else, whose presence he rapidly forgets.

Then, he asks, 'Should I … Have the strength to force the moment to its
crisis?' ('after tea and cakes and ices') and we wonder, 'what moment?', 'what
crisis?' This might have something to do with his mysterious, perhaps even his
imagined, companion – male, female, us, who knows? – but it might not. We are
never sure because here and at so many other crucial significant moments of
personal conjecture in the poem, the speaker soon loses interest and moves on

to something else. He seems habitually drawn to metaphor and high cultural name dropping ('my head ... brought in upon a platter' is an affected reference to John the Baptist, while the 'eternal Footman' seems the gateman to an eternity of his own devising) and with this evidence we could take him as an educated, idiosyncratic, artistic figure either close to a nervous breakdown or extemporizing on the unstructured pointlessness of his life. At the same time, our speculations on the nature of this enigmatic shadowy presence are undermined by the fact that he is embedded in a structure that is patently impersonal and inauthentic. Certainly, his rather fickle, irresolute failure to give coherent shape to his metaphor and the overall impression that he is suffering from some high cultural variant of attention deficit disorder cause him to appear more engagingly ordinary than most literary creations, particularly in poems. Yet it is entirely implausible that a genuinely uncontrived interior monologue would contain rhyme and there is even a small concession to that other basic principle of poetic design, metre. The lines vary in length and the stress pattern is irregular but it is possible to detect occasional echoes of the iambic pentameter just as we might discern a harmonic undertow in a piece of improvised jazz music. Again, while Eliot's poem differs enormously from the other three pieces considered so far – particularly in terms of our impression of the speaker and the poet's implied artistic raison d'être – it achieves its singularity by the employment of the defining characteristic of all poems; an interaction, juxtaposition or interplay between specifically poetic devices and features common to all linguistic texts, the double pattern.

I recognize that the argument advanced so far is unlikely to convince every reader – as we will see, some are ideologically and temperamentally ill disposed towards the very notion of finding a definition for poetry – but as the book progresses and involves detailed engagements with such issues as the history and transmutations of poetry and the critical ideas that inform our perceptions of it, the value of the double pattern as an anchor point in an otherwise perplexing torrent of ideas will become self-evident. At this point, it would be useful to pose a number of fundamental questions, which will be readdressed at greater length in due course.

If one accepts the premise that the double pattern exists as the definitive feature of verse, then it might hold some clue as to why exactly poetry is written: to borrow an analogy from the sciences, if we can identify the predominant active constituent of a chemical substance, then we have taken a crucial step towards explaining why, for some, that substance is addictive.

We will consider literary theories in depth in Part III, but here I shall offer some general observations on the raw material of poetry, language. Throughout the history of Western culture, we have been encouraged, often obliged, when using language – spoken or written, for purposes political, religious, legal or social – to attend to certain abiding precepts: clarity, transparency and the faithful communication of what is deemed to be or can be verified as the truth. The music of language, its decorative possibilities or its user's predilection towards elegance or stylistic sophistry, all these are permissible within strict limitations. If the message or the argument is attended by passionate commitment – declarations of love, hellfire-and-brimstone-type religious sermons or political speeches for example – then rhetoric is deemed acceptable, provided that it buttresses the speaker's conviction and sincerity rather than mesmerizes or calculatedly deceives the listener. The only sphere of linguistic communication in which devices that purposely disrupt transparency are not only permitted but can be deployed without regulation or limitation is literature, and the genre in which these are used most self-consciously and intensively is poetry. Most official accounts of why this licence is available for verse state that verse performs no serious function in the affairs of man. It is, at its most elevated, an art form, a diversion from the routines and demands of the real world in which language is the means by which we organize our daily lives and plan our futures. Some have claimed for poetry properties that place it on a par with philosophy or spiritual and personal enlightenment – most notably the Romantics – but while such claims are intriguing, the fact is that beyond the coterie of those who made them, they have not altered the status of poetry as an ineffectual annex to real language.

Here we encounter a number of paradoxes. Few poets, however self-deprecating, unpretentious or modest they might be, would consign their craft to the subordinate status of a mere entertainment, a slightly refined counterpart to television or football. And while good poets are possessed of extraordinary intellectual gifts, only a small minority perceive their poems as contributions to the sum of human knowledge. There is a general consensus, involving poets themselves, on what poetry is not and what it does not do, but rarely, if ever, is there ventured a thesis on how its difference from everything else occasions its addictive qualities, both for practitioners and readers, and, most importantly, grants it significance. The reason for this is both beguiling and outstandingly simple. Consider again Wollheim's twofold thesis, involving the interplay between subject (the thing or idea represented) and object (the actual painting itself). The composite materials that make up the latter – paint, brushes, canvas and so on – to create the former are relatively impersonal, in the sense that before the artist gives them shape, they are formless, inconsequential matter. The poetic object is made of language, the material that animates our lives, the units that enable us to meet our husbands, wives or partners, that we teach to our children, that document our status as drivers, workers, homeowners, living beings and, in the end, dead ones. Language is our intimate, an ever present feature of our conscious existence, its particularities as familiar to us in the way we use it as our physical bodies. Yet there is only one area in which we are permitted, by convention, to be limitlessly creative with it, to turn it into patterns of sound and rhythm that would be deemed distractions in the real world, to make extravagant leaps from one level of meaning to another by using metaphor simply because we want to without paying heed to the rational or the logical. Because the material that we draw upon to make poems is also the stuff of wills, death certificates, constitutions and declarations of undying love between very real people, our breaking and rewriting of the rules that govern non-poetic language are much more than indulgence or entertainment.

As I made clear at the opening of Chapter 1, poetry is unlimited with regard to subject or perspective: any type of speaker can address any topic in any manner. But unlike its non-literary counterparts, the subject of the poem will always in part also be its object, its medium. There are poems about every known subject and some unknown, and each one of them will also be about language. Poetry also, however, permits its practitioners and connoisseurs to set up a tension between the regulated function of language as a channel for information and its curious potential to defy the rational and the orderly. Every time we speak or write, even when we are doing so in a formal or impersonal manner – filling in a form, answering a telephone – we always, sometimes despite ourselves, feel a sense of personal, exclusive empathy with our medium, but we know also that we must share its conventions, its material, with everyone else. Some of us are proud of our accents and idioms as the badges of region and background, others evolve stylistic idiosyncrasies in speech and writing that are meant to evince some special personal characteristics. We are constantly aware that the medium that is part of our consciousness is capable of extinguishing our sense of individuality. In the real world, our struggles against this are predicated upon allowable idiosyncrasies and variations: articulacy, eloquence and a rich lexicon might mark us out as special, if only to ourselves, but in truth there will be many others who can perform just as well. We escape one set of depersonalizing conventions to join yet another, albeit more elite, branch. Poetry, however, offers a sphere, a means of expression, in which uniqueness seems attainable. It does so by providing a catalyst between two independent networks of conventions, the intrinsically poetic and those that poetry shares with non-poetic language. Despite poetry's apparent abundance of depersonalizing conventions and regulations, its opportunity for independence, a sense of being able to control, even transcend the system is hugely extended. The double pattern involves an interaction between two programmes of composition, which means that the poet, if sufficiently skilled, can gain release from the ultimate control of each.

It was clearly Williams' intention in 'Spring and All' to free himself completely from the cloying legacies of traditional poetry, so why, we must ask, did he not make that final gesture of detachment by abandoning that last formal convention that bound, indeed tied, his text to the very tradition that he disavowed, the poetic line? The question is rhetorical, at least to the extent that the poem which survives testifies not only to his choice to write in lines but also to the unique effect that this decision brought about. Williams is long deceased and we have no record of the intuitions and thoughts that attended the composition of the poem. Nonetheless, it is evident from the words and lines themselves that he was as much preoccupied with the process of recording and communicating experience – language – as he was with the prelinguistic images themselves. He was not simply deploying the line as a cursory acknowledgement of a convention now stripped of its formal characteristics. Rather, the line becomes, for him, a means of generating nuances of meaning that cannot be accounted for in terms of the standard rules of semantics and syntactic coherence. His raw material comprised the same basic units to which everyone else has access and, at a localized level, he felt obliged to use these in accordance with roughly the same regulations that govern any assembly of two or more words. At the same time, however, the line provides him with a supplementary register, a second level of signification. It does so by generating impressions of uncertainty, hesitation, even evanescence that are imitative, in the sense that we are given the opportunity to witness, uniquely, the poet at work as the sentient intermediary between language and prelinguistic experience and perception.

In this respect, Williams' poem is more an extension of, rather than a break from, the conventions of regular verse. As Donne showed in 'The Flea', it is possible to set up counterpoints between apparent spontaneity and improvisations – ordinary language – and a pattern entirely comprising a mosaic of phonemic and rhythmic schema. As a consequence, the characters are caught in a curious hall of mirrors, somewhere between the peremptory, temporal sphere of time involving the imponderables of decision, response and consequence and a frozen purely representational state, like figures in a painting. It is an effect that can only be achieved via the double pattern but it is not merely a recreational diversion. It raises questions as to our relationships with the medium that, some would argue, confers upon us our sense of being, language.

In *The Republic* (1888), Plato has much to say about poetry. In Book 10 an exchange takes place regarding the nature of imitation and representation: the subject is ostensibly art, but the originary motive is as usual the determining of the nature of truth. By the end of the dialogue Socrates has established a parallel hierarchy of media and physical activities. The carpenter makes the actual bed, but the idea or concept behind this act of creation is God's. The painter is placed at the next stage down in this creative hierarchy: he can observe the carpenter making the bed and dutifully record this process. The poet, it seems, exists in a somewhat ambiguous relation to this column of originators, makers and imitators:

> Perhaps they [poets] may have come across imitators and been deceived by them; they may not have remembered when they saw their works that these were but imitations thrice removed from the truth, and could easily be made without any knowledge of the truth, because they are appearances only and not realities. (Plato, 1888, p. 312)

In short, the poet is capable of unsettling the hierarchy that sustains the clear relation between appearance and reality. Poets, as Aristotle and Plato recognized, are pure rhetoricians: they work within a kind of metalanguage which draws continuously upon the devices of rhetoric but which is not primarily involved in the practical activities of argument and persuasion. As the above quote suggests, they move disconcertingly through the various levels of creation, imitation and deception, and as Plato made clear, such fickle mediators were not the most welcome inhabitants in a Republic founded upon a clear and unitary correspondence between appearance and reality.

While Plato's stern indictment of poetry has never been officially sanctioned, his sense of it as a dissolute aberration from the conventions of non-poetic discourse has endured. He was the first commentator to note that poetry is a law unto itself, capable of creating trajectories of signification that transgress the consensually agreed contract between what he terms *dianoia/pragmata* and *lexis/taxis*, reality and language. He had postulated a forerunner to the double pattern. Roman Jakobson, a more recent critic, whose work on poetry we will consider in detail in Chapter 9, was more precise on how poetry achieves its aberrant status. Jakobson (1960, p. 39) states: 'The poetic function projects the principle of equivalence from the axis of selection into the axis of combination.' Jakobson's notion of 'equivalence' corresponds closely with Plato's contract between *dianoia/pragamata* and *lexis/taxis*. In non-poetic discourse this is dominated by the 'axis of selection'. When we use language, we choose individual words from the axis of selection and assemble them according to the conventions of the 'axis of combination' or, in basic terms, grammar. It is possible to create a nonsensical yet grammatically correct sentence:

I am song but a shameful sea must soon be inside the pastry.

The pronouns, connectives, adjectives, verbs and nouns follow the abstract rules for grammatical coherence but because the relationship between key individual words bears no resemblance to the rational and logical connectedness between their equivalents in the prelinguistic world, the sentence appears absurd and incoherent. The axis of selection refers to the choice we make when we choose each consecutive word in the construction of a sentence. We know we have to use a verb or a noun or a pronoun, but which one? Our decision is influenced primarily by general principles of clarity and coherence, so we opt for a word that corresponds as closely as possible to the idea or fact we wish to communicate; we attempt to close the gap between language and reality. The poet, however, chooses words not according to a sense of duty to an extrinsic frame of reference. Instead, the chain of meanings and connections becomes possessed of its own internalized anti-logic; the poem is a law unto itself, with the relationship between images and ideas within the text superseding any responsibility to notions of order and reason that prevail outside it. This is what Jakobson means when he refers to the 'principle of equivalence' shifting from the axis of selection to that of combination. The selective axis is the mechanism that anchors specific linguistic utterances or writings to a broader consensus on what word is appropriate in a given context or most suitable for the apparent purpose of a statement. When we write or, indeed, read a text, we focus on how each word reacts with others in the sentence and also on how the image created by the syntax corresponds with our sense of the actual or the plausible. In Jakobson's model of poetic writing, this second register, anchoring the text to an extrinsic frame of reference, is subordinated to a more powerful mechanism where words and images shed their allegiance to the normative conventions outside the poem and create their own internalized dynamic. Consider the opening stanza of Craig Raine's 'Professor Klaeber's Nasty Dream':

> High September hedges,
> and the sun's great golden vowel
> beating gold on turquoise paper.

The first line establishes what appears to be the context – tentatively, a rural scene – and the subsequent reference to the sun maintains a degree of continuity. So far the poem has not disturbed the balance between the two axes and Raine's choice of words from the axis of selection reinforces our accustomed expectations of the description of a late summer landscape, but then we come upon 'vowel'. The word, a noun, is grammatically correct but in terms of our standard conception of the prelinguistic world, it is incompatible with the context. Suddenly a new set of images has intruded upon the opening phrase: 'the sun's great golden vowel/beating gold on turquoise paper'. The notions of writing and language have now become interwoven with the denotation of sunshine and landscape and, as the poem proceeds, the two patterns of imagery continue to intersect. We are told that the 'hedge's medieval manuscript' is 'wild with dog rose'; 'pollen' is made up of 'soft asterisks' and the 'brambles' are 'wound in an endless diphthong'. 'September', Raine concludes, is like an engrossing text, 'undecipherable', possessed of 'unreadable beauty,/beyond all letters'. The broader thematic foci of the countryside and language are distinguishable, in the sense that we encounter them as the prevailing thematic polarities of the poem, but their relationship corresponds with no rational or empirical state outside the text. The combinative axis – the internal self-governing chain of connections – has taken over from its selective counterpart.

In a work of fiction, a biography, perhaps an essay, it would be possible to suggest some idiosyncratic or psychological link between an individual's experience of the countryside in late summer and their preoccupation with language. Such a proposition would inevitably invoke a framework of causality, the need to rationalize, or at least establish as a fact, the subject's state of mind. In Raine's poem, however, the two referential complexes are neither explained nor logically connected; they become part of a rolling, contrapuntal dynamic whose existence as the core of the poem excuses it from any responsibility to account for itself as coherent or logical, at least in terms of the way we accept those ordinances in the real world.

Poetry, as we are continually reminded, is prone to the excessive use of metaphor and other figurative devices but given that these are permissible in all other discourses, this is more a case of excess and abundance than a definition. There is, however, a difference. In non-poetic language, excursions from the rational are the exception rather than the rule, deployed when thought useful as a means of persuading the reader or listener of some explanation or truth. In poems, the relationship between the existence we assume we know and the one created by the words is less predictable. The poem draws upon the lexicon of ordinary language but assembles the words in a manner that invokes yet does not assent to accepted reality.

Let us return to the question posed above: why is it that poetry is a compulsive, addictive discourse that seems to have no consensually agreed function? Poetry, through the double pattern, enables the poet to engage with the standard public conventions of language while undermining their authority. The poet controls separate levels of linguistic organization – some peculiar to verse and others common to verse and all other non-poetic discourses – and is, as a consequence, able to create a limitless number of permutations upon effect and meaning through their interaction. For both its creator and reader, the poem obtains the ultimate state of expressive freedom.

There are, then, three elements of the double pattern. The first involves the normative consensual realm of writing, perception and reason that the poem shares with the world beyond itself, a covenant ratified by the fact that poetry and all other discourses draw upon the same lexicon as indivisible units, words, and honour the same conventions of grammar. The second and third, involve, respectively, the material of language – its sounds, rhythms, shapes – and its capacity to create a mental universe that absconds from any responsibility to our sense of the real or the actual. The common factor, the feature that unites the various dimensions of the double pattern is their raw material, language. The factor that divides them is the question of how language corresponds to everything else, the primitive basic notion of who we are. Poetry continually challenges easy solutions to this question for the simple reason that it confronts us with the contrast between our sense of presence – ourselves in relation to others and the world – and the means by which we secure and stabilize this – language.

In Part II we will consider how, over the past four centuries, poets and critics have dealt with this unsettling conundrum.

PART II

HISTORY: THE RENAISSANCE TO POSTMODERNISM

3

The Renaissance

I have chosen to begin this history in the 16th century for the simple reason that far more verse was written during the 100 years between the beginning of the reign of Elizabeth I and the mid-17th century than in the previous four centuries. It is quite possible that, prior to the 16th century, the poetic output of those inclined to write verse was widespread and prolific but we will never know because very little was preserved. In purely chronological terms, we have roughly one significant text for every five years of the 14th and 15th centuries. Profusion is not, of course, a guarantee of significance or quality, but the self-evident diversity and individual intricacy of the verse produced from the mid-16th century onwards provides us for the first time with a comparative index to the genre, a sense of common objectives, of competitiveness and a consensus on cultural affinities shared by similarly disposed individuals. Also, the 16th century saw the first ever treatises on literary criticism, albeit few and fragmentary, which provide us with some indication of contemporaneous ideas regarding the nature and function of poetry. Finally and significantly, poetry in this period played a major part in the emergence of literature as something produced for and consumed by the general public. Virtually all Renaissance English drama, to a large extent, comprises verse.

Measure for Measure is generally regarded as one of William Shakespeare's 'problem' plays. The principal problem for the reader or member of the audience is that it offers a series of questions that remain largely unanswered. It does not inscribe a reliable formula against which we can properly judge the violation of moral norms or the subversion of political, religious or social absolutes. How should we judge Isabella's decision to preserve her own code of virginity and consequently to endanger her brother's life? Is Angelo merely a disagreeable individual or a symptom of a more widespread form of social and moral corruption? Is the Duke obliged to temporarily abdicate, disguise himself and engage with the murky practices of his fiefdom because autocratic monarchy is no longer a practical institution?

Like many of Shakespeare's more tendentious dealings with the state and the individual, the context is shifted safely to a time and a place that are not early 17th-century London. However, the questions of government and of administering the judicial system faced by the Duke bear a more than accidental resemblance to a number of ideas addressed by James I (before whom the play was first performed) in his tract *Basilicon Doron*. The image of Vienna as a city-state threat-ened by criminality and incipient moral anarchy could just as easily apply to the expanding capital of the new trading and mercantile powerhouse of England.

The play comprises partly prose and partly blank verse. Before Milton's *Paradise Lost* (1667) legitimized blank verse as a vehicle for non-dramatic poetry, the form was treated by consensus as a hybrid. It was poetic in the sense that it adhered to the abstract template of the iambic pentameter and by custom its use was accompanied by an unprosaic abundance of rhetorical devices. The absence of rhyme and, in general, other sound patterns lent a little credibility to the speaker on stage, someone who, if they conversed with others or addressed the audience in couplets or stanzas, would seem ostentatiously unreal. We will never know if Shakespeare or his contemporaries succeeded in creating an authentic copy of the spoken improvised prose of the period, since no actual or vicarious record of the latter survives, but the evidence of the plays themselves, involving colloquialisms, slang and casual syntax, indicates that this was their intention. What these plays provide, then, is a working model of the relationship, then perceived, between poetry and ordinary language. *Measure for Measure* and all Shakespeare's other plays confirm our expectation that poetry is, in general, the preserve of the mercantile classes, the gentry and the aristocracy. Poetry was, irrespective of one's thoughts on its value, the badge of cultural sophistication. Non-poetic language, then and today, is the pragmatic medium in which opinions are straightforwardly expressed and arrangements made, with priority given more to the effective transference of the message than to the eloquence of the exchange; prose is the language of Shakespeare's lower orders. I should qualify the above with the term 'predomi-nantly' because while in most instances these two types of expression reinforce social stereotypes, there are also considerable overlaps, where people from one class borrow the linguistic garment of the other. It is even more intriguing when the two genres operate as part of the same dialogue. In these instances, Shakespeare provides a far more compelling and eloquent thesis on the relative capacities of poetry and ordinary language than will be found in any contem-porary prose work that attempts to address the same topic.

The following extract is from Act I, Scene ii, lines 118–28. Angelo, in the Duke's absence, is busily enforcing laws on public and private behaviour, including sexual morality; his rationale being that a ruthlessly enforced code of personal ethics will result in a collective attendance to order and stability. Every member of Shakespeare's audience would have recognized parallels between this albeit largely secular ordinance and the programmes endorsed by extreme branches of Protestantism, particularly in King James's home country, Scotland. Claudio, a young gentleman, tells Lucio, a resourceful opportunist of no obvious social rank, of his arrest for having had premarital sex with his fiancée:

Lucio   Why, how now, Claudio! Whence comes this restraint?
Claudio   From too much liberty, my Lucio, liberty:

As surfeit is the father of much fast
So every scope by the immoderate use
Turns to restraint. Our natures do pursue –
Like rats that ravin down their proper bane –
A thirsty evil, and when we drink we die.

Lucio   If I could speak so wisely under an arrest, I would send
for certain of my creditors. And yet, to say the truth, I had
as life have the foppery of freedom as the morality of
imprisonment. What's thy offence, Claudio?

Lucio's 'Whence comes this restraint?' is a straightforward enquiry as to why Claudio has found himself in the custody of the Provost and his officers. But instead of answering him directly, as one might expect of someone detained, threatened with a death sentence and for whom the actualities of life are all too tangible, Claudio launches into an extravagant melee of rhetorical flourishes, all of which involve profound observations on his existential state, while seeming to provide little useful information.

In purely rhetorical terms, Claudio's florid response involves a combination of euphuism (the extended use of balance and paradox), synoeciosis (expanded paradox), progressio (advancing by steps of a comparison) and syncrisis (comparing contrary elements in contrasting clauses), all interlaced with metaphor.

I document and specify these devices not because I see them as being of much use in your social or intellectual life, dear 21st-century reader, but because Shakespeare was offering the Claudios in his audience, and indeed the Lucios, something more than the next stage in his enthralling plot. For those with even a rudimentary grammar school education, Shakespeare included, Claudio's speech would have seemed very familiar, similar to the kind of exercise they were obliged to perform in the classroom. The basic textbooks for rudimentary instruction on the devices and mechanisms of language were derived from Horace's *Ars Poetica*, translated into Italian and French in the 15th century and plagiarized in a variety of English manuals in the 16th. Horace and his successors rarely reflected on the reasons why people might write poetry or on its ultimate or even practical purpose; instead he and they offered voluminous instructions on its mechanics – metre, structure, rhetorical devices – and the potential effects of these upon the listener or hearer. Poetry was a means by which language could project you into another world, one where the actuality of everyday life was dispersed into various states of figurative speculation. In this regard it is not entirely implausible to see Shakespeare here as presenting poetry as a refuge from uncomfortable reality. Rather than face the blunt facts that he is under arrest and might soon be executed, he uses rhetoric, poetry, as a comforting, intellectually respectable escape. Lucio, replying, casts a somewhat sceptical eye upon his friend's performance: 'If I could speak so wisely under an arrest, I would send for certain of my creditors.' Such droll irony: verbal dexterity will not, he knows, undo reality.

As I have stated, many in Shakespeare's audience would recognize that the playwright had here annexed another agenda to his story of governance, love and justice. Those who were literate might well have come upon Puttenham's *The Arte of English Poesie* (1589). This was the Rough Guide to everything that anyone might wish to know about verse. Puttenham even went so far as to 'translate' the original Latin terms for rhetorical devices into what he deemed their familiar English equivalents, sometimes hilariously (*micterismus*, the 'fleering frumpe'; *paradoxon*, 'the wonderer'; *antitheton*, 'the quarrelor' and so on). Readers of Puttenham and even of his more respectable high cultural competitors would have seen in Lucio something both familiar and disturbing, a man who has become an impressive rhetorician and versifier but who seems incapable of recognizing that his skills are but an avoidance of truth and contingent fact. Puttenham frequently assembles his lists of rhetorical devices as one might an armoury of weapons (see Wimsatt and Brooks, 1957, p. 234):

> Mezozeugma, or the Middlemarcher
> Sillepsis, or the double supply
> Parison, or the figure of even
> Traductio, or the tranlacer
> Antitheton, or the quarreller
> Ploche, or the doubler
> Ironia, or the drie mock
> Meiosis, or the disabler
> Micterismus, or the fleering frumpe
> Charientismus, or the privie nippe
> > ('These be souldiers to the figure *allgoria*
> > and fight under the banner of dissimulation.')
> Paradoxon, or the wonderer
> Synecdoche, or the figure of quick conceit
> Noema, or the figure of close conceit

One cannot help but notice the uncomfortable similarity between this marshalling of linguistic forces and Lucio's disciplined, and desperate, retreat from actuality into the apparent safety of rhetoric. Shakespeare's audience too would have observed this, and some might well have recalled Puttenham's remarks on what rhetoric and poetry achieve:

> ... they deceive the ear and also the mind, drawing it
> from plainness and simplicity to a certain doubleness,
> whereby our talk is the more guileful and abusing.

He continues:

> And ye shall know that we dissemble, I mean speak
> otherwise than we think, in earnest and well as in

> sport, under covert and dark terms and in learned
> and apparent speeches ...

Claudio seems to be dutifully implementing Puttenham's directive on the creation of 'doubleness', 'dissembling', a deliberate 'drawing' away from 'plainness and simplicity'. Puttenham, although willing to expand upon the immediate effects and consequences of poetry, never ventures a thesis on why exactly or for what purpose anyone might wish to use language in this way and nor indeed do any of his more elevated, high cultural contemporaries. Sir Philip Sidney's *The Defence of Poesie* (1595) is far more discursive and polemical than Puttenham, more a gentleman's essay than a textbook. Sidney parades his familiarity with his classical antecedents, Plato, Aristotle, Horace et al., and attempts with languid unsuccess to reach some conclusion of his own on the value of poetry. Typically, he says:

> Poesy, therefore, is an art of imitation, for so Aristotle termeth it in his word mimesis, that is to say, a representing, counterfeiting or figuring forth; to speak metaphorically, a speaking picture, with this end, – to teach and delight.

Sidney not only distorts and misrepresents Aristotle's conception of mimesis, he also embarks upon an audacious perversion of logic, contending that representation, counterfeiting and 'figuring' (the use of metaphor) are but stages in the veritable process of truth telling and transparency. His so-called 'defence' of poetry is a tissue of fabrications and self-contradictions. One cannot question his motive; he wishes to rescue verse from its status as a fickle testimony to the unreliability of language. But in attempting to argue that it is a vehicle for unalloyed fact and truth, he becomes the victim of his own flamboyant desperation. For a more honest account, go to Shakespeare's juxtaposition of the haplessly adventurous Claudio with the pragmatic Lucio and to Puttenham's description of verse as 'guileful' and 'abusing', the motor of 'dissembling', 'covert dark terms' and 'dissimulation'.

It is difficult to accept – but accept it we must – that the man ranked higher than any other in the field of English poetry perceived his medium as fickle and by its nature unreliable. There is a passage in Act II, Scene ii where Isabella, novitiate nun and sister of Claudio, argues with Angelo over the ethical and judicial validity of her sibling's death sentence. Lucio, at her shoulder, offers encouragement and guidance, rather in the manner of a theatre director:

Isabella	We cannot weigh our brother with ourself:
	Great men may jest with saints; 'tis wit in them,
	But in the less foul profanation.
Lucio	(*Aside to Isabella*) Thou'rt i' th' right girl: more o' that.
Isabella	That in the captain's but a choleric word
	Which in the soldier is flat blasphemy.
Lucio	(*Aside to Isabella*) Art advis'd o' that? More on't.
Angelo	Why do you put these sayings upon me?

Isabella   Because authority, though it err like others
                    Hath yet a kind of medicine in itself
                    That skins vice o' the top. Go to your bosom;
                    Knock there, and ask your heart what it doth know. (126–37)

Isabella and Angelo, as befits their social rank, converse in blank verse, marshalling orotund rhetoric devices to service their opposing arguments. Lucio, the pragmatist, commentates:

> Ay touch him; here's the vein (70)
> Ay well said (89)
> That's well said (109)
> O, to him to him, wench! He will relent: (124)

Wryly, Shakespeare leaves us uncertain as to what aspect of Isabella's performance Lucio feels is deserving of such unreserved commendation. He might of course admire her intellectual gravitas and linguistic versatility but it eventually becomes evident that he senses that these are actually of little practical use in the world of instinct and contingency. He suspects that Angelo is not so much persuaded by her argument as entranced by her physical presence and, because of her vocation, her elusiveness. And Lucio is correct. Angelo, supposedly guardian of high principles, does indeed offer Isabella a reprieve for her brother, provided that she has sex with him. The Duke, in disguise, arranges a 'bed trick' when Angelo's ex-fiancée Mariana is substituted for Isabella and Angelo becomes entrapped by his own hypocrisies.

It would be misleading and do a grave injustice to Shakespeare's superlative intellect to treat *Measure for Measure* as a play that addresses itself only to the intractable problems of morality, justice and governance. It has a second agenda, not unrelated to its more conspicuous themes, but which establishes it as a work of beguiling originality. It is about writing, specifically the difference between poetry and everything else. The plot's engine, its motivating force, is the dynamic relationship between contingency, desire and action. Ideas, abstract principles and beliefs are continually invoked but rendered laughably ineffectual by the power of actuality. Ideals and their intellectual and spiritual appendices are always addressed in verse, while events, the opportunity to do something or effect change, are occasioned exclusively by prose.

Act III, Scene i is a wonderful composite of the play as a whole. Its two most memorable passages involve Claudio alone in his cell contemplating the nature of death:

> Ay, but to die, and go we know not where;
> To lie in cold obstruction and to rot;
> This sensible warm motion to become

> A kneaded clod; and the delighted spirit
> To bathe in fiery floods, or to reside
> In thrilling region of thick-ribbed ice; (116–21)

Removed from the context of the play, this could, credibly, be offered as a lyric poem on mortality – plenty of similar ones were being written at the time. Figurative excursions and lurid imagery become substitutes for grisly unalterable fact. Shortly after this, in the same scene, the Duke explains how he intends to effectively entrap, indeed blackmail, Angelo with the bed trick:

Duke	Have you not heard speak of Mariana, the sister of Frederick, the great soldier who miscarried at sea?
Isabella	I have heard of the lady, and good words went with her name.
Duke	She should this Angelo have married; was affianced to her by oath, and the nuptial appointed. (215–17)

The exchange between the Duke and Isabella, in prose, is governed entirely by the nostrum that facts, some of them distasteful, are what determine our lives and prospects; language enables us to acknowledge them, particularize our intention to deal with them, but they, rather than it, set the agenda for what we can be and do. Poetry, however, both in exchanges and in such monologues as Claudio's, is by its nature delusional. We can build metaphoric universes from simple ideas, but in the end all we have produced is a piece of language; entrancing, wonderful, beguiling, even persuasive, but in the end absolutely futile.

On only one other occasion did Shakespeare make writing as much the subject of his work as its vehicle and this, significantly, was in the play that most regard as his last, his goodbye note to the trade. Nearly all of Act I, Scene i of *The Tempest* is in prose, as the Boatswain, his crew and passengers desperately attempt to keep their vessel afloat in the storm. Prose seems appropriate, given that their world is now composed exclusively of contingent, unpredictable and deadly facts – there is little opportunity for imaginative speculation.

They do not, of course, die but find themselves on Prospero's island, a place just as fantastic and hypothetical as the Afterlife. On the island, everyone apart from the seamen and the ordinary passengers speaks in blank verse. Even Caliban, a figure able to acquire aspects of the human but originating from a much lower point in the chain of being, is comfortable with the sophisticated nuances of the form. At one point, he plots with Stephano, the drunken butler, and Trinculo, a jester, an assault on his master Prospero (Act III, Scene ii, lines 88–101). They speak in prose, while he declaims, elegantly, in the high cultural idiom taught to him by Prospero. Indeed, he knows no other form of speech:

Trinculo	I did not give thee the lie: Out o' your wits and hearing too? A pox o' your bottle! This can sack and drinking do. A murrain on your monster, and the devil take you fingers!
Caliban	Ha, ha ha!
Stephano	Now forward with your tale – Prithee stand further off.
Caliban	Beat him enough: after a little time, I'll beat him too.
Stephano	Stand further – Come, proceed.
Caliban	Why, as I told thee, 'tis a custom with him I' the afternoon to sleep: there thou may'st brain him, Having first seiz'd his books; or with a log Batter his skull

The concluding enjambment reminds one of the counterpoint between improvisation and design in Donne's 'The Flea'. The syntax cuts across the two pentameters but the slight pause at the line ending preserves their formal architecture. Caliban hesitates and in that brief moment reflects, perhaps savours, the exact nature of his intent. There is, of course, something superbly incongruous about the refinement, the pure artistry, of the passage and its content:

> with a log [he pauses and reflects]
> Batter his skull ...

What sort of creature is this who has become so well assimilated to the conventions of high art while being still, essentially, subhuman? He is, at least in part, the creation of Prospero, the ultimate autocrat who not only governs his domain but within it enjoys a sense of other-worldliness, controlling creatures who are not quite real but who nonetheless converse admirably in the idiom allotted to them by their master. Prospero's closest counterpart in the real world is the literary writer, the playwright and poet.

Shakespeare, aside from his designated status as the greatest writer in English, was also, albeit obliquely, an immensely shrewd critic. In his plays, he continually raised questions regarding the nature and function of poetry and, most astutely, left them unanswered. In doing so, he diagnosed and reflected the mood of his age.

The poets who are thought to have best embodied the spirit of the English Renaissance are those of the so-called Metaphysical School. They thrived in the early 17th century and their most celebrated representatives are John Donne, George Herbert, Henry Vaughan, Robert Herrick, Richard Crashaw, Thomas Traherne and Andrew Marvell. The two most astute summaries of what the verse of these men involved came from figures who held antithetical views on its value. Samuel Johnson (1779–81, pp. 46–7) stated:

> But wit, abstracted from its effects upon the bearer, may be more rigorously and philosophically considered as a kind of *discordia concors*; a combination of dissimilar images, or discovery of occult resemblances in things apparently

unlike. Of wit, thus defined, they have more than enough. *The most heterogeneous ideas are yoked by violence together* [emphasis added]; nature and art are
ransacked for illustrations, comparisons, and illusions; their learning instructs,
and their subtlety surprises; but the reader commonly thinks his improvement dearly bought, and, though he sometimes admires, is seldom pleased.

Johnson objects to, as he sees it, the overadventurous and irresponsible use of
figurative language (or 'wit' as he puts it). In this respect, as we shall see, Johnson
was speaking on behalf of the general consensus of 18th-century ideas regarding
poetry. His principal point is that the Metaphysicals deliberately used language
to undermine orderly perceptions of reality. By the phrase 'heterogeneous ideas
are yoked by violence together' he meant that ideas, concepts and images that
had no natural or logical relation to each other were caused to seem as though
they did; the innately paradoxical was made to seem self-evidently logical and
plausible. In his 'Second Anniversary', Donne tells of how

> her pure and innocent blood
> Spoke in her cheeks, and so distinctly wrought
> That one might almost say her body thought

Typically he engages with that perennial debating point of philosophers and
theologians, the relationship between the corporal and the spiritual and,
although one might take issue with Johnson's use of the term 'violence',
there is without doubt a hypnotizing 'yoking together' of 'heterogeneous
ideas'. Johnson and his contemporaries were aware that figurative language
was a collateral feature of all poetic writing but in their view it should be
used with discrimination and as a means of clarifying or buttressing a point
of logical disputation. Donne, however, performs the verbal equivalent of
illusionism, causing her cheeks to speak and her body to think. T.S. Eliot
(1921, p. 2024) stated:

> It is the difference between the intellectual poet and reflective poet. Tennyson
> and Browning are poets, and they think, but they do not feel their thought as
> immediately as the odor of a rose. A thought to Donne was an experience; it
> modified his sensibility. *When a poet's mind is perfectly equipped for its work, it
> is constantly amalgamating disparate experience* [emphasis added]; the ordinary
> man's experience is chaotic, irregular, and fragmentary. The latter falls in
> love, or reads Spinoza, and these two experiences have nothing to do with
> each other, or with the noise of the typewriter or the smell of cooking; in the
> mind of the poet these experiences are always forming new wholes.

Eliot agrees almost exactly with Johnson on the nature of Metaphysical technique: 'A thought to Donne was an experience'. But Eliot regards the ability to
undermine the logical and empirical specifications of reality as the essential
calling of the poet; to use poetic language to oblige us to re-examine our rational

processes of thinking and our perceptions of actuality. For Johnson, the 18th-century Rationalist, the distinction between, say, bodily sensations and the workings of the intellect should be maintained as much in poetry as in a philosophical essay. For Eliot, it is the duty of the poet to challenge, even undermine, such orthodox classifications: 'in the mind of the poet these experiences are always forming new wholes'. While these two critics differ with regard to the value of Metaphysical writing, they agree precisely on its character and effect. What they did not do, however, was to propose an explanation for this period of imaginative excess.

Aside from its ostensible topic, every poem of the period betrays the poet's sense of perplexity. This is at once a desire to master the formal demands of verse along with an implicit eagerness to create from the artefact something neither sanctioned nor available in other forms of writing. It often seems that each is involved in a question, an experiment. Each knew how poetry worked and from experience and rhetorical handbooks had a reasonably clear knowledge of its capacities, yet none seemed sure of its ultimate purpose. English poets of this period had inherited no legacy from their immediate precursors against which to test their own ambitions and intuitions. In the 15th and 16th centuries, critics such as Tasso, du Bellay, Scaliger and Sidney tried their best to adapt the principles of classical verse to the contemporaneous indigenous languages and cultures of Europe, but though heroic in their intentions, the task was beyond them. Irrespective of its veneration of classical ideas, post-medieval Christian Europe, torn apart by the Reformation and the emergent commercialism of the nation state, bore no resemblance to its classical precursor. The mechanisms of 16th- and 17th-century verse, in terms of rhetoric and formal structure, were closely comparable to those of its classical antecedents, but its subject matter, the material which poetry variously consumed and transformed, was utterly different. English poetry, as we properly understand it, was born in the late 16th century but it came into the world without a familial inheritance. It had immense explosive potential but no one to advise it on how and why this might be employed. Very few poems of the period directly addressed issues such as religious division, theological and philosophical polarities and political instability, yet these universal public controversies were telescoped into vivid private evocations of chaos and irresolution.

Donne's 'The Relic' begins as follows:

> When my grave is broke up again
> Some second guest to entertain,
> (For graves have learned that woman-head
> To be to more than one a bed)
> 　　And he that digs it, spies
> A bracelet of bright hair about the bone,
> 　　Will he not let us alone,
> And think that there a loving couple lies,

Who thought that this device might be some way
To make their souls, at the last busy day,
Meet at this grave, and make a little stay?

The line 'a bracelet of bright hair about the bone' was celebrated by Eliot as a brilliantly cogent example of 'the amalgamation of disparate experience'. It involves images that celebrate lived experience – the wearing of a 'bracelet', the beauty of 'bright hair' – but they are attached to a bone, all that remains of a life no longer lived. It sets the tone for the rest of the piece, in that the speaker seems intent upon convincing himself, and us, that something of his transient relationship with the woman will survive their deaths. Thus far, the speaker appears to be the kind of sublimely inventive overreacher indulged by the conventions of verse, a man who is capable of marshalling his creative skills into a defence against grim ineluctable fact. Read on, however, and we find that Donne sews into his monologue questions, doubts about the mental stability of the speaker. In the final stanza, for example, he discloses, almost unwittingly, that the woman might never actually have spoken to him:

Difference of sex we never knew,
No more than guardian angels do;
Coming and going, we
Perchance might kiss, but not between those meals;
Our hands ne'er touched the seals
Which nature, injured by late law, sets free.

The conditional – 'might', 'perchance' – informs the stanza and so predominant is this sense of ambivalence that we begin to wonder why he has never in the poem referred specifically to anything resembling even a conversation between them, let alone a relationship. Gradually, as we read the poem again and again, our suspicions grow regarding this man. The woman exists, certainly, but the speaker seems more a fantasist than her lover. At the same time, however, he is a gifted lyricist and rhetorician, and here Donne poses a question, not unlike Shakespeare's when he equipped Caliban with similar resources. The verbal architecture of poetry might be worthy of esteem but what lies beneath it?

Donne's speaker has become subservient to the mechanism of verse. In one respect, it enables him to project his rather tragic delusions into a realm of persuasive, perhaps self-deluding artifice, while at the same time it protects him from a truth he seems unable or unwilling to confront. By implication, Donne raises the question of whether poetry can do anything more than this.

George Herbert, in 'Jordan (I)', addresses it more explicitly:

Who says that fictions only and false hair
Become a verse? Is there in truth no beauty?
Is all good structure in a winding stair?

> May no lines pass, except they do their duty
> Not to a true, but painted chair?

The question is rhetorical and his apparent distress of having betrayed principles of truth and transparency is feigned. The speaker is a magnificent paradox, a man who will not cease to torment himself with the fact that his medium is a vain delusion, yet who rejoices in his ability to master its complexities. 'Jordan (I)' is an exercise in finely crafted masochism; the speaker inhabits, loves, controls his verse form while seeking forgiveness for enjoying its largesse, its ability to project him beyond the mundane, the ineluctable, even the standard nostrums of scripture.

In 'Jordan (II)', Herbert begins by admitting to poetry as his calling and the passage is penitential in mood. He seems ashamed of this passion:

> When first my lines of heavn'ly joyes made mention,
> Such was their lustre, they did so excel,
> That I sought out quaint words, and trim invention;
> My thoughts began to burnish, sprout, and swell,
> Curling with metaphors a plain intention,
> Decking the sense, as if it were to sell.
>
> Thousands of notions in my brain did run,
> Offering their service, if I were not sped;
> I often blotted what I had begun:
> This was not quick enough, and that was dead.
> Nothing could seem too rich to clothe the sun,
> Much less those joys which trample on his head.
>
> As flames do work and wind, when they ascend,
> So did I weave my self into the sense.
> But while I bustled, I might hear a friend
> Whisper, 'How wide is all this long pretense!
> There is in love a sweetness ready penned:
> Copy out only that, and save expense.'

His account in the first two stanzas of how he revelled in the minutiae of composition, corralled language and imaginative indulgence into art is an almost exact anticipation of Johnson's and Eliot's descriptions of the techniques of the period. Herbert, however, comments also on the fundamental issue of how he feels. His 'friend', in truth his conscience, reminds him that there is more truth and sincerity in unadorned transparent statements than in any form of verse.

Andrew Marvell is seen as the only poet of any worth who maintained the Metaphysical tradition into the later 17th century. He was born in 1621, roughly 10 years before the deaths of Herbert and Donne. His most important, enigmatic poem is 'The Garden'. Its eponymous subject is a variation upon the original garden, Eden, an unusual version customized by Marvell for his own purposes. The speaker, and we can assume it is Marvell, imagines himself as the first human being, Adam. But this is not just Adam before the Fall – a routine idyllic projection – this is Adam before Eve, before any contact with God and indeed before language:

> Meanwhile the mind from pleasure less
> Withdraws into its happiness;
> The mind, that ocean where each kind
> Does straight its own resemblance find;
> Yet it creates, transcending these
> Far other worlds and other seas
> Annihilating all that's made
> To a green thought in a green shade

The mind would at this point be freed from such distractions as love and sex ('pleasure less'). It would withdraw into itself, 'Annihilating all that's *made*', leaving behind the rational and empirical world, which Marvell suggests is as much a fabrication as a state of being, and attaining a final moment of transcendence, 'a green thought in a green shade'. In 17th-century cultural lore, green was treated as the purest colour, emblematic of uncontaminated solitude.

In this stanza, Marvell addresses the same issues as Herbert. These are poems about language, or, to be more accurate, the relationship between language and the various spiritual, moral and intellectual ideals to which we all aspire. They rehearse continually a central unifying paradox. Poetry offers a licence to do with language what in other contexts would be deemed absurd or incongruous, yet this invitation brings with it a proviso; the reminder that without language, we effectively cease to exist.

One reason why the poetry of the late 16th and early 17th centuries was marked by such an obsessive yet uneasy preoccupation with verbal and formal exuberance has already been indicated; it was a rudderless genre without substantial guidelines or precedents with regard to its purpose. One should note also that these poets were faced with a world that was at every level bifurcated by contentious, antithetical postulations on what truth and actuality involved. The most profound and obvious cause of this was the Reformation. Even though the politics of England from Elizabeth I onwards were dominated by a Protestant ethic and outlook, a widespread knowledge of, and sometimes an affiliation to, Catholicism endured into the late 17th century. For the first time, at least in Western Europe, Christianity was divided between two diametrically opposed models of the human condition and man's relation to God, a division exemplified in the certainty among Catholics that the sacrament at Mass became literally the body of Christ, as opposed to the Protestant insistence that the sacrament was but an emblematic symbol of the embodiment of the Almighty. Both

branches of faith faced challenges from the nascent sphere of rational empiricism, conclusions based upon experimental observation; notably the contention
made first by Copernicus and later Galileo that the relationship between the
Earth and the Sun was the exact opposite of the Ptolemaic model adopted by the
early Christians. Indeed, the Earth itself appeared to be altering virtually every
year as news arrived of new topographical discoveries and hitherto unimagined
races. The English Civil War (1642–51) was a watershed in the history of European politics, but during the 50 years that preceded it, when the Metaphysicals
flourished, the ideas that fuelled the military conflict were already beginning to
threaten the secure assumptions that had dominated European monarchical
governance for the previous five centuries. James I's *Basilicon Doron*, with which
Shakespeare engaged, albeit implicitly, in *Measure for Measure*, challenged its
author's own right to unaccountable sovereignty.

Not only did the Metaphysicals have no clear sense of their genre's purpose, their
raw material, the world in which they existed, seemed at every level provisional,
determined as much by competing perceptions and opposing beliefs as by verifiable
fact. In those circumstances, figurative language – in Johnson's and Eliot's terms 'the
most heterogeneous ideas yoked by violence together', the 'constant amalgamating
[of] disparate experience' – might be seen as an unexceptionable even appropriate
response in poetry to the world outside the poem. The ostentatious use of figurative
devices was the most obvious means of causing language to usurp the unsteady
contours of reality but, equally, the brief revival by poets such as Herrick and
Herbert of the so-called 'Pattern Poem' indicates a desire to turn words into prelinguistic truths. The following is Robert Herrick's 'The Pillar of Fame':

> Fame's pillar here, at last we set
> Out-during marble, brass, or jet,
> Charmed and enchanted so
> As to withstand the blow
> Of o v e r t h r o w :
> Nor shall the seas
> Or o u t r a g e s
> Or storms o'rebear
> What we uprear,
> Tho' kingdoms fall
> This pillar never shall
> Decline or waste at all;
> But stand for ever by his own
> Firm and well-fix'd foundation.

Herrick spins out the figurative resonance of the word 'pillar' as something
'Charmed and enchanted so/As to withstand the blow' and which 'never shall/
Decline or waste at all', while shaping this linguistic pattern into a visual represen-
tation of the theme of the poem. The most intense evocations of natural and

human impermanence occur in the narrow shaft of quartosyllabic couplets. Just as this compacted economy of syntax and metrical structure imitate a sense of tightening and strain, so we are also aware that, in architectural and purely visual terms, the shaft is the point at which the load-bearing function of the pillar is most concentrated; and the final couplet both closes the figurative play and becomes, almost literally, the 'Firm and well-fix'd foundation' of the visual image. In a more conventional Metaphysical poem, the use of the concept of a pillar as the vehicle for figurative speculations on the relationship between notions of permanence and transience would be a routine strategy. Herrick supplements this by pressing his words into service as an image of the concepts they represent. In this respect, the Pattern Poem, while something of a rarity, was consistent with the poetic mood and temper of the time. It raised fundamental questions about the relationship between language and prelinguistic truth. (See also Herbert's 'Easter Wings' whose 'theme', the ascent to heaven of Christ at Easter, is invoked in the shape of the poem on the page; its two stanzas resemble pictures of birds in flight.)

Throughout this period, the two dimensions of the double pattern were continually, self-consciously foregrounded and counterpointed and this exemplified a broader consensus on the relationship between verse and everything else. Verse could appropriate the profound and the routine and make worlds of its own, worlds and states of mind at once beautiful, fixating, contradictory and unjustifiable. It was, in this regard, mimetic.

T.S. Eliot claimed, infamously, that the decline of Metaphysical technique and sensibility, occurring at some point during the later 17th century, marked the death knell for the quintessence of English poetic achievement. For Donne, Shakespeare and their contemporaries, thought and emotion, the intellectual and the visceral aspects of our mental universe, were the catalysts for poetry. After the Civil War, according to Eliot's model of literary history, a 'dissociation of sensibility' set in. At one extreme, the Augustans, the 18th-century poets and theorists, turned poetry into a genre where intellect and rational sensibility held sway, conferring logic upon and controlling its imaginative excesses. At the other, the Romantics, and their latter-day Victorian descendents, idolized and eventually became habituated to the magical ingredients of emotion, imagination and inspiration, giving little attention to intellectual rigour. Eliot's thesis becomes unconvincing when he attempts to offer a historical and political rationale for the changes he discerns. In the pre-Civil War period, according to Eliot, sensation and intellect had existed in a content, unselfconscious state of harmony and imaginative largesse was thus the natural expression of the poetic temperament. Here he is wrong. In an inordinate number of poems written at the time, it is evident that the poet is indeed self-consciously, sometimes guiltily, aware of the peculiarity of his enterprise; each admits to its addictive capacities but none perceives it as a collateral artistic expression of spiritual, intellectual or moral harmony. Although Eliot is correct in his characterization of poetry in the subsequent two centuries, he misdiagnoses the causes for this. Certainly, external factors played a part – the brief 'elevation' of the poet to the status of political commentator in the 18th century, and the fervour of the late 18th century as fuel for the rebellious complexion of Romanticism are examples. But the most profound influential feature in the history of English poetry is the double pattern, the awareness, by poets, that verse incorporates, preys upon and often transforms language. The alterations in the nature and character of verse during the 300 years following the Metaphysicals are radical and complex. All, however, are underpinned by the simple question that faces all poets. They are aware of the character of poetry, they know in formal terms what it is and what it might do, but the question as to what this means to them or the reader remains unanswered. The history of poetry is an index to this search for purpose.

Milton exemplifies this impulse while remaining remote from the collective habits and tradition of his period. A number of his predecessors and near successors, notably Herrick and Herbert, preoccupied themselves with the delicate issue of how the somewhat vulgar disestablished practice of poetic writing could be reconciled to the profoundest questions of all, involving God. Herbert, as we have seen, exemplified a sense of irresolution by setting his consummate poetic skill against his commitment to his faith, while all the time reminding himself of their incompatibility. Milton, throughout his early career as a poet, showed no comparable feelings of unease regarding his ability to consolidate poetry with theology. He was, in truth, preparing himself for what is arguably the most important epic, narrative poem in English, *Paradise Lost* (1667). *Paradise Lost* tells the story, in 12 books, of the creation of mankind and the reasons for our ongoing perilous state. The poem is essentially the book of Genesis in English verse and Milton had set himself a gargantuan task. In some respects, his poem resembled a lengthy dramatic work, with around 20 dramatis personae, principally Adam, Eve, God, Satan and an assembled crew of other angels, fallen and unfallen. It differs from a play in that the author also appears in it, performing the same tasks that would eventually be undertaken by the narrator in fiction; choreographing the action, introducing the characters, contextualizing their state of mind, commenting on their actions and moving the narrative forward. The only comparable attempt to achieve something quite so monumental in English verse was Spenser's *The Faerie Queene* and in this the only voice is that of the poet, in exclusive control of characterization, description, digression and comment. All poets, Spenser included, faced the problem of accommodating a sense of presence, including all the correlatives of idiom, mood and authenticity, to the abstract formal structures that defined poetry. Milton aggravated and intensified this by dividing up the poem between so many speakers with such fundamentally distinct roles, himself included. These were figures, moreover, who were inscribed deeply in everyone's basic conception of the nature of humanity – and indeed the difference between genders – and our relationship with God. It had long been a custom for poets to address God in lyric poems, but here for the first time ever God would answer back, in verse. The test of good poetic writing lay in the poet's ability to make the arbitrariness of his form and the individuality of his voice appear apposite and congruous and for Milton this would have seemed all but impossible. Whatever form he chose, even if, like Spenser, he had invented a stanza of his own to match the grandeur of the occasion, the repetitive formulaic nature of the text would have ebbed away at each character's claim upon selfhood. His solution marked a change in the history of English poetry comparable with the invention of free verse at the beginning of the 20th century.

Non-dramatic poems had before this been written in blank verse, notably by Surrey, but they were very few in number and treated as curiosities, aberrations; poetic in manner yet not in the strictest sense poems. In the late 17th century, the opportunities by which the opinions of those involved in literary writing could be made public were limited. Literary journals did not exist. However, a year after Milton's Christian epic appeared, John Dryden published his *Essay of Dramatick Poesie* (1668), which, on the topic of poetic and non-poetic language particularly, is regarded as an accurate reflection of the consensus. In Dryden's opinion, blank verse is a hybrid form – he calls it *prose mesurée* – suitable for passages in drama containing a profligate amount of figurative language but not acceptable in non-dramatic verse. If it did not rhyme, contended Dryden, then that vital, definitive component of poetry, the line, would become inaudible and effectively non-existent. Milton, in his second edition in 1674, responded with a prose note on 'The Verse', claiming that, in his poem, 'sense' would be 'variously drawn out from one verse into another', a brief, apparently gnomic phrase that was loaded with significance. To draw sense out from one line into another presupposes that two verbal structures are in operation simultaneously and in a manner that is recognizable to the reader. He is invoking the double pattern.

The debate on whether or how Milton achieved his stated ambition in practice continues today, and in the last century and this, Ricks (1963), Hollander (1975) and Bradford (2002) arrived at something close to an agreement on this matter. Milton supplemented the flimsy structure of the unrhymed pentameter with a complex network of syntactic devices. He imitated the relation between hesitation and progress in ordinary speech yet choreographed this with the structure of each line. If the line did not end with a grammatical pause, then he would create a contrapuntal relationship between the apparent completion of a statement at the tenth syllable and the continuation of the sentence into the next line, a device Hollander called *contra-rejet*. A well-known example of this occurs in Book IV:

> .... now conscience, wakes despair
> That slumbered, wakes the bitter memory
> Of what he was, what is, and what must be
> Worse (23–6)

On the one hand, each line appears to work as a support for what is an apparently intense, though cautious and improvised speech. The potential pauses after 'despair' and 'memory' reinforce the impression that the speaker, Milton himself, is intent on finding the most apposite phrase. At the same time, however, one could argue that the lines themselves are buttressed and maintained by the ebb and flow of the speech. The two parts of the double pattern are self-evidently present but prior to Milton no one had caused them to interact in such a manner that it was almost impossible to decide on whether the poetic or the non-poetic dimension predominates. This becomes most apparent at lines 25 and 26 where there at first seems to be an echo of the prayer book formula 'what must be' while the syntax moves on to connect this with a more compelling non-doctrinal state, 'Worse'. Close the gap at the line ending and the prayer book formula seems to disappear in the sweep of the syntax but since we have already taken note of its, potential, existence, some residue of it remains.

Paradise Lost is an outstandingly important poem not only because of its engagement with the Old Testament but also as an exemplar of the relationship between change and continuance that marks every stage in the history of poetry and contributes to a clearer perception of why and how poetry is different from all other forms of speech and writing. Milton effectively rewrote the rules of verse – after *Paradise Lost* blank verse was accepted as a suitable vehicle for poetry and flourished in the 18th and 19th centuries – but what he did not do was to challenge the necessity for such conventions. *Paradise Lost* altered perceptions of what poems could or could not be but reinforced the requirement that interaction between poetic and non-poetic devices was its heartbeat. Milton, brilliantly, pioneered a new model for what the former actually involved and in doing so secured its presence as something obtuse, arbitrary, yet absolutely vital to the identity of the poem. As we shall see, every major break from established convention in the history of poetry – be this collective or individual – involves a similar desire to move away from the consensus on how poems should be written. The motives and causes of change vary; some perceive their contemporaries and predecessors as hidebound and restrictive, others wish to inform apparent anarchy with a sense of order. The constant in this flux of rebellion and refashioning is the addictive capacity of the double pattern. The credos and manifestoes on the purpose, value and capacity of poetry that accompany its post-Renaissance history are diverse and often contradictory but in the poems themselves the chameleonesque presence of the double pattern persists. The question of why exactly this is so has never been subjected to lengthy scrutiny, and I shall do so following this brief tour of the history of verse, but for the time being I shall return to a theme addressed in Part I. The raw material of language, its identity purely as sound, stress and marks on the page, plus its capacity to liberate or disrupt meaning, is in non-poetic discourse acknowledged but treated with a mixture of caution and almost puritanical anxiety. Poetry allows for interplay between the ordered rational dimension and its impulsive, messy, unlicensed counterpart and this, the double pattern, is what makes poetry so mesmeric and irresistible. It is the impulse that both sustains it and defines it.

Milton was a maverick in the sense that, although he created what amounted to a poetic subgenre of his own, he played no significant part in the enormous collective change in the nature of English poetry that occurred between the mid-17th century and the restoration of the monarchy in 1660.

4

The Restoration and the 18th Century

From the 1660s to the 1750s, poetic writing was dominated by the generic and functional notion of the public poem. This could range from the direct engagement with contemporary political issues (the so-called 'poem on affairs of state') to the more discursive 'georgic' mode, in which matters such as architecture, dress sense, the sanitary conditions of the streets or the practice of sheep husbandry would function as the subject of all or part of the poetic discourse. Poems about real people and events were, of course, written before the Civil War, but in the post-Civil War period, poems themselves and writings about poetry began to focus more upon the stylistic and formal conditions that would establish poetry as the literary counterpart to the political or philosophic essay. The events and circumstances that prompted and sustained this change in emphasis were political, social and intellectual. The 1688 bloodless coup, also known as the Glorious Revolution, the Triennial Act 1694 and the Septennial Act 1716, ensuring parliamentary elections at three- and seven-year intervals respectively, the lapse of the Licensing Act in 1695, creating the opportunity for relative press freedom and the proliferation of pamphleteering – all these and many other factors, not least the increase in commercial printers and publishers, established the conditions for the emergence of the new social and cultural phenomenon of the professional writer – often disparagingly referred to as the 'hack'. The hack would not necessarily earn his money from sales of published material. As elections became more frequent, the ambition to control Parliament became stronger; party lines hardened and the arena of conflict shifted from private mansions into the open street. Ideas had to be transmitted quickly and persuasively and the poem was just as important a medium for such purposes as the essay. It would be wrong to assume that all the best-known poets of the period (Dryden, Swift and Pope for example) were political puppets and hirelings, but it is certainly the case that their objective of using poetry as an instrument for reflecting and influencing public opinions was partly fuelled by these broader changes in status of the poet and the poem.

The intellectual mood of the period was closely related to its turbulent politics. The Royal Society was founded after the Cromwellian Protectorate during the first months of the Restoration and in the succeeding decades established itself as a kind of barometric guide to developments in the key areas of thinking and writing. Its best-known and most widely quoted statement of purpose occurs in Thomas Sprat's 'The History of the Royal Society' ([1667]1908) (and for 'history', we might read 'manifesto'):

> The resolution of the Royal Society has been ... to reject all amplifications, digressions, and swellings of style; to return back to the primitive purity and shortness, when men deliver'd so many *things* almost in an equal number of words. They have extracted from all their members a close, naked, natural way of speaking, positive expressions, clear senses, a native easiness, bringing all things as near the Mathematical plainness as they can, and preferring the language of Artizans, Countryman, and Merchants, before that of Wits or Scholars. (pp. 117–18)

Sprat respects the status of language as an arbitrary self-determined medium of representation (words are not things), but his promotion of the language of 'Artizans, Countrymen and Merchants' over that of 'Wits and Scholars' emphasizes the need for a matching or unitary correspondence between our chief representative medium and the concrete and verifiable continuum of events and conditions that determine our condition.

Poetry, in establishing itself as a medium for public debate, was readily responsive to such terms and objectives, and in 1677 Dryden restates Sprat's proposition as a manifesto for the poetic deployment of wit: 'the definition of wit ... is only this: that it is propriety of thoughts and words; or, in other terms, thoughts and words elegantly adapted to the subject'. Or, as Pope later put it in his *An Essay on Criticism; Part II*:

> True wit is nature to advantage dressed
> What oft was thought, but ne're so well expressed.

Here we come across the principal distinction between the poetry of this period and the style of the Metaphysicals. For the Augustans, the imaginative instinct, that which creates metaphors, is essentially a sorting and cataloguing process by which things and ideas that are already regarded as discrete and separate can be assembled in a manner that reflects their prelinguistic condition. Thus we find, almost a century later, Johnson objecting to the Metaphysical tendency to create correspondences and parallels within language that would change or distort the broadly accepted relations between language and reality: language, including poetic language, was held in the 18th century to be a means of clarifying and validating the relation between abstractions and verifiable facts, not as a means of disturbing this balance and shifting the linguistic continuum towards new and unsubstantiated fields of speculation.

The heroic couplet (heroic designating it as an appropriate vehicle for the epic) had been widely used before the Restoration but in its post-1660 manifestations, it obtained a far more orderly and symmetrical character. For example, Pope effectively rewrote a number of Donne's *Satyres*, rather in the manner of a tutor correcting the work of a talented but undisciplined pupil:

Donne:	I more amaz'd than Circe's prisoners, when
	They felt themselves turn beasts, felt myself then
	Becoming Traytor, and methought I saw
	One of our Giant Statutes ope his jaw
Pope:	Not more Amazement seiz'd on *Circe's* Guests,
	To see themselves fall endlong into Beasts,
	Than mine, to find a Subject staid and wise,
	Already half turned Traytor by surprise. (Pope, 1939–69,
	vol. IV, 38–41)

Donne's sentence cuts an unruly path through the structure of the two couplets, setting up a discordant relationship between the parallelism of the form and the apparently unpredictable, prolix nature of the speech. Pope turns improvisation into a logical sequence. The argument moves forward gradually, purposively and is choreographed with the metre, the caesurae and the rhyme scheme of the form. The two halves of the double pattern are made to cooperate and contribute to a shared purpose.

Consider the following sequence of statements. 'I like dogs. My whole family likes them. At least, most of them do. We used to have six.' None of these sentences can be properly understood without reference to the others. The 'them' of the second sentence ties into 'dogs' of the first; 'most of them do' (third) ties into 'family' (second). Virtually all statements in speech or prose comprising more than two sentences involve a comparable pattern of links, whereby subjects are specified, expanded upon and digressed from while remaining part of a chain that gives the text coherence. The following is a verse paragraph from Pope's *Essay on Criticism: Part I*:

> But you who seek to give and merit fame,
> And justly bear a critic's noble name,
> Be sure yourself and your own reach to know
> How far your genius, taste and learning go;
> Launch not beyond your depth, but be discreet,
> And mark that point where sense and dulness meet. (46–51)

The principal difference from the prose sequence is that Pope's passage involves a single complex sentence, yet each extended subclause only becomes intelligible through some tie between it and an already specified topic. For example, 'yourself', 'your genius' and 'your depth' are all anchored to the opening specification of the poem's main subject, 'you ... a critic'. Significantly, the couplets operate as a supplement to syntax. Each new expansion upon and illustration of the model of criticism is contained discretely in every consecutive couplet. Pope has altered completely the relationship between the purely poetic and the non-poetic dimensions of verse that had obtained until the late 17th century. Previously, there had been a persistent contrast, an irregular dynamic between the repetitive, predictable structures of verse and the flow of speech. Now, however, the couplet has become a means of controlling and regimenting syntax. For the only time in its history, in the Augustan period, poetry could lay a greater claim upon logic and order than prose.

John Rice, a mid-18th-century critic, offered an account of what had effectively become the rules for verse composition:

> In reading poetry, if the Numbers interfere with the Harmony of the Period, there is a Defect in the Composition: For though the Harmony of Prosaic Periods is different, or will admit a greater Latitude and Variety than those of Poetry; yet the Laws of Diction require that the Sense and Meaning of the Writer should be consistent with both. (1765, p. 17)

In Rice's opinion, the 'Numbers', that is, the formal structure of verse, should supplement and buttress 'Sense and Meaning', and his views were endorsed by the vast majority of 18th-century critics (see Bradford, 2002).

Pope shows how poetry can offer a logical superstructure for an abstract thesis, but in the descriptive verse of the period there was an equally rigid orchestration of form and meaning. This is Jonathan Swift's 'A Description of the Morning':

> Now hardly here and there a hackney-coach
> Appearing, showed the ruddy morn's approach.
> Now Betty from her master's bed had flown,
> And softly stole to discompose her own;
> And slipshod 'prentice from his master's door
> Had pared the dirt, and sprinkled round the floor.
> Now Moll had whirled her mop with dext'rous airs,
> Prepared to scrub the entry and the stairs.
> The youth with broomy stumps began to trace
> The kennel-edge, where wheels had worn the place.
> The small-coal man was heard with cadence deep,
> Till drowned in shriller notes of chimney-sweep.
> Duns at his lordship's gate began to meet,
> And brickdust Moll had screamed through half the street.
> The turnkey now his flock returning sees,
> Duly let out a-nights to steal for fees.
> The watchful bailiffs take their silent stands,
> And schoolboys lag with satchels in their hands.

Each couplet introduces another character to the cast, and it is as though he is placing a new photographic transparency upon the previous one so that the scene becomes more densely populated. Swift achieves an exquisite balance between movement, with characters apparently entering or leaving the street, and a sense of stasis comparable to a painting of the scene. He does so by transforming the couplet from an arbitrary formal structure into an efficient instrument of representation.

Matthew Arnold classified Dryden and Pope as 'classics of our prose', his point being that they did their best to curtail the extravagant potentialities of poetry and made it attend to the implicit criteria of order, transparency and coherence that governed well-written prose. Donald Davie (1955) divided poetry into five stylistic types: subjective, dramatic, objective, like music, like mathematics. Augustan verse is, in his view, predominantly objective, with a nuance of the mathematical: 'it follows a form of action, a movement not through any mind but through the world at large' (p. 79). This is an apt account of Swift's achievement and Davie sums up concisely the general 18th-century ordinance that by not allowing the poet, or the poem, to interfere with the 'world at large', verse would play its part in strengthening the predominant contemporary ideals of order and coherence in politics, society, architecture and philosophic thought. Laura Brown (1985, p. 7) noted:

> Pope's art is at once a mode of representation and an act of adjudication through which an elaborate and sophisticated linguistic structure, emulative of the Imperial age of Roman culture, shapes a 'world' where rhetoric, belief and morality perfectly intersect.

Brown offers an astute diagnosis of the bifurcated nature of Augustan verse, which some might perceive as ambidextrous and others as duplicitous. The pursuit of order and transparency was invoked as the predominant article of faith but it was rarely conceded that this required contrivance as much as disclosure. In terms of what was expected of 18th-century poetry, the modern equivalent would be something of a hybrid, involving the assiduous attention to fact and authenticity that is supposedly beholden of journalists along with the opportunity to dress the topic in the unostentatious manner of the short story. Robert Tatersal's 'The Bricklayer's Labours' (1734) is an exemplary piece. It does not address the grand themes of Pope's *Essays* – it is no more or less than a chronicle of a day in the life of the average bricklayer – yet in design and manner, it is self-evidently of the same species. It begins:

> At length the soft nocturnal minutes fly,
> And crimson blushes paint the orient sky;
> When, by a kind of drowsy stretch and yawn,
> I ope my eyes, and view the scarlet dawn;
> But stealing sleep my vitals still surprise,
> And with a slumb'ring softness seal my eyes,
> Till open light corroborates the day,
> And through the casement darts his signal ray;
> When up I start, and view the eastern sky,
> And by my mark find six o'clock is nigh.

Then hanging on my threadbare coat and hose,
My hat, my cap, my breeches and my shoes,
With sheepskin apron girt about my waist,
Downstairs I go to visit my repast,
Which rarely both consist of more than these:
A quartern loaf and half a pound of cheese.
Then in a linen bag, on purpose made,
My day's allowance o'er my shoulder's laid:
And first, to keep the fog from coming in,
I whet my whistle with a dram of gin;
So thus equipped, my trowel in my hand,
I haste to work, and join the ragged band.

The demands and limited options of the bricklayer's day are meticulously cata-logued, with the couplet sequence resembling the movement of a giant clock face, in front of which we watch the man and his companions ply their trade:

And now refreshed again we mount on high,
While one calls 'Mortar', others 'Bricks' do cry,
And then 'A line, a line' 's the constant sound;
By line and rule our daily labour's crowned,
While to divert the sultry hours along,
One tells a tale, another sings a song.
And now the sun, with full meridian ray,
With scorching beams confirms the perfect day.
Full twelve o'clock, the labourers cry, 'Yo-ho',
When some to sleep, and some to dinner go:

Noon occurs shortly after line 60, almost exactly halfway through the poem. Pope customarily deals with such concepts as taste and aesthetic perfection but his technique is almost identical to that of Tatersal's portrait of the jobbing builder. What might, in truth, be discordant or disorderly details or ideals are provided in the poem with what appears to be shape and cohesion.

The following example of double-edged satire by John Ellis throws light upon the prevailing consensus regarding the function of poetry:

Sarah Hazard's Love Letter

To the printer of the Chester Courant

December 10, 1747

The following epistle I met with at a neighbouring seaport, and showed it to our curate, who said that the girls' sentiments were much the same with those of Ovid's heroines, were theirs to be stripped of poetical decorations. A day or two afterwards he brought it to me, as likewise an attempt to versify it; both which I herewith send you, and am

Your friend and servant,

G.Z.

Lovin Der Charls,

This with my kind lov to yow, is to tel yow, after allowr sport and fon, I am lik to pa fort, for I am with Child, and were of mi Sister Nan knose it, and clas me hore and bech, and is rady to ter mi sol owt, yet Jack Peny kics hur every tim he cums ashor, and the saaci Dog wud a lade with me to, but I wud not let him, for I will be alwas honest to yow, therefore Der Charls, cum ashor, and let us be mared to safe me vartu, and if yow hav no munni, I will pawn mi new staies, and sel the smocks yow gav me, and that will pa the Parson, and find us a diner, and pra, Der lovin Charls cum ahor, and, Der Charls, don't be fraad for want of a ring, for I hav stol my sister Nans, and the naaty tode shal never hav it no more, for she tells about, that I am going to hav a basterd, and god bless yowr lovin sol cum sune, for I longs to be mared accordin to yowr promis, and I wil be yowr own der vartus wife tel deth,

SA. HAZARD.

P.S. Pra don't let yowr messmate Jack se this, for if yow shud, he'l tel owr Nan, and ther wil be the Divil to do.

DEAR object of my love, whose pow'rful charms
With bliss ecstatic filled my clinging arms!
That bliss is past; and nought for me remains,
But foul reproach, and never-pitied pains!
For (nature baffling ev'ry art I tried)
My sister has my waxing waist decried,
And brands me oft with each opprobrious name,
Though the crack's conscious she deserves the same:
Her loose associate, sated, from her flies,
And oft, though vainly, to seduce me tries;
True as a wife, I only want the name;
O haste to wed me, and restore my fame.
No lack of coin our union shall defer,
For my pawned stays will well supply my dear;
And those good smocks which once your fondness gave,
Those smocks I'll sell, or any clothes I have:
What these produce will pay the coupling priest,
And furnish dainties for our nuptial feast.
O how I long my loving Charles to see,
Haste then, my life! To happiness and me;
Nor anxious be 'bout that material thing,
For I've just stol'n my saucy sister's ring:
In vain she may expect me to restore;

No! faith, the slut shall never have it more.
Come quick, my love, for fare she spreads my shame;
Come, patch my virtue, and defend my fame.
Take me, and make me soon thy lawful spouse,
Then heav'n shall bless thy due regard to vows,
And will reward thee with what lasts for life,
A tender, duteous, fond and faithful wife.
P.S.   These earnest dictates of my anxious heart
        I beg you would not o your friend impart;
        For oft beneath fair friendship's specious show
        Lurks the false, trait'rous, undermining foe. (1747)

What is clear from the correspondent's story is that poetry is regarded as a transformative medium, not in a spiritual or ethical sense – that would be the province of the Romantics – but rather as a means of imposing order and coherence upon a world otherwise threatened by those who have not benefited from the disciplinary ordinances of education. It also exposes the complex sociocultural fabric that underpins this consensus. Notably, the letter writer is female and can therefore be conveniently catalogued as a subject of poetic discourse rather than a practitioner. She is compared with one of 'Ovid's heroines … stripped of their poetical decorations'. Just as Ovid created the female-speaking presences of his verse, so the curate takes it upon himself to recreate the actual semi-literate woman as an extended and exceptionally well-ordered conceit.

There were, of course, a number of educated women poets of the 18th century (see Chapter 14) but they all laboured against the general view that since poetry was now regarded as a serious discipline, demanding all the intellectual strength and coherence of the essay or the political speech, its natural stewards were men. Pope's 'To a Lady' begins:

> Nothing so true as what you once let fall
> 'Most women have no characters at all'
> Matter too soft a lasting mark to bear,
> And best distinguished by black, brown or fair.

One might, mistakenly, assume that there is at least a hint of self-caricature in this brutally misogynistic statement but read on and you will find that Pope deploys all of his considerable classical erudition in presenting women as variously shaped by mythological prototypes and conforming to a predictable series of formulae. His opinions might be somewhat abhorrent, at least to us, but they sit comfortably within the cultural infrastructure epitomized by the unforgiving rigour of the couplet.

Statistically, the heroic couplet was used in more than half the poems published between 1660 and 1750. It was regarded as the trademark and guarantee of order, but even when poets of the period chose more flexible or complex designs, one discerns a collateral attendance to the working principle that elucidation, classification and documentation must overrule imaginative intemperance.

Although Milton had licensed the use of non-dramatic blank verse, its 18th-century manifestations were, by comparison with *Paradise Lost*, atrophied and predictable. The following is from James Thomson's *The Seasons*:

> The dripping Rock, the Mountain's misty Top
> Swell on the Sight, and brighten with the Dawn
> Blue thro' the Dusk, the smoking Currents shine;
> And from the bladed Field the fearful Hare
> Limps, awkward: while along the Forest-glade
> The wild Deer trip, and often turning gaze
> At early Passenger. Musick awakes,
> The native voice of undissembled joy;
> And thick around the woodland hymns arise.
> Roused by the cock, the soon-clad shepherd leaves
> His mossy cottage, where with peace he dwells;
> And from the crowded Fold, in order drives
> His flock to taste the Verdure of the Morn. (54–66)

Thomson pays lip service to Milton in that in both poems the relationship between the line and the syntax seems shifting and irregular but apparent parallels are overwhelmed by contrasts. Milton uses the line to variously contain and release the often-troubled relationship between apprehension, thought and speech. We move through *Paradise Lost* following what appears to be each speaker's coherent outlook or preoccupation but often finding ourselves caught between what we intuit as the mental animus of the words and what the speaker actually goes on to say. Milton's outstanding achievement is to counterpoint design and expression, tangibly the line and the sentence, to create a fabric of tension and unresolved dilemmas, to provide a very human dimension for the story of how humanity originated. Thomson tailors his material with far more regularity, attempting to ensure that his words record with seamless transparency a curiously regimented vision of the rural landscape. While Milton's use of the line break at 'what must be/Worse' leaves us wondering about Satan's own sense of certainty, Thomson uses the line as a supplement to a meticulous delineative programme of description. Often the syntax is carefully sown with pre-emptive clues, warnings even, of what will be encountered in the subsequent line. It is not surprising that the *fearful* Hare/Limps, that the '*soon clad* shepherd leaves/His mossy cottage' or that from the '*crowded Fold*' he 'drives/His flock'. Although there are obvious differences between the parallelism of the heroic couplet and Thomson's use of blank verse, both employ the generic devices of poetry as a secondary grammatical system, a means of further clarifying and particularizing the message.

The Augustans represent the single historic school of poets and critics whose collective imperative was to subjugate the disruptive, innately poetic aspect of the double pattern to the objectives of order and transparency. Even during the later 18th century when lyrical subjectivity underwent something of a revival, most famously in the odes and elegies of Thomas Gray, William Collins and Oliver Goldsmith, there was a notable reluctance to release the resources and conceits of verse as vehicles for chimerical excursions from fact. In Gray's 'Elegy Written in a Country Churchyard', the poet contemplates the ordinary people of the parish as both embodiments of unfulfilled greatness and the reliable mainstays of rural life. Gray does not point up the contrast between what might have been and what is or allow himself impassioned reflections, perhaps on the tragic inconsequentialities of lives endured and, but for their gravestones, left unrecorded. Instead, we find sentiment and emotion eloquently anaesthetized, displayed for scrutiny in much the same way that Tatersal's tradesman lays his bricks:

> Far from the madding crowd's ignoble strife
> Their sober wishes never learned to stray;
> Along to cool sequestered vale of life
> They kept the noiseless tenor of their way.
>
> Yet even these bones from insult to protect
> Some frail memorial still erected nigh,
> With uncouth rhymes and shapeless sculpture decked,
> Implores the passing tribute of a sigh.

The neat, four-line stanzas, as tightly regimented if slightly more spacious than the couplet, operate as cabinets for each display of cautiously rehearsed empathy.

Modern criticism has always faced something of a dilemma when caused to deal with the preoccupations and self-denying routines of 18th-century verse. Of late, that is, since around the 1970s, an embargo has been placed upon criticism that admits of aesthetic hierarchies, the possibility that one poet or group of poets is superior to or more valuable than another (and we will discuss the reasons for this in Part III). As a consequence, one looks in vain for recent criticism that offers an evaluative survey of Augustan poetry. Instead, studies such as Brown (1985), Easthope (1983) or Gilliland (2001) approach the period laterally, considering poems as one aspect of a dense fabric of cultural and ideological forces. For opinions on their worth, one has to go back to the time of F.R. Leavis (1936, p. 97):

> it is a period in which something has gone wrong. It appears unprosperous … in the sense that the prevailing modes and conventions of the eighteenth century did not on the whole tend, as those of the seventeenth did, to bring into poetry the vitality of the age.

But even Leavis and his peers were reluctant to venture some explanation for why 'something' went 'wrong' or even offer a clear account of the nature of the period's deficiencies. Obviously there are parallels between the ambitious and widespread belief that 18th-century Britain could re-enact classical ideals of sensibility, behaviour, governance and culture and the overarching desire for order and restraint in verse. At the same time, one should take into account that English poetry at the end of the 17th century was a genre that lacked a precipitate sense of tradition or any coherent notion of its value and purpose. It was, as a collective enterprise, barely a century old, and, if one accepts Johnson as a reliable spokesman for Augustanism, viewed as a potentially dissolute, unlicensed excuse for verbal and imaginative excess unlikely to purchase respect for itself as anything more than a form of recreation.

If we are to particularize so broad a species as an inclusive genre, then the unifying feature of the Renaissance poem is its independence as an aesthetic object. We can, of course, draw parallels between what we find in the verse and what is known of the experiences, even the predispositions, of its author – the imprint of Herbert's and Vaughan's lifelong callings as devout clergymen upon the intense arguments with belief in the poems is an obvious case – yet even at their most impassioned and authentic, these lyric presences become dissipated by an abundance of invention. The poems that contain them are such masterpieces of baroque style, involving interpolations of spontaneity and meticulous craft, that we are continually reminded that the speaker can never be disentangled from the artefact. The poet – Donne, Herbert, Marvell et al. – might have made the poem but each has done so with such an intoxicated preoccupation with artistry that he will always stand outside it.

The Augustans, from the interpretive satiric voices of the public poems to chroniclers of the landscape and elegiac apologists for its weary inhabitants, set about establishing the poem as equalling the essay or pamphlet in its claim upon profound and serious attendance to its topic and matching the public oration as a tribute to the presence of the speaker as its legitimate, eloquent and learned originator. In reinstalling the poet within the poem, however, they frequently displayed an overcautious concern with stylistic exuberance, attempting to make the definitively poetic features of verse – predominantly metrical devices and figurative language – compatible with conventions and obligations of non-poetic discourse. Augustan poetry was limited by the self-contradictory nature of its rationale: to establish poetry as the equal of more exalted forms of writing while scrupulously regulating, even sublimating, those features which defined it as verse.

At the close of the 18th century, the pendulum would swing again towards the ostentatiously poetic aspect of the double pattern, although the causes were very different from those of the Renaissance, as were the consequences.

5

Romanticism

The Romantic poets present us with a series of problems that demand the cooperation of literary scholarship and linguistic analysis. W.H. Auden, writing as a
somewhat sceptical heir to the legacies of Romanticism and Modernism, summarized our difficulties. In memory of Yeats, he wrote: 'Poetry makes nothing
happen.' What he meant is that, unlike most other forms of linguistic representation or interpersonal exchange, the poem is confined within the vacuum of its
own self-determined formal conditions. It can issue orders, promote one particular moral or ethical position above others, or enable its perpetrator to complain
about their own existential condition or that which they share with the rest of
humanity, but it forbids itself from entering the same functional circuit of
personal, social or political exchange as the letter, the philosophical thesis or the
manifesto for the envisaged rights of man. The problem, from which no poet or
reader is immune, is of how to balance the paraphrasable, functional message of
the text with its specificity as literary discourse, its self-conscious deployment of
linguistic properties and conventions which create patterns of signification that
poems do not share with non-poetic discourses. Poetry is never immune from
the uncertain relation between textual content and extratextual context, but in
the period occupied by the Romantics, we encounter a particularly difficult
interrelation between purpose, aesthetics and poetic form.

It could be argued that Romanticism, at least in its somewhat confined desig-
nation as a change in the history of English poetry, was a response to an unprecedented pattern of intellectual, social and political developments. The effects of
the Enlightenment were felt in the theoretical underpinnings of both the French
and American Revolutions. Writers such as Voltaire, Rousseau, Diderot, Paine
and Godwin had begun to challenge and threaten the distinction between the
literary and political-social functions of writing in ways that went far beyond
the Augustan, neoclassical precondition that the text should be grounded upon
the empiricism of what is established, precedented and verifiable. Late
18th-century Britain, a country already shaken by war and anarchic economic
cycles, was beginning to experience the social unrest that had overthrown the
French social order and, in the USA, established a new one. On top of this was
what we now refer to as the Industrial Revolution: individual social functions
and instincts were becoming marginalized by a more powerful system of urbani-
zation, rural dispossession and labour-intensive means of production. The

English government under which Blake, Coleridge and Wordsworth lived was engaged in either Continental warfare – mostly with the French – or in suppressing internal dissent (see Woodring, 1970).

What, you might inquire, has all this to do with the arcane, internalized world of poetic form and language? Auden might be correct in his assertion that poetry 'makes nothing happen', but he also infers that because of its independence from the discourses enslaved to the empirical, the demonstrable and the ineluctable, it might be capable of providing an extraordinary perspective on matters that have exceeded the ability of ordinary language to comprehend them. Romanticism is customarily and misleadingly associated with the Age of Revolution but Romantic poetry does not involve manifestoes for change, or at least any that a pragmatic individual, irrespective of their radical inclinations, would take seriously. Instead it sets about overturning the 18th-century fixation upon verse as a lens, an ordering principle of perception, in favour of poetry as a catalyst, a new way of seeing, which will consequentially cause us to question the very nature of apprehension and quiddity.

The *Lyrical Ballads, with a Few Other Poems* (a collection of poems by William Wordsworth and Samuel Taylor Coleridge, first published in 1798) is taken by most to be the inaugurating moment of Romantic verse, and it embodies the perversities and unresolved paradoxes that inform all aspects of the movement. In the second edition, published in 1800, Wordsworth, in the newly added Preface, proclaims that his intention is to make available in poetry 'the real language of men', to catch the unmediated 'spontaneous overflow of powerful feeling'. He is, however, somewhat guarded and obtuse on how exactly he intends to realize these objectives. The vast majority of the poems in the collection concern the lives and experiences of the uncultured denizens of the rural landscape of late 18th-century England. The best-known and most widely discussed are 'The Idiot Boy', 'Simon Lee' and 'The Mad Mother'. Wordsworth presented these figures as possessed of an intrinsic wisdom uncomplicated and undiminished by the intellectual constraints of the educated city-dweller, and the poems that caused the most controversy among early reviewers of the collection (see Jordan, 1976, p. 107) were those that centred upon characters who were neither quaint nor particularly heroic and who presented the reader with few opportunities to reflect upon their dire state as being the cause of some tangible form of social injustice or symbolic of an ungenerous branch of fate. They simply existed, and Southey (1798), in a much-cited review, sums up the puzzling unprecedented character of this exercise. 'The Idiot Boy', he claimed, 'resembles a Flemish picture in the worthlessness of its design and the excellence of its execution.' 'Worthlessness' should not be mistaken as evidence of Southey's complete disapproval; he meant that the poem lacks any sense of allegory or pregnant meaning, that it is simply a naturalistic portrait of fact without comment. Similarly, Dr Burney in *The Monthly Review* (1799) compared the rural ballads with 'pictures', 'as dark as those of Rembrandt'. The principal subjects of these poems, Johnny in 'The Idiot Boy', Martha Ray in 'The Thorn', the unnamed

Mad Mother or the eponymous Simon Lee, are never the commanding presences of their pieces. Sometimes their speech is reported but the story is always told by someone else, never quite the same person but serving a similar purpose in Wordsworth's sociocultural confidence trick. His speakers are intermediaries between his own condition of high cultural erudition, a condition he regrets but from which he knows he can never detach himself, and a region unpolluted by art and philosophy where tactile experience and emotion enjoy unostentatious purity. His poems, then, would be despatched in the 'real language of men', ordinary men with no great literary ambitions but at the same time not quite so ordinary as their semi-literate subjects. Here, though, a practical problem arose. To have had his speakers adopt, say, the Horatian ode, the accepted repertoire of stanzaic formulae, blank verse or the couplet would have involved a clash between the stylistic tradition he was attempting to overturn and his inartistic subject. The former would rob his characters of their essential vitality, turn them into curiosities rather than independent, inspirational presences. As a compromise, Wordsworth appropriated the ballad from its customary low cultural status as a vehicle for folk tales in verse. Robert Mayo (1954) showed how late 18th-century publications, such as the *Monthly Magazine*, the *European Magazine* and the *Gentleman's Magazine*, regularly included versified short stories which gave unashamed prominence to the bizarre and ghoulishly attractive experiences of rural life. Wordsworth's achievement becomes evident when we compare his 'The Idiot Boy' with what appears to be a similar ballad called 'The Idiot' (published in *The Sporting Magazine*, October 1798). In the latter, the teller of the tale dwells on the details of the eponymous orphan's mental incapabilities, particularly his inability to understand that his mother is dead and his attempts to preserve her decomposing corpse. In Wordsworth's poem, the speaker recounts, with respectful detachment, the story of how Betty Foy sends out her son Johnny to seek assistance for her sick friend Susan. Johnny, much to the distress of the two women, seems to have lost his way but at the end he returns safely with help and his only comment on the entire episode is that 'the cocks did crow to-whoo, to-whoo/And the sun did shine so cold'. Unlike the subject of 'The Idiot' and indeed those of virtually all the other ballads of the magazines, Johnny is not treated as a morbid spectacle, someone who at once satisfies the prurient interest and confirms the intellectual superiority of the reader. Instead, a kind of modest dignity is conferred upon Betty, Susan and most of all Johnny himself. Indeed, Johnny's image of the moon as a 'sun' that 'shines so cold' has a quiet eloquence about it.

Wordsworth was aware, however, of the limitations of his ventures with the ballad form. The use of rural figures as delegates in his re-establishment of 'the real language of men' would, he knew, become something of a curiosity and was essentially a postponement of the voice of William Wordsworth as the commanding presence of his poems. The inclusion within the collection of 'Tintern Abbey' is an indication that the ballad experiments were a grand aberration of and eventual destiny of Romanticism:

> Once again
> Do I behold these steep and lofty cliffs,
> That on a wild secluded scene impress
> Thoughts of more deep seclusion; and connect
> The landscape with the quiet of the sky. ('Tintern Abbey', lines 4–8)

Wordsworth's poem was the most unashamed and ambitious revisitation of Milton's radical precedent in more than a hundred years. It is, it seems at first, the 'cliffs' that physically 'impress' upon the 'scene', until, after the line ending, the focus shifts from the visual to the ratiocinative: 'impress/ Thoughts'. They, the cliffs, literally 'connect' the landscape with the sky, but also in the mind of the perceiver, an emotional connection occurs between 'deep seclusion' and the 'quiet' of the sky. Milton's brilliant and subtle implementation of the unrhymed pentameter as a means of creating two apparently simultaneous levels of meaning is Wordsworth's model but there is a difference. We will search in vain for a subject or a predominant theme in 'Tintern Abbey'. Common sense and scholarship tell us that Wordsworth's familiarity with the gorge near where the River Wye enters the Severn provides it with a context of sorts, but similarly configured rivers, hills and ruins would have sufficed. Wordsworth at no point apportions some numinous significance to that particular location. There is no narrative but nor is there, as one would find in such 18th-century landscape poems as Thomson's *The Seasons*, a deference to impartial chronicling and description. The prevailing impetus of 'Tintern Abbey' – but one is reluctant to call this its topic – is the unpredictable, oscillating, subjective state of mind of the perceiver. It is a poem informed by the dynamic between experience, thought and language, but Wordsworth does not go on to fossilize this, to detach himself from it and contemplate its significance.

Although there are apparently overriding incongruities between 'Tintern Abbey' and the ballads – notably, they position themselves at opposing ends of the sociocultural spectrum – all are involved in attempts to realize Wordsworth's objective, stated in the Preface, to bring poetry closer to both spontaneous, spoken discourse and to prelinguistic experience. The unfortunate corollary of this ambition, addressed rather chaotically in the Preface, is that it is founded upon a paradox. Wordsworth asserts that 'there neither is nor can be any essential difference' between 'the language of prose and metrical composition'. Rarely has an eminent literary figure made such a self-evidently absurd claim, as his erstwhile friend and companion Coleridge would point out, albeit diplomatically, in his *Biographia Literaria* (1817). Indeed, later in the Preface, Wordsworth himself implicitly acknowledges the self-contradictory nature of his case. He asks: 'why, professing these opinions, have I written in verse?' By stating that he has chosen to write in verse rather than prose, he has already demolished his previous claim that the two forms are indistinguishable. To his self-addressed question, he answers that:

it will be answered, that a very small part of the pleasure given by Poetry depends upon the metre, and that it is injudicious to write in metre unless it be accompanied by other artificial distinction of style … and by such devia-tion [that is, the abandonment of metre, rhyme, figurative language and so on] more will be lost by the shock which will be thereby given to the Reader's associations than will be counterbalanced by any pleasure which he can derive from the general power of numbers.

He begins by conceding that poetry by its nature imparts a certain amount of pleasure, implying that this is but a slight and perhaps vulgar aspect of its grand duty, and goes on to claim that the reader should be spared the 'shock' of being offered something that is neither, technically speaking, poetry, nor what they would usually expect of prose.

He also concedes that there is an irreconcilable fissure between the Romantic ideal and what was obtainable in practice:

The music of harmonious metrical language, the sense of difficulty overcome, and the … pleasure which has been previously received from works of rhyme or metre of the same or similar construction, an indistinct perception perpet-ually renewed of language closely resembling that of real life, and yet, in the circumstance of metre, differing from it so widely.

He admits that poetry is an autonomous self-determined system of rules and conventions whose '[close resemblance] to real life' is arbitrary and disingen-uous, and here one might return to his question as to why he had elected to write in verse. In truth, he had no choice. Poetry might be an unsatisfactory medium but all other available genres were even less suitable. Coleridge, in the *Biographia* (1817), foregrounds the paradox:

[the best part of human language] is formed by a voluntary appropriation of fixed symbols to internal acts, to processes and results of imagination, the greater part of which has no place in the consciousness of uneducated man.

Roughly translated: poets might idolize the guileless sublime but poetry is and can only be a high cultural game played by trained sophisticates.

Coleridge picks up on his friend's account of why definitively poetic features are unavoidable. The 'communication of pleasure' achieved only by the 'super addition' of such devices is, he contends, insufficient. That would simply involve either some decorative effect or an imposition of arbitrary structure upon the unalloyed material of perception and expression, and in this regard, Coleridge clearly has in mind the Augustan preoccupation with order, both within the poem and as an improvement upon its subject. He revised Wordsworth's formula: 'A poem … is opposed to works of science'. Its objective is the achieve-ment of symbiosis 'by proposing to itself such delight from the *whole* as is compatible with a distinct gratification from each component *part*' (Coleridge, 1817). Poetry should involve abstract formal structure not only as custom or as deference to orthodoxy but also as an index to what Coleridge (1817, p. 81) calls the text's 'legitimacy':

> [A] *legitimate* poem ... must be one, the parts of which mutually support and explain each other ... the reader should be carried forward, not merely or chiefly by the mechanical impulse of curiosity, or by a restless desire to arrive at the final solution; but by a pleasurable activity of mind excited by the attraction of the journey itself.

This comes as close as anything extant to a manifesto for Romantic poetry.

Romantic odes frequently involve stanzas, or more accurately 'strophes', where line length and rhyme scheme, although conspicuous by their presence, are almost infinitely unpredictable; form, rhythm and structure existed but are subject to improvisation and variation, the poetic equivalent of traditional jazz. One of the best examples is Wordsworth's 'Ode: Intimations of Immortality', of which the following is the opening strophe:

> There was a time when meadow, grove, and stream,
> The earth, and every common sight,
> To me did seem
> Apparelled in celestial light,
> The glory and the freshness of a dream,
> It is not now as it hath been of yore;
> Turn wheresoe'er I may,
> By night or day,
> The things which I have seen I now can see no more.

This is an instance of what Coleridge meant by his notion of a symbiotic involvement of the 'parts' with 'the whole'. Neither the minutiae of form nor the broader sweep of syntax obtain control; instead, there is a persistent contrapuntal relationship between them. There is self-evidently a close correspondence between this and Coleridge's template for logical progression and narrative, that it is the 'journey', the dynamic of the poem, rather than any sense of 'solution' or 'arrival' that should excite the mind. The generic feature of the Romantic poem is its apparently unfinished or unfocused nature. Wordsworth's ballads are stories, of a sort, but they propose no obvious philosophic or moral truisms, and other examples of Romantic narrative display a similar reluctance either to complete their tales or allow us to unravel their collateral enigmas. Coleridge's 'The Rime of the Ancient Mariner' and 'Christabel', Keats's 'Eve of St Agnes', even Byron's satirical but equally inconclusive *Don Juan*, all take us through a series of consecutive events but seem unable or unwilling to close this progress with reflections on what these events might actually signify.

The following is from Percy Bysshe Shelley's 'Ode to the West Wind':

> Thou on whose stream, mid the steep sky's commotion,
> Loose clouds like earth's decaying leaves are shed,
> Shook from the tangled boughs of Heaven and Ocean,
>
> Angels of rain and lightning: there are spread
> On the blue surface of thine airy surge,
> Like the bright hair uplifted from the head
>
> Of some fierce Mænad, even from the dim verge
> Of the horizon to the zenith's height,
> The locks of the approaching storm.

In *Revaluation* (1936, p. 346), F.R. Leavis subjected the poem to the kind of scrutiny that we might expect of a prosecuting barrister offering the court a statement taken from a befuddled, slightly intoxicated defendant. In what way, he asks, are the 'Loose clouds' like 'decaying leaves' and how can 'Heaven and Ocean' be comprised of 'tangled boughs'? How can clouds be 'shed' and how can the 'blue surface' of the sky 'surge'? Leavis was fully aware that poetry licenses and indulges unorthodox combinations of words and ideas but he felt that Shelley had taken this too far, that he suffered from, or rather had allowed himself to suffer from, 'a weak grasp upon the actual'. If one were to employ Leavis's criteria on how the poet should make due concessions to 'the actual', then such exemplary Romantic pieces as Coleridge's 'Kubla Khan', 'The Eolian Harp' and 'Limbo' and Keats's 'Ode to Psyche' involve comparable dislocations between what occurs in the poem and our sense of it as engaging with a familiar cognisable notion of reality.

Keats's 'Ode on a Grecian Urn' typifies the problematic nature of what was effectively a new poetic subgenre. The urn itself, decorated with symbolic representations of the natural world, love and eternity, is the vehicle for a medley of abstract speculations on the nature of existence and indeed the role of poetry in such enquiries. The closing two lines seem to contain a conclusive maxim but the famous five words in quotation marks have resisted attempts by two centuries of critics to explain what exactly they mean:

> 'Beauty is truth, truth beauty,' – that is all
> Ye need to know on earth, and all ye need to know

Nothing like this had occurred before in the history of English poetry. Certainly, the more adventurous writers of the 16th and 17th centuries had created unusual confections of logic and inventive exuberance but in each case the contrast between the actual and the imaginative or hypothetical had been the keynote of the poem. The Romantics excused themselves from any obligation to an orthodox acknowledgment of the real or the rational.

In the *Biographia Literaria* (1817), Coleridge wrote:

They [images] become proofs of original genius only as far as they are modified by a predominant passion; or by associated thoughts and images awak-
ened by that passion ... when a human and intellectual life is transferred to
them from the poet's own spirit.

In *A Defence of Poetry* (1819), Shelley stated: 'Poets are the hierophants of
unapprehended inspiration; the mirrors of the gigantic shadows which futurity
casts upon the present; the words which express what they understand not.'

It is evident that Wordsworth's rubric of the 'real language of men' is predicated upon a different notion of the 'real' from that of his Augustan predecessors. For the Augustans, reality was classifiable according to the logical order of a
grammar and semantics, exemplified in prose but obtainable in poetry provided
that its more licentious propensities were subjected to a strict regime of order.
The Romantics, conversely, treated poetry as uniquely capable of apprehending
a more subliminal, elemental state. Their problem was how to transform this
belief into practice.

To appreciate the essential difference between Romantic poetry and verse
written during the Renaissance and the Augustan period, attention should be
given to what linguists term 'deictics'. When we are speaking face to face in
familiar circumstances to someone we know well, deictics are of virtually no
significance. They are those aspects of a statement or a text that provide us with
vital clues to its context, everything from the identity of the person uttering or
writing the words to the broader circumstances in which this occurs – personal,
social, historical and so on. Donne's 'The Flea' is abundant with deictic pointers to
the context of the utterance, to the speaker's apparent state of mind, gender and
motivation and even to the silent response of the listener. The typical speaker in
the 18th-century public poem was, in general, a predictable presence able to
address the subject and inform the text with requisite erudition and wit. The
manner of such poems generally conformed to a standardized recipe regarding
the nature of the speaker and his, rarely her, choice and treatment of their topic.
The deictic features of verse are what enable us to position the poem in relation to
the world of actual people, events and objects, an operation that we perform
instinctively when confronted with any text whose origins and prefiguring
circumstances are not self-evident, and we could include in this category essays,
short stories, novels and even letters and diaries. Deictics are those aspects of the
poem that are not innately poetic, those elements of the double pattern that
poetry shares with non-poetic texts and statements; they provide the channel that
links the poem with the real world. The Romantic ode blurred this link. Never
before had the speaker of the poem seemed so amorphous and ill-defined and
neither had there been so few indications as to the poem's rationale or pretext.

It is largely impossible to encounter a published version of 'Kubla Khan'
without also coming upon Coleridge's prose description of its inspiration and

compositional genesis: he claims it to be the record of a probably opium-induced dream 'in which all the images rose up before him as things with a parallel production of the correspondent expressions, without any sensation or conscious-ness of effort'. This statement counterposes the Romantic ideal with its almost tragic unattainability. He asks us to believe that the poem came into being spon-taneously. The 'things' – by which he means the constituent parts of the prelin-guistic vision – became 'expressions', or, rather, words without 'consciousness of effort'. The burdens of intellectual and cultural orthodoxy, embodied in the protocols of thinking and writing, have, he claims, been bypassed; the poem is an unsullied record of a pseudo-mystical experience. It is of course impossible to entirely disprove Coleridge's claim. Indeed, a monument to critical credulity exists in John Livingstone Lowes' *The Road to Xanadu: A Study in the Ways of The Imagination* ([1927]1978), a masterpiece of scholarly source-hunting, in which Lowes attempts to trace each of the poem's references to mysticism and Middle Eastern culture back to Coleridge's own reading, experience and private frame of reference. The book is based on the premise that the prose preface to the poem should be interpreted literally. Lowes attempts to reconstruct in minute detail the process through which Coleridge's disparate conscious and subconscious thoughts were suddenly reconstituted, indeed spontaneously assembled, as the poem. One point that Lowes ignores, rather like the proverbial elephant in the room, is that the poem itself is made up of carefully constructed, immensely complex five-line stanzas, complemented by a dense circuitry of assonance and alliteration. Certainly, the overall effect is of what we might term the pure music of language sidelining any concessions to easily decodable sense, logic or coher-ence. In short, the poem sounds like an invocation of the irrational and the improvised. But we must then ask ourselves if we can take seriously the notion of so complex a fabric of stanzas and formal devices as coming together 'without consciousness' or 'effort'. 'Kubla Khan' opens

> In Xanadu did Kubla Khan
> A stately pleasure-dome decree:
> Where Alph, the sacred river, ran
> Through caverns measureless to man
>   Down to a sunless sea.

and proceeds to repeat the same stanzaic formula again and again with admi-rable precision. Can we believe that even an individual so attuned to the devices of poetic writing could produce this effortlessly and without pause? Or have we come across another manifestation of the paradox inherent in Wordsworth's ballads, where we are expected to accept the myth that poetry is a medium for the purity of experience, while ignoring the fact that it is also, by its nature, the most blatant manifestation of the unavoidable arbitrariness of language?

In 'The Immortality Ode', the first person 'I' carries us quixotically from abstract speculations on the nature of truth and eternity through fragments of imagined or recollected experience, a kaleidoscope of reference points, of which none can claim to be the predominant focus of the poem. The only dependable feature of the text is its persistent concession to metre and rhyme, which is ironic, given that the collective, stated purpose of Romantic writing was the desire to unshackle verse from such totemic orthodoxies.

William Blake both exemplifies yet transcends the Romantic paradox. His early twin collections *Songs of Innocence and Experience* (1789–1805) beg comparison with *Lyrical Ballads*, notably because, like Wordsworth, Blake borrows from a low cultural subgenre, specifically, the popular type of poem/hymn published and distributed by dissenting preachers, poets and hymn writers of the 18th century, often for the religious and moral instruction of children. But the *Songs* are far more calculatedly perverse than the *Ballads*. While Wordsworth usually employed an uncomplicated intermediary presence as a link between his own creative oligarchy and the unfalsified ordinariness of his subjects, Blake's speakers are unapologetic versions of himself and unlike no others previously encountered in the history of poetry. This is 'London' from *Songs of Experience*:

> I wander thro' each charter'd street,
> Near where the charter'd Thames does flow.
> And mark in every face I meet
> Marks of weakness, marks of woe.
>
> In every cry of every Man,
> In every Infants cry of fear,
> In every voice; in every ban,
> The mind-forg'd manacles I hear
>
> How the Chimney-sweepers cry
> Every blackning Church appals,
> And the hapless Soldiers sigh,
> Runs in blood down Palace walls
>
> But most thro' midnight streets I hear
> How the youthful Harlots curse
> Blasts the new-born Infants tear
> And blights with plagues the Marriage hearse.

Scholars have toiled for decades over the strange syntactic and semantic transformations wrought by the poem. For example, 'mark' could simply denote appearance, or it could be meant to invoke comparison with the biblical 'mark' upon the victimized, downtrodden inhabitants of Jerusalem (Ezekial, 9:4; a passage with which Blake was compulsively familiar). 'Charter'd' might be intended to provoke a recollection of the much-referred to 'chartered rights of Englishmen', frequently used in invectives against the repressive regime of Pitt, or it might also refer to the urban topography, the Thames included, as literally 'charted'; owned, confined, mapped out, designated for commercial use. 'Ban' might refer to a prohibitive feature of government legislation or it might be an ironic allusion to the similarly binding obligations of the marriage announcement.

The *contra-rejet* between the last line of the second stanza and the opening of the third, the exact mid-point of the poem, is one of the most complex ever devised. The phrase 'I hear' seems initially to complete the previous four-line sentence, abundant as this is with audible sensations: the 'cry' of every Man, the fearful 'cry' of Infants and the 'mind-forg'd manacles' that constrain 'every voice'. At the same time, it appears to initiate the bizarre sequence in which visual and auditory images vie for prominence. How can the speaker 'hear' that every 'blackning church' is 'appalled' by the 'Chimney-sweepers cry' (appals in any event involves both its modern figurative sense as 'disgusts' and its earlier literal use as draping with a pall, usually after death)? Even more extraordinary is the 'sigh' that 'Runs in blood down palace walls'. By the closing stanza, the juxtaposition of grotesque and shocking images appears to have replaced the logic of syntax. 'I hear', he tells us

> How the youthful Harlots curse
> Blasts the new-born Infants tear
> And blights with plagues the Marriage hearse.

Never before had a poem involved such a dense fabric of semantic and figurative contrasts; it is the verbal equivalent of Surrealism, more than a century before that movement's aesthetic inception. It prompts comparison with 16th- and 17th-century verse but the Renaissance conceit had improvised upon the sturdy backbone of logic and classic rhetoric; Blake allows language to undermine rational thought. We should not, however, treat his work as evidence of capricious indulgence. His purpose becomes apparent when we compare 'London' with a piece written more than 50 years earlier addressing, apparently, the same anarchic metropolis. This is John Bancks' 'A Description of London':

> Houses, churches, mixed together,
> Streets unpleasant in all weather;
> Prisons, palaces contiguous,
> Gates, a bridge, the Thames irriguous.
>
> Gaudy things enough to tempt ye,
> Showy outsides, insides empty;
> Bubbles, trades, mechanic arts,
> Coaches, wheelbarrows and carts.
>
> Warrants, bailiffs, bills unpaid,
> Lords of laundresses afraid;

Rogues that nightly rob and shoot men,
Hangmen, aldermen and footmen.

Lawyers, poets, priests, physicians,
Noble, simple, all conditions:
Worth beneath a threadbare cover,
Villainy bedaubed all over.

Women black, red, fair and grey,
Prudes and such as never pray,
Handsome, ugly, noisy, still,
Some that will not, some that will.

Many a beau without a shilling,
Many a widow not unwilling;
Many a bargain, if you strike it:
This is London! How d'ye like it?

Bancks is unsparing in this presentation of the city as an untidy confection of
order and chaos, but he differs from Blake in the manner of his portrait; his is a
catalogue of random phenomena and while he attempts neither to apportion
blame nor explain the spectacle, Blake's vision of London is so horrifying that it
impairs even the dispassionate mechanisms of description.

The feature that the two poems have in common, a regular stanzaic and
metrical formula, also serves to emphasize their difference. In Bancks' piece,
syntax, metre and rhyme schema cooperate to provide an inventory of contrasts
and contradictions. It is almost as though formal coherence offers both the poet
and the reader protection against the otherwise unpleasant subject of the poem,
a characteristically Augustan procedure. Blake's jaunty trochaic rhythm and neat
four-line stanzas seem absurdly incongruous with a collage of images that are,
by varying degrees, terrible and ineffable.

In his later work, Blake elected to take the route that Wordsworth and
Coleridge contemplated but rejected as self-destructive, the gradual abandonment of the formal features that both defined, and in Blake's view confined,
poetry. He states his case in the Introduction to 'Jerusalem':

When this Verse was first dictated by me, I considered a Monotonous Cadence,
like that used by Milton and Shakespeare and all writers of English Blank
Verse, derived from the Modern bondage of Rhyming, to be a necessary and
indispensable part of Verse. But I soon found that in the mouth of a true
Orator such monotony was not only awkward, but as much a bondage as
rhyme itself. I therefore have produced a variety in every line both of cadences
and of number of syllables. Every word and every letter is studied and put
into its fit place; the terrific numbers are reserved for the terrific parts, the

mild and gentle for the mild and gentle parts, and the prosaic for inferior parts; all are necessary to each other. Poetry Fetter'd Fetters the Human Race. (Blake, 1966, p. 434)

In 'Jerusalem' and many of his other later works, Blake abandoned all concessions to metrical regularity but retained that single token of a poem's difference from all other genres, the line, albeit in a manner that was infinitely variable and which satisfied no abstract formula. He had created his own idiosyncratic brand of free verse, a century prior to its official gestation as a token of literary Modernism. In doing so, he foregrounded the enigma that had dogged poetry since the Renaissance, which would be more profoundly addressed with Modernism and which remains unresolved. From the 16th century onwards, poetry acquired its own self-referring network of formal conventions, the features that defined it and whose deployment was debated by successive generations of commentators, usually poets themselves. What it lacked, however, was a clear sense of purpose. Gradually, from the late 17th century through the period dominated by Pope, it attained the status of a hybrid; it was by its nature and character literary, yet it was deemed worthy of addressing the kinds of topics that were generally the preserve of non-literary discourses. One might contend that Romanticism, as an act of literary revolution, was motivated by the fact that, during the 18th century, poetry had attained this level of respectability; it was, technically speaking, still poetry but it had, in all other respects, been annexed by the non-poetic establishment. It held a junior role in the collocation of discourses dedicated to maintaining a rational, almost prescriptive command of the world. The Romantics dedicated themselves to a search for a radical, unaffiliated status for poetry and reached something close to a consensus on its capacity to reveal and address fundamental truths of existence, truths that conventional language either denied or failed to apprehend. Their manifesto was that poetry should be restored to its role as the vehicle for passionate extremity, as the form of expression most suitable for capturing prelinguistic experiences and sensations. Here we, and they, encounter the paradox. If poetry is possessed of this extraordinary, almost visionary capacity, then it must by some means maintain its status as poetry, as a form that is recognizably different from non-poetic discourses. The only means by which it could do so was its retention of arbitrary, formal characteristics, the intrinsically poetic aspect of the double pattern. Wordsworth, in *The Prelude* (lines 46–54), came tantalizingly close to conceding that the entire enterprise of Romanticism was founded upon a self-contradiction:

> Thus far, O Friend! did I, not used to make
> A present joy the matter of a song,
> Pour forth that day my soul in measured strains
> That would not be forgotten, and are here

> Recorded: to the open fields I told
> A prophecy: poetic numbers came
> Spontaneously to clothe in priestly robe
> A renovated spirit singled out,
> Such hope was mine ...

If, as Wordsworth states, this is the memory of a moment of poetic inspiration, are the 'measured strains', 'here/Recorded' an admission that the original experience is irretrievable, a chimera made concrete only via the transformative power of 'poetic numbers'?

6

Victorian Poetry

The Victorian poets, by whom I mean those whose reputations were made and sustained between the 1830s and 1890s, are often celebrated as the most skilled and meticulous stylists of post-Renaissance English verse. They were eclectic, while preferring versatile orthodoxy to experiment. The techniques and formal paradigms that the Victorians inherited from three centuries of writing would be perfected, extended, even challenged, but they would not in any significant way be altered. In this regard, Alfred, Lord Tennyson and Robert Browning (born 1809 and 1812 respectively) and Matthew Arnold (1822), Algernon Swinburne (1837), Thomas Hardy (1840) and Gerard Manley Hopkins (1844) are effectively the second and third generations of Romanticism. The Romantic dichotomy between a belief in verse as the supremely subjective medium for expression and a begrudging recognition of it as an abstract system of rules and devices became, after the 1830s, the accepted precondition for writing. Correspondingly, there was a discernable institutionalization of what had once been a radical mood. The Romantics treated the poem as a medium for enquiry, a site for exploration, capable of extending the orthodox limits of knowledge and experience, while their successors rehearsed such gestures while accepting implicit constraints, limitations and boundaries. Profound questions are addressed in the quintessential poems of the mid- to late 19th century, but in each instance there is an attendant predisposition to concede that all that can ever be recovered from such imaginative excursions is an acceptance of the given, a resigned contemplation of disillusionment, loss and often despair.

Tennyson's *In Memorian AHH* foregrounds a number of tensions, predominantly the Romantic dilemma regarding the nature and purpose of poetry. It is a long poem, addressing itself to the death of Tennyson's friend Hallam while maintaining this single event as the correlative for explorations of the meaning of life, death, love, art and all manner of permutations upon the relationship between subjective existence and the events that control and determine this condition.

Milton in *Paradise Lost* and Wordsworth in *The Prelude* tread an uncertain path between an extended narrative, respectively, the Christian epic and autobiography, and the minimalist capacities of verse to concentrate moments of lyrical intensity into perhaps no more than five lines. Both employed blank verse, the most flexible of all pre-Modernist forms, which enabled them to better control the tempo of their poems; the unrhymed line could be used both to focus and intensify moments of perplexity and also to release the narrative into lengthier passages of description or reflection. Tennyson's poem, however, comprises compact stanzas (iambic octosyllables, rhyming a bb a), which creates a far more uneasy relationship between broader thematic development and intense localized foci.

The predominant themes of *In Memorian AHH* – Tennyson's and Hallam's lives, their friendship and the latter's death – are indicated in the opening stanzas and thereafter each swims in and out of focus and, significantly, they underpin, anchor, the poem's excursions into more general observations on the meaning of life, and the nature of death. Section XV, for example, appears to focus exclusively upon the unforgiving spectacle of night-time, autumn, and the coming of winter:

> Tonight the winds begin to rise
>   And roar from yonder dropping day;
>   The last red leaf is whirled away,
> The rooks are blown about in the skies;

The theme of a landscape, one full of life but now made barren by the ineluctable force of nature, dominates the next five stanzas and read out of context the section might easily be mistaken for a lyric on the capricious nature of the seasons. But we know that soon, in fact in the subsequent section, we will be returned yet again to a particular instance of change and loss, specifically the death of Hallam and its effect on his friend.

The poem seems driven by a compulsive, fetishist state of mind in that regarding the particulars of his relationship with Hallam and his subsequent sense of loss, little is or can be said beyond Tennyson's feeling that the latter surpasses explanation and the former is too sacred for easy comprehension.

Section V is effectively the poem's manifesto, or, to be more accurate, a self-addressed apology for a piece of writing that could well have gone on for as long as Tennyson was able to add more stanzas to it:

> In words, like weeds, I'll wrap me o'er,
>   Like coarsest clothes against the cold:
>   But that large grief which these enfold
> Is given in outline and no more.

He admits that these 'words', the poem, are at once a means by which he can explore his grief and also his protection from it. In the preceding stanza, he writes:

> But for the unquiet heart and brain,
>   A use in measured language lies;
>   The sad mechanic exercise,
> Like dull narcotics, numbing pain.

This is a candid summary of the post-Romantic condition. Tennyson is fully aware of the heroic failure of the previous generation. Their ambition, to obtain in poetry something inconceivable in rational discourse, was noble but self-abnegating because poems would always be enclosed, self-referring worlds made up entirely of linguistic devices. Now, instead of engaging radically with life, poems had become a refuge from it: 'a use in measured language lies ... like dull narcotics, numbing pain'. T.S. Eliot charged the post-Renaissance tradition of English verse with a 'dissociation of sensibility', an inability or unwillingness to synthesize in poetic language the disparate and, in rational terms, unrelated elements of our lived experience, and his point, as Tennyson confesses, is valid. The speaker of *In Memoriam* is both the self-consciously ineffectual poet lamenting the very real departure of his friend and the poet's alter ego, the reflective craftsman composing an elegy if not on the death of poetry then at least on its grand ambitions of half a century earlier.

The questions faced by Tennyson and his contemporaries are addressed by Arnold in his classic essay 'The Study of Poetry' (1880). Arnold examines the perennial problem of the relationship between what poetry is and what it can and ought to achieve, and his argument involves a fundamental contradiction. He contends that the post-Shakespearean lexicon of forms and devices is diverse, profligate and effectively complete; the question is, what should its 19th-century inheritors do with it: 'poetry is at bottom a criticism of life ... the greatness of a poet lies in his powerful and beautiful application of ideas to life – the question: How to live' (p. 376). The phrase 'poetry is ... a criticism of life' is one of those mantras that is by equal measure all-encompassing and fatuous. It might be taken as a plea for a return to the relevance and accessibility of the Augustan public poem, but elsewhere in the essay Arnold dismisses Dryden and Pope as 'classics of our prose'; in short, in Arnold's opinion, such poetry had annexed itself to the routines of empirical language and as a consequence relinquished the unique capacities of verse. At the same time, Arnold does not re-endorse the Romantic claim that poetry might serve some quasi-revolutionary purpose by reacquainting the jaded intellectual with the uncontaminated essentials of exist-ence. He adds:

> More and more mankind will discover that we have to turn to poetry to interpret life for us, to console us, to sustain us. Without poetry, our science will appear incomplete; and most of what now passes with us for religion and philosophy will be replaced by poetry. (Arnold, 1880, p. 376)

Note that in the first sentence, the ideal of poetry as an activating force, promi-nent in all Romantic theses, is exchanged for a passive role – poetry has now become a way of coping, or, as Tennyson put it, a 'sad mechanic exercise, Like dull narcotics, numbing pain'. The 'science' to which he refers involves every-thing from the growth of Darwin's empiricist explanation for existence to the pragmatics of the Industrial Revolution. This, he implies, has sidelined religion and orthodox philosophy but we should regard with some scepticism a literal reading of his claim that poetry can 'complete' the questions raised by science and 'replace' the void created by the retreat of conventional belief systems. Throughout the essay and indeed in Arnold's other writings on literature and education, poetry is treated as a recuperative resource, a means of preserving a special yet ineffable kind of spiritual integrity; a bourgeois, domesticated brand of Romanticism, something to be treasured by those precious souls able to write and appreciate it.

The deictic features of Arnold's best known poem 'Dover Beach' are elegantly diffuse. We can say with some certainty that the ebb and flow of the waves on the pebble beach, the cliffs of the Kent coast and the moonlit seascape are its tangible points of reference. Beyond that, the speaker folds all manner of figurative, religious, abstract, historical and emotional registers into a tour of his evidently melancholic state of mind. He hints that he might be addressing his thoughts to a particular individual ('Come to the window', 'Listen! you hear the greeting roar') but this presence is so unspecific as to allow for the possibility that he might be addressing us, the reader, or even himself. When he opens the final strophe with

> Ah love, let us be true
> To one another! For the world which seems
> To lie before us ...

'love' might be a term of affection, attached to a specific person, or he might be addressing 'love' itself as an ideal, an abstraction. When the poem closes, our uncertainty remains.

The poem appears to perpetuate the precedent set by the Romantic ode, with subject and focus in a unfixed, continuously oscillating state, but a subtle alteration has occurred. The Romantics – calculatedly or guilelessly, we will never be sure – created in their most celebrated odes a flexible, seemingly improvised relationship between the poet's imaginative, emotional and artistic resources. Arnold, however, offers us something far more disingenuously crafted. In the penultimate strophe, we witness the original concrete image gradually yet meticulously refashioned into a lament for the lost spirit of the age:

> The Sea of Faith
> Was once, too, at the full, and round earth's shore
> Lay like the folds of a bright girdle furled.
> But now I only hear
> Its melancholy, long, withdrawing roar,
> Retreating, to the breath
> Of the night-wind, down the vast edges drear
> And naked shingles of the world.

As a metaphor, this has none of the bravado of the Renaissance conceit nor has it the sturdy mechanics of an Augustan figure; it works by inference and accretion. Yet, at the same time, there is an orotund profundity about it – particularly its prophetic tone of loss and absence, a civilization in decay – that would have seemed anathema to the Romantics, at least during their reckless early years.

The prosodic structure of 'Dover Beach' seems also to declare an allegiance to Romantic unorthodoxy, with each of the four strophes comprising a varying number of lines of shifting, unpredictable length and an irregular rhyme scheme. The metre is predominantly iambic but with sufficient variations to hint at improvised speech. It is, however, a testament to Arnold's skill as a versifier that the flexibility of mood and theme is perfectly framed by the equally fluid structure: in both cases spontaneity is borne of understated contrivance.

Dante Gabriel Rossetti's 'Sudden Light' (1870) is more regular in form than Arnold's poem, although its three identical stanzas incorporate a somewhat baroque design (each involving lines of 6, 8, 8, 4 and 10 syllables and rhyming a b a b a):

> I have been here before,
>> But when or how I cannot tell:
> I know the grass beyond the door,
>> The sweet keen smell.
> The sighing sound, the lights around the shore.
>
> You have been mine before, –
>> How long ago I may not know:
> But just when at that swallow's soar
>> Your neck turned so,
> Some veil did fall, – I knew it all of yore.
>
> Has this been thus before?
>> And shall not thus time's eddying flight
> Still with our lives our love restore
>> In death's despite,
> And day and night yield one delight once more?

In terms of their creation of an interplay between concrete specificity, albeit lightly sketched, and an ill-defined sense of loss or vulnerability, both poems seem to follow almost identical formulae. The 'here' to which Rossetti's speaker has been 'before' carries an approximation of actuality with references to 'the grass', 'the door', the 'smell', 'the shore', but after the opening stanza this gradually disperses, with the introduction of a person who might well have shared the speaker's experience of the place and whose turned 'neck' he recalls as an image transposed with that of a 'swallow's soar'. The 'veil' that 'did fall' is almost certainly a figurative one, disclosing as it does nothing actual but rather a blurred combination of fantasy, recollection and longing. This evocation of a quasi-visionary moment is nonetheless informed by the presence of Rossetti the poetic strategist. The adverb 'before' ends the first line of each stanza and functions as an axis between the hypnotic rhyme scheme and the thematic shift from the past to the apparent present of the spoken utterance: 'before', 'door', 'shore'; 'before', 'soar', 'yore'; 'before', 'restore', 'more'. Again the catalogue of Romantic credos is rehearsed: the presence of the speaker seems to elide with an unspecified notion of the sublime; nature appears on the verge of disclosing a glimpse of the eternal; love and beauty are nuanced but never particularized. At the same time, however, the poet's meticulous craftsmanship is self-evident and undisguised. The conflict between design and immanence addressed by Wordsworth and Coleridge has in Rossetti become an exercise in choreography.

Browning's most notable contribution to the lexicon of poetic formulae and subgenres is undoubtedly the dramatic monologue. At first, this form seems to be a radical departure from the Romantic lyric, in that each of Browning's first-person speakers builds into their account a meticulously detailed, apparently authentic picture of their status, profession, tastes, day-to-day routines and even the objects that surround them as they deliver their piece; there is an abundance of deictic clues. In this regard, they resemble the creations of Donne, Marvell, Herbert and others of two centuries earlier. Browning's creations differ in their more rounded, often disturbing, psychological complexity. In 'My Last Duchess' and 'The Bishop Orders His Tomb', we find ourselves drawn gradually yet inexorably into the mental firmament of figures whose grasp upon the rational and the logical becomes suspect, an effect made all the more unnerving by their erudition and intellectual versatility. As the speaker of 'My Last Duchess' contemplates the portrait of his departed eponymous partner, his eloquent command of what exactly he is saying is gradually undercut by our suspicion that we are witnessing a terrible form of insanity. In this respect, Browning invites comparisons with the genre that had by then overtaken poetry as a means of mediating the world outside the text, the novel. His poems resemble first-person short stories, yet differ from them in one crucial respect. Browning's speakers address us variously in the heroic couplet, blank verse and complex, meticulously regular stanzas. The speaker of 'My Last Duchess' is just as frozen, just as detached from the world outside the text as the image of his late wife, an excellent representation but self-evidently no more than a work of art.

In 1889, Walter Pater argued that the 'chaotic variety and complexity of the modern world' could not be properly mediated by the 'restraint proper to verse form', that the 'special art of the modern world was imaginative prose'. We should not treat this as a foretelling of the death of poetry because Pater did not hold that poetry was incapable of dealing with the 'variety and complexity' of contemporaneous life; rather, that it would be inappropriate for a genre, in whose gift were such steadying absolutes as truth and beauty, to trouble itself with a world which seemed, at least to Pater, a dreadful medley of the mundane and the nihilistic. By 'restraint', he meant the capacity of poetry to create for itself a capsule in which events, ideas and feelings would coexist but which would be at a self-evident, aesthetic remove from their unrefined interactions beyond the poem; essentially, the double pattern would contain and disinfect them.

It is noticeable that, as well as being enclosed within their beautifully constructed material and stanzaic components, none of Browning's monologists exist in the present. All are drawn from the late medieval-Renaissance period and each exists at the core of Renaissance culture, not in England but on the European continent. Browning was pre-empting Pater's ordinance on the discordancy between poetry and the untidy garishness of contemporary life. Browning's speakers are subject to horrifying mental torments and emotional crises but at the same time spared the distasteful contingencies of the here and now. In this regard, they preserve an essence of the Romantic ideal, albeit one that its originators would, in their incautious youth, have abhorred.

In his numerous commentaries on art and life, Arnold (1865a) never tires of deriding the many organs of middle- and lower class culture for their voracious hunger for horrible fact:

> this paragraph on which I stumbled in a newspaper ... 'A shocking child murder has just been committed at Nottingham. A girl named Wragg left her workhouse there on Saturday morning with her young illegitimate child. The child was soon afterwards found dead on Mapperly Hills, having been strangled. Wragg is in custody.'
>
> Nothing but that; but ... how eloquent, how suggestive are those few lines! 'Our old Anglo-Saxon breed, the best in the whole world!' – how much that is harsh and ill favoured there is in this best! Wragg! If we are to talk of ideal perfection, 'of the best in the whole world', has anyone reflected what a touch of grossness in our race, what an original shortcoming in the more delicate spiritual perceptions, is shown by the natural growth amongst us of such hideous names – Higginbottom, Stiggins, Bugg! (see Wimsatt and Brooks, 1957, pp. 440–1)

Arnold seems uncertain as to whether it is the likes of the girl 'Wragg' or the apparent appetite for reports of her class that disgusts him most. One cannot help but note the parallels between Ms Wragg and Wordsworth's 'The Mad Mother', one of the most celebrated *Lyrical Ballads*, yet there is also a crucial difference that disqualifies the former from the kind of elevation to tragic grandeur bestowed by Wordsworth. The dispossessed of Arnold's world, as his quotation infers, are no longer part of some primitivist fantasy but products of a new industrial urban landscape (in this instance Nottingham and its many workhouses) and, as a consequence, no longer suitable for poetry.

Adelaide Anne Procter's 'Philip and Mildred' (1864) is a fascinating piece of work but not because it is unusual in its manner; rather, it exemplifies an insufficiency endemic to almost all Victorian verse. Contemporary and more recent commentators take it for granted that the narrative involves the eponymous couple divided by ungenerous circumstances. They meet, and live, in the countryside – the opening stanzas offer references to 'the valley' and 'the shady lime walk' – where, one surmises, they have spent their courtship. Then a 'learnèd Traveller', a man who 'had gained renown, '[comes] there', notes a corresponding potential in Philip and advises him that his future lies 'in London'. Philip's subsequent success condemns Mildred to a form of ill-defined spinsterhood – their engagement is never formally ended, but it seems clear that he will never properly return – and she dies alone.

My summary is as accurate as the poem allows but it should, nonetheless, be treated with some caution. While there are no suggestions that Philip and Mildred's story occurs at any point other than the time of writing, the 1860s, the poem is mysteriously devoid of contemporaneous detail. Apart from the reference to London, all other particulars are surrendered to a fabric of affective abstractions and generalizations. Many complex psychological and moral issues are mooted, including the tension between the public and private worlds of individuals and the emotional commitment bestowed by the making of vows; and indeed very few contemporaneous readers would not be alert to the tension between economic forces, which drew the destitute and the ambitious to urban centres, and whatever personal or emotional commitment might preside elsewhere. However, while the poem is subject to such contextual resonances, it neither contains nor explicitly invokes them. It does not, like Browning's monologues, conspicuously exempt itself from engagements with mid-19th-century Britain by appropriating different mythologies of place and time, but it creates a comparable effect. The world of the poem, involving its registers and personnel, is at once evocative yet independent of the one in which Proctor and her peers and readers spent their lives. The vacuum created by the scrupulous avoidance of minutiae, incident or contingency is filled by the vagaries of bathos and resignation, the causes of which are not disguised but nor are they clearly evoked. When Philip returns, it is evident that whatever emotion attached to their original relationship is now dissipated but one searches in vain for an answer to such questions as why the marriage will never now occur or what either of them actually expect. Instead our attention is shifted towards emotive but comfortably unspecific imagery. Consider, for example, the opening two lines of this stanza, where a question is raised regarding the apparent dissolution of their relationship:

> What was wanting? He was gentle, kind, and generous still, deferring
> To her wishes always; nothing seemed to mar their tranquil life:

The lines seem pregnant with the anxiety and tension that underpin any relationship challenged by seemingly implacable circumstances, but instead of an insight either into the cause of their despair or its effects, we get

> There are skies so calm and leaden that we long for storm winds stirring,
> There is peace so cold and bitter, that we almost welcome strife.

Procter's Anglicized version of the classical hexameter – alternately 17 and 15 syllables in length – is flexible, ponderous, enough to sometimes resemble prose but this impression of release into the discursively unpoetic is false. There is a stiffening regularity underpinning the apparent looseness. The 17-syllable lines all carry a resounding double rhyme as security against the loss of the inter-vening single rhymes in the sweep of the irregular rhythm. The devices and artifice of verse are not ostentatious – conceits are implicit rather than mani-fest – yet the design of the text is self-evident and persistent. There is, in this regard, a consistency between the poem's avoidance of particulars and its detachment from the discourses of the real world.

By the mid-19th century, virtually every form of linguistic mediation – scien-tific papers, political essays, the journal, the magazine and the newspaper, and of course the novel – was busily recording the gradual and incessant fragmentation of orthodox systems of belief and social organization and the transformation, over little more than a generation, of the way life was lived, the latter driven by the Industrial Revolution. Marx and Engels, among others, were collapsing the pre-19th-century distinctions between philosophical, historical and political discourses. Thomas Huxley, Charles Lyell and Charles Darwin were subjecting to the merciless empiricism of science subjects that had once been protected by theological absolutes. The novels of Dickens, Thackeray, Eliot, the Brontës and Hardy exchanged the ordering principles of art for the arbitrariness of existence. Arnold, always the most reliable spokesman for his age, addressed this in his Cambridge lecture called 'Literature and Science' (published in 1882). He concedes, with a somewhat resigned and begrudging air, that Darwin and Huxley, who he mentions, and those in politics of the rational humanist disposition, had finally dispossessed society of what, in the Middle Ages, was 'supposed knowledge':

> The middle age could do without humane letters, as it could do without the study of nature, because its supposed knowledge was made to engage its emotions so powerfully. Grant that the supposed knowledge disappears, its power of being made to engage the emotions will of course disappear along with it – but the emotions will remain. Now if we find by experience that humane letters have an undeniable power of engaging the emotions, the importance of humane letters in man's training becomes not less, but greater, in proportion to the success of science in extirpating what it calls 'mediaeval thinking'. (see Wimsatt and Brooks, 157, pp. 449–50)

In short, poetry (aka 'humane letters') must bridge the chasm left by the disap-pearance of immutable belief and 'the emotions' must become – although Arnold would not have admitted as such – a placebo, a means of comforting the sensitive individual otherwise left only with a nihilistic void of unbelief and frightening empiricism.

The Romantic impulse has now come full circle from the time of its inchoate radical genesis in the Age of Enlightenment and Revolution to a state where its

tryside – the opening stanzas offer references to 'the valley' and 'the shady lime walk' – where, one surmises, they have spent their courtship. Then a 'learnèd Traveller', a man who 'had gained renown, '[comes] there', notes a corresponding potential in Philip and advises him that his future lies 'in London'. Philip's subsequent success condemns Mildred to a form of ill-defined spinsterhood – their engagement is never formally ended, but it seems clear that he will never properly return – and she dies alone.

My summary is as accurate as the poem allows but it should, nonetheless, be treated with some caution. While there are no suggestions that Philip and Mildred's story occurs at any point other than the time of writing, the 1860s, the poem is mysteriously devoid of contemporaneous detail. Apart from the reference to London, all other particulars are surrendered to a fabric of affective abstractions and generalizations. Many complex psychological and moral issues are mooted, including the tension between the public and private worlds of individuals and the emotional commitment bestowed by the making of vows; and indeed very few contemporaneous readers would not be alert to the tension between economic forces, which drew the destitute and the ambitious to urban centres, and whatever personal or emotional commitment might preside elsewhere. However, while the poem is subject to such contextual resonances, it neither contains nor explicitly invokes them. It does not, like Browning's monologues, conspicuously exempt itself from engagements with mid-19th-century Britain by appropriating different mythologies of place and time, but it creates a comparable effect. The world of the poem, involving its registers and personnel, is at once evocative yet independent of the one in which Proctor and her peers and readers spent their lives. The vacuum created by the scrupulous avoidance of minutiae, incident or contingency is filled by the vagaries of bathos and resignation, the causes of which are not disguised but nor are they clearly evoked. When Philip returns, it is evident that whatever emotion attached to their original relationship is now dissipated but one searches in vain for an answer to such questions as why the marriage will never now occur or what either of them actually expect. Instead our attention is shifted towards emotive but comfortably unspecific imagery. Consider, for example, the opening two lines of this stanza, where a question is raised regarding the apparent dissolution of their relationship:

What was wanting? He was gentle, kind, and generous still, deferring
To her wishes always; nothing seemed to mar their tranquil life:

The lines seem pregnant with the anxiety and tension that underpin any relationship challenged by seemingly implacable circumstances, but instead of an insight either into the cause of their despair or its effects, we get

There are skies so calm and leaden that we long for storm winds stirring,
There is peace so cold and bitter, that we almost welcome strife.

duty is to protect the civilized elite from an encroaching sense of disorder. The paradox that had beset Romanticism, of how the 'real language of men' could be reconciled with a medium that was self-evidently separate from 'real' discourse, had become the poem's means of self-preservation; the double pattern was the Victorian poet's hiding place from an otherwise unforgiving world of actuality.

The Victorian poets were almost neurotically eclectic in their permutations on every given structural formula, and Arthur Hugh Clough went as far as anyone previously had done towards abandoning all concessions to abstract form, but in his epistolary *Amours de Voyage*, the correspondence between his characters never quite submits to unconstraint. It is still written in lines, worn like vestments, testaments to a faith at least in the poetic ideal, if not its precise doctrine. Swinburne indulged himself with images that, as far as the period allowed, were implicitly sexual but his rampant use of alliteration, assonance and every other branch of rhythmic emphasis and sound pattern to foreground his innuendoes turns his poems into late 19th-century portents of *Carry On* film scripts. He too was making use of the mechanisms of the double pattern as a means of absorbing and blunting what he knew would be otherwise unmentionable. Hopkins, the most celebrated avant-gardist of the period – but whose work did not enter the public sphere until the 20th century – was in truth a guardian of formal tradition. His creation of frantically irregular metrical structures – notably sprung rhythm – and his outrageous foregrounding of metaphor and sound pattern were unprecedented but judiciously conservative. This is stanza 28 from 'The Wreck of the Deutschland':

> But how shall I … make me room there:
> Reach me a … Fancy, come faster –
> Strike you the sight of it? look at the loom there,
> Thing that she … there then! the Master,
> Ipse, the only one, Christ, King, Head:

He was reworking and consolidating the intrinsically poetic conventions of the double pattern, albeit at the expense of coherence.

Between the 1830s and the 1890s, every form of the double pattern was variously reworked, revived, dismantled and reassembled. The patently formal devices of poetry clothed and protected a mannered solipsism, while its practitioners treated those same devices as a means of maintaining the essential significance of literary art. For the Victorians, the maintenance of the double pattern was comparable with the institution of marriage; in each instance, passion and the pure physicality of existence were at once sanctioned, institutionalized and quarantined.

The period is the terminus of traditionalism in verse, the double pattern was exhausted and had nowhere else to go, and in this regard Victorian verse played a significant peremptory role in causing the most cataclysmic change in the history of poetry.

7

Modernism and After

What is free verse? This question has taxed the interpretive resources of critics and poets since the 1900s and has resulted in a rich variety of solutions. None of these can claim to be a comprehensive, abstract definition of what free verse is or of how it works and many remain as angry attempts to dismiss the validity of their competitors. Free verse is the most significant contribution by poetry to the formal aesthetics of Modernism, and in this chapter I shall attempt to provide a thorough account of how it began, why it persists and its influence upon orthodox poetic writing. In the process, we will be forced to reconsider the standard, conventional perceptions of how language works and, more significantly, of how poetic language can claim to be different from its non-poetic counterparts.

Consider the following task. Choose a poem and then define the metrical, prosodic form in which it is written. Most people will be able to identify *The Rape of the Lock* as a sequence of heroic couplets, *Paradise Lost* as blank verse and Shakespeare's sonnets as indeed sonnets. At the irregular end of the spectrum, the Romantic ode, Hopkins' sprung rhythm or Coleridge's accentualist experiment in 'Christabel' will make concessions to identifiable patterns of syntax, alliteration, rhythm or rhyme scheme – their flexibility is validated by their invocation of regular precedent. But with Williams' 'The Red Wheelbarrow', Pound's 'In a Station of the Metro' or Eliot's 'Ash Wednesday', we can agree to designate all three as free verse only because they persistently evade the abstract patterns of regular verse. We know what they are because of what they are not. It might be possible to draw up a diagram of stress patterns and line lengths, but this would not represent an abstract formula for free verse, only a plan of the particular free verse poem that we happen to be reading.

The only unifying element in the free verse canon is the use of the poetic line – the so-called prose poem can be dismissed as an intriguing aberration. But what is a poetic line? If it does not establish its formal identity in deploying a regular or irregular pattern of sound (metre, rhythm, rhyme, assonance, alliteration) it cannot, at least in the abstract, be said to exist. We might shift our focus from the metrical to the non-poetic aspect of the double pattern and still be disappointed: there is no rule or convention that obliges the free verse poet to construct their lines according to any particular syntactic formula. The line might consist of a complete sentence or a single word (adjective, noun, verb, connective) whose relation to the structure of preceding and succeeding lines is infinitely flexible. By establishing this peculiar precedent, the free versifiers have caused a number of problems for readers, critics and other poets. At the root of these problems is the relation between the tangible presence of the free verse line – the fact that it exists on the page is de facto proof that the poet intended it to play a part in how the poem works – and its capacity to alter, even create, meaning. The three writers whose postulations on the structure and purpose of free verse encouraged the most vociferous debates were Ezra Pound, Amy Lowell and Harriet Monroe. Monroe founded the Chicago-based journal *Poetry: Magazine of Verse*, which from 1912 provided an outlet for innovative US poets and London-based Imagist groupings whose most prominent early members were Ezra Pound, Richard Aldington, F.S. Flint and T.E. Hume – soon to be joined by T.S. Eliot and William Carlos Williams. Lowell moved from Boston to London in 1914 and went on to edit and write prefaces to three annual anthologies of *Some Imagist Poets* (1915–17) – although scholars are still uncertain about the relative contributions of Lowell and Pound to these ground-breaking proposals. The poets published in these volumes are often divided by conflicting personal and aesthetic affiliations, but it is possible to identify a number of recurrent questions and issues raised by the poems themselves and in the critical debates that attended them.

The ex cathedra writings of the leading Imagists, particularly Pound, Lowell and Monroe, address many of the same issues as the Romantics but with uncompromising conviction and intent:

> To create new rhythms – as the expression of new moods – and not to copy old rhythms, which merely echo old moods. We do not insist upon free verse as the only method of writing poetry. We fight for it as a principle of liberty. We believe that the individuality of a poet may often be better expressed in free verse than in conventional forms. In poetry a new cadence is a new idea. (Lowell, 1915)

The Romantic impatience with the inhibiting conventions of form is again invoked but while the poets of a century earlier were unable to resolve the question of how poetry could rid itself of its confining regulations and still be poetry, the Imagists proposed to write in a manner that is at once poetic yet unprecedentedly radical. Nonetheless, the exact nature of this new way of writing is left to the surmise of the reader. In the next volume of *Some Imagist Poets, 1916*, they (the Preface was thought to have been co-authored by Lowell and Monroe) attempt a more prosaic account of what free verse involves. Instead of such abstract principles as 'the foot, the number of syllables, the quantity, or the line', the poetic dimension of the text, that which distinguishes it from prose, is to comprise 'the cadence' and 'the strophe'. The exact distinction remains unclear but an analogy is suggested, wherein a person is asked to run, walk, stroll around a circle but to complete the process within a given time. They can vary their pace almost limitlessly but the act of completing the circle will provide the irregularities of progress with a sense of organic resolution. The analogy was provocative, adventurous and in pragmatic terms meaningless. What it did disclose was that while it seemed difficult to arrive at a formula for what the new line in free verse would actually involve, it indicated a release from the abstract formulae that had governed verse, English and classical, for its entire history.

Pound stated in 'A Retrospect' (1918):

> *Rhythm* – I believe in an 'absolute rhythm', a rhythm, that is, in poetry which corresponds exactly to the emotion or shade of emotion to be expressed. A man's rhythm must be interpretative, it will be, therefore, in the end, his own, uncounterfeiting, uncounterfeitable. (in Faulkner, 1986, p. 64)

The structure of the line must, it seems, be a reflection of the prelinguistic moment of inspiration. He rejects pure impressionism and formlessness and proposes instead that the formal or aesthetic features of the poem should over-rule the delineative function of language. Ingeniously, he attempts to resolve the Romantic paradox by arguing that the poetic function is not, as previously perceived, a decorative adjunct to ordinary language but the means by which we come closest to unfettered transparency. Amy Lowell later suggested that the line should be shaped by 'a rhythmic curve … corresponding roughly to the necessity of breathing' (Lowell, 1920). Again we find echoes of the Romantic (and Hopkins') ideal of spontaneity and transparency, but the Modernists attempted to realize what for the Romantics, with the notable exception of Blake, had been aspiration and hypothesis. But what did the former actually achieve?

A poem that is often regarded as the archetype for both the Imagist movement and Ezra Pound's later experiments in *The Cantos* is his 'In a Station of the Metro', published in *Poetry*, April 1913:

> The apparition of these faces in the crowd;
> Petals on a wet, black bough.

It is known that when this and a number of similarly clipped and enigmatic pieces were written, Pound was deeply interested in the Chinese and Japanese ideogram (see Kenner, 1972, pp. 195–7). In 1913, Mary Fenollosa sent Pound the unpublished manuscript of her late husband Ernest's essay on the relation between Chinese and Western poetry, which Pound eventually edited and published in 1919 as *The Chinese Written Character as a Medium for Poetry*. Hugh Kenner has called this document 'the *Ars Poetica* of our time' and Donald Davie has compared its influence with that of Wordsworth's Preface to *Lyrical Ballads* and Shelley's *Defence of Poetry*. Why? Fenollosa claims that the Chinese written sign, the ideogram, is capable of representing single images and relations between them in a way which bypasses the systematic, successive rules of Western language. For example, the three ideogrammic signs, roughly translated as 'man sees horse', consist of three visual figures, and in each of these the pictorial image of legs is represented: man is a thing with two legs, the movement of his eyes is (metaphorically) represented by moving legs and the horse is denoted as a figure with four legs. The attraction for Pound and others of this method of representation lay in its apparent ability to transcend the refractory nature of language (a persistent post-Romantic ideal). In the English version, 'man sees horse', the matrix of subject, verb and object is deterministic. We could transform the sentence into 'Horse is seen by man' but we will never be able to escape from the dominant function of the verb 'to see' in the relation between the two syntactic functionaries, man and horse. In the Chinese version, the movements and the objects perceived and the act of perception are interwoven. One element of the experiential condition (legs) is shared by all three signs, thus the processes of witnessing (seeing) and existing (man on two legs, horse on four) become interdependent elements of a single unit of meaning. Pound's problem – not unlike Wordsworth's – was how to make this ideal of transparency and immediacy correspond with the conditions of Western language. He could hardly abandon words in favour of purely visual images. What he did was to transform the poetic line from its conventional function as a foregrounding of sound patterns into a unit whose means of signification could be accounted for neither in purely syntactic nor purely prosodic, metrical terms.

Consider 'In a Station of the Metro' with this programme in mind. It is a sentence without a main verb or proposition. The two parts of the text (indicated by its division into lines) operate as the Western linguistic counterpart to ideogrammic visual images, but how do we go about documenting and describing the effect of their juxtaposition? Harvey Gross (1964, p. 162), in a respected study of Modernist verse form, gives us an example of how to interpret this poem, and in doing so subverts what we know or assume about Pound's intention:

> No harm comes if we want to see this as vaguely analogous to Chinese writing; the two images have spatial and emotional relationships. Grammar, however, is not missing; it is automatically supplied by the reader.

Gross goes on to claim that the phrase 'are like' is 'implied' by the syntactic and semantic constituents of the two lines. The problem, which Gross does not address, is that by 'automatically supplying' the missing grammatical component, the reader is negating the effect that Pound was attempting to achieve. Gross's reading imposes a grammatical structure upon a juxtaposition of images that attempts to transcend such structures. For example, it would be equally plausible to claim that Pound perceived the faces in the urban crowd as sadly and tragically 'unlike' the life-enhancing images of the petals on the bough. Perhaps we should forego the search for the 'correct' interpretation, given that Pound's intention was not to offer us a rational (that is, grammatical) link between the two images but to preserve the original multiplicity of impressions that occur prior to the imposition of an unambiguous linguistic structure.

Pound's enthusiasm for the multidimensional immediacy of the ideogram is echoed in the ex cathedra writings of his contemporaries.

T.E. Hulme (1908) called Imagist poetry 'the new visual art' consisting of 'the succession of visual images'. 'It builds up a plastic image which it hands over to the reader, whereas the old art endeavoured to influence him physically by the hypnotic effect of rhyme.' In practical terms, the poetic line should be constructed as a 'method of recording visual images in distinct lines'.

This ideal of immediacy, the snapshot of prelinguistic experience uncontaminated by the inheritance of metrical structure, also underpinned observations on figurative language and poetic idiom. The following quotations are from Jones (1972):

1 Direct treatment of the 'thing' whether subjective or objective.
2 To use absolutely no word that did not contribute to the presentation. (F.S. Flint, *Poetry*, March 1913)

Use no superfluous word, no adjective, which does not reveal something. Don't use such an expression as 'dim land of *peace*'. It dulls the image. It mixes an abstraction with the concrete. It comes from the writers not realising that the nature object is always the *adequate* symbol. (Ezra Pound, *Poetry*, March 1913)

1 To use the language of common speech, but to employ always the *exact*, not the nearly exact nor merely the decorative word …
2 To produce poetry that is hard and clear, never blurred nor indefinite. (Preface to *Some Imagist Poets 1915*)

Pound's 'In a Station of the Metro' would seem to meet all these criteria, its only excursion from the purely nominative being the appellation of 'wet' and 'black' to the condition of the bough. T.E. Hulme in 'Images' is a little more indulgent:

> Old houses were scaffolding once
> > and workmen whistling.
> >   *
> Sounds fluttered
> > Like bats in the dusk.
> >   *
> The flounced edge of skirt,
> > Recoiling like waves off a cliff.

There are certainly juxtapositions and contrasts here: the unspecified 'sounds' and the fluttering of bats; the 'edge of skirt' and the 'waves off a cliff'. But these hardly belong within the same rhetorical sphere as the metaphors and symbols that featured routinely in pre-20th century verse. Images are placed alongside each other but they are not linked by anything resembling the syntactic counter-logic and imaginative extrapolation that drive even the most orthodox conceits of Romanticism.

H.D.'s 'Oread' seems at first to flout the ordinances of anti-metaphoric Puritanism:

> Whirl up, sea –
> Whirl your pointed pines,
> Splash your great pines
> On our rocks,
> Hurl your green over us,
> Cover us with your pools of fir.

I.A. Richards (1936) has provided the most succinct account of how metaphor works with his distinction between the 'tenor' of the device – specifically, the literal, grounded frame of reference – and the 'vehicle', the point of comparison carried over from a very different context. In pre-Modernist verse, we are usually able to discriminate between the operations of tenor and vehicle, with the former grounding the conceit in immediate observations and the latter functioning as the channel for imaginative excess. In H.D.'s poem, however, the distinction is uncertain. The seascape could be the tenor and the woodland the vehicle or vice versa. While concessions are made to the capacities of metaphor to redirect the trajectory of logic, the orthodox relationship between the literal and the figurative is transformed into a fluid dynamic interaction between two sets of images.

T.E. Hulme achieves a similar effect in 'Autumn':

> A touch of cold in the Autumn night –
> I walked abroad,
> And saw the ruddy moon lean over a hedge
> Like a red-faced farmer.
> I did not stop to speak, but nodded
> And round about were the wistful stars
> With white faces like town children.

Before transposing the image of the moon with that of the red-faced farmer, Hulme slips into the description the anthropomorphic term 'ruddy'. The comparison between the planet and the human visage is unforced and guileless, and in the closing three lines, the heavenly panorama as a spectrum of human faces seems to have evolved naturally. It is metaphoric writing but not of a type previously practised. Prior to this, metaphor was an instrument, a device initiated and executed by the controlling presence of the speaker/poet. Now the speaking presence becomes as much the subject of the metaphor as its guide.

An even more radical example of the surrender of rational control occurs in Pound's 'A Girl':

> The tree has entered my hands,
> The sap has ascended my arms,
> The tree has grown in my breast –
> Downward,
> The branches grow out of me, like arms.
>
> Tree you are,
> Moss you are,
> You are violets with wind above them.
> A child – *so* high – you are,
> And all this is folly to the world.

One of the persistent, apparently irresolvable quandaries of Romantic and post-Romantic verse was of how to consummate, in language, the much-venerated ideal of man as at one with the natural world. The problem, principally, was that despite his best intentions, the poet would always be in command of the material that he supposedly revered. Pound, commendably, attempts to short-circuit the taxonomy of intellect, language and subject. The speaker is not so much addressing the beauty or separateness of the tree as dissolving the distinction between observer and subject. He does not comment on the external world in the abstract reverential mode of the 19th century; he attempts to dismantle the distinction between the perceiver and the perceived, to integrate the act of representation with its object.

The early Modernists, primarily the Imagists, had engaged with the ideals and objectives of the Romantics and, in practice, had been far more pioneering and radical in their attempts to realize them. In terms of the catalogue of devices that constituted the intrinsically poetic constituents of the double pattern – metre, sound pattern, abstract stanzaic structure, persistent and ostentatious figurative constructions – they had eschewed precedent, detached themselves from the accumulated legacy of literary history. Yet their achievement, by its nature, sowed the seeds of their demise. The obsessive concern in early Modernism with the unalloyed, transparent, almost transcendent image involved not only the disavowing of orthodox design and convention but also the exclusion from the poem of a discernable authorial presence. By minimalizing the formal mechanisms of poetry, Modernists had alienated the speaker or the poet from the text. One of the axioms that attends the history of poetry is that for a poem to engage the interest of the reader, it must be informed by a presence that we recognize, a figure distracted or perplexed by a range of concerns – from the mundane to the apocalyptic – similar to our own; one of us. A testament to the authenticity of this figure and a guarantee of our interest in them is their ability to variously control, fashion and inform the architecture of the poem. If we minimalize these formal structures, then, as a consequence, we diminish our cognisance of their practitioners. Despite its radicalism and the shock of its arrival, Modernism began, from the 1920s onwards, to dissipate, to become marginalized by a re-emergent, although flamboyantly modified, brand of traditionalism and this issue would begin to divide Modernism after its pre-1920s heyday. For example, the spirit of Imagism would be kept alive in the US by such second-generation champions of its principles as Charles Olson, Robert Creeley, Robert Duncan, Gary Snyder and Cyd Corman. Olson's 'Projective Verse' (1950) echoes and radically re-endorses the credos of the early Imagist anthologies. He distinguishes between 'closed' poetry – frozen by the abstract formulae of rhyme, metre and conventional figurative language – and the 'open' text:

> Every element in an open poem (the syllable, the line, as well as the image, the sound, the sense) must be taken up as participants in the kinetic of the poem just as solidly as we are accustomed to take what we call the objects of reality; and these elements are to be seen as creating the tensions of a poem just as totally as do those whose objects create what we know as the world. (p. 20)

The poem, while not a purely transparent medium, should at least accommodate and be shaped by the dynamic of forces that make up the prelinguistic world and our attendant acts of perception. This is Fenollosa revisited, and the following, from Olson's *Maximus* letters, indicates what he has in mind:

> I have this sense
> that I am one
> with my skin
>
>
> Plus this – plus this:
> that forever the geography
> which leans in
> on me I compell
> backwards I compell Gloucester
> to yield, to change
>   Polis
> is this

Olson uses the free verse lines not simply as rhetorical devices; they record the progress and vacillation of the poet's ratiocinative faculty, become a chronicle of his mind changing direction. 'I compell backwards I compell Gloucester to yield' is ungrammatical and the line endings are a register of the unresolved possibilities and indecisions that occur at the interface between impression and language.

E.E. Cummings was a near contemporary of Olson with similarly radical leanings but his technique developed in an antithetical manner. The following is from his *95 Poems*:

l (a

le
af
fa

ll

s)
one
l

iness

In common with Olson, Cummings has rejected the orthodox relationship between the line and syntax but rather than allowing design to be shaped by and subordinated to experience makes it the determinant of meaning. In purely technical terms, he has supplemented the effects created in traditional verse by the relationship between the line and syntax. Now, however, the 'line break' does not so much bifurcate a single trajectory of meaning as actually take over from syntax and semantics. The bracketed sentence 'a leaf falls' is literally inter-woven with the truncated single word, 'loneliness'. Differently deployed, the two components of the poem could recall 'In a Station of the Metro':

a leaf falls
loneliness

But Cummings has combined this echo of Imagist transparency with a delib-erate invocation of the pure arbitrariness of poetic structure.

For both Olson and Cummings, the double pattern is still present, but while the former reduces the poetic function to the bare minimum, the latter relishes and foregrounds its perversity. William Carlos Williams, as we have seen in Chapter 2, stands between these two extremes, creating an impression of trans-parency while subtly integrating the line as a counterpoint to improvisation. By far the most important figure in this realignment of the avant-garde with cautiously preserved aspects of orthodoxy was T.S. Eliot.

Eliot's earliest, most discussed blend of the radical and the conservative is 'The Love Song of J. Alfred Prufrock' (1917), a passage from which has already been scrutinized as an example of the double pattern at work (Chapter 2). The poem invites comparison with Browning's dramatic monologues, and does so calculatedly to point up its double-edged invocation and refashioning of prec-edent. While the Imagists were determined to cut themselves free from the established corpus and formal lexicon of verse, Eliot worked by infiltration and subversion. Browning's monologues attempted to strike a balance between their status as verse, with the speaker split between a framework of metre and rhyme that was self-evidently unreal, and a fabric of locative and private references to circumstance that lent him some credibility. This is Eliot's opening verse paragraph:

> Let us go then, you and I,
> When the evening is spread out against the sky
> Like a patient etherised upon a table;
> Let us go, through certain half-deserted streets,
> The muttering retreats
> Of restless nights in one-night cheap hotels
> And sawdust restaurants with oyster-shells:
> Streets that follow like a tedious argument
> Of insidious intent
> To lead you to an overwhelming question …
> Oh, do not ask, 'What is it?'
> Let us go and make our visit.

The 'I' is obviously the speaker, but who is the 'you'? It might be us, the reader, invited to join him on this journey through his own rather troubled consciousness. But we cannot be sure. He might be addressing someone else within the imagined situation of the poem, not necessarily someone present at the moment that he utters the words but a figure with whom he is nonetheless preoccupied; he might even be addressing himself, constructing an alter ego or situating his uneasy state of mental and emotional division as separate pronouns. Our attempts to solve this puzzle by further examining the details of the text intensify rather than decode the mystery. Is the 'patient etherised upon a table' a figurative reference to 'you' – whomever that might be – 'I' or 'the sky'? Is the question to which we, he or they will be led, the succinctly existential 'What is it?' Or is the speaker advising his companion, or himself, not to ask what the question is? Are the streets and restaurants that lead to this unasked or unanswerable question literal and real – perhaps the question and its circumstantial pre-emptings will become clearer when we reach a specific destination – or do they represent a figurative journey through fragments of memory and consciousness comprised of half-recollected places with private associations?

Read on beyond this passage and become even more confused. Particular and locative clues begin to accumulate ('my hair', 'my head', 'the cups', 'the marmalade', 'the tea', 'my trousers'), but this tentative offer of a sense of the speaker's tangible presence is undermined by a bewildering collage of references to literature, the Bible, history, nature, art and all manner of impersonal allusion that might have gathered in the mind of a particular individual or might just as easily invoke a collective, albeit bourgeois and educated, consciousness. In the broader aesthetic context of Modernism, we might find links between the diso-

rientating shifts of the poem and the prose techniques of the interior monologue developed by Joyce and Woolf. But there is a difference. The interior
monologue (aka stream of consciousness) attempts to realize in language the
multidimensional tension between the inner and outer dimensions of consciousness – the condition of our mental and perceptual worlds prior to the ratiocinative processes of thought and conventional linguistic organization. Eliot,
although creating a similar effect, qualifies his concession to impressionistic
formlessness with a persistent and self-conscious use of form – the poetic dimension of the double pattern. The metrical structure and the rhyme scheme are
irregular but they are continuously present. They function as a bridge between
an evocation of pre-rational chaos and a tenuous sense of order. This provision
is the feature that links the poem with the cultural and aesthetic legacy from
which the early Modernists had attempted to distance themselves.

Metaphor, the conceit, the figure, the trope, all had, like metre, been the
mainstays of verse but no one before 'Prufrock' had used them as Eliot does:

> The yellow fog that rubs its back upon the window-panes,
> The yellow smoke that rubs its muzzle on the window-panes,
> Licked its tongue into the corners of the evening,
> Lingered upon the pools that stand in drains,
> Let fall upon its back the soot that falls from chimneys,
> Slipped by the terrace, made a sudden leap,
> And seeing that it was a soft October night,
> Curled once about the house, and fell asleep. (lines 15–22)

The fog and the sinister animal, species undisclosed, vie for prominence – in
Richards' terms, we are never quite sure which is the vehicle and which the
tenor – and the speaker seems equally muddled and careless with regard to
prosody. There is a rhythmic undertow, apparently relaxed and uncommitted,
along with a rhyme scheme that seems little more than a casual, rather lazy
acknowledgement that he is writing a poem. In the second line, he appears to be
searching for a way of articulating his impression but does not have the energy
or inclination to avoid repeating himself: 'rubs its back'; 'rubs its muzzle';
'window-panes', 'window-panes'. Blake, in 'London', had fractured convention
with his chain of shocking juxtapositions yet his was a calculatedly radical
disorder. Eliot, for the first time in literary history, invents us a speaker who is
irresolutely out of control, a disorientated unfocused figure who never enables
us to identify his prevailing theme or even diagnose a cause for his troubled
state. The only aspect of the poem that is persistent and unremitting is the
speaker's self-conscious role as the choreographer of its formal features, and he
performs this role in a manner of someone caught perplexedly between an allegiance to the traditional legacy of what writing verse involves and a palpable
sense of discomfort with these duties. Eliot stated in 'Reflections on "Verse
Libre"' (1917, p. 101):

> We may formulate as follows: the ghost of some simple metre should lurk behind the arras even in the 'freest' verse; to advance menacingly as we doze, and withdraw as we rouse. Our freedom is only freedom when it appears against the background of artificial limitation.

This captures perfectly Prufrock's oscillation between a half-acknowledged attendance upon tradition and his insouciant disrespect for its demands. In 'Tradition and the Individual Talent' (1919, p. 84), Eliot expands upon his thesis:

> The poet has not a 'personality' to express, but a particular medium ... in which impressions and experiences combine in peculiar and unexpected ways ... The emotion of art is impersonal. And the poet cannot reach this impersonality without surrendering himself wholly to the work to be done.

In Eliot's view, the paradox that had troubled poets since the Romantic period and been confronted more ruthlessly by the early Modernists was an inescapable precondition for all poetic writing. The long-cherished ideal of the poet – or 'personality' – freeing themselves of the binding conventions of the 'medium' in order to offer some unalloyed, perhaps ultimate, vision was a contradiction in terms. Without 'the medium', the 'personality' of the writer becomes subject to the contingencies and commonplaces of non-literary communication and is no longer recognizable as a poet. He showed in his verse that it was possible to fragment and undermine the monoliths of tradition and he averred that to pretend tradition could be dispensed with meant that one was no longer writing poetry. Eliot is, in effect, endorsing the double pattern.

The Waste Land, that presiding monument to Modernism, is a collage of perspectives, voices, snatches of German poetry, Hindu and Christian scripture, allusions to Goldsmith and Marvell, juxtaposed with visions and sounds from 1920s London. 'These fragments I have shored against my ruins' says the 'speaker' (Tiresias? The Fisher King? Eliot? Everyman?) at the end of the poem, and the only point of stability for the reader of this ahistorical multicultural assembly is the means by which the fragments have been so desperately 'shored'. The dominant, ever-present element is the poetic line and its faithful companion the trope. The famous opening verse paragraph reproduces the Shakespearean/Miltonic device of the blank verse *contra-rejet*. The line structure is governed by the anxious foregrounding and splitting of verb phrases, with 'breeding', 'mixing', 'stirring', 'covering' and 'feeding' shifting us uneasily between the literal and the figurative notions of spring and life. Throughout the rest of the poem, we are hastened through four centuries of metrical and figurative precedent and it is against this patchwork of tradition that the purely Modernist gesturing of the poem becomes evident.

In Section III, 'The Fire Sermon', one part begins as an echo of the Imagist ordinance of structure as subservient to impression:

> The river sweats
> Oil and tar
> The barges drift
> With the turning tide
> Red sails (266–70)

But gradually, perhaps addictively, the speaker begins to allow the poetic 'medium' – in this instance a very irregular rhyme scheme – to impose upon the impressionistic fragments:

> Wide
> To leeward, swing on the heavy spar.
> The barges wash
> Drifting logs
> Down Greenwich reach
> Past the Isle of Dogs. (270–5)

The poetic line is the organizing principle of the text, something from which the speaker seems unable or unwilling to detach himself. Two lines of the original manuscript were rewritten by Pound, and echo the juxtaposed pattern of 'In a Station of the Metro':

> Unreal City,
> Under the brown fog of a winter dawn (60–1)

They re-emerge in the rest of the poem almost as a refrain,

> Unreal City
> Under the brown fog of a winter noon (207–8)
> …
> Falling towers
> Jerusalem Athens Alexandria
> Vienna London
> Unreal   (373–6)

The poetic line becomes the speaker's guide through a wilderness of images, ideas and memories and also the means by which he can shift in and out of focus, at once the subject of the text's chaotic fabric and at the same time its anxious erudite choreographer.

The Waste Land can be regarded as the first self-conscious exploration, although certainly not the first instance, of that elusive and friable concept, the 'postmodern'. Limitations of space do not permit a full discussion of the postmodern: it seems to mean different things to architecture theorists, literary critics, political commentators and practically anyone with anything to say about the 20th century. But mercifully, the enclosed field of poetry allows us a more confident grasp of how it informs and defines the aesthetic object. I'll begin with a general thesis: the postmodern poem involves the acknowledgement and deployment of devices drawn from the recognized archetypes of Modernist and pre-Modernist form.

If we are to test this against alternative perceptions of 20th-century literature, we must start with an implicit paradox. In short, the Modernist and the postmodern poem are the same thing. The most obvious and explicit break with traditional form involves a total rejection of the conventional elements of the double pattern, but the single feature that had once been the organizing principal of these elements, the line, is maintained. No other aesthetic genre, linguistic, visual or musical, involves the same degree of formal continuity. True, Modernist fiction will usually make some concession to the organizing principle of the sentence, and abstract, surrealist or post-impressionist paintings often share with their traditional predecessors a hierarchical disposition of units, colours or shapes, but none can claim to have preserved a formal unit that is so persistently conspicuous and so influential upon the broader stylistic manner of the piece. A poem written by one of the leading figures of the first generation to follow the arrival of Modernism is as revealing an insight into early 20th-century literary history as any essay. It is W.H. Auden's 'In Memory of W.B. Yeats'.

Yeats was one of the few major poets whose work bore the imprint both of late 19th-century traditionalism and Modernism, although it must be said that his own affiliation to the latter was prejudiced by his use of it as a vehicle for his private visionary preoccupations. Auden pays due respect to the reputation of his eminent co-practitioner but in truth the poem is a thesis on the history of poetry over the previous half-century. It is a distilled chronicle of late 19th-, early 20th-century poetry played backwards, and it begins in Section I with an exercise in free verse of the type that is conspicuously uneasy with its own unfettered state. There are concessions to such abstractions as regular iambic movement but the most self-evident emphatic units of syntax, the verbs, nouns and adjectives that command each sentence, obtain something close to repetitive spacing,

> He disappeared in the dead of winter
> The brooks were frozen, the airports almost deserted

imparting to each line a shadow of formal cohesion and intimating at some symbiotic, rather than purely random, relationship between the line and the sentence. Similarly, conceits take shape gradually, as if we are being asked to witness them forming in the mind of the speaker. In the second stanza, for example, the images of 'wolves', 'forests', 'a river', 'fashionable quays' could, for those who knew anything of Yeats's life and work, be taken as referring to the dichotomy between the urbane Anglo-Irish sophistication of his background and the primitive landscapes and cultures that he later fetishized. Then suddenly, in the closing line, this disparate account of his state of mind is gathered into compact and superbly resonant conceit:

> The death of the poet was kept from his poems.

The works that will preserve his legacy are at once unaffected and completed by his demise. Throughout Section I, there is a tangible sense of the conspicuous poetic aspects of verse stirring uncomfortably beneath a superficially unstructured format and, in Section II, the balance shifts towards the former. The rhythmic undertow of each line, although still irregular, is more confidently persistent, and the language, becoming self-evidently figurative, indicates conspicuous invention. Also, the poem's double agenda is evident. 'Poetry', mentioned once only in Section I, the part of the poem that is, stylistically, the least poetic, now shifts into the foreground, and becomes as much the focus of the piece as its ostensible subject:

> For poetry makes nothing happen: it survives
> In the valley of its own making ...

Poetry, by its very nature, must be a law unto itself, and in order to perform its uniquely unspecified role must detach itself from the world in which language is the instrument of action and record. Section III almost contradicts this mantra – almost. Anyone reading this shortly after it was written, effectively the beginning of the Second World War, would not need to have explained to them the exact nature of 'the dogs of Europe', the 'nations' sequestered in their 'hate'. The poem ends in a manner that the avant-gardists of a generation earlier would have treated as obdurately archaic, a trochaic ballad form incorporating a declamatory metaphor:

> With the farming of a verse
> Make a vineyard of the curse,
> Sing of human unsuccess
> In a rapture of distress;
>
> In the deserts of the heart
> Let the healing fountain start,
> In the prison of his days
> Teach the free man how to praise.

While deferring to the achievement of Yeats, Auden's real subject is poetry, specifically, its purpose at a time when most of the civilized world seemed on the brink of an all-consuming apocalyptic moment in its history. His conclusion, if so simplistic a formula can be applied to the poem, is that while poetry can do and change nothing, it can, by preserving its unique characteristics, remain at least the repository for the conscience of the individual, something which 'survives/In the valley of its own making', the implied coda being that the only means by which it can ensure its survival is to preserve its uniqueness, to maintain the double pattern.

Auden produced his best-known early poems during the 1930s. The Imagist revolution had occurred two decades earlier, and figures such as Eliot, Pound and Williams had in various ways been transformed from iconoclasts to icons. In British poetry, this period has come to be known as that of the Auden generation, whose most celebrated members were Auden's contemporaries at Oxford – Louis MacNeice, Stephen Spender and C. Day Lewis (see Tolley, 1975). To generalize further would be to obscure the rich complexities of this 'next stage' of Modernism, but two issues should hold our attention. First, the poets who began writing in the late 1920s and 1930s were the inheritors of a literary tradition that includes Modernism, and, as a consequence, they felt able to draw upon both the stylistic innovation of their immediate predecessors and pre-Modernist conventions. Second, they initiated a change in the status and objectives of post-1900s poetry. Early Modernist writing, particularly poetry, centred upon the individual consciousness as a means of perceiving, recording and communicating experience while remaining largely immune from the imperatives of order, judgement, classification or rational objectivity. The poetry of the 1930s began to forge more tangible links between the individuality of the speaking subject and the broader social, political and existential conditions that the speaker shared with the reader – consider how Auden's 'In Memory of W.B. Yeats' combines the destiny of speaker and hearer as inhabitants of a continent on the brink of war. These two factors, stylistic eclecticism and a desire to re-establish poetry as a channel between private experience and public discourse, have dominated British poetry since the late 1930s up to the present day. The two poets who represent the most divergent engagements with those issues in the mid- to late 20th century are Dylan Thomas and Philip Larkin.

Thomas's 'After the Funeral' and 'A Refusal to Mourn the Death, by Fire, of a Child in London' begin with suggestive prepositions, 'After' and 'Never', and as we wait for these to connect with a pronoun or a subject, we are bombarded with a cascade of surreal images and conceits – 'Windshake of sailshaped ears', 'the salt ponds in the sleeves', 'flower/Fathering and all humbling darkness' and so on. Verbs and verb phrases appear, but few indulge coherence or contribute to a broader sense of continuity. We are left to wonder who or what 'Fathers the humbling darkness', 'Tells with silence', 'Tap[s] happily of one peg' or 'Shakes a desolate boy'. Eventually 'After' appears with 'I stand', 'never' and 'Shall I let pray' but if we assume that this confers a general state of intelligibility on what has happened in the interim, we are deceiving ourselves. The potential for self-deceit is provided by the pattern of assonance, alliteration and rhyme, and irregular metre, supplemented in the case of 'A Refusal to Mourn' by a regular stanzaic formula. Thomas has swamped the poem's referential function with a discontinuous montage of images. In a prose passage, such a technique might be written off as meaningless and self-indulgent but Thomas frames his shambolic chiaroscuro within the pattern of sounds and rhythms that we associated with regular, intelligible verse. Read 'Fern Hill', 'Do Not Go Gentle Into That Good Night' and 'When, Like a Running Grave' and consider how Thomas's 'baring the device' of versification operates as a replacement for the ordinary function of syntactic and semantic coherence.

Thomas was not the only British poet to make extravagant use of Eliot's early precedent – see also the work of W.R. Rodgers – but by the late 1940s he had become the most conspicuous target for a new generation of British anti-Modernists. Novelists, poets and critics such as Kingsley Amis, John Wain, Philip Larkin, D.J. Enright, Donald Davie and Robert Conquest would eventually come to be classified by literary historians as members of The Movement (see Blake Morrison's study, 1980). These writers were a more determined and confident manifestation of the Auden generation. In 1955, Davie published *Articulate Energy: An Inquiry into the Syntax of English Poetry*, and this could stand as a disguised and sophisticated manifesto for The Movement poets: 'in free verse and in Dylan Thomas's complicated metrical stanzas the articulation and spacing of images is done by rhythm instead of syntax' (Davie, 1955, pp. 126–7). What was needed, Davie implied, was poetry that restored plain language and syntactic coherence as the consolidating structures against which poetic devices could be counterpointed. This would not necessarily involve the rejection of Modernist innovation and precedent – free verse and obtuse, idiosyncratic locutions and images were still permissible – but these would not be the guiding principles of writing, would indeed be available as options within a range of technical devices, both radical and conventional.

Philip Larkin is without doubt the most eminent figure in the contra Modernist generation of postwar poets. He is routinely classified as a conservative, both in outlook and manner, but he could lay claim to setting a precedent in the history of English verse by his employment of an idiomatic mood and temper that is more unpoetic than anything previously recorded. His 'Vers de Société' begins:

> My wife and I have asked a crowd of craps
> To come and waste their time and ours; perhaps
> You'd care to join us? In a pig's arse, friend.

Thereafter the poem becomes the occasion for reflections on how such gatherings prompt him to reflect on how life is largely a catalogue of equally pointless routines, variously customized to reinforce the illusion that something might matter. He is pithily contemptuous of another evening with 'a crowd of craps', including the 'bitch/Who's read nothing but *Which*' and the 'ass' with his 'fool research', but the alternative involves something that he cannot quite bring himself to describe. He circles it, using such phrases as 'Funny how hard it is to be alone', and comes closest to disclosure with:

sitting by a lamp more often brings
Not peace, but other things.
Beyond the light stand failure and remorse
Whispering *Dear Warlock-Williams: Why, of course* –

He splits the semantics of the two words 'failure' and 'remorse' so that we are
never certain if they refer to the grim social obligations that irritate him, but
from which he cannot fully disengage, or whether they carry traces of those
'other things' that haunt his solitariness. The casual laconic drift of the language
picks resonances from a variety of informal registers – a letter to a friend, a
private diary entry, a conversational disclosure to someone of similar disposition. Ironically, the calls made so frequently by Wordsworth onwards for a
poetic idiom unshackled by poetic convention appear to have been answered at
last by a writer who despised the avant-garde. Such a claim on Larkin's behalf
would have to be qualified, however, by our recognition that this stylistic informality is set against the structure of traditional form. His achievement is to
make the latter elegantly conspicuous but unobtrusive.

Larkin's technique does not of itself exemplify a predominant trend because
after the 1950s poetry entered, has entered, a unique stage in its post-Renaissance
trajectory. Literary history is now complete, by which I mean that the alterations
so far recorded in the nature and status of poetry have brought us to a point from
which no further progression is possible. From the Renaissance onwards, poets
have experimented with and expanded the accepted lexicon of devices that
constitute the formal character of verse and altered the agenda for the poem's
cultural and epistemological status. With Modernism, these shifts between stasis
and refashioning reached an end point. There have between been revisionist
exercises that are creditably refreshing, such as those by Larkin, and the flame of
radicalism and experiment has been kept alight by figures as diverse as the reso-
lutely impenetrable J.H. Prynne and Charles Bernstein and the more tractable
Edwin Morgan. Charles Tomlinson and Geoffrey Hill are each, by degrees,
inscrutable and public poets, rejoicing in their mastery of technique while
undermining its routine demands. The Black Mountain school of restless experiment pioneered in the US by Charles Olson and Robert Creeley lives on in the
work of such contemporary British writers as Tom Raworth, Catherine Walsh
and Geraldine Monk, while Tony Harrison, Hugo Williams, Kit Wright, Glyn
Maxwell and Simon Armitage are heirs to the tradition of Larkin. Craig Raine
founded his own subgenre, the so-called 'Martian School' of verse, whose best
known co-practitioner is Christopher Reid. Their trademark is the preponderant
self-conscious use of conceits, with the speaker displacing himself from the
poem and working outside it as would an artist with their canvas. Consult
Armitage and Crawford's *Penguin Book of Poetry from Britain and Ireland since 1945*
(1998) and you will encounter a bewildering abundance of techniques alongside
an equally unpredictable range of perspectives, subjects and idioms. All can be
traced to a precedent in the history of poetry but none is revisionist or imitative.

Adjustments are made, familiar and recondite devices from the long distant past are combined with contemporary locutions and states of mind. At the same time, gestures that were once pioneering and ground-breaking are employed as trusted mannerisms; experimental devices are now more like shibboleths than gateways to uncharted territories of invention. There can never be another alteration in the character of poetry because everything possible and achievable is already available. Every potential variation on what the poetic line actually involves, on how tropes function and how the presence of the speaker might be variously consumed or alienated by the body of the poem is licensed and available to the poet. There can, of course, be limitless combinations and permutations upon each of these but none in their own right will ever again involve a break with convention.

I shall close with a definition of Modernist poetry that draws together a number of issues already raised.

Modernism and, more specifically, Modernist poetry represent the terminus of literary history. All subsequent and forthcoming developments – postmodernism included – are extensions, mergers or revivals of established Modernist and pre-Modernist precedents. In making this claim, I do not rule out the possibility that poems to come will possess a sufficient degree of originality, stylistic and thematic brilliance to earn them the title of 'classics' of their period. What I do claim is that formal experimentation has reached, to borrow a phrase from popular culture, the final frontier. In the 18th or 19th centuries, the poems by Eliot, Thomas and Williams discussed above would not have been accepted as poems – or they would have been treated by the more tolerant as engaging eccentricities. They would have violated the accepted conventions of the poetic corpus. The strange and deviant patterns embodied by these texts have now become part of the readjusted lexicon of verse technique. Further adjustments cannot and will not occur. How do I know? Consider the premise established at the beginning of this study – the double pattern. Poetry, whatever else it might be or say, can only be accepted as poetry if it supplements the organizational framework shared by all other linguistic genres with a fabric of effects that are arbitrary and specific to the poem itself, and we have reached the limits to which this relationship can be pressed. The line can now consist of a single letter (see E.E. Cummings); it need not even follow the linear progress of syntax (see Concrete Poetry); it can be organized around patterns of pure sound that defy syntactic or lexical coherence (see the poems of Edith Sitwell, Robert Lax or, in some cases, Dylan Thomas). My point is that, in the early decades of the 20th century, poets could move beyond precedent and consequently disrupt the conditioned expectations of the competent reader, but today a paradigm can be found for any form of innovation and, if the reader is interested, an essay, book or thesis can be provided to inform us of the best way to make sense of this phenomenon.

Pure innovation might be a thing of the past but there is one elusive and compelling question that demands the attention of critics and literary historians. The double pattern at once defines poetry and foregrounds the paradoxical nature of poetic writing. It involves limitless tensions and cooperations between the referential function of language – what it does – and the material identity of its sounds and shapes – what it is. The rules and conventions that govern this relationship have, from Shakespeare to E.E. Cummings, been extended, amended, revised and abandoned, but the relationship endures. Why? The possibility that linguistic and prelinguistic experience are inseparable and mutually dependent dimensions of the human condition has held centre ground in recent poststructuralist-deconstructionist controversies, but the tenacious attraction of the double pattern for writers and readers of poetry provides us with a much more engaging perspective on this question. Language is not simply a means of mediating our condition, it is part of our condition and poetry allows us to experience rather than just ponder this relationship. With this in mind, we turn to the activity that plays an intermediary role in our encounters with verse, criticism.

PART III

CRITICISM AND CONTEXTS

8

New Criticism

The literature of classical Greece and Rome, predominantly poetry and dramatic poetry, has been studied in the older European and US universities since their formation. The study of modern, post-medieval literary writing – again almost exclusively poetry – gained a foothold in higher education in the late 19th century and, as a consequence, literary criticism obtained some credence as a respectable intellectual discipline. Poetry had previously been written about, principally, by those who were themselves poets, but the tentative acceptance of English as a subject worthy of academic study signalled the arrival of the professional critic. The US and British academics, who from the 1920s onwards involved themselves in attempts to establish literature as a respectable university subject, earned themselves the collective title of the 'New Critics'. However, Matthew Arnold, 19th-century poet and education theorist, is acknowledged as the originator of a number of precepts and maxims that sustained English studies in its late Victorian infancy and which survive in today's debates on the national curriculum and English in universities. Arnold argued that the study and appreciation of literature – and by literature he referred exclusively to verse; the novel being, in his view, a vulgar surrender of aesthetics to populist entertainment – would inform and, mysteriously, harmonize the fragmented ideology and social disunity of modern British society. Poetry would supplement, perhaps even replace, the Church as the touchstone for intellectual and social cohesion: it would cultivate or 'hellenize' the new and potentially philistine influence of the middle classes; for the working class, it would promote sympathy and fellow feeling with those who might be better off but who shared with their lower brethren a deep admiration for the universality and classless beauty of verse (see Baldick, 1983).

The rather vague Romantic ideal of poetry as a prophetic balsam had been formalized, but the evangelical passion of Arnold's programme is unequalled in its intellectual vacuity. Apart from affirming his belief in the capacity of verse to procure intellectual, cultural, even moral benefits, he raised the question of how exactly it might do so. He implied, and only implied, that because poetry was absolved of the tedious practicalities of logic and rationality, it might, like religious faith, provide access to an elevated, transcendent state of awareness, but his apparent reluctance or inability to establish a tenable link between what poetry is and what precisely it might achieve would resurface continually in the work of the New Critics.

T.S. Eliot claimed in 'The Metaphysical Poets' (1921, p. 2024) that

a poet is constantly amalgamating disparate experience; the ordinary man's experience is chaotic, irregular, fragmentary [falling love, reading Spinoza, the noise of the typewriter, the smell of cooking]; in the mind of the poet these experiences are always forming new wholes.

Eliot's definition of poetry would be preserved and elaborated by the New Critics. Arnold himself had pre-empted it. The 'grand power' of poetry, he claimed, was not in its 'explanation of the mystery of the universe' (activities devolved to philosophy and religion) but in its ability to 'awaken in us' a sense of being in contact with the 'essential nature' of ordinary, mundane events and objects: 'to have their secret, and to be in harmony with them' (Arnold, 1865b, pp. 157–8).

Eliot and Arnold promoted poetry as a vehicle for harmony and unification; not as a practical solution to disagreements in theology or morality or as offering some insight into the problems of social and political disunity, but rather as a kind of personal, intellectual palliative, a discourse that involved a retreat from the utilitarian paradoxes of the real world to a world created by the poet, the literary text, in which the 'chaotic, irregular, fragmentary' material of experience would be coerced into 'new wholes'. Both writers posit a theological link between form and effect that is ambitious and some might say delusional. Essentially, they are contending that devices such as metaphor, where two levels of meaning or reference not routinely or logically connected are forced into a catalytic relationship, take us beyond the sphere of literary aesthetics to that of enlightenment and revelation. It is possible that both thought it too vulgar or simplistic to undertake an explanation of how this occurs; in any event none was forthcoming.

I.A. Richards was the first British literary critic to ground such speculations in the pragmatics of reading and understanding verse, basing his findings upon his work in the Cambridge English Faculty. He argued in *Principles of Literary Criticism* ([1924]1966) that although poetry is able to engage with the same issues and particulars as are available to non-poetic language – that is, anything and everything – it does so by promoting their purely *emotive* effects: 'the question of belief or disbelief, in the intellectual sense, never arises' (p. 277). Instead of engaging with the poet's philosophical credence or religious integrity, the reader or critic should pay attention to the experience that is unique and particular to the reading of the poem. The critic should not paraphrase the poem or be overly concerned with its social or historical contexts but should concentrate instead on what Richards called the 'relevant mental condition' ([1924]1966, p. 1) shared by poet and reader. In *Principles of Literary Criticism* and later in *Practical Criticism* ([1929[1964), he gives detailed accounts of how this 'condition', apparently unique to poets and their readers, is made available; that is, through a taxonomy of stylistic devices, predominantly conceits and metrical patterns, which separates the language of poetry from all others acts of communication. Although Richards stops short of Arnold's and Eliot's vision of poetry as a means of opening doors to perception and intuition, he shares with them a model of it as uniquely capable of absorbing and telescoping the diversities of the real world into a special zone that is at once a version of and elevated from the actualities of life outside the poem.

The common feature of these theories is the idea that poetry is both relevant to the modern condition, in its ability to absorb and compress the diversities of life into particular poems, and perversely elevated from the puzzling and sordid actualities of that condition. This double assertion permeates New Critical thinking and manifests itself in a number of ways.

American New Criticism gained much of its cohesion and unity from a group of academics working in Vanderbilt University, Tennessee during the 1920s: principally, John Crowe Ransom, Allen Tate and Robert Penn Warren. Ransom's essay 'Criticism Inc' ([1937]1972) economically summarizes the concerns and objectives of the group. Ransom lists those elements that contribute to but which should not dominate the critical enterprise; and the subtext of his list of exclusions is his desire to isolate literary studies from the encroachment of other academic disciplines – particularly history, philosophy, linguistics and the newly emergent social sciences:

- 'Personal registrations' (tears, humour, desire, excitement) can be procured by the chemist or the Broadway producer.
- 'Synopsis and paraphrase' are the stuff of 'high school classes and women's clubs'.
- 'Historical studies' tell us about the poet and his circumstances but are of no necessary relevance to the particular effect of the poem.
- 'Linguistic studies' might assist with a 'perfectly logical' understanding of 'content', but not with a proper understanding of the poem.
- 'Moral studies': 'moral content is not the *whole* content' (p. 236).

Ransom claims that although the critic may inform himself of these materials 'as possessed by the artist', his real business is to 'discuss the literary assimilation of them' (p. 236). The poem is a 'desperate ontological and metaphysical manoeuvre' in which the normal registers of language, fact, logic and emotion are transformed by its 'living integrity' (p. 238).

Given that we accept that poetry is capable of uniquely refracting and transmuting the commonly perceived world, the problem remains of what the critic should do with all of the (in Ransom's view) extraneous information that will affect their reading; very few people read poems by Donne, for example, without some prior knowledge of the religious, marital and professional aspects of his life. In 'The Intentional Fallacy' (1946) and 'The Affective Fallacy' (1949; both reprinted in Wimsatt's *The Verbal Icon*, 1954), Wimsatt and Beardsley set about tackling this problem. They asked: If we can clarify the 'intention' or the 'affective' (that is, emotional) register of a non-poetic statement by inquiring into its context or motivation, why not do so with literary statements? Their answer, although more detailed and better illustrated, was the same as Ransom's: literature involves the material of non-poetic discourse, but cuts itself off from the cause-and-effect relations which govern that discourse.

The New Critical programme of focusing upon how poetry distorts and alters ordinary perceptions of the world is consistent with their earliest objectives of establishing literary studies in the university: as I have stated, we can reinterpret Ransom's catalogue of exclusions in terms of the potential threat to the integrity of literary criticism posed by other academic disciplines.

The best-known and most widely discussed examples of New Criticism in action are William Empson's *Seven Types of Ambiguity* (1930) and Cleanth Brooks' *The Well-Wrought Urn* (1947). In his first chapter, Empson discusses the ways in which the sound patterns of poetry create a fabric of meaning that can both supplement and deviate from the conventional structures of grammar, syntax and semantics. At one point, he considers an extract from Browning:

> I want to know a butcher paints,
> A baker rhymes for his pursuit,
> Candlestick-maker much acquaints
> His soul with song, or haply mute,
> Blows out his brains upon the flute.

Empson observes that the stanza is ambiguous, in that it connotes at least three levels of meaning. He notes their operations in the first line:

> I want to know what the whole class of butchers paints,
> I want to know what some one butcher paints,
> I want to know personally a butcher who paints.

Empson comments (1972, p. 56):

> The demands of metre allow the poet to say something which is not normal colloquial English, so that the reader thinks of the colloquial forms which are near to it, and puts them together; weighing their probabilities in proportion to their nearness. It is for such reasons as this that poetry can be more compact, while seeming to be less precise than prose.

His argument is founded upon two principles:

1 Metre and rhyme provide a system of organization that centralizes what, in prose, would be unfocused.
2 Unlike in prose, where we attempt to resolve the ambiguity into a specific referential meaning, we should regard poetic ambiguity as a fluctuating dynamic element.

In *The Well Wrought Urn* (1947), Cleanth Brooks employs a similar method in relation to poetic paradox. Below are the closing two lines of Wordsworth's sonnet 'Composed Upon Westminster Bridge', followed by Brooks' discussion of them:

> Dear God! The very houses seem asleep;
> And all that mighty heart is lying still!

> To say they are 'asleep' is to say they are alive, that they
> Participate in the life of nature ... It is only when the poet sees the city under the semblance of death [heart is lying still] that he can see it as actually alive. (cited in Lodge, 1972, p. 294)

Brooks regards the entire poem as underpinned by a fundamental set of paradoxes (principally, awake/asleep, life/death). In ordinary language, we attempt to distinguish between them; in poetry, they are stylistically telescoped into delicate nuances of contrast and combination.

To sum up the points that have arisen so far, we can say that the New Critical enterprise involves two dimensions of literary interpretation:

1 Attention to the constituent features and operations of the literary text – those which characterize it as different from non-literary texts.
2 The capacity of literature, particularly poetry, to give us rich and 'concrete' apprehensions of experience, while remaining immune from the determinate conditions of politics, society, philosophical and religious discourse.

There are self-evident parallels between many of the New Critical postulations on the character of poetry and the double pattern. The principal difference is in their reluctance or failure to move from tangential or particular observations to a general thesis. For example, Ransom, Wimsatt and Beardsley are all concerned with establishing lines of demarcation between the fabric of meaning generated by the poem and the world beyond it and, as a consequence, they fail to acknowledge that poetry secures its unique status by blurring such lines. Similarly, Empson and Brooks succeed in identifying features that are persistently present in poetry – specifically ambiguity and paradox – but which in non-poetic discourse are generally ascribed to such aberrant tendencies as deception or equivocation. What they do not go on to do, however, is consider how the reader might reconcile their engagements with these uniquely poetic effects to their broader assumptions on what poetry is supposed to be and to do. These questions, left largely unaddressed by the New Critics, are brought into clearer focus by the double pattern, in that we are obliged to consider the persistent interaction between the intrinsically poetic features of the text and its broader frame of reference.

A classic instance of this New Critical dilemma is the long-running debate prompted by Keats's 'Ode on a Grecian Urn'. For much of the poem, Keats creates a fabric of cultural, symbolic and metaphoric nuances, puzzling in themselves but grounded upon the relatively incontrovertible fact that these excursions are prompted by his, the speaker's, encounters with representations, on the exterior of the ancient vase, of purity, nature, love and eternity. As a consequence, critics could strike a balance between the figurative and formal extravagances of the text itself – the meat and drink of New Critical definitions of poetry – and a stabilizing context: this is a speaker, indeed a poet, using Greek mythology as a springboard for personal, subjective or often intuitive comments on the nature of existence. A problem arose, however, with the poem's much-quoted concluding apothegm:

> 'Beauty is truth, truth beauty,' – that is all
> Ye know on earth, and all ye need to know.

Dozens of early to late 20th-century critics – all by degrees adherents to the nostrums of New Criticism – toiled over, disagreed upon and were often infuriated by these lines. (See Stillinger, 1971, pp. 167–73 who documents the work of more than twelve critics.) The questions that arose most frequently were: Why were the five words in inverted commas? Did this indicate that 'the urn' was speaking to him? Or was he reframing, for whatever reasons, his own reflections for 'Ye' the reader? And what did that five-word gnomic mantra actually mean? T.S. Eliot declared the lines 'a serious blemish on a beautiful poem', going on to confess that 'the statement of Keats ... seems to me meaningless; or perhaps, the fact that it is grammatically meaningless conceals another meaning from me'. Leaving aside the fact that Eliot might easily be commenting on a passage from his own verse, what irked and unsettled critics was the fact that Keats had disrupted the equitable balance between what went on inside the poem – metaphoric excursion, mythological and symbolic frame of reference and so on – and our ability to make sense of what the poet was actually attempting to achieve. As we shall see, the procedure by which we interpret poetic extravagances such as paradox and ambiguity and draw these back into the realm of the rational and the logical has become known as 'naturalization'. The New Critics practised this, with varying degrees of success, but never properly acknowledged or admitted to doing so. Their reluctance can be explained by the disputes and controversies that surrounded Keats's two lines. If Keats had written the entire poem in the obscure, opaque manner exemplified by the concluding lines, then critics would have adopted a less interrogatory problem-solving stance, treated it more as an anticipation of Pound's *The Cantos*. What unsettled them was his shift in tempo from one level of textual complexity to another. Both were manifestly poetic but since they occurred in the same poem, the already uncertain notion of what exactly an interpretation of the strange mannerisms of poetry might involve was further skewed.

An immensely informative and probably tongue-in-cheek account of the problems engendered by 'Ode on a Grecian Urn' can be found in 'Who Says

What to Whom at the End of "Ode on a Grecian Urn"?' (Appendix III, Stillinger, 1971). Stillinger, brilliantly, documents the bizarre spectrum of the debate, from disputes on who exactly prepared the final manuscript for publication – punctuation might well have altered the entire register of the lines – to speculations by close readers on who exactly is speaking. Stillinger's point – implied rather than specified – is that despite the fact that the New Critics celebrated the peculiarities of poetry, they had still not reconciled this with an incongruous instinct to clarify and make sense of poems: in short, to rob the artefact of its defining feature.

F.R. Leavis, based along with I.A. Richards at Cambridge, has had a formative influence upon English studies in British universities. Like his contemporaries in the US, Leavis believed that literary criticism rests upon the engagement of intuitive and irreducible values (variously described by him as 'felt life', 'maturity', 'humanity', 'sensitivity' and 'profound seriousness'), which are at once addressed and concretized in our encounters with literature and which also underpin our sense of social responsibility and commitment. He describes the activity of criticism as follows: 'The critic's aim is, first, to realize as sensitively and completely as possible this or that which claims his attention; and a certain valuing is implicit in the realizing' (Leavis, cited in Lodge, 1972, p. 623). The 'this or that' can be anything, from the dominant theme of the text (the fall of Man in *Paradise Lost*, for example) to the distribution of particular images or ideas in a poem (the city and nature, life and death in Wordsworth's 'Ode on Westminster Bridge'):

> As he matures in experience of the new thing he asks, explicitly and implicitly: 'Where does this come? How does it stand in relation to ... ? How relatively important does it seem?' and the organisation into which it settles as a constituent in becoming 'placed' is an organisation of similarly 'placed' things, things that have found their bearings with regard to one another, and not a theoretical system or a system determined by abstract considerations. (Leavis, cited in Lodge, 1972, p. 623)

The questions that Leavis cites for the putative critic are those which would be raised in practically all our encounters with statements on God, life, love, society, politics, philosophy – the 'this and that which claims [our] attention'. In poetry, however, our response must be qualified by the realization that the organization (that is, the textual structure) into which those issues 'settle' and are 'placed' obliges us to give attention as much to other elements of the same text ('things that have found their bearing with regard to one another') as we do to 'systems' outside the text.

You will recognize similarities between this argument, Ransom's exclusion of literary criticism from contextual matters and Eliot's notion of the 'new wholes' that constitute the fabric of poems. You might also recognize dissimilarities between it and your own experience of literature. If you are a woman, you might find it difficult to completely dissociate Donne's treatment of women characters from the 'systems' of gender role and displacement that have endured outside and beyond literary texts since the 17th century. The 'placing' of an issue in a literary text does not necessarily strip it of the polemical, oppressive or unjust associations that it carries in the real world.

The quotation from Leavis is part of his response (later published in *The Common Pursuit*, 1952) to a letter written to the journal *Scrutiny* by René Wellek. Wellek, while admiring Leavis's book *Revaluation* (1936), observed that Leavis had failed to state explicitly and defend systematically his implicit assumptions regarding the nature and value of poetry. Wellek (1937) asked Leavis to become 'conscious that large ethical, philosophical and ... ultimately aesthetic *choices* are involved' in poetry criticism. What Wellek was seeking was an abstract, theoretical model which would specify the form and function of poetry as distinct from other discourses, and which would enable us properly to distinguish between 'ethical and philosophical' choices of the real world and those that are transformed by the 'aesthetic' of literature.

This objective had, to an extent, been pursued by critics such as Richards, Empson and Brooks but it was more firmly rooted in the European tradition in which Wellek (born in Vienna, 1903) had developed as a critic. And it is to this tradition that we now turn.

9

Formalism and Structuralism

Formalism originated in Russia with the founding of the Moscow Linguistic Circle in 1915 and its St Petersburg counterpart Opayaz in 1916. Its most influential founding members were Viktor Shklovsky, Vladimir Propp and Roman Jakobson.

Formalism involves the reversal of the traditional relation between form and content. In classical and in post-16th-century European thought, definitions of literature were drawn principally from the discipline of rhetoric. Rhetoric involves the classification of linguistic devices (metaphor, antithesis, metre, sound pattern, pun, repetition and so on) that variously amplify and distort ideas and concepts. It is underpinned by the belief that prelinguistic ideas and concepts (content) exist as immutable entities, and that language enables us to decorate, document, clarify or promote them (form). Literary language, principally poetry, is more prone to the use of formal devices than its practical, utilitarian counterpart. In short, literature is licensed to foreground form at the expense of content.

The Formalists challenged this assumption by arguing that language, be it literary or non-literary, is a formative rather than a reflective or transparent system of representation. All classical and post-classical modes of Western thought are founded upon the assumption that reality (involving tangible objects and events, empirical and speculative reasoning, and programmes of belief) exists before and outside its representation in words. Formalism proposes that the structure of reality is effectively determined and shaped by language: form predetermines content. (Ferdinand de Saussure's contribution to this idea will be discussed in Chapter 10.)

The concept that underpins all Formalist work on literature is *ostranenie*, variously translated as making strange or defamiliarization. Donne's subtle metaphor, 'a bracelet of bright hair about the bone' makes strange familiar connotations of life (the wearing of a bracelet, having bright hair) and death (the fleshless bone) by compressing them into a single image. The Formalists did not regard *ostranenie* as a perverse distortion of reality: since reality is a construct of language, *ostranenie* foregrounds and exposes this interdependency.

Some critics whose work originated in Formalism have sought to find empirical proof for a difference between poetry and non-poetic language and the most influential of these was Roman Jakobson (1896–1982). Jakobson began his work on linguistics and poetry during the Formalist heyday of the 1900s to 1920s, but the Anglo-American branch of literary studies only became fully aware of his ideas with his 1960 paper called 'Closing Statement: Linguistics and Poetics'. Jakobson's most quoted and widely debated statement is his definition of the so-called 'projection principle': 'The poetic function projects the principle of equivalence from the axis of selection into the axis of combination' (1960, p. 39). These two axes can be represented as follows.

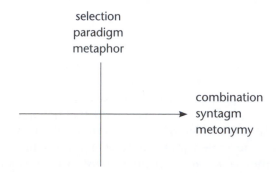

selection
paradigm
metaphor

combination
syntagm
metonymy

The axis of combination involves the system of rules and conventions (grammar and syntax) through which individual words are combined into larger units of meaning: the dominant, all-purpose unit of combination being the sentence, or in Jakobson's terms, the 'syntagmatic chain'. The axis of selection involves the choices made at each stage in the syntagm from the different words available for each grammatical class or type – in Jakobson's terms, 'paradigmatic selection'. For example, in order to describe the progress of a woman along the street, we might use different verbs to describe the same activity: the woman walks; the woman strolls; the woman moves; the woman strides. We can choose different verbs from the selective axis while maintaining the same syntagmatic-combinative formula (article-noun-verb).

The principle of equivalence involves the matching of the two axes; first, in terms of the rules of the syntagmatic chain ('Its woman is walk' is grammatically incorrect), and second, in terms of the agreed 'equivalent' relation between the rules of the syntagm and the perceived relation between language and the prelinguistic world. If I stated that 'A tree walks', I would have satisfied the rules of the syntagm ('walks', like 'grows' or 'lives' is a verb used in its correct gram-matical position), but I would have disrupted the perceived or equivalent rela-tion between language and the prelinguistic world: trees as far as we know cannot and do not walk. This unusual and unexpected use of the selective axis is the basic principle of metaphor.

Jakobson claims that 'for poetry, metaphor – and for prose metonymy – is the line of least resistance and consequently the study of poetical tropes is directed chiefly toward metaphor' (Jakobson and Halle, 1956, pp. 95–6). This does not mean that all prosaic language is metonymic; rather that metonymy is more indicative of the logic of prose while metaphor embodies the fundamental illogic of poetry. Metonymy involves a comparison between two conditions or elements that have a pre-established connection in the empirical world. We frequently refer to elements of monarchical government in terms of 'the crown' (crown forces, crown lands and so on); and we might refer to a person's car as 'their wheels'. Metonymy involves the substitution of one element of an object or condition for its entirety, and, as Jakobson argues, it embodies the governing principle of prosaic, non-poetic language; that language should reflect and articulate the perceived condition of the prelinguistic world. Metaphor, conversely, uses the selective axis to variously disrupt and refocus the perceived relation between language and reality.

The continuous and persistent use of metaphor in a text does not automatically define it as a poem:

> The principle of similarity underlies poetry; the metrical parallelism of lines or the phonic equivalence of rhyming words prompts the question of semantic similarity or contrast; there exist, for instance, grammatical and antigrammatical but never agrammatical rhymes. (Jakobson, 1987a, p. 114)

Along with their projection of the axis of selection into the axis of combination (metaphor), poems also create a continuous level of interference between poetic form (metre, rhyme, assonance and alliteration) and the practical, non-poetic registers of syntax and semantics. Consider the way in which the internal and external rhymes of Donne's 'The Flea' tend to fix our attention upon the tenor (the flea and fleabite) of the metaphor: 'this flea', 'in this', 'me is', 'Me', 'thee', 'be', 'this flea', 'and this', 'temple is', 'kill me', 'added be', 'killing three', 'guilty be', 'from thee', 'fears be', 'to me', 'from thee'. The principal themes of the speaker's argument are drawn into a network of semantic and phonetic associations – mainly 'this flea', 'is', 'thee', 'be', 'me' – that creates an almost subliminal counterpart to the metaphor. As Jakobson states, the logical meaning of the words of a poem are tied into a system of phonemic and rhythmic similarities and parallels: in this case, the persuasive echoes of the rhyme scheme insinuate themselves into the rhetoric of the extended metaphor.

Jakobson (1960, p. 50) describes the combined effect of metaphor and sound pattern upon the poetic function:

> Not only the message itself but also its addresser and addressee become ambiguous ... The supremacy of the poetic function over the referential function does not obliterate the message but makes it ambiguous. The double sensed message finds correspondence in a split addresser, in a split addressee as well as in a split reference.

Jakobson uses the term 'ambiguous' differently from its application by William Empson (see Chapter 8). He does not refer only to instances of uncertain or paradoxical meaning, but rather to a more general 'split' between what happens in the poem (who is speaking to whom and with what intention or effect) and our expectation of how such transferences of meaning would be achieved in non-poetic language.

In Donne's 'The Flea', this split becomes apparent when we attempt to submit the poem to the circumstantial terms and conditions of non-poetic language. We know that it is a first-person, present tense discourse that draws upon immediate events and circumstances (the proximity of the addresser and addressee and their shared experience of the fleabite), and which shows the ability of the speaker to adjust and improvise his argument according to ongoing events: he clearly responds to the woman's attempt and eventual success in crushing the flea. The split becomes evident when we recognize that the real-world conditions of spontaneity and improvisation are at odds with the baroque complexity of the text. No one could improvise a stanzaic structure consisting of three couplets, each involving an octosyllabic followed by a pentameter line, which terminates with a triplet of one octosyllabic and two pentameter lines. Jakobson's point is that, on the one hand, we need to decode a poem in terms of its paraphrasable meaning (its 'referential' function – in this case, a man responding verbally to a woman's silent rejections), while, on the other, we should recognize that its 'poetic' function is particular to the structure of the text in question and untranslatable into the terms and conditions of non-poetic discourse (in this case, the addresser and the addressee are effectively constructs of an unimprovised, self-consciously contrived system of metrical and rhyming patterns).

At a more complex level, 'the split' presents a problem for the analysis of such poems as Romantic odes. The subject of the latter, their referential function, is very often an issue more readily associated with philosophy or theology and, as a consequence, critics tend to read them as they would tracts by Wordsworth or Keats on fundamental existential questions. The dilemma, which Jakobson's thesis points up, is how to reconcile an interpretative agenda governed by the inclination to tease out what exactly the poet postulates on matters such as eternity, death, beauty or the mystical purity of nature with the recognition that the poem, the speaker, the addressee and indeed the message are each the product of an aesthetic artefact.

Jakobson's work incorporates the multidisciplinary strands of modern literary studies. He held that in order to understand the distinction between poetic and non-poetic discourses, we must first conduct an exhaustive survey of the operations and the material constituents of language. His (and Jones') analysis of Shakespeare's Sonnet 129 (1970, reprinted in Pomorska and Rudy, 1987) reflects his consistent assertion that poems concentrate and crystallize the more diffuse, practical operations of non-poetic language: metaphor becomes the subject rather than the instrument of communication; metre, rhyme and sound pattern promote the phoneme and the syllable from the status of pragmatic bridges between sound and meaning to the procedure by which the sound of a poem organizes its meaning. On the one hand, his working principle that literary studies needs the assistance of linguistics in order properly to understand literature goes against many of the New Critical doctrines of isolation. On the other, many of the more recent structuralist and poststructuralist critics have condemned Jakobson's work for advocating what they regard as the institutional elitism of literature as 'different' from ordinary discourse (see Culler, 1975; Chapter 10).

Jakobson's model of the 'split' underpins my own theory of the double pattern. In due course, I shall show how the double pattern clarifies a number of problems that Jakobson left unresolved, the first of which involves the process of naturalization. Naturalization is a term used by post-1960s literary theorists and critics to describe the process of interpreting verse and it is borrowed from its more familiar usage of when an individual transfers their allegiance from one national, cultural and social context to another; it is effectively the reversal of the Formalist notion of defamiliarization or *ostranenie*. The latter presents the poem as a text that has deliberately alienated itself from the standard non-literary conventions of exchange. Naturalization is what happens when the poem is refamiliarized with the world in which ordinary language obtains, the working principle of all conventional criticism. Even in its most subtle and nuanced forms, the exercise of criticizing poetry incorporates explanation and paraphrase; we make sense of what is palpably unusual and drag the poem back into the rational, logical frame of the real world. Although this begs comparison with the practice of translation from one language to another, it is a far more complex transaction. For example, Samuel Levin (1962, 1971), a devotee of Jakobson, evolved a theory of naturalization that he called 'coupling'. Following Jakobson's general thesis on 'the split', Levin identified those features of poetry that are 'cognitive' – predominantly, the standard grammatical, semantic and referential dimensions of the poem that differ little from their use in non-poetic language – and those that are 'conventional', or specific to poetry as a genre, such as the various permutations upon rhythm and sound pattern that make up the poetic line. According to Levin, coupling occurs at those points where the cognitive and the conventional elements clash. The most obvious example of this would be a pair or sequence of rhyme words. In ordinary language, we avoid rhyme where possible because the repetition of sound draws the listener's attention away from the logic of syntax and semantics; we might find ourselves giving disproportionate attention to two words whose relationship in the sentence is arbitrary or counter-logical. Rhyme, being a persistent feature of most conventional poems, must, one assumes, be intended to create just such bifurcation of focus or, in Levin's term 'coupling', but having identified this uniquely poetic process, Levin does not fully explain how we deal with it when we naturalize a poem. For example, the opening couplet of Pope's 'Epistle to Dr. Arbuthnot'

> Shut, shut the door good John fatigued I said
> Tye up the knocker, say I'm sick, I'm dead

could be treated as a classic instance of coupling. The sardonic insouciance of telling an intermediary to inform others that you no longer exist is framed first by the metrical symmetry of the two lines, which points up the contrast between what he is and what he says he is, and cemented in the counterpoint between two words that sound almost identical while drawing upon antithetical frames of reference, specifically, the ability to speak and oblivion.

Yet there are problems with this model of naturalization that Levin, perhaps understandably, does not acknowledge. First, I should concede that my rather brief naturalization of Pope's couplet has involved approximately 30 minutes of scrutinizing the text on the page and recording my findings. I have offered a laborious account of how the cognitive and conventional features of the poem interact but can this be treated as an accurate reflection of what happens when we read it? Some poets and critics have maintained that verse is, or should be, a predominantly spoken medium, best appreciated when listened to and 'performed' by someone alert to its stylistic and rhythmic nuances. Perhaps, but the ideal of the spoken poem is entirely at odds with the practice of the vast majority of 20th- and 21st-century critics, irrespective of their theoretical allegiance, whose work, one would assume, is to disclose the essential qualities and meaning of the poems to which they have turned their attention. Naturalizing Pope's complete poem in the manner demonstrated above is comparable to scrutinizing an ordnance survey map of a region, while the spoken/aural model of appreciation is the equivalent of travelling through it. The former enables one to assess and compare vast numbers of facts and details from a commanding, almost omniscient perspective, while the latter minimalizes the focus to what can be apprehended and recalled in a very short space of time.

Michael Riffaterre (1966) was the first critic to draw attention to the potential discrepancy between our ability to document the minutiae of stylistic interaction and the ability of the average reader to appreciate that all these things are happening at the same time. Riffaterre coined the term 'Superpoem' to account for the immensely complex phenomena disclosed by the work of Jakobson, Levin and other linguist critics, and he invented the notion of a 'Superreader' to account for a putative and very unreal presence who is capable of accommodating these effects simultaneously, along with an ex cathedra knowledge of who the poet is, and how this particular poem relates to work by the same poet and by other writers.

Riffaterre proposed that the Superpoem and the Superreader are illusions, a means by which traditional theorists, Jakobson included, sustained their presuppositions on the nature of poetry and the sensibility of the poet and the reader. There is some truth in this, in that to give full attention to every minute feature of a passage of verse, we need to operate like a pathologist, to turn the text into a static, three-dimensional framework and to move across and through it, shifting our investigative focus and drawing conclusions as we see fit; perhaps moving forward from line five to line eight and then back again to a semantic crux in line one, recalled by a sound echo in line eight. This process of dissection cannot be undertaken simply by reading a poem from beginning to end and retaining an impression of its complex interwoven fabric, let alone hearing it read by someone else. The human brain simply does not have the capacity to both retain and analyse such a volume and density of material. If computers had reached a state of maturity comparable to those of today when Riffaterre invented the Superreader in 1966, he would probably have transposed his unreal hypothesis with an all-consuming behemoth from the world of IT.

Riffaterre's dismantling of the traditional model of interpretation was at once radical in a manner that would come to be termed 'poststructuralist' yet founded upon a number of conservative presumptions. He was correct in assuming that the Superpoem and the Superreader bore a closer resemblance to vast catalogues or cross-referenced indexes of information than to individuals, however learned and accomplished, involved in almost instantaneous intuitive appreciation of poems. What he did not acknowledge was that since the end of the 18th century and particularly during the 20th century, the processes of reading, interpreting and, most crucially, writing verse had involved a tacit but rarely acknowledged acceptance that while poems can be enjoyed in performance, full knowledge of their complex aesthetic can be obtained only when they are scrutinized over long periods, as static artefacts on the page. This essentially was the working principal of the technique of interpretation routinely associated with the New Critics and the Formalists: 'close reading'. Arguably the most impressive sustained example of close reading in action was Christopher Ricks' *Milton's Grand Style* (1963), in which he links detailed analyses of brief passages of *Paradise Lost* with reflections on the poem's universal themes. These 20th-century critics might have perfected close reading as an academic practice but in truth they inherited it. Even during the 18th century, when the poem in performance was venerated as its true and authentic manifestation, critics were in practice relying upon the written text, the stalled poem, in order to make their detailed observations on how form refracts meaning (see Bradford, 2002). We shall return to this topic of what the reading and interpretation of verse actually involves in Chapter 13, Deconstruction, but for the time being, in Chapter 10, we will examine an aspect of Riffaterre's thesis that has since grown into the doctrine that informs and in many ways contaminates the academic study of poetry.

10

The Role of the Reader
and Poststructuralism

Two years after Riffaterre's article appeared, Roland Barthes published a piece that is now treated as a landmark in the progress of cultural and literary theory, 'The Death of the Author' (1968). The demise of the text's creator was not, he argued, literal since this was to be experienced as much by living writers as their long-deceased predecessors. What would be extinguished, so Barthes contended, was the image of the author as the active and conscious creator of everything that the reader discerns within and extracts from the literary text. In Barthes' view, the Superreader – although he does not use the term – imposes upon the text a vast repertoire of expectations gleaned from their study of aesthetics, interpretive theory and other literary works.

In *Is There a Text in this Class? The Authority of Interpretive Communities* (1980), Stanley Fish took reader-centred theory a stage further by introducing us to the notion of 'literary competence', an adaptation of Noam Chomsky's concept of 'linguistic competence'. We acquire linguistic competence as much by habit and experience as by the intensive study of grammar. We listen to elementary linguistic phrasings and formations used by our parents and peers, and without necessarily being able to reduce these to abstract rules, we implement them in our own habits of communication. Obviously, our accent, routines of phrasing and even the esteem that we impart to particular words will reflect the community and circumstances in which we acquired linguistic competence, disclosing features such as class, ethnic affiliation and region. In Fish's model of literary competence, a similar network of influences operates in what he calls the 'interpretive community' of the education system and its broader cultural contexts. It is here that we acquire a familiarity with the constituent features of literary texts and once we are able to name their parts, we extend this to a knowledge of how these operate. This is as fundamental to our perception of how literature works, argues Fish (1980, p. 171), as is our linguistic competence to our ability to understand and reply to other people:

> Interpretive communities are made up of those who share interpretive strategies not for reading (in the conventional sense) but for writing texts, for constituting their properties and assigning their intentions. In other words,

these strategies exist prior to the act of reading and therefore determine the shape of what is read rather than, as is usually assumed, the other way around.

For example, the interpretive community equips us with a grammar and vocabulary of interpretation to deal with the local stylistic effects of poetry. Let us return to the opening lines of Milton's *Paradise Lost*:

> Of man's first disobedience, and the fruit
> Of that forbidden tree, whose mortal taste
> Brought death into the world ...

The interpretive community teaches us that the break between the first and second lines is called 'enjambment'. Our experience of how critics deal with enjambment will encourage us to expect the production of a double meaning; and indeed the line break at 'fruit' does seem to suggest a momentary hesitation between literal meaning (the actual fruit of the tree) and the eventual disclosure of its figurative usage (the consequence of eating the fruit which 'Brought death into the world'). Fish (1980, pp. 165–6) claims, in relation to a similar effect in Milton's *Lycidas*, that:

> line endings exist by virtue of perceptual strategies rather than the other way around. Historically, the strategy that we know as 'reading (or hearing) poetry' has included paying attention to the line as a unit, but it is precisely that attention that has made the line as a unit ... available.

A New Critic or Formalist would argue that Milton's lines do exist, that the iambic pentameter is a verifiable phenomenon. Fish would reply that while we might recognize the presence of linguistic phenomena, our account of how they produce effects is based not upon empirical evidence but upon acquired habits of interpretation.

In 1970, two texts were published that reflect the differences between traditional – that is, New Critical and Formalist – method and its poststructuralist, reader-centred counterpart. Jakobson and Jones produced what has become an archetype of Formalist analysis in their dissection of Shakespeare's Sonnet 129 (see Pomorska and Rudy, 1987). In this, they document every instance of what Levin calls 'coupling'. They examine how the quatrains and stanzas of the sonnet variously enclose and underpin its binary themes (life/death, heaven/hell, body/spirit) and how its metre and sound patterns create extra-syntactic parallelisms between practically every word of the text. In *S/Z: An Essay* (1975), Barthes employs a similarly exhaustive stylistic programme in his analysis of Balzac's novella *Sarrasine*. He divides the text into 561 lexies, irreducible units of prose structure, comparable with Jakobson's notion of the phoneme and syllable as the basis for metre and sound pattern. Barthes then examines how the lexies are combined in Balzac's text to produce five levels of effect and response, which he categorizes as the hermeneutic, semic, symbolic, proairetic and cultural codes. These codes are comparable with Jakobson's tracing of relationships between the metrical, syntactic, phonemic, morphological and referential features of the sonnet.

These similarities of method are misleading, because Barthes' work is effectively a parody of Jakobson's. Barthes' 561 lexies can comprise anything from a single word to a series of sentences. He virtually invites the reader to question these classifications, perhaps to consider alternatives. Barthes, tongue firmly in cheek, justifies his division into lexies by claiming that each lexie foregrounds a particular engagement with one or more of his five codes. At the same time, his own use of these codes brings their validity into question. Frequently he digresses upon the kind of reader who would be especially interested in the operation of particular codes. Digression number LXXI focuses upon lexie 414, in which Sarrasine embraces a castrato in the mistaken belief that he is a woman. Barthes acknowledges that the code in operation here will depend upon the disposition of the reader: one reader might emphasize the proairetic (narrative) code and be interested in what happens next; another might give most attention to the cultural code, particularly in relation to their own experiences of sexuality and its cultural formations.

Barthes's *S/Z* is a demonstration of his thesis that the stylistic patterns and effects of texts are non-empirical, in a constant state of formation and change according to the circumstances of interpretation and the condition of the reader.

A more straight-faced critique of Jakobsonian, Formalist interpretation is found in Jonathan Culler's *Structuralist Poetics* (1975, pp. 55–75), where Culler applies the formulae of coupling and parallelism that Jakobson had used on Shakespeare's sonnet to an extract from Jakobson's own critical prose. Culler's exercise is convincing and persuasive, and he claims that linguistics

> does not solve the problem of what constitutes a pattern and hence does not provide a method for the discovery of patterns. *A fortiori*, it does not provide a procedure for the discovery of poetic patterns. (1975, p. 65)

The validity of Culler's claim can only properly be discussed after a careful reading of his book and the work of Fish, Jakobson and Barthes, but the relatively uninformed and undecided reader will notice an obvious flaw in his thesis. It is certainly the case that Jakobson's methods of stylistic analysis are founded upon developments in linguistics that have occurred beyond and outside the production of its literary subjects. But surely Culler cannot question the actuality of a text consisting of fourteen iambic lines and divided into three rhymed quatrains and a couplet. The sonnet must 'constitute a pattern' that is far more common in poetry than it is in everyday conversation, or – re Barthes and *Sarrasine* – in discursive prose. It does not require a 'procedure' for its 'discovery'; it exists.

The quarrel between those critics who founded their engagement with poetry upon a belief that it is possessed of intrinsic, definitive features – who for the sake of convenience we shall hereafter refer to as the 'textualists' – and those who insist that our cognate or intellectual knowledge of verse is derived primarily from a system of expectations and strategies that are independent of the text – let us call them the 'contextualists' – reached its climax during the 1970s and 80s. The contextualists were the victors but not because their arguments were proved to be more valid or because they exposed flaws in those of their competitors – quite the opposite, as we shall see – but as a consequence of a much broader, fundamental shift in the power base of literary critical ideas, or at least those practised within universities. It is impossible to offer a summary of what happened that is both accurate and concise, except to state that what has come to be known as 'literary' or 'critical theory' established itself as the intellectual benchmark to which all ambitious academics and precocious students sought to aspire. Let us return to the contextualist ideas on reader-centred interpretation, with a view to ascertaining exactly the kind of reader these theorists have in mind.

In 'How To Recognise a Poem When You See One' (1980), Stanley Fish describes how, when teaching a course on the religious lyric, he asked his class to interpret a modern lyric chalked on the classroom blackboard. This 'text' is actually a list of surnames left over from the previous class on linguistics (to add a sardonic edge, the names are those of major US literary linguists of the 1960s and 70s):

Jacobs – Rosenbaum

Levin

Thorne

Hayes

Ohman (?)

His students demonstrated an apparent literary competence (Fish, 1980, p. 324):

The first line of the poem (the very order of events assumed the already constituted status of the object) received the most attention: Jacobs was explicated as a reference to Jacob's ladder, traditionally allegorised as a figure for the Christian ascent to heaven. In this poem, however, or so my students told me, the means of ascent is not a ladder but a tree, a rose tree or rosenbaum. This was seen as an obvious reference to the Virgin Mary who was often characterised as a rose without thorns, itself an emblem of the immaculate conception.

Fish's description of their analysis continues for a further 500 words. This experiment, which Fish claims to have performed with similar results in '9 or 10 universities in 3 countries', supports his claim that 'acts of recognition, rather than being triggered by formal characteristics, are their source' (Fish, 1980, p. 326).

Fish's thesis is that his students have been programmed to interpret the tensions and paradoxes allegedly inherent in verse but that this procedure is in truth something that they impose upon the text once key signals – specifically line divisions – prompt them to accept that what they encounter is a poem.

His exercise is sardonic, almost convincing, yet it is also deeply fraudulent. He informs them that the text on the blackboard is a poem and its typographic structure might indeed invite comparisons with more radical pieces by Cid Corman, Robert Creeley, or even E.E. Cummings. What he does not do, however, is to ask them to express an opinion on this 'poem'; that is, to offer an account of what the poet is attempting to achieve and an evaluation of their success. Had he done so, it is quite possible – given his students' self-evident familiarity with Modernist technique and its offshoots – that someone might well have contended that the anonymous blackboard poet was clearly inferior to a figure such as William Carlos Williams. What had they achieved by abandoning anything resembling syntax when Williams, in pieces such as 'Spring and All' (see Chapter 2), had shown how to challenge the regularities of syntax and line structure by making use of them radically and not by leaving them out? This might well have prompted another of Fish's precocious charges to wonder how anyone might enjoy, admire, or even be stimulated by a 'poem' that apparently required not even linguistic, let alone creative, competence to write. Warming to this theme, another might suggest that they go through the New York telephone directory, throw it in the air several times and on each occasion select at random a surname from the opened page. It is likely, they could aver, that in six 'lines' one could assemble a richly laden trajectory of social, ethnic, cultural and religious reference points. But if anyone can do this, is the resulting text worthy of being called a 'poem'?

We will never know why Fish did not invite his students to go beyond recognition and cold interpretation to evaluation but there is a good deal of circumstantial evidence to allow for conjecture. Literary theory in this period did not allow for evaluation. Its prevailing doctrine was that poetry is one of many discourses and that its claim to aesthetic pre-eminence is a delusion; therefore how could one literary text be aesthetically superior to another if the independence of poetry as an art form was itself a bourgeois fantasy?

In *Literary Theory: An Introduction* (1983), Terry Eagleton contends that the ideal of separating poetry from other modes of expression, defining it, leads to a dangerously apolitical brand of literary criticism. The textualist notion of poetic style as non-pragmatic, self-referential language causes us to detach the literary text from the real world of political and ideological discourse. A preoccupation with aesthetics prevents us from recognizing that what we might value as good verse is effectively a reflection of the ideological prejudices and preconditions of a particular society or period: 'Literature, in the sense of a set of works of assured and endurable values, distinguished by certain shared inherent properties, does not exist' (Eagleton, 1983, p. 11). Eagleton goes about proving its non-existence by employing the same teleology as Fish: by 'disclosing' intrinsically poetic features of language in texts that are self-evidently non-poetic. In one instance, he fixes upon the Formalist notion of estrangement as elicited by language that is perversely unusual, specifically, the effects of ambiguity or paradox that Empson and Brooks, respectively, identified as the persistent defining features of verse:

> Consider a prosaic, quite unambiguous statement like the one sometimes seen in the London underground system: 'Dogs must be carried on the escalator'. This is not perhaps quite as unambiguous as it seems at first sight: does it mean that you *must* carry a dog on the escalator? Are you likely to be banned from the escalator unless you can find some stray mongrel to clutch in your arms on the way up? Many apparently straightforward notices contain such ambiguities: 'Refuse to be put in this basket', for instance, or the British road-sign 'Way Out' as read by a Californian. But even leaving such troubling ambiguities aside, it is surely obvious that the underground notice could be read as literature. … Imagine a late-night drunk doubled over the escalator handrail who reads the notice with laborious attentiveness for several minutes and then mutters to himself 'How true!' What kind of mistake is occurring here? What the drunk is doing, in fact, is taking the sign as some statement of general, even cosmic significance. By applying certain conventions of reading to its words, he prises them loose from their immediate context and generalizes them beyond their pragmatic purpose to something of wider and probably deeper import. (Eagleton, 1983, p. 11)

His thesis is as flawed, and as calculatedly fraudulent, as Fish's. Certainly one might 'find' effects and devices customarily ranked as poetic almost anywhere, but the fact that they are notable for their rarity, exceptions to the general condition of non-poetic writing, testifies to their status as accidents or curiosities. In poems, they form a consistent element of the stylistic fabric of the text, something deliberately and calculatedly fashioned by the poet and which distinguishes the poem from the sphere of non-poetic discourse. Unwittingly, Eagleton's invention of a drunken close reader undermines both his own and Fish's argument. In both instances, the reader is a faintly absurd hypothesis. Fish's students are erudite, commendably articulate versions of Pavlov's dogs, while Eagleton's drunk is, one assumes, someone no longer able to discriminate between something that was intended as a literary text and a sign on the underground. This raises the question of why neither of these theorists themselves admits to being unable to distinguish 'real' poetry from accidents or randomly assembled groups of words. If, as they contend, poetry is to a large extent a construction of the sociocultural conditions in which it is apprehended, then where does this leave professors of English? They seem intent upon rejecting their predecessors' maxim that poetry is definable and recognizable in terms of its intrinsic features, yet they appear equally reluctant to place themselves in the position of the hypothetical readers of their exercises who are incapable of making a rational distinction between what is and what is not poetry.

During the 1970s and 80s, the exercises undertaken by Culler, Fish and Eagleton became the equivalent of a Masonic handshake; an acknowledgement of shared affiliation to a new programme of perceiving and classifying poetry. Along with his 'reading' of a piece as prose or the equivalent of a Jakobsonian analysis of a sonnet, Culler redrafted a sentence from W.V. Quine's philosophical treatise *From a Logical Point of View* as a free verse poem to show how the iconic foregrounding of words gives the false impression that 'intrinsic irony or paradox', characteristically poetic features, are its presiding template. Hence: 'We are dealing less with a property of language than with a strategy of reading' (Culler, 1975, p. 163). Forrest-Thompson (1978) redrafted a *Times* leader article on the new chairman of the BBC as a Poundian lyric and interpreted it accordingly. Hawkes (1977, pp. 139–40) reversed this procedure, albeit with the same objective, and argued that William Carlos Williams' 'This Is Just To Say' has only been interpreted as a poem because critics are prompted to impose such readings in response to its shape and the prestigious status of its author.

Like Culler and Fish, each of these theorists projects their strategies of reading onto putative figures who are, if not quite as tangible as the students or the drunk, certainly not the theorists themselves. Again, this enables the theorist to operate in a vacuum, or, to be more accurate, from a position of omniscient security: better informed than their delusional textualist predecessors but at the same time able to stand outside the deluge of competing discourses that denies poetry the right, as Eagleton puts it, to 'exist'.

To answer the question of why so many academics have over recent years seemed determined to undermine the status of poetry as an autonomous discourse or literary genre, we must look even deeper into the background of modern theory.

Most would agree that the inaugurator of modern literary theory was Swiss linguist Ferdinand de Saussure (1857–1913). Saussure died early and during his lifetime published little, but his lecture notes were transcribed by his students as the *Course in General Linguistics* ([1916]1959). The phrase that sent reverberations through communities of linguists, literary critics and indeed philosophers for the subsequent century was that 'in language there are only differences without positive terms'. What he meant by this was that language is not simply a means of engaging with or representing the non-linguistic world, reality, but that without language, the world, the non-linguistic realm, call it what you will, exists only as a private, incognisant, incommunicable blur. His model of language as a structure dependent entirely upon 'difference' can only be properly understood in relation to his concept of the 'linguistic sign'. The 'signifier' is the tactile, concrete literary sign, spoken or written, and the 'signified' is the concept represented by the sign. A third element is the 'referent', the prelinguistic object or condition that stands beyond the signifier–signified relationship. This tripartite function is, to say the least, unsteady. The atheist and the Christian will share a largely identical conception of the relation between 'God' (signifier) and 'God' (signified), but the atheist will regard this as a purely linguistic state, a fiction sustained by language, and without a referent. For such an individual, the signifier God relates not to a specific signified and referent, but to other signifiers and signifieds – concepts of good and bad, eternity, omniscience, omnipotence, the whole network of signs that enables Christian belief to intersect with other elements of the human condition. In Saussure's terms, the signified 'God' is sustained by the differential relationship between itself and the other words and concepts, and this will override its correspondence with a 'positive term' (the referent). The implications of Saussure's thesis were exceptional and unprecedented. It undermined the conventional assumption that language plays a subsidiary functional role as a medium for communication and expression, while the complex spectrum of the actual – from abstract ideas, thoughts and beliefs to the nature of physical objects – exists independently of linguistic acts. The relevance of Saussurian linguistics for the study and understanding of poetry is twofold; one aspect of his programme underpins the poststructuralist project, while another offers sustenance to the traditional model of poetry as unique aesthetic genre.

Any understanding of the former must begin with Saussure's distinction between *langue* and *parole*. The *langue* is the system of rules and conventions that governs the operation of a language, at its most elementary, a combination of grammar and semantics. The *parole* is a particular instance of linguistic usage, generally with self-defining parameters. We can ask for a telephone number in a single sentence, which would constitute a *parole*, as would a far more gigantic sequence of sentences, all of which are in some way interconnected, and in this respect a novel also could be seen as a *parole*.

One of the most contentious issues to emerge from the various uses and investigations of this *langue–parole* or structure–event formula is in the threat it presents to the notion of originality, individuality, or in current phraseology, the autonomy of the subject. If, when using language, we need to draw upon the vast impersonal structure of the system in order to be understood, then it would seem that what we say or write is by no means unique to our personal, prelinguistic experiences or perceptions; rather, it is something made available from a shared system of enabling conventions that constitute and delimit the varieties of discourse. If we accept that a sentence in English can have meaning only by virtue of its relations to other sentences and abstract deep structures within the conventions of the language, then when we supplement syntactic structure with the arbitrary codes of rhythm, metre, rhyme and lineation, we are imposing even more limitations upon the identity and individuality of the subject represented within or speaking through poetic language. Consequently, if we commend poetic discourse for allowing us to represent hesitation and uncertainty within the text, without contextual interjections, we also face the contention that this imagined speaker who pauses and hesitates becomes more a function of the text itself and less an individual who inhabits the world outside the text.

This question does not arise only from the special instance of enjambment. Most poems, whatever their immediate provenance or concern, will at some point engage with issues of perception, truth and identity that we would usually associate with the non-literary spheres of philosophy, psychology, theology and sociology. Within these discourses, it is permissible to use devices that are more ostentatiously foregrounded in poetry: metaphor, allegory, analogy, symbolism, irony, parody. However, in non-poetic language, these devices are employed for purely pragmatic reasons, variously as instruments of persuasion or elaboration. In poetry, they have no manifest function, but rather are symptomatic of the poet's preoccupation with language itself. Moreover, the one feature of poetry that will not be found in the philosophic theorum or the essay on psychology is the use of metre, rhyme and lineation. So when, in the 'Immortality Ode', Wordsworth states that

> The sunshine is a glorious birth;
> But yet I know, where'er I go,
> That there hath past away a glory from the earth.

we can accept that he is making a profound statement about his own existential vision. But had Kant or Wittgenstein made such a statement in rhyme and metre, we would assume that they had taken a day off from their more serious philosophic conjectures. Why? There are several interrelated responses to this. We could claim that if Wordsworth's single objective was to communicate his model of mortality and existence, then there are surely better ways of clarifying such issues than dressing them up in metre and rhyme. Why then did he choose poetic form? It might be that the 'music' of metre and rhyme have some almost subliminal, persuasive effect upon the addressee. If so, this is not so much a statement, but more an exercise in deception. To complicate matters, we find that in adopting this traditional perception of what poetic form is and does, we have further compromised the equally traditional notion of the poet as the source, the originator of a thought or an image. If his message registers as an impressive vision of life and reality, particular to Wordsworth, it does so at least partly because of its ability to draw upon the same system of conventions and techniques shared by other poets and other poems. Northrop Frye observes that 'poems are made out of other poems', and if we accept that the prosodic material of construction plays some part in the generation of specifically poetic meaning, we would also have to concede that the poetic identity of William Wordsworth is similarly 'made out of other poems'.

This, essentially, is the reasoning behind Barthes' concept of the dead author and the working principle for those who propose that the poem is not the vehicle for the author's message or aesthetic design but rather a template of triggers upon which the competent reader imposes coherence and continuity.

Conversely, one might invoke the sequence of choices and actions executed by the poet as teleological proof that the poet is involved in a premeditated decision to create something manifestly different from all other linguistic acts. If one accepts this premise, then one must also concede that the poetry is not simply one of many impersonal discourses, a *langue* with a subordinate regiment of *paroles*. It transcends this status because, uniquely, it can borrow from every literary or non-literary subgenre – everything from dialogue through correspondence to shopping lists have appeared in poems – while supplementing this limitless abundance of linguistic registers with characteristics that are exclusively poetic: the double pattern. The variations between and permutations upon the relationship between these two elements are infinite and unpredictable. Hence the *parole* can exceed the limiting power of the *langue* for the simple reason that two different species of *langue*, comprising the same raw material, are being combined in ways that subvert the calculable mechanisms of each. The poet, therefore, is returned to their conventional status as the independent creator of the poem. It is, in the end, up to you to choose which thesis you find more convincing, and in Chapter 11 we will encounter further examples of their claims to precedence.

11

History, New Historicism and Cultural Materialism

The Saussurian seed would also germinate into a branch of theory known as New Historicism. Its best-known advocate is Stephen Greenblatt, whose collection *Shakespearean Negotiations: The Circulation of Social Energy in Renaissance England* (1988) is frequently cited as the exemplar of New Historicism in practice. Consider the most perturbing implications of Saussure's model: that language and whatever is extraneous to language are locked into an interdependent relationship, that we do not simply make use of language to express and represent ideas and facts but that without language, ideas and facts will be inexpressible and incognizable.

The most controversial, radical heir to the Saussurian legacy is Jacques Derrida. We will examine Derrida's invention, deconstruction, in Chapter 13 but for the time being we will consider what amounts to his concise and uncharacteristically accessible summation of Saussurian linguistics: 'There is nothing outside the text' (il n'y a pas de hors-texte) (1976, pp. 158–9). By 'text' he means anything spoken or written, and by 'nothing' he contends that the essential meaning or character of a given text can only be engaged with, challenged, illuminated, clarified, expurgated or simply explained by the creation of another text. We might, for example, refer to an ultimate, transcendent, eternal reality which exists beyond the linguistic realm, but that is all we can do, refer to it. We might pretend that the sequence of signifiers that we are citing or explaining is the bridge between presence and truth, but in order to do so we are obliged to build our thesis from yet another formation of signifiers. This process, Derrida argues, is endless and circular; any pursuit of a prelinguistic ultimate truth will only involve the creation of other new texts consisting entirely and exclusively of language.

We are left, then, with a model of the human condition, and society, as made up of a fabric of texts or discourses. Each will be deemed to serve a given function, in the sense that all utterances or writings fall into generic categories – casual speech act, formal enquiry, letter, novel, telephone bill, religious pamphlet and so on – with conventions of manner and style that accord with their accepted purpose. But according to Derrida, 'the text' (or to be more accurate the texts) constitutes our knowledge and experience of the world. This is the point at which the New Historicists engage with the Saussurian and Derridian thesis; we, as individuals, exist only in relation to the complex, ever competing fabric of discourses that enable us to engage with and rationalize our world. The intrinsic nature of each and their relationship to one another fluctuate through history, and the New Historicist programme is focused exclusively upon this sense of mutation and dynamic. Conventional historians work according to the principle that documents of all types provide evidence from which we can construct an authentic account of occurrences and individual experiences. Their orthodox, literary counterparts, while giving special attention to literary texts, premise their work upon a similar differentiation between documents and actuality, the latter usually made up of a hypothetical rationale for why the poet elected to write in a particular manner, influenced as they were by specific historical conditions. The New Historicist, however, deals with history as constituted exclusively of texts. They would not deny that real people existed or that actual events occurred at around the time these texts were written and disseminated, but they would aver that an attempt to reconstruct them involves the self-deluding procedure of assembling yet another text while claiming that this provides access to the ultimate prelinguistic truth underpinning the rest.

Greenblatt's work is concerned predominantly with the Renaissance, specifically with the relationships between Renaissance drama and other contemporaneous discourses. An exact and comprehensive account of his methodology and technique, particularly with regard to Shakespeare's plays, would require at minimum another chapter and is, in any event, only marginally relevant to the remit of this book. I shall, therefore, focus upon one part of his programme that does concern us, poetry. Greenblatt's notion of a tension between discourses borrows significantly from Marxist concepts of power and exchange. He presents Shakespeare's plays as engaged in a struggle with other texts and rituals of the period; they, among other things, appropriate and reshape rhetorical devices, recreate analogous versions of non-literary ceremonial or political customs and so on. The opening chapter of *Shakespearean Negotiations* (1988) begins in an almost contritional manner, admitting that as a callow, traditional critic, he had become preoccupied with hearing the voice of the long dead Shakespeare in his magnificent plays. He does not doubt that the plays 'were in large part written by the supremely gifted alumnus of Stratford grammar school' but now he recognizes that, by focusing on their author, he was eclipsing the process that vouchsafes them their energy and power, that is, the tension that exists at 'the boundaries ... understood to be art forms and other, contiguous, forms of expression'. Examples include the practice and manner of issuing royal pardons and a comparable disposition of power and mercy in *Measure for Measure*, and in *A Midsummer Night's Dream* the Catholic rituals involving holy water and the anointing of marriage beds reworked as magic and fantasy. Oddly, however, Greenblatt either fails to notice or deliberately omits from his account a tension, a meeting of textual boundaries that is a persistent, even defining feature of the plays of Shakespeare and his contemporaries, that is, the tension between blank verse and non-poetic speech. I have already shown how, in *Measure for Measure*

(Chapter 3), the characters themselves are aware of how poetry functions differently from non-literary discourse, of how extended conceits distort any rational correspondence between language and truth. One reason why Greenblatt might have overlooked something whose relevance to his thesis is striking is that it raises serious questions about the validity of his project and those of his fellow New Historicists and their close allies the Cultural Materialists. First of all, it is understandable that in his plays Shakespeare incorporates a significant number of self-referential engagements with the status of poetry, particularly regarding its relationship with the more pragmatic function of ordinary language. Lucio's sardonic comments, in prose, on how Claudio, speaking in verse, seems unable to offer a coherent, transparent account of his predicament is a case in point (see Chapter 3). What Shakespeare is doing here is replicating in miniature the contemporaneous state of uncertainty – evidenced in the prose writings of Puttenham and Sidney (see Chapter 3) regarding the significance and character of poetry. This would be troubling for Greenblatt to acknowledge because, on the one hand, it brings our attention back to Shakespeare the individual, the specific creator of a text that declares its independence from Greenblatt's model of the dynamic kasbah of competing discourses. Moreover, we encounter Shakespeare speaking to us – that voice from the dead that Greenblatt dismissed as a delusion – of the essential difference between poetry and everything else, proclaiming that the former is a unique and special discourse, operating in a self-consciously inventive realm of its own. Hearing the voice once sought and then dismissed as a foolish caprice is bad enough but listening as it undermines the premise upon which your methodology is founded would, for Greenblatt, have been unendurable.

No New Historicists have addressed themselves exclusively to poetry and verse only features within the margins of ground-breaking New Historicist writings, which causes one to suspect that they, by this omission, recognize that a discourse so belligerently different from all others in its character and with no given function will, at the very least, prove to be a subversive aberration from their notion of textual interdependence; its peculiarity proclaims its autonomy. This suspicion is borne out in Bennett and Royle's lauded, student-targeted *An Introduction to Literature, Criticism and Theory* (1995), in which the authors embark upon a New Historicist interpretation of Wordsworth's 'Alice Fell, or Poverty'. As they point out, a poem whose ostensible subject is poverty and deprivation invites comparison with contemporaneous texts that deal with related topics, such as Adam Smith's *The Wealth of Nations* (1776), and, at a more impressionistic level, they consider a passage from Wordsworth's sister Dorothy's journal in which she offers what we can assume to be an authentic account of the dire, impecunious condition of a real woman called Alice Fell. This 'join the dots' exercise, where correspondences are located between the poem and other discourses, is fascinating, but it skews a number of New Historicist claims. What we are offered is a conventional, biographical and empirical, account of how Wordsworth's poem might well have borrowed details from a real experience and an equally orthodox comparison between the way the poet Wordsworth deals with economic inequality and its treatment by political philosophers such as Smith. Bennett and Royle undo their own exercise and, unwittingly, the branch of theory, New Historicism, they are attempting to exemplify and defend. They move, with confident agility, between the three texts – Wordsworth's, Dorothy's and Smith's – without even considering that poetry is not simply another discourse but rather one governed by arbitrary conventions in which the responsibilities to notions of truth or sincerity, perceived or privately intuited, which govern Dorothy's journal and Smith's pamphlet, no longer obtain.

It is intriguing to compare Bennett, Royle and Greenblatt's interpretive method with that of Christopher Hill, a critic and historian of the previous generation. New Historicism and Cultural Materialism are generally treated as poststructuralist in technique but ideologically aligned with Marxist literary theory. Marxist approaches to literature range from the so-called 'vulgar' Marxism of Luckács, in which novels are treated as transparent records of social and economic change, to the Bakhtinian thesis of 'dialogism', which examines fiction as an unwitting polyphony of competing discourses, each indicative of various forms of social disturbance, unease or self-interest. It would not be entirely inaccurate to treat the New Historicist/Cultural Materialist model of poetry as derivative of Bakhtinian dialogism, the difference being that Bakhtin's text is the novel, while the New Historicists treat all discourses, including poetry, as contributory features to the all-encompassing social text. The poem, like the character or voice in the novel, is autonomous only insofar as the text that creates and contains it allows it to be, that is, not at all. Hill too was a Marxist critic but his methodological approach to poetry was very different from that of his New Historicist successors. For example, Hill begins his 1946 essay 'Society and Andrew Marvell' with a lengthy summary of non-poetic accounts of contemporaneous social and political events and more specific references to Marvell's own career as tutor, minor civil servant and MP. It soon becomes clear that, for Hill, Marvell is primarily a poet with a separate life as a figure who witnessed and played a minor role in the transformative political events of the late 17th century. His interest, primarily, is in how Marvell distils his complex and varied experiences into a discourse that is, by its nature, non-pragmatic and defamiliarizing – poetry. Hill regards Marvell's poetry as a form that demands an interpretive approach very different from the one we bring to the extant documents that enable us to build a picture of the social and political conditions of the period. Here, Hill (1946, pp. 68–9) describes his approach:

The existence of a conflict of some sort in Marvell is apparent from the most careless reading of his poems. At the risk of alienating readers by an excessively crude and oversimplified statement, I wish to say briefly and dogmatically what I think may have underlain this conflict, and then to try to prove and illustrate this thesis. The suggestion is that Marvell's poetry is shot through with consciousness of a conflict between subjective and objective, between the idea and the reality, which it is perhaps not too far-fetched to link up (very indirectly, of course) with the social and political problems of his time. This conflict takes many forms, but we can trace a repeated pattern, a related series of symbols, which suggests that fundamentally all the conflicts are interrelated, and that this 'double heart' (Marvell's phrase) is as much the product of a sensitive mind in a divided society as is Day Lewis's 'divided heart'. That of course is one reason why Marvell and the other 'metaphysical' poets have so attracted our generation.

Hill's method – shared by the vast majority of his contemporaries, irrespective of their ideological affiliation – is to treat poetry as a prism through which the world is uniquely reflected. It is taken for granted that poetry functions in this way because of its intrinsic difference from other discourses.

The New Historicist thesis, at least in relation to its implications for poetry, is deeply flawed. It is intriguing that New Historicism took root in and has, since the 1980s, focused predominantly upon what is generally termed the 'early modern' period of literary history, running from the early 16th to the mid-17th century, the epoch dominated by Shakespeare. This was not a random choice. The Renaissance suits New Historicism perfectly because, for the first time, surviving literary texts from a period are accompanied with an abundance of other documents and records that address its religious, political and sociocultural ethos. At the same time, although the fabric of raw material for scrutiny is far more dense than would be encountered even from the 15th century, the close of the Middle Ages, it is fragmented and incomplete compared, say, with documents that allow us access to the 18th or 19th centuries. Literary writers of the Renaissance, and indeed their eminent non-literary peers, are spectral figures. For most, there are some accounts of the fact that they existed, sometimes even of their activities or experiences, but since printing was in its infancy and the official, bureaucratic practice of documenting facts involved little more than threadbare parish records of births, marriages and deaths, what we know is buttressed by a good deal of surmise and speculation. The most famous example is, of course, Shakespeare, the most eminent author in English whose biography, at least in terms of undisputed, verifiable facts, fills little more than a page. This, therefore, is ideal territory for theorists who hold that textualism overrides the traditional notion of the real autonomous author whose inspiration and purpose is evident in their writing. If there are very few reliable accounts of the latter and their circumstances, then the model of a historical period consisting exclusively of a dynamic relationship between texts becomes all the more convincing.

Another related problem with New Historicism involves its reluctance to test its methodology against established theories of historical change and development. This, as we shall see, is particularly relevant to any clear understanding of the relationship between poems and their historical contexts.

During the 1920s, Jakobson, Mukarovsky and other Formalists engaged with Saussure's ideas on how language alters through time; specifically, how the phonetic and semantic registers of individual words mutate from one period to the next. Their conclusion, briefly summarized, was that no single moment of alteration can ever be identified, even when speech is recorded electronically or in the tribal memory. Language, from individual words to agreed grammatical formulae, is in a constant state of flux, with some parts remaining immune to change and others altering in varying degrees at different velocities. Regarding the causes of change, these too are almost infinitely variable and unpredictable. The political and cultural annexation of one nation by another will, of course, initiate change, but such occurrences cannot be predicted nor their consequences for language foreseen. Jakobson and Mukarovsky borrowed the two axes from their model of language per se for a representative diagram of historical change.

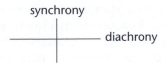

The synchronic axis represents the passage of time, while its diachronic counterpart involves that state of a language at a given point in time. This interactive relation could, he argued, be more accurately represented by a prism. (This model was adapted by Jakobson in 'Zur Struktur des Phonems' [1939]1971; see Bradford, 1994, p. 145).

```
            diachrony

a – – – > b – – – > c – – – > d – – – > e        s
          ¦         ¦         ¦         ¦         y
          a         b         c         d         n
                    ¦         ¦         ¦         c
                    a         b         c         h
                              ¦         ¦         r
                              a         b         o
                                        ¦         n
                                        a         y
```

What this diagram seeks to demonstrate is that the clinical distinction between synchrony and diachrony is a necessary methodological fiction that must, in turn, be qualified by our awareness that, at any putative point in time on the diachronic scale, there is a continuous tension between elements of the linguistic past and the present, with the implication that our more extended and active awareness will produce an increasingly complex present.

This diagram was intended to account not only for the particulars of lexical syntactic or phenomic change but also for the more complex alterations in the constitution of larger generic formations of language, everything from conversational etiquette through letter writing to ceremonial formulae and the composition of books, essays and treatises.

The exception to this process of reformation and flux is poetry. This is Jakobson (1987b) on 'the dominant':

> The dominant may be defined as the focussing component of the work of art: it rules, determines, and transforms the remaining components. It is the dominant which guarantees the integrity of the structure.

> Inquiry into the dominant had important consequences for Formalist views of literary evolution. In the evolution of poetic form it is not so much a question of the disappearance of certain elements and the emergence of others as it is a question of shifts in the mutual relationships among the diverse components of the system, in other words a question of the shifting dominant ... the hierarchy of artistic devices changes within the framework of a given poetic genre; the change, moreover, affects the hierarchy or poetic genres, and, simultaneously, the distribution of artistic devices among the individual genres. Genres which were originally secondary paths, subsidiary variants, now come to the fore, whereas the canonical genres are pushed toward the rear. (Jakobson, 1987b; see Bradford, 1994, p. 152)

The dominant is the element of the poetic function, which, at any particular synchronic point, preserves its essential difference from other linguistic discourses and which consequently ensures that the synchronic-diachronic shifts that occur within the history of poetry are governed as much by the definitive and inherent nature of the dominant as by external, contextual elements such as politics and sociocultural change. The dominant is effectively Jakobson's definition of the poetic function as 'the focus upon the message for its own sake' viewed from the sociohistorical perspective, and, in immediate, textual terms, is the double pattern.

This model is antithetical to that of the New Historicism and other poststructuralist theses, which relegate the poet from the role of aesthetic initiator to that of functionary or producer. Consider, for example, Wordsworth's use of the ballad form in *Lyrical Ballads* (see Chapter 5), which involves a deliberately disorientating confluence of intertextual and historical axes. At the end of the 18th century, the ballad was an icon of subliterary popular culture and Wordsworth's deliberate juxtaposition of this with issues and themes more readily associated with the high cultural status of the lyric or even with the philosophical essay caused a disruption of expectation: matters such as natural justice and existential angst were being addressed in rustic circumstances by low-life personae. In this instance, the dominant is the ballad form, which carries with it specific social and cultural associations but whose predominant allegiance is not to the diachronic axis of competing texts and forces but to a specific genre, both contemporaneous and locatable at any point in recorded history as far back, in Western culture, as classical Greece. It is essentially and self-evidently a poem, a category of text whose defining feature might undergo changes but which will remain secure in its separateness from other utterances and discourses. It can mutate through history but not sufficiently to alter its enduring character; in this regard it is ahistorical. The dominant, the double pattern, undergoes altera-tions, the most significant of which are seen as the key transitional moments in the history of poetry – the unseating of the Augustan couplet by the lyric-centred eclecticism of the Romantics, the 20th-century free verse revolution and so on – and it is certainly the case that factors external to the purely poetic realm play an influential part in these metamorphoses. There was no single factor that caused poets in the late 17th and early 18th centuries to place restraints upon the poetic function with a view to producing more coherent and transparent verse, but the broader aspirations towards neoclassical ideals of order and symmetry in culture and society were influential. At the same time, the poets of the period were self-consciously aware that the predominant consensus on how poems should be written had been inaugurated by them, that they were altering what had gone before and were attempting to maintain a new order (see Chapter 4). The double pattern, guaranteeing the independence of poetry from the arbi-trary fluctuations to which other texts and discourses are subject, also confers upon the poet a special sense of responsibility. The ability to change or preserve the relationship between the poem you are writing and its predecessors, while acknowledging their shared affiliation to the double pattern, enables the poet to achieve autonomy beyond the dehumanizing flux in which the status of a given text depends exclusively upon its interdependent relationship with others. Greenblatt, the critic, might lament the lost voice of his hero Shakespeare, but poets speak and listen to other poets; the message from one to another is encoded in a manner that transcends the temporal flux of existence and discourse. The poet writing today will know that their version of the double pattern will be picked up and recognized by a poet two centuries hence, rather like a Morse code message discharged into space and received via satellite long after its sender has died. Similarly, that same poet will be engaged in a dialogue with their predecessors, fellow practitioners of this unique atemporal *langue*, alluding to, challenging, referencing but never quite abandoning the factor that links them, the double pattern.

Poetry, as I have stated, is unlimited in its range of subjects and this func-tional rootlessness frees it from the contingent relationships based upon 'power' that Greenblatt, incorrectly, posits as a feature of all discourse. Its only affiliation is to itself and in this regard I should revise my claim that poetry is irresponsible, limitless and heterogeneous in terms of a given purpose. In the end it is preoc-cupied with the material from which it forms itself. Its subject is that which it preys upon constantly and self-consciously. It is about language, and with this in mind we should turn to another strand of structuralist and poststructuralist theory, psychoanalysis.

12

Psychoanalysis

Any proper appreciation of the relevance, or otherwise, of psychoanalysis to the study of poetry must involve some knowledge of the parallels between the ideas of Freud and the linguistic theories of Jakobson. The following is from Freud's 'The Interpretation of Dreams' (1900, pp. 277–8):

> Suppose I have a picture-puzzle, a rebus [Freud describes the dream as a rebus], in front of me. It depicts a house with a boat on its roof, a single letter of the alphabet, the figure of a running man whose head has been conjured away, and so on. Now I might be misled into raising objections and declaring that the picture as a whole and its component parts are nonsensical. A boat has no business to be on the roof of a house, and a headless man cannot run [etc.] … But obviously we can only form a proper judgement of the rebus if we put aside such criticism as these of the whole composition and its part and if, instead, we try to replace each separate element by a syllable or word that can be represented by that element in some way or other. The words which are put together in this way are no longer nonsensical but may form a poetical phrase of the greatest beauty and significance. A dream is a picture-puzzle of this sort.

There seems to be a close connection between Freud's notion of transference of images from the latent dream to its manifest counterpart in language and Jakobson's distinction between ordinary language and the poetic function. Freud's pictorial dream image of a headless man running is nonsensical but it acquires a degree of 'beauty and significance' when realized in language. What is inconceivable in any real, prelinguistic situation can be translated into a 'fixed' semantic unit. But the relationship between Freud's model of transference from dream images to language and Jakobson's concept of the poetic function is uneasy and potentially contradictory. Jakobson's most significant reference to Freud occurs in his essay 'Two Aspects of Language' ([1959]1971, p. 258):

> A competition between both devices, metonymic and metaphoric, is manifest in any symbolic process, be it intrapersonal or social. Thus in an inquiry into the structure of dreams, the decisive question is whether the symbols and the temporal sequences used are based on contiguity (Freud's metonymic

'displacement' and synecdochic 'condensation') or on similarity (Freud's 'identification' and 'symbolism').

Jakobson does not provide an answer to this 'decisive question' because, in his view, Freud's model blurs the distinction between the involuntary creation of metaphoric images – we do not determine their content – and the subsequent realization of their verbal counterparts. Moreover, Freud remained unclear regarding how exactly the chiaroscuro of symbols and images retained after the dream would be picked over and catalogued by the kind of person disposed to turn them into a poem. In Jakobson's model, the poet chooses to emphasize the selective or the combinative axis. Their choice might well be based on, as Freud put it, 'a (disguised) fulfilment of a (suppressed or repressed) wish' (1900, p. 160), but surely if a choice is made, the 'wish' must be manifest at least to the poet themselves.

It was not that Jakobson did not believe in Freud's model of conscious and unconscious activities; rather that Freud's consistent argument that creative writing, literature, is analogous to and sometimes an example of dream manifestation undermines Jakobson's conception of poetry as a medium where the poet consciously marshals and choreographs the devices and is fully aware of their effects. Obviously, there is some connection between the dream stories of Freud's patients and the more respectable cultural activity of literary writing, but there is a conflict between Freud's all-embracing classification of creative writers and Jakobson's distinction between ordinary and literary language and, most significantly, between poetry and prose. In 'Creative Writers and Day Dreaming', Freud (1908) gave particular emphasis to the type of 'egocentric' novel in which the activities, the psychological condition and the speech patterns of 'His Majesty the Ego, the hero' betray some symbolic relationship with the unconscious drives and conflicts of the author. Of secondary interest was the 'eccentric' novel in which the central character plays a less active part in the events of the story (Zola is cited as an example). Freud's psychoanalytic model of the centralized and decentralized author-hero would seem to correspond with Jakobson's formulaic connection between 'metonymy as the leading trope in epic poetry' (and, by implication, in the novel) and 'metaphor as the inherent trope in lyric poetry'. 'In this connection, the lyric poet, we note, endeavours to present himself as the speaker, whereas the epic poet takes on the role of a listener who is supposed to recount deeds learned by hearsay' (Jakobson, [1959]1971, p. 297). However, these two classifications of literary genre are diametrically opposed. Jakobson's apparent extension of the 'egocentric' author-hero of the novel to the commanding presence of the poetic lyric voice is anti-Freudian. The Freudian author-hero is a figure for whom the story is a double-edged deployment of literariness: on the one hand, it corresponds with the real-world context of sequences and events, and on the other, it mediates the unconscious, repressed fabric of drives and conflicts. Jakobson's lyric poet similarly creates two patterns of signification. The poem is referential, in the sense that it is bound to refer to something, but it also creates an internalized, reflexive pattern of significations from its network of interactions between sound and meaning and through its unlicensed metaphoric and figurative range. The difference between these two figures is that while the former exerts partial control over unconscious and conscious determinants of the narrative, the latter consciously and deliberately controls the relation between the metonymic and metaphoric axes and the pattern of metre and sound with which these are interwoven. One could cite as an example Donne's 'The Flea', in which the addresser at once submits to an egocentric fantasy of sensual metaphors while the poet deploys the metrical scheme as a reminder that the entire text is a contrived, self-mocking exercise (see Chapter 2). Freud often uses the terms 'poetic language' and 'poetical effects', but we must assume that he means any type of extravagant verbal invention. His patients resemble novelists in the sense that both create self-evident stories in which there is a tension between invention and credibility, but none of them, as far as we know, enclosed their dream stories within a persistent metrical or sound pattern.

When Freud offers accounts of how he deals with the disclosures of his patients, his technique appears to be remarkably similar to the intentionalist or author-centred model of literary criticism dismantled so convincingly by Wimsatt and Beardsley (1946) in 'The Intentional Fallacy' (see Chapter 8). Freud reads through their 'manifest' account – that is, their verbal summary of the images of the dream – in an attempt to decode its significance at a primal prelinguistic level, and, more significantly, as a symptom of their state of mind. Freud himself never fully extended his technique to detailed readings of literary texts, but some of the earliest examples of how his model of psychoanalyst/patient was adapted by others to the relationship between critic, text and poet disclose the inherent problems of such approaches.

One of Swift's most notoriously puzzling poems is 'Cassinus and Peter: A Tragical Elegy' (1731). The two eponymous figures are Cambridge undergraduates. Peter finds his friend in a state of almost suicidal despair, unwashed, delirious and weeping continually. He asks:

> Why, Cassy, thou wilt dose thy pate:
> What makes thee lie a-bed so late?
> The finch, the linnet, and the thrush,
> Their matins chant in every bush;
> And I have heard thee oft salute
> Aurora with thy early flute.
> Heaven send thou hast not got the hyps!
> How! not a word come from thy lips?

His distress, it seems, derives from his beloved, one Celia:

> O Peter! beauty's but a varnish,
> Which time and accidents will tarnish:
> But Celia has contrived to blast
> Those beauties that might ever last.
> Nor can imagination guess,
> Nor eloquence divine express,
> How that ungrateful charming maid
> My purest passion has betrayed:
> Conceive the most envenomed dart
> To pierce an injured lover's heart.

Peter assumes that something horrific has occurred and tries, with little success, to have his friend disclose the exact nature of these events. Is Celia ill? Has she left him? Is she, God forbid, dead? Cassinus only seems capable of offering eloquent, and imprecise, evocations of a tragedy that seems to defy definition:

> And on the marble grave these rhimes
> A monument to after-times –
> "Here Cassy lies, by Celia slain.
> And dying, never told his pain."
> Vain empty world, farewell. But hark.
> The loud Cerberian triple bark:
> And there – behold Alecto stand,
> A whip of scorpions in her hand:
> Lo, Charon from his leaky wherry
> Beckoning to waft me o'er the ferry:
> I come! I come! Medusa see,
> Her serpents hiss direct at me.
> Begone: unhand me, hellish fry:
> "Avaunt – ye cannot say 'twas I."

Eventually, however, poor Cassinus can no longer contain himself and confides the terrible truth to Peter:

> Nor wonder how I lost my wits;
> Oh! *Celia, Celia, Celia* sh–!

A number of so-called 'vulgar' Freudian critics – that is, those who treat the author as the equivalent of the patient – seized upon 'Cassinus and Peter' as evidence of Swift's mentally disturbed state:

From the psycho-analytical standpoint one would describe his neurotic behaviour as an inhibition of normal potency, with a lack of courage in relation to women of good character and perhaps with a lasting aggressive tendency towards women of a lower type. (Ferenczi, 1926)

Swift was a neurotic who exhibited psycho-sexual infantilism, with a particular showing of coprophilia, associated with misogyny, misanthropy,
mysophilia and mysophobia. (Karpman, 1942)

One gets the impression that the anal fixation was intense and binding, and
the genital demands so impaired or limited at best that there was a total
retreat from genital sexuality in his early adult life, probably beginning with
the unhappy relationship with Jane Waring, the first of the goddesses.
(Greenacre, 1955)

These quotations are from an essay by Norman O. Brown called 'The Excremental Vision' (1959) (reproduced in Lodge, 1972, p. 512). Brown points out,
convincingly, that it is both peremptory and self-contradictory to treat Swift as a
figure whose various unconscious drives and repressions rise unbidden to the
surface in this poem, as though he were a patient offering a guileless improvised
account of either his dreams or private fears. Brown does not provide a detailed
alternative reading to those of the Freudians but consider the following
interpretation.

It could be argued that the 'patient' in this scenario is not the poet Swift, but
his creation Cassinus. The poem is touched with a degree of black comedy in
that Cassinus's histrionics, his self-possessed tragic performances veer between
the pathetic and the farcical, especially when we consider their cause. At the
same time, however, it is possible to perceive him as the exemplification of a
widespread but rarely acknowledged contemporary paradox. This was an age
that presented itself, to itself, as the re-creation of the great civilizations of Rome
and Greece. Neoclassical architecture, art and, of course, poetry embodied the
ideals of order, symmetry and coherence. The paradox inheres in the fact that
the idealization of a new purity in aesthetics, culture and the intellect contrasted
spectacularly with the day-to-day life of the rapidly expanding urban centres
such as London. The latter were captured with merciless honesty later in the
century in paintings by Hogarth, with the streets of the capital awash with
prostitutes, drunks, beggars, disease and, yes, excrement. Cassinus, self-evidently,
is a figure who has immersed himself in the world of classical learning,
mythology and aesthetics; he seems incapable of addressing facts, returning
continually to florid rhetoric and hyperbole. It is possible, then, to interpret his
apparently bizarre fixation with his girlfriend's bodily functions not as evidence
of mental disorder but of an overabundance of purblind intellectualism; he sees
her, and indeed everyone else, less as a real human being than a fabric of ideal-
ized expectations, a near spiritual presence who transcends the ordinariness of
corporal existence. In this regard, Swift becomes the analyst rather than the
patient, someone who recreates in Cassinus symptoms of disequilibrium he has
observed in his peers.

Let us turn now to a figure whose influence rivals that of Freud, at least in
terms of the literary critical branch of psychoanalysis, Jacques Lacan.

Lacan inserted himself into the fissure between Freudian and Jakobsonian theories of the sign, and in his essay 'The Mirror Stage' (1949) he lays the groundwork for the lecture 'Discourse at Rome' (1953) and maps out his post-Freudian concept of language and the unconscious. Lacan sees the unconscious as coming into being simultaneously with language. In his view, desire, the driving force towards prelingusitic instinctual satisfaction, can only be properly understood in terms of the tension between the subject and 'that condition which is imposed upon him by the existence of the discourse to cause his need to pass through the defiles of the signifier' (1949, p. 264). In brief, desire, far from being an element of our prelinguistic unconscious condition, is actually the result of our being 'born into language'. In the Freudian scheme, the unconscious exists as a mass of instinctual representations; in Lacan's scheme, the unconscious is the product of the structuring of desire by language. The signifier invests desire with meaning. As a consequence, the material signifier becomes the focus of subjectively felt needs and is in a constantly 'sliding' state above the continuum of the signified.

Jakobson ([1959]1971, p. 672) acknowledges that the psychoanalytic endeavour to 'disclose the *privata privatissima* of language [the fundamental level of inner speech] may find stimulation in Lacan's attempts to revise and reinterpret the correlation between *signans* and *signatum* in the mental and verbal experience of the patient', but his use of the conditional term, 'may', and his implication that mental *and* verbal experiences are not the same thing signals a degree of tension between Jakobson and Lacan. In Lacan's 1957 lecture at the Sorbonne 'The Insistence of the Letter in the Unconscious' (reproduced in Lodge, 1988), this tension becomes strikingly evident. At one point, Lacan refers to the 'law of the parallelism of the signifier' in verse, but his intended meaning is selective and one-dimensional (p. 88). For Lacan, the parallelism of the phonic and metrical patterns of the signifier is what enables verse to foreground and disclose the more general 'notion of an incessant sliding of the signified under the signifier' (p. 87), and again we encounter a distortion of Jakobson's theory. Jakobson's point is that verse projects the material signifier into a second level of organization, which supplements but does not displace the balance between signifier and signified in non-poetic discourse. So, in verse, the relation between signifier and signified is not one of 'incessant sliding' but of a productive, multi-dimensional tension between what language is and what language does. Lacan shares with Jakobson the belief in poetry as a medium that isolates and foregrounds general elements in the nature and function of language, but for Jakobson this process requires a conscious and intensive manipulation of the agreed relation between signifier, signified and referent, while for Lacan it discloses the uncontrollable structuration of signified and referent by the signifier in both the conscious and the unconscious continua. Lacan's notion of literature, and poetry in particular, as a condition or a symptom, rather than a deliberate, self-aware practice, is one of the more trenchant of all the various poststructuralist attacks upon the autonomous status of the author, and Julia

Kristeva, in 'The System and the Speaking Subject' (1986), picks up where he leaves off. Kristeva endorses the Formalist thesis that poetry complicates the standard relationship between signifiers and signifieds:

> first [by] rhythmic and stylistic markings [which replace] logic as the motivation of the signifier ... secondly [by] operations which disturb the syntactic chain by means of ellipses and indefinite emboldings of grammatical categories. (p. 215)

She complicates the distinction between the former and the latter (whose most notable manifestations in verse are, respectively, metre/rhyme and metaphor) by examining how each can exemplify the 'semiotic' and the 'symbolic'. In Kristeva's schema, the 'semiotic' corresponds with Freud's description in 'Beyond the Pleasure Principle' (1920) of how his grandson dealt with separation from his mother by throwing a spool tied to a string over the edge of his crib while shouting 'Oooo' – 'Da', 'Fort!' – 'Da!' ('Oooo' – 'Here', 'Gone!' – 'Here!'). For the child, the signifier – yelled and palpably experienced – was a substitute for a sense of loss, a compensation achieved mainly because at his age the distinction between the logic of language and its primitive tactile pleasure of making sounds is blurred. Kristeva contends that, in poetry, the licensing of sound pattern and illogical conceits as deviations from the orderly structure of sense is the adult equivalent of a lost infantile experience. The 'symbolic', while allowing of the same devices and techniques as the 'semiotic', involves a far more calculated and premeditated use of them: in this regard, the poet is suppressing, displacing or substituting aspects of their unconscious. Kristeva suggests that the semiotic manifests itself principally in unorthodox and avant-garde poetry, while the symbolic is more evident in conventional verse. She refers exclusively to French verse but to adapt her thesis to English one might contend that with the arrival of Romanticism, the semiotic began to replace the symbolic as at once the paradigmatic and most extreme instance of the poetic function. For example, Coleridge's 'Kubla Khan' could be regarded as a sophisticated enactment of the 'pleasure' that Freud's grandson derived from his game with the sounds of words. The poem involves an inconclusive chain of fantastic images and conceits, accompanied by a rhyme scheme and an alliterative/assonated pattern so dense as to almost eclipse syntactic continuity. However, the question raised, although not satisfactorily addressed, by Freud remains. To what extent is Coleridge aware not merely of what he is creating but of its potential as a release mechanism for what Kristeva calls 'a crisis of rationality' (1986, p. 219)? It seems presumptuous in the very least to infer that without poetry of the type exemplified by 'Kubla Khan', Coleridge's alleged emotional or intellectual 'crisis' would have intensified. Consider the fact that during the century before Romanticism, pieces such as this were virtually non-existent, the rationale for verse being the implementation of poetic devices as a secondary layer of logic and symmetry. Were poets of a similar temperamental disposition to Coleridge condemned pre-1800 to suffer in a form of creative inertia, even imprisonment? Significantly, Kristeva also contends that the semiotic and the symbolic are gender related, with male writers dominating the former and women more inclined toward the latter. (See Chapter 14 for a study of gender and style.)

In 1985, Geoffrey Hartman published an essay called 'The Interpreter's Freud', which, as its title indicates, addresses itself principally to the founder of psychoanalysis, but the presence of Lacan informs the piece. Hartman concentrates on the postulation by Lacan, and indeed Derrida, that language is essentially unstable, involving the perpetual 'sliding of the signified under the signifier', an endless deferral of determinate meaning, and poses the question of whether human beings can be aware of this and indeed address it in verbal form. This is a conundrum that psychoanalysts have caused but not resolved: if figures such as Lacan are alert to the 'sliding of the signified under the signifier', why should they assume that this knowledge is exclusive to them? In short, utterances or texts that psychoanalysts treat as involuntary symptoms of the sliding signifier might well be premeditated, calculated engagements with this same phenomenon; and the most obvious contender for this ranking would be poetry. Poems involve a persistent and endemic preoccupation with the arbitrary relationship between the materiality of language and any assumed or postulated notion of conclusive meaning. They deploy the sounds, rhythms and shapes of language as a metatext, alongside but not subservient to the standard conventions of syntax and semantics. Moreover, they create internalized patterns of signification that invoke the frames of reference of non-poetic discourse yet refuse to comply with their implicit requirement for closure or clarification; in both instances, we are dealing with the double pattern.

Hartman (1985, p. 376) quotes from the notebooks of Coleridge and Keats:

'My thoughts crowd each other to death,' Coleridge wrote. He finds himself in the grip of what he named 'the steamy nature of association'; in his Notebooks, especially, not only the dream he puts down but also his speculative etymologies and related word chains accelerate into a futile 'science of the grotesque'. ... Or Keats, in a light-hearted vein: 'I must be quaint and free of Tropes and figures – I must play my draughts as I please ... Have you not seen a Gull, an orc, a Sea Mew, or any thing to bring this Line to a proper length, and also fill up this clear part; that like the Gull I may dip – I hope not out of sight – and also, like a Gull I hope to be lucky in a good sized fish – This crossing a letter is not without its associations – for chequer work leads us naturally to a Milkmaid, a Milkmaid to Hogarth Hogarth to Shakespeare Shakespeare to Hazlitt – Hazlitt to Shakespeare and thus by merely pulling an apron string we set a pretty peal of Chimes at work.'

He is intrigued by both poets' self-conscious awareness of an abundance of unattached verbiage, their sense of language as persistently present but at the same time insufficient to sate their desire for a state of calm or closure. What he does not note is the remarkable parallel between these disclosures and the utterances of Freud's grandson. In both respects, a spontaneous encounter with language as a route to as yet undisclosed potentiality is self-evident, but the poets go on to rationalize this, create from their primitive moments of inchoate chaos an aesthetic imitation of the experience – poems.

Hartman concentrates upon Wordsworth's 'A slumber did my spirit seal' and looks at how the poet refuses to allow us to fix upon a specific signified. Sleep and death, continuance and finality, transcendence and annihilation: the oppositions are continually played upon in the poem but no matter how many times we read it, we will only ever encounter counterpoint and tension; finality is restlessly deferred.

Hartman does not venture to resolve the unsteady association between psychoanalysis and poetry but I will pursue the implications of his paper. Poems are commentaries upon the peculiar, almost fetishistic relationship between language and the prelinguistic tangible world. In Freud's and Lacan's model, language becomes detached from its routine referential function only at an elemental subconscious level; in dreams or suppressed fantasies, condensation and displacement, the constituent features of figurative language, unfold unwittingly; in moments of stress, inspirational excess or at the infantile stage when we exert no command over the shared conventions of discourse, sound and rhythm overdetermine the conventions of coherence. The double pattern is present but unconfined and unfocused. Neither Freud, Lacan, Kristeva, nor indeed other theorists who consider the parallels between psychoanalysis and poetry have properly examined the possibility that the poet might be as alert as analysts to the potentialities of the sliding signifier, that practitioners of the double pattern might have pre-empted the discoveries of Freud. It is indisputably the case that poetry involves an interaction between two linguistic registers, one that we perceive as a rational, calculated orchestration of register and meaning and the other which allows the innate, distorting capacities of words and their interactions to disturb the coherence of the former. Kristeva engages with this issue tangentially, but ventures no clear distinction between the premeditated volitional model of poetic writing and the author as subject of a discourse. For more than a century, psychoanalysts have debated and failed to reach a consensus on how these two features correspond with conscious or subliminal states of mind. Poets, although not explicitly addressing the question, have disclosed a solution. The poem is the point at which the rational and the illogical are caused, deliberately, to coexist and interact, an experiment initiated and orchestrated by the poet.

13

Deconstruction

Deconstruction has grown out of the interwoven fabric of European linguistics, philosophy and semiotics. It draws on Saussure's model of the differential nature of language, the sense of meaning as an indeterminate condition that depends upon the relation between linguistic signs rather than a direct and unitary correspondence between individual signs and their apparent foundation in immutable units of reality. Deconstruction takes Saussure's thesis a stage further. First, it holds that language and reality are largely indistinguishable; that the flow and counterflow of signification between linguistic units is what constitutes reality. Second, and most significantly, it contends that language functions as our means of persuading or deceiving ourselves that what we are talking or writing about exists as an independent, prelinguistic entity or system. The activity of deconstruction is concerned principally with exposing this double process of fabrication: it operates from the premise that what lies outside language is unknowable (or in some instances non-existent) without language; it discloses the means by which a particular text, utterance or discourse uses the resources of signification to persuade itself and its recipient that it is involved in addressing some stratum of prelinguistic truth rather than involved in constructing it.

Derrida claims that the idea of the sign as comprising a signifier and a signified is a false supposition inherited from the traditional, pre-Saussurian notion of the mode of representation providing access to the thing represented. In his early work, Derrida often referred to this philosophical assumption as 'the metaphysics of presence', a generic state of mind that anchors all Western thinking to a 'desire for presence', a belief that signs will ultimately provide access to a prelinguistic referent.

Derrida's modified account of the nature of the sign leads him to a radical undermining of Saussure's notion of 'difference'. In Saussure's model of language, the difference between signifiers, concrete signs, enables us to stabilize the otherwise shifting fabric of signifieds. Famously, Derrida invented the portmanteau word *différance*, involving a conflation of *différence* (difference) with *différant* (differing). His point is that while we, and Saussure, routinely assume that the tangible difference between signs – their different sounds and appearance on the page – secures a collateral lexicon of prelinguistic ideas and concepts, signifieds, our search for the latter actually involves a constant and ultimately futile process of deferral. When we seek a clearer definition or account of an idea, we effectively exchange one set of signifiers for another. In Derrida's view, this exchange of an inadequate account for one more suitable and allegedly accurate is symptomatic of our continuous 'desire for presence' or our search for prelinguistic truth, but what actually occurs is a deferral of meaning; the pursuit of a meaning behind the fabric of signifiers is infinite and perpetual.

Individual 'texts' – and by this Derrida means anything from a brief spoken statement to a work of philosophy – involve attempts by their authors to secure them as reliable encodings of truth and meaning but within each text will be a blind spot, a 'flaw', which exposes its reliance upon the relationship between signifiers as a substitute for its declared or implied disclosure of actuality. Deconstruction, then, involves the location of this flaw, which will yield meanings and strategies within the text that often contradict its manifest purpose: all texts are capable of deconstructing themselves and require only the attention of a reader alert to Derrida's insights to expose this process.

Consider Derrida's theses in relation to the double pattern. According to Derrida, all non-poetic discourses are, unless deliberately fraudulent or misleading, premised upon the objective of disclosing or clarifying meaning. As such, in various ways they disguise their dependence upon the relation between signifiers, a dependence that deconstructionists set out to reveal. Poetry, on the other hand, involves a continual tension between the referential aspect of language, features that the poem shares with non-poetic discourses, and its disruption of any clear or unitary meaning. The latter can involve anything from a spiralling metaphor that seems to turn the poem into a self-contained fabric of effects, detached from any grounded notion of truth or specificity, to the interference of metre, rhyme and sound pattern in the standard conventions of syntax and semantics. Derrida (1981, p. 26) could have been referring to this when he wrote that in all texts 'the play of differences supposes, in effect, syntheses and referrals which forbid at any moment, or in any sense, that a single element be *present* in and of itself, referring only to itself'. However, most critics, and indeed most poets, would treat the 'syntheses and referrals' of the double pattern that seem to suspend any clear or unambiguous sense of what is meant as deliberate contrivances, consciously and meticulously orchestrated by the poet. In Derrida's model, the writer is at best only in partial control of this process: 'The reading must always aim at a certain relationship unperceived by the writer, between what he commands and what he does not command of the patterns of language that he uses' (1976, p. 158). By 'command', Derrida means those forces and instincts of prioritization that effectively govern our composition of a text. In short, he argues that the process of reading or interpreting will involve patterns of signification that cannot be properly accounted for by the straightforward, a priori objective of specifying exactly what Donne or Wordsworth meant by this word, or line or stanza. Such means-to-ends procedures should be replaced by a 'teas[ing] out [of] the warring forces of signification within the text itself'. For the more sceptical critic, this sounds like a procedural cop-out: instead of trying to solve the puzzle of the poem, we should happily embrace its incessant and irresolvable paradoxes. So what did the deconstructors of poetry actually do?

Paul de Man has called attention to the closing line of Yeats's 'Among School Children': 'How can we know the dancer from the dance?' De Man (1979) argued that practically all readings perceive this as a figurative or rhetorical question. We already know that we cannot distinguish dancer from dance; this playful inter-animation of object and experience is the central theme of the poem. He went on to argue that it is just as valid to regard this question as literal and non-figurative (p. 12):

> in which the final line is read literally as meaning that, since the dancer and the dance are not the same, it might be useful, perhaps even desperately necessary – for the question can be given a ring of urgency, 'Please tell me, how *can* I know the dancer from the dance' – to tell them apart.

To understand what is happening here, you should look back to Chapter 9 and the problem of reconciling the devices and effects of the text with the normative patterns of ordinary discourse and understanding (aka naturalization). De Man argues that each interpretation – figurative or literal – involves a form of naturalization that brings the text into line with what we think it is trying to do. Instead of choosing one or the other, he urges us to accept that both are vital to a proper critical engagement with the text: in Derrida's terms, an acknowledgement that neither we nor the poet can 'command' the text's shifts between an apparent desire for an answer and its implications that an answer is inappropriate, unnecessary or impossible.

Does this mean that deconstructive criticism should simply respond to, perhaps rejoice in, the indecipherable complexities of the poem? Geoffrey Hartman (1980), a deconstructor, seems to think so: 'literary commentary may cross the line and become as demanding as literature: it is an unpredictable or unstable genre that cannot be subordinated, a priori, to its referential or commentating function'.

The critics who seized upon deconstruction as a literary critical strategy in the 1960s and 70s (notably Geoffrey Hartman, J. Hillis-Miller and Paul de Man) saw it as offering another, untested avenue for literary studies. For the New Critics, the process of bringing literary criticism into line with the more respectable disciplines of the social sciences and humanities had involved a difficult and apparently unresolvable conflict between treating poetry as one of many historical, political or philosophic discourses and maintaining that it is intrinsically different from all these. Deconstruction offered the possibility of doing both: interpreting literature, particularly poetry, as a nexus, a forum of tensions between what we seem or want to know, and the means (language) by which we investigate, disseminate and celebrate this knowledge. However, one cannot help but note some parallels between what the deconstruction of poetry actually involves and a number of the exemplary New Critical theories on its essential character. Empson, for example, in *Seven Types of Ambiguity* ([1930]1961) more than fulfilled the promise of his title by picking out patterns of calculated equivocation in poems from the Renaissance to the mid-20th century. At the end of his study, he reflects upon the pragmatics of recognizing and acknowledging that a passage from a poem is ambiguous ([1930]1961, p. 234):

> all the subsidiary meanings must be relevant, because anything (phrase, sentence, or poem) meant to be considered as a unit must be unitary, must stand for a single order of the mind. In complicated situations this unity is threatened; you are thinking of several things, or one thing as it is shown by several things or one thing in several ways ... More generally one may say that if an ambiguity is to be unitary there must be 'forces' holding its elements together, and I ought then, in considering ambiguities to have discussed what the forces were, whether they were adequate.

He does not aver that the ambiguity should be resolved or that one level of meaning should, for whatever reason, be classified as the most authentic or valid to the exclusion of others. The significant difference between his position and de Man's is that Empson argues that there are predominant and subsidiary meanings and offers explanations for the persistent use of ambiguity in poems. In his view, in 'complicated situations', which are the natural territory of verse, 'unity is threatened'. In short, poems are mimetic, deliberately imitative of intellectual and emotional anxiety and indecision. What the critic should seek, in Empson's view, is a perception of the state of mind captured by the poem. Hartman's version of ambiguity is 'indeterminacy' (1980, p. 270):

> Indeterminacy does not merely *delay* the determination of meaning, that is, suspend premature judgements and allow greater thoughtfulness. The delay is not ... [merely] a device to slow the act of reading till we appreciate ... its complexity. The delay is intrinsic: from a certain point of view, it is thoughtfulness itself, Keats's 'negative capability', a labor that aims not to overcome the ... indeterminate but to stay within it as long as is necessary.

The reason for the enthusiastic annexation of deconstruction by a generation of US literary academics who had inherited the grand but rather untidy legacy of New Criticism is indicated in Hartman's term 'thoughtfulness itself'. He perceives poems, very conventionally, as the record or trace of a 'process' of mediation. All other discourses are shackled to the collateral objective of making sense of their subject or, at a more complex level, reaching some conclusion as to its state. Poetry, according to Hartman, 'labor[s] ... not to overcome the ... indeterminate' and we might note the parallels between Hartman's notion of indeterminacy and Empson's: 'In complicated situations ... unity is threatened; you are thinking of several things'.

The difference is evident in Empson's use of 'you'. Empson, like all non-poststructuralist critics, holds the poet to be the initiator and orchestrator of the various levels of meaning that operate within the text. Hartman perceives the poem as, like all texts, part of a chain of intertextual deferrals and interactions. The critic should not attempt to resolve the ambiguities and uncertainties of the poem or propose an answer to the questions raised by it; they should instead become one half of a dialogic relationship with the poem's irresolvable state of indeterminacy. The ideal is beguiling but the practice raises a number of problems and questions.

First of all, when we talk or write about poetry, we must recognize that our discourse will have a lot more in common with the structure of non-poetic texts (including novels and plays) than it will with poetry.

The densities of poetic form and language, the constant shifts between patterns of signification within the text, are effectively stratified and catalogued in critical writing. The simultaneous interactions in a poem between a rhyme scheme, a metaphor and the referential objective of the language are turned by criticism into a linear framework of casual relations: 'The rhyme reacts with the metaphor to create the effect of ...'. This raises a major problem for deconstruction, and one that has not been decisively resolved. Hartman (1980, p. 201) argues for a criticism which 'cross[es] the line' so that 'the perspectival power of criticism, the strength of recontextualization, must be such that the critical essay should not be considered a supplement to something else'. Recontextualization, criticism as a 'supplement' to the object text, involves the prioritization of the fact-finding, puzzle-solving impetus of ordinary discourse above the complexities and perversities of the text. Hartman's general point that such an opposition should be broken down is attractive, but he tends to ignore the practicalities of such an activity – particularly for poetry criticism. Unless we write criticism in a form that allows us some generic link with the poem – interrogating *Paradise Lost* in the blank verse and the idiomatic pattern shared by all its characters, or writing about Pope's verse in the heroic couplet manner of his own 'Essay on Criticism', for instance – we will always face the problem of translating parallels and simultaneities of form and effect into a linear, discursive framework.

In order to resolve the potentially unbridgeable divide between the theory of deconstruction and the more pragmatic activity of talking and writing about verse, we should fix upon the next two propositions that I shall attempt to validate: that poems are, by their nature, self-deconstructive. More significantly, I shall argue, against the grain of orthodox deconstructive thinking, that the poet is the conscious premeditated source of these acts of auto-deconstruction.

Deconstructionists contend that any attempt to naturalize or close down the shifting dynamic of the poem is but a hidebound falsification of what actually occurs in the text. In all of this, the poet is treated with sympathetic respect as the guileless artisan, someone as fascinated as the critic by the arbitrary relationship between signifiers, signifieds and the referent; neither, however, is able to exert control over this process either as its choreographer or decoder. With this in mind, consider the following passage from Wordsworth's 'Home at Grasmere' (i, 574–7):

> Dreamlike the blending of the whole
> Harmonious landscape, all along the shore
> The boundary lost, the line invisible
> That parts the image from reality.

An elementary naturalization or recontextualization of this would have Wordsworth causing the unambiguous notions of sky, sea and land to merge into a 'dreamlike whole', the 'line' of what was once the horizon becoming 'invisible' and, in the process, supplementing 'the real' with a numinous 'image'. This would correspond with a standard perception of the Romantic ideal of the natural world, as something possessed of a neo-mystical pantheistic significance. Having established this correspondence between the text and its apparent referent, we might begin to suspect that another pattern of signification is alive within the former. Specifically, 'the lost boundary' and the 'invisible line' that 'parts the image from reality' could also refer to a more literal strategy of reading the poem. If we choose to ignore completely the line endings and give more attention to the broader rhythmic sweep of the verse, key stylistic nuances disappear, such as the *contra-rejet* at 'whole/Harmonious', where the line oscillates between completion and progression: 'whole' is transmuted from what at first appears to be a noun – 'the whole' – to its more equivocal function as an adjective; 'whole Harmonious landscape'. In this respect, then, significant terms within the passage – 'blending', 'whole', 'shore', 'boundary' and 'line' particularly – move beyond their purely referential status, as providing nouns, verbs and connectives for Wordsworth's account of the landscape, to discharge a supplementary self-referential function: they are also 'about' the poem that contains them.

Few poems are as explicitly self-referential as this but at the same time Wordsworth is drawing attention to a feature of poetry that is endemic and definitive: the fact that we can read through the text to its apparent paraphrasable meaning while being aware that, in the process, we are doing a grave injustice both to the effects created and our encounters with them. Poems, through the double pattern, employ language to refer to things, events and sensations and simultaneously expose language as an arbitrary network of unfixed signifiers.

In *Of Grammatology* (1976, pp. 7–8), Derrida gives close attention to the materiality of language, particularly the relationship between speech and writing:

> The privilege of the *phonè* does not depend upon a choice that might have been avoided. It corresponds to a moment of *economy* (let us say the 'life' of 'history' or of 'being-as-self-relationship'). The system of 'hearing (understanding)-oneself speak' [*s'entendre parler*] through a phonic substance – which *presents itself* as the nonexterior, nonworldly and therefore nonemper-

ical or noncontingent signifier – has necessarily dominated the history of the world during an entire epoch ...

Speech, because it appears dependent upon a rational living presence as its source, suppresses any suspicion that the relationship between the signifier (the phoneme) and signified (the thought, idea or image) and eventually the referent is arbitrary. And here we should note the intriguing parallels between Derrida's observations and a rarely observed but endemic paradox involving poetry and interpretation. All pre-deconstructive criticism, by implication, privileges speech as the working principle for the pursuit of a conclusion regarding the poem's significance or meaning. Poetry has, of course, long been celebrated as a primarily aural medium, both in terms of its gestation and performance, and this mythology has been sustained in traditional verse by the pre-eminence of quasi-musical aspects of the double pattern – rhyme, metre, sound pattern and so on. What is rarely acknowledged is that the spoken poem, as a compositional imperative and a key aspect of appreciation and interpretation, is a falsehood. As Words-worth has shown, literally, the complex architecture of poetic design has barely a nominal connection with the ideal of what Derrida calls 's'entendre parler', that moment of apparent spontaneity when apprehension, sensation, ratiocination and linguistic expression are simultaneously fused. Famously, Coleridge accompanied his poem 'Kubla Khan' with a brief prose description of its compositional genesis: he claims that it is the record of a probably opium-induced dream, 'in which all the images rose up before [me] as *things* with a parallel production of the correspondent expressions, without any sensation or consciousness of effort'. On awakening, he wrote these down. On the one hand, Coleridge seems here to endorse Derrida's opinion that the mythology of speech as a guarantee of presence is a form of 'auto affection ... the suppression of difference'; in short, a delusional belief that prelinguistic experience can be made evident in spoken language. However, one only has to read the poem itself to encounter Coleridge deliberately undoing this premise in one of the most explicit, poetic, acts of auto-deconstruction. The poem is obsessively self-referential. It makes use of proper names from classical and Middle Eastern mythology (Kubla Khan, Alph, Xanadu, Mount Abora and so on) and less identifiable references to unnamed rivers, chasms, fountains, a pleasure dome and an Abyssinian maid. However, every tentative referential pointer to a world outside the poem is subsumed by a far more powerful internal network of alliterative, assonated and rhyming patterns linking virtually every noun phrase to another within the text, plus a fabric of conceits from which no clear notion of a tenor or grounding is detachable from the incessant shifts from one vehicle to another. For some, the sound of this short poem, when recited, might be mesmerizing but, in truth, it is the ultimate testament to poetry as writing. We do not need to peruse Coleridge's manuscripts to know that – contra his prose description – only an immensely complex, time-consuming operation with pen and paper, involving numerous revisions and planning, could have brought the poem to its final published form.

The distinction between speech and writing holds the key to a proper under-standing of the relationship between poetry and deconstruction.

The following, from *Of Grammatology* (1976, pp. 287–8), are Derrida's musings on how and why the practice of recording language has gone through many curious mutations:

> The furrow is the line, as the ploughman traces it: the road – *via rupta* – broken by the ploughshare ... How does the ploughman proceed? Economi-cally. Arrived at the end of the furrow, he does not return to the point of departure. He turns ox and plough around. And proceeds in the opposite direction ... Writing by the *turning of the ox – boustrophedon* – writing by furrows was a movement in linear and phonographic script. At the end of the line travelled from left to right, one resumes from right to left. Why was it abandoned at a given moment by the Greeks for example? Why did the economy of the writer (scripteur) break with that of the ploughman? Why is the space of one not the space of the other?

Derrida does not propose a solution to the question of why writing developed as an arbitrary, non-linear form, effectively detaching itself from the economies of speech. But consider this: the break at the end of each written line is consistent with the contemplative, premeditated nature of writing. When we write, we can stop at any point, correct what we were about to state, even abandon the script and begin again. Obviously, we do not discipline ourselves to allow for a period of revision and/or contemplation at exactly the point where the pen or the illuminated script reaches the right-hand margin of the page, or screen, but nonetheless one can discern a correlation between the mechanics of writing and its advantages over speech as a form that allows one to transcend the demands of immediacy and linear progression. However, as Derrida points out, the margins of the page and the field are merely routine and unavoidable phenomena, but the poet, both in traditional and free verse, chooses to stop, turn and begin again. This moment of control, of the intervention of the poet in the conventional routines of language, exemplifies a much broader range of opportunities in which the linear, referential function of language is counter-pointed against a more internalized fabric involving the use of the material of language in metre, sound pattern and the concrete structure of the line or the creation of tropes and conceits: the double pattern. One might, of course, treat my endorsement of the authorial power and autonomy of the poet as naive conservatism, but consider the following from an essay by one of the most eminent contemporary poets, Geoffrey Hill, on his own experience of writing (quoted in Griffiths, 1989):

> The true realisation of the poet's voice comes from a blending or a marriage of the silent and the spoken forms. If we put this into the shape of a figure of speech, if we conceived of the voice as it reads the poem as being on the

horizontal plane, and if we thought of the text on the page, as it were, going down vertically, then I think that the listener should follow the spoken poem in the way that a listener follows a string quartet with a score. I think only by being most keenly sensitive to that moment when the horizontal of the spoken voice comes into contact with the formalities, with the restraints, with the restrictions that are there printed in the text, only by recognising with immediate sensitivity those moments of contact, of harmony or of hostility, only then can the reader, the listener, truly appreciate how the poet's voice is being realised in the most minute, intimate, and yet profoundly rich, prosodic forms.

Hill, with great subtlety, refers here both to the literal processes of reading and writing – the movement of the eye and the placing of words across and down the page, devices of which Wordsworth, above, makes ample use – and also to the more complex, less easily quantifiable aspect of 'writing', the 'formalities ... restraints ... restrictions ... moments of contact, of harmony', the intrinsically poetic dimension of the double pattern. He compares the reader's awareness of this with the listener who follows a musical performance with 'the score' in hand and is thus able to note the complex interrelationship between the transient performance of the piece and its complex formal architecture. This is a perfect analogy for the way in which poetry transcends and encompasses the strict division between speech and writing and, more significantly, complicates the relationship between the text and the critic. The former is involved in what I call 'auto-deconstruction' – I prefer this term as an alternative to the more frequently used 'self-deconstruction', given that, in my view, this procedure involves the conscious volition of the poet – causing the process of naturalization to involve two trajectories, one involving an awareness of what the poem does, or appears to do, and the other demanding far more sensitivity to the unique capacities of the double pattern.

Consider our encounters in Chapter 2 with Donne's 'The Flea' and Williams' 'Spring and All'. For both we are required – or rather require ourselves – initially to conduct a very elementary naturalization involving a search for answers to such questions as: What is the poem's principle subject? What can we discern from the words about their apparent context (contemplative? spontaneous? and so on)? From such evidence, what impressions can we form of the speaker and their apparent state of mind or intention? Naturalizing poems at this very basic level is a necessity, an instinct: only from this primary knowledge or set of assumptions can we proceed to more complex and sophisticated conjectures. Initially, then, the poem falls into the same category as the opening page of a novel, a shopping list, an email, or a message on the telephone answering machine: for all, our first encounter coincides with an instinctive urge to make sense of the message. Next, however, our interpretative encounters with the poem diverge radically from those with any other non-poetic or non-literary statement or text. We begin to engage with the complex fabric of effects and devices that enable the poem to set up a tension between its poetic and non-poetic functions; the double pattern. Existing as we do in the realm of non-poetic, linear discourses, we will, sometimes despite ourselves, attempt to reconcile the errant, arbitrary potential of the former with the rational, problem-solving capacities of the latter. A deconstructive reading would involve an acknowledgement that the two dimensions are not reconcilable, they exist in a perpetually oscillating relationship with one another. How, then, do we conduct a deconstructive critical interpretation, given that deconstruction treats the very process of interpretation as inimical to the nature of the text? We must achieve, in critical discourse, a form of double reading that accommodates, rather than closes down, what actually occurs in the poem. In one respect, we will offer a self-consciously insufficient analysis of what the poem does, but in the process we must interrogate our own predatory interpretive acts, interrupt ourselves, even contradict our own trajectory of naturalization. In short, as we move towards an account of the poem's apparent meaning and objectives, we should remain alert to the fact that it continually eclipses, complicates or overrides such conclusions.

Orthodox criticism is involved in a prioritization of oppositions of the type that deconstructors attempt to unsettle – or rather to show how they unsettle themselves. Consider the following columns:

Criticism	Poetry
Linear discourse	Density and simultaneity
Meaning	Signification
Recontextualization	Indeterminacy
Interpretation	Puzzle
Facts	Effects
Writing	Speech

How can the necessary objectives and formal determinates of the left-hand column be made to accommodate rather than immobilize and impose order upon the shifting, kinetic elements of the right? This is the question that must be addressed in any deconstructive reading of poetry.

As we have seen, the material of language – its sounds and its appearance on the page – enables both the poet and the poem to transgress, even transcend, orthodox linguistic conventions, but figurative devices can also project the poem beyond non-poetic discourse to the comparable level of an aesthetic object that we can appreciate but never, in the interpretive sense, dominate. Craig Raine is variously acclaimed and disparaged as the inaugurator of a trend in 1970s British verse that came to be known as 'Martian' poetry, and the poem 'A Martian Sends a Postcard Home' (1979), from which the subgenre gained its title, offers a vivid exemplification of Martian technique:

> Caxtons are mechanical birds with many wings
> and some are treasured for their markings

they cause the ice to melt
or the body to shriek without pain.

I have never seen one fly, but
sometimes they perch on the hand.

The poem plays games with our routine, familiar linguistic registers. 'Caxton' is not a noun that we will previously have encountered, except of course as the surname of a specific individual, who invented the printing press. What are we to make of this generic brand of caxton – 'birds with many wings', 'treasured for their markings', which 'cause the ice to melt', the 'body to shriek without pain' but which, unlike their avian cousins, don't fly and only occasionally 'perch on the hand'. It is impossible to predict the point, or time, at which this grammatically correct, formally coherent but in every other respect oblique passage opens itself to a second level of meaning, but once a single clue is decoded, the rest follow in rapid order. Caxtons are books. Imagine what happens when you allow the pages of a book to spring open in a semi-circle, they do indeed resemble birds, and peacocks in particular come to mind. Like birds, they are treasured for the markings, specifically the words on their pages. Some 'cause the ice to melt' – bring joy or perhaps, more literally, prompt tears – and others make us laugh; shrieking without pain is a wonderfully vivid picture of laughter. Others, when read, will indeed be perched on our hand. One might also point out that there is nothing overly obtuse or mischievous in naming a thing or activity after a particular individual; vacuum cleaners are routinely referred to as Hoovers, the surname of the man who founded probably the most famous manufacturers of the machine. Similarly, we use the term 'Biro' as frequently as 'ballpoint pen' and rarely reflect on the fact that, like Hoover, the former is the title of a manufacturer, not the object itself. Routinely, particular, often iconic, objects are substituted for more general conditions: 'the crown' for the monarchy is one of the best known. As noted in Chapter 2, this is called 'metonymy', or what might be described as logical metaphor, in which one term already associated with another is substituted for it.

Once we have become attuned to Raine's persistent, incessant practice of figurative substitution, the clues become a little easier to uncover. 'Model T', we are told, is 'a room with the lock inside', a slightly puzzling juxtaposition of registers, or at least until we come upon the next image, the 'key'

Turned to free the world,
for movement

Suddenly we find a connection between Henry Ford's first mass-produced car and the routine habit of turning the ignition key. The 'world' outside the 'room' does indeed seem to move independently of the interior of the car. We appear to witness the stationary landscape suddenly brought into motion, 'so quick there is a film/to watch for anything missed'. The image of a wristwatch or clock in which time is imprisoned, ticking with impatience, is a small delight, but a little more puzzling is the 'haunted apparatus' that 'snores when you pick it up', 'cries' when we 'carry it' to our lips, 'soothe to sleep' with sounds and 'wake' with our 'finger'. The imagery is tactile and sensuous, and it is only gradually that we shake free of these mildly erotic registers and fix upon something, an activity, that is also habitual and commonplace. Aside from our partner, or children, the only physical object upon which we confer such prehensile attention is, we realize, the telephone. Raine continues with a reminder of our discomfort regarding the necessary act of defecation, for which we 'go to a punishment room', there to 'suffer ... alone', 'with water but nothing to eat'.

'No-one is exempt/and everyone's pain has a different smell'. The closing conceit brings us to night-time 'when all the colours die' and members of this curious species 'hide in pairs' to 'read about themselves –/in colour, with their eyelids shut'; a trenchant, thought-provoking juxtaposition of reading and dreaming, both of which involve an element of otherness and fantasy.

The conceit that the poem is authored by a person from another world, a 'Martian' become conversant and familiar with our linguistic customs but remaining unrehearsed in our incurious habits of thinking, naming and perception, is something more than intellectual exhibitionism on Raine's part. There is a subtext: the 'Martian' is in fact the archetypal poet, constantly re-examining, and causing us to re-examine, the means by which language filters or reflects familiar aspects of the world. Adjust this relationship, as does Raine, and although we understand the language at a basic cognitive level of knowing what the words and sentences mean, there is discordance between this register and our routine sense of the real and the actual. There is no evidence of Raine having read Derrida before writing this poem and even if there were the temptation, for some, to suggest that it drew upon the intellectual fabric of poststructuralism and deconstruction, this is invalidated by the simple fact that it owes its allegiance to a much older tradition, poetry. Poetry, as Raine shows, is the exemplification of what deconstruction can only postulate. Moreover, this poem preserves the status of the poet as the sole autonomous designer of effects which, deconstructionists contend, are the endowment of language itself. In it, Raine gives such meticulous and continuous attention to the transformative power of language that when we naturalize it, in effect paraphrase it, we all but destroy it. Metaphor is not only a device employed by Raine, it is both the subject and animus of the poem; when we explain the metaphor, we drain the poem of its energy and eradicate its substance as a work of art. The dilemma is best illustrated by the two columns listed above. The left-hand column is comprised of aspects of non-poetic discourse, in effect the foundation for any explanatory critical analysis. If we describe how Raine's, or rather his putative Martian's, figurative excursions operate, we will inevitably invoke the restraints and preconditions of the left-hand column; aka naturalization. We might also attempt to be sympathetic to the aberrant peculiarities of the work – its refusal to conform to the routine correlation between language and meaning – but what we must accept is that we cannot elucidate or document what actually happens when we read the poem. This experience involves a fluid, dynamic interaction between the two columns. It is something we experience but which is, by its nature, alien to the conventions of critical prose. This is what I mean by auto-deconstruction. We can witness, as we read the text, the process by which the poem deconstructs itself, and refuses to give total allegiance either to the left- or right-hand columns. We cannot, however, describe what we have experienced because critical discourse, even in its most unorthodox, radical state, will always be allied to the left-hand column.

Christopher Reid, a near contemporary of Raine, achieves a comparable, subtly nuanced effect in 'A Holiday from Strict Reality', which begins:

> Here we are at the bay
> of intoxicating discoveries,
> where mathematicians
> in bathing trunks ...

It is almost as though Reid has pondered I.A. Richards' classification of metaphor as made up of 'tenor' and 'vehicle' and decided that it was both inaccurate and authoritarian. In Wordsworth's famous line 'I wandered lonely as a cloud', the tenor is the apparent subject of the speaker walking through the field, conscious of his isolation, and comparing this state of loneliness with the impersonal disembodied image of the cloud, the vehicle. As Reid demonstrates, however, it is possible to unbalance this relationship. We might well be inclined to treat the tenor of this extended conceit as some faintly exotic location – the 'bay of intoxicating discoveries', a 'gilded paradise' littered with 'white yachts', and bohemians such as the 'beach bum/who lives under an old boat'; all gazed at from a lofty 'high glass balcony'. At the same time, these anchoring images of location, people and hedonistic languor become themselves the subject of a potentially more powerful theme: the topic of geometry and mathematics. We begin to wonder if the particulars of the holiday location are the background to a reflection on abstract spatial relationships or whether the latter are the predominant themes of the poem, with the 'set squares' of the 'white yachts', the 'angles' traced by speedboats and the 'decimal point' described by the 'restless volleyball' a richly illustrative background. In short, the speaker's priorities are unclear: is he someone with a temperamental predilection for mathematics and geometry whose psyche imposes this template upon an otherwise formless sequence of images or does he suddenly find that the randomness of the beach scene has acquired a mesmerizing structure of its own? It is the linguistic equivalent of those illustrations in which the central, white silhouette seems to resemble a vase, and at the same time it could equally represent the space between two identical profiles of human faces; the effect that it creates for the reader corresponds closely with that of the poems discussed above. We attempt to naturalize the poem because this procedure is an inevitable concomitant of our encounter with a text that differs radically from the routines of ordinary language; as we read it, we cannot help but try to make sense of it. Our problem is caused by its constant changes in emphasis from context to predominant topic, and vice versa, and the recovery process, the technique of recontextualization, is continually skewed.

   The question of how we might deconstruct a poem such as this, or for that matter those of Wordsworth and Raine, is based upon a fallacy. Deconstruction is what we experience or witness, not what we do, which leaves us with the practical problem of how we deal in language – particularly if we are writing an essay or article – with something that is immune from the descriptive logic of the left-hand column. It must be acknowledged that the process being undertaken – criticism – is insufficient, a falsification of a complex shifting panorama of effects that, by their nature, defy the delineative preconditions of explication. Moreover, the process must be supplemented by what amounts to an appendix, a self-conscious commentary upon the features of the poem that variously elude or defy critical analysis. In short, deconstructive criticism must involve a double perspective, one which picks over and explains the workings of the text and another as a commentary upon this procedure, a reminder that what is being stated diverges from the complex dynamic of the double pattern, the unpredictable interplay between the left- and right-hand columns, which we experience as readers but can never accurately record.

   'Deconstruction' is a term widely misunderstood because of its frequent misuse. 'Deconstruct' is not an active verb and the procedure of deconstruction is not something purposively undertaken by the critic in the manner that, say, a New Historicist or a feminist critic would bring to the poem an analytical or ideological framework of interpretation. Deconstruction is, so deconstructionists contend, a generic feature of all linguistic acts and texts. Everything we write or speak contains the seeds of its own deconstructive dissolution, it is not something that has to be provoked or perpetrated by an external agent. I would contend that this is a valid thesis, with one exception. Poetry is the only discourse that involves two separate linguistic registers simultaneously, registers that can coexist within the text but which are divided by their allegiance, respectively, to the purely poetic function – arbitrary features of language with no standard role in the clarification or production of meaning – and to the non-poetic register with which the poem must engage in order to make some basic claim upon comprehensibility – fundamentally the conventions of semantics and syntax. In this respect, poetry is not like other discourses, self-deconstructive; instead, it enables the poet to perplex the reader by refusing to allow the text to affiliate exclusively either to self-reference or the discharge of paraphrasable meaning. It borrows from the material shared by all other discourses but disposes this material in a manner that guarantees self-determination. The poet and the poem cooperate in a unique form of auto-deconstruction.

To summarize, deconstruction is less a technique of analysis than a focus for the vast number of questions that have attended poetry criticism over the past century. Most significantly, we are obliged to acknowledge that the various forms of naturalization devised and proposed by earlier critics are, by degrees, tangential and inadequate formulae for describing what happens when we read poems. The simple answer to the putative question 'how do I deconstruct this poem?' is that you do not. You show how the poem deconstructs itself. The double pattern is the definitive characteristic of poetry and if you refer to the two columns given earlier, it is evident that criticism has more in common with the non-poetic features of the double pattern than those which are specific to verse. To demonstrate how the poet makes use of the poem as a self-deconstructive act, you must pay specific attention to the dynamic of resistance between these two elements, the extent to which the linguistic structure of the text itself interferes with its apparent or avowed referential function. Most significantly, you must acknowledge and comment upon the fissure between your own discourse and that of the poem; address but do not reach conclusions on those parts of the poem that have obtained a condition of autonomy through their shifts between the two columns, the two dimensions of the double pattern.

Where, then, does this leave the reader and the critic? With regard to the former, I would argue that auto-deconstruction is the factor that has secured our, albeit perplexed, fascination with poetry since it was first produced. It draws us into a hinterland beyond the orthodox realm of purposive, rational linguistic functions, a zone in which words still generate meaning but are also licensed to operate as objects, like pieces of sculpture or aspects of a painting, or to interact in a manner that prompts us to witness or simply enjoy the processes of signification rather than to clarify or decode the message.

For the critic, burdened with the task of describing this dynamic subjective experience, problems seem to abound, and so they should. The critic, with regard to the auto-deconstructive aspect of verse, must offer some record of the poet's and the poem's shifts in allegiance, from the text itself to the world and the network of discourses beyond it. No final conclusions can be sought – as deconstructionists correctly aver, this alters the status of the poem to that of, say, the enigmatic treatise on philosophy – but what should be pursued are questions regarding the poet's competence, motivation, perhaps even pure brilliance as they shift between the two levels of the double pattern. This will be the subject of Chapter 16, a sphere of critical analysis rarely if ever acknowledged let alone scrutinized: evaluation. In short: is the poem, or the poet, any good?

14

Gender

The following is Andrew Marvell's 'To his Coy Mistress', a poem published in 1681, but thought to have been written in the 1650s:

> Had we but world enough, and time,
> This coyness, Lady, were no crime.
> We would sit down, and think which way
> To walk, and pass our long love's day.
> Thou by the Indian Ganges' side
> Shouldst rubies find: I by the tide
> Of Humber would complain, I would
> Love you ten years before the Flood:
> And you should, if you please, refuse
> Till the conversion of the Jews.
> My vegetable love should grow
> Vaster than empires, and more slow.
> An hundred years should go to praise
> Thine eyes, and on thy forehead gaze.
> Two hundred to adore each breast:
> But thirty thousand to the rest;
> An age at least to every part,
> And the last age should show your heart;
> For, Lady, you deserve this state,
> Nor would I love at lower rate.
>   But at my back I always hear
> Time's wingèd chariot hurrying near;
> And yonder all before us lie
> Deserts of vast eternity.
> Thy beauty shall no more be found,
> Nor, in thy marble vault, shall sound
> My echoing song: then worms shall try
> That long preserved virginity,
> And your quaint honour turn to dust,
> And into ashes all my lust:
> The grave's a fine and private place,

But none, I think, do there embrace.
          Now therefore, while the youthful hue
Sits on thy skin like morning dew,
And while thy willing soul transpires
At every pore with instant fires,
Now let us sport us while we may,
And now, like amorous birds of prey,
Rather at once our time devour
Than languish in this slow-chapt power.
Let us roll all our strength and all
Our sweetness up into one ball,
And tear our pleasures with rough strife
Thorough the iron gates of life:
Thus, though we cannot make our sun
Stand still, yet we will make him run.

To describe what happens when we read this poem, we must consider the way in which its style affects its meaning. It is written in octosyllablic couplets, and the relationship between metre, rhyme scheme and syntax is rather more relaxed and unpredictable than in the later couplet poems of the Restoration and 18th century. There is no continuous pattern that governs the relation between the structure of the couplet and the disposition of noun and verb phrases. The two syntactic units of lines 5–7 involve an identical framework of subject, object and verb, but these do not run parallel with the structure of each couplet:

Thou by the Indian Ganges' side
Shouldst rubies find: I by the tide
Of Humber would complain.

Throughout the poem there is a tension between two stylistic registers. The metrical pattern is a repetitive feature of the text that inscribes it within a tradition of literary conventions and practices. But the syntax pulls against this impersonal, arbitrary scheme, embodies the hesitations, thoughts and idiosyncrasies of a specific speaking voice and links the text with the non-literary sphere of dialogue.

The opening lines suggest a condition of immediacy and improvisation, of an utterance generated by the particular experience of the speaker and listener. The subject is '*this* coyness', not the general problem of coyness or a particular memory or hypothesis, but the hearer's apparent reluctance to submit to the speaker's sexual advances at this moment. When we consider the latter's rhetorical strategy, this sense of immediacy and urgency becomes even more apparent. The mood and the syntactic character of the first paragraph is conditional and speculative. The metaphoric excursions are fantastic: her body and his contemplation of it – both invoking the ephemeral nature of mortal existence and sensual pleasure – are transformed into almost limitless expanses of space and time. The second paragraph maintains the extravagant figurative tone, but changes from the conditional to the specific and possessive mood: 'my back', 'before us lie', 'Thy beauty', 'your quaint honour', 'my lust'. The third paragraph confirms a much-debated feature of the text. Its organization into three premises follows the formula of the philosophical syllogism: there is this, and there is that; therefore there must be ... . Again we find that the speaker combines a device drawn from the non-literary sphere of scholastic philosophy with a pattern of overtly poetic conventions.

So far, I have emphasized the stylistic features that enable us to consider the effect of the poem and to identify its context. Let us now shift the emphasis further towards this imagined contextual situation. The hearer is undoubtedly female: how does this affect our status as critics and readers? Thus far, my observations about the stylistic devices of metre, metaphor, structural organization and contextual positioning have been impartial and objective, but it becomes difficult to maintain this approach when we consider the effects of these upon the hearer. The only mental or emotional attribute conceded to her is her apparent inclination to coyness. Every other verbal, adjectival or nominal feature is physical. The pseudo-religious concept of purity and 'virginity' preserved beyond mortal existence is compromised by an image of physical violation: 'then worms shall try/That long preserved virginity'. And the concept of her eternal 'honour' is similarly tainted by a familiar contemporary pun: 'quaint' was frequently substituted for 'cunt'. The speaker's ingenious rhetorical strategy rests upon the assumption that the woman is a person whose sense of identity is a function of her physical attractiveness. In the first paragraph, the speaker raises the tantalizing possibility that this might be preserved beyond the normal span of human existence, and in the second, he presents her with the disagreeable fact that it cannot. The entire text confirms and sustains the most extreme version of ascribed gender roles and it opens up a whole range of perspectives on the relation between literary style and the representation of gender.

Consider the following riddle:

In a motorway accident a man is killed and his son severely injured. The boy is rushed to a casualty ward and the unit's most eminent specialist in the treatment of physical trauma is summoned. The surgeon arrives with a retinue of assistants, hesitates and explains, 'I can't operate on him. He's my son.'

Not all listeners find this puzzling, but many admit to a slight feeling of shock at the surgeon's disclosure. Prior to her statement, the surgeon is an ungendered subject, but many listeners admit that they naturalize this figure – eminent, active, dominant, involved in the stark physicality of life and death – as male.

Now let us consider what the writing of regular poetry requires. It involves the ability to coerce an unlimited range of linguistic and referential registers into an arbitrary pattern of metrical rules and conventions. The control exerted by

Marvell's speaker over his stylistic material (and, it is implied, over the listener) is explicitly related to maleness. But even if the topic and the speaking present of the poem are ungendered (which is usually the case), intellectual control is a significant feature of the act of writing. Just as we frequently associate the role of the heroic figure who cuts, binds and repairs the human body with notions of maleness, so we might similarly assume that an anonymous presence who displays an aggressive, confident control of two linguistic registers is a man.

Virginia Woolf, in addressing the question of why there are more pre-20th-century women novelists than poets, claimed in *A Room of One's Own* (1929) that 'the novel alone was young enough to be soft in [their] hands' (quoted in Eagleton, 1986, p. 7). In short, the 18th- and 19th-century novel was exploring and establishing its own stylistic conventions; it was 'young' enough to maintain a distance from a male-dominated cultural heritage. In *The Madwoman in the Attic* (1979), Sandra Gilbert and Susan Gubar qualify this thesis with a practical consideration: women, if they were to write at all, would by the late 18th century have been more likely to generate a professional income from the sale of novels than from the publication of poems. But they also agree that women poets faced the intimidating prospect of participating in a stylistic field whose registers and cultural associations were predominantly male.

Gilbert and Gubar (cited in Eagleton, 1986, p. 110) refer to the historically and theologically sanctioned association of 'the poetic passion' with mysterious inspiration, divine afflatus and bardic ritual – an aesthetic manifestation of the priesthood: 'But if in Western culture women cannot be priests, then how – since poets are priests – can they be poets?' But the most influential determinant of the genre/gender relationship is stylistic:

Finally, and perhaps most crucially, where the novel allows – even encourages – just the self-effacing withdrawal society has traditionally fostered in women, the lyric poem is in some sense the utterance of a strong, assertive 'I'. Artists from Shakespeare to Dickinson, Yeats and T.S. Eliot have of course qualified this 'I' emphasizing, as Eliot does, the 'extinction of personality' involved in a poet's construction of an artful mask-like persona, or insisting, as Dickinson did, that the speaker of poems is a 'supposed person'. But, nevertheless, the central self that speaks or sings a poem must be forcefully defined, whether 'she' or 'he' is real or imaginary. If the novelist, therefore, inevitably sees herself from the *outside*, as an object, a character, a small figure in a large pattern, the lyric poet must be continually aware of herself from the inside, as a subject, a speaker: she must be, that is, assertive, authoritative, radiant with powerful feelings while at the same time absorbed in her own consciousness – and hence, by definition, profoundly 'unwomanly', even freakish. (Gilbert and Gubar, 1979, cited in Eagleton, 1986, p. 111)

Gilbert and Gubar present us with a new and intriguing perspective on Jakobson's theory of the poetic function. Jakobson argues that there is a constant, irreconcilable ambiguity between the textual addresser and their contextually determined counterpart, but that they share the imperative of projecting the speaking voice into the impersonal network of poetic conventions and devices. Gilbert and Gubar show that this same act of projecting is an aesthetic manifestation of the traditionally prescribed role of the male in a variety of linguistic and social functions, a role that is 'profoundly "unwomanly"'.

Let us now consider how this concept of gender/genre relations relates to a number of issues already considered in our examination of poetry and literary history. The part played by the woman in the 17th-century amatory lyric is straightforward. She might feature as an embodied correlative for the contextual detail of the text or as the inspiration for some of its metaphoric excursions. Inevitably, she will remain silent. In drama, where the female can answer back, her function is usually marginalized by an imposing complex of contextual elements. We have already noted in Chapter 3 that Isabella in *Measure for Measure* becomes more a functionary of the text than, like her male counterparts, an arbiter in the shifting relations between style and meaning. Her brief one-to-one exchange with Angelo in which they battle over the true meaning of that elusive signified, justice, is rapidly exchanged for her role as an exploitable and transformable signifier: the Duke, rather like Marvell's speaker, plays a textual game with her physical presence. A similar function is played out by Portia in *The Merchant of Venice*. She operates as an active linguistic and physical presence only in the world of Belmont, a world safely detached from the unreliable signifiers of Venice. She does, of course, transform and reinterpret the plot and its moral/judicial underpinnings, but she does so as a man. One might even compliment Shakespeare for his prescient analogue of the woman writer in the 18th and 19th centuries: Belmont and Isabella's convent, as Gilbert and Gubar (cited in Eagleton, 1986, p. 111) write of the novel, 'allows – even encourages – just the self-effacing withdrawal society has traditionally fostered in women'; while 'the utterance of a strong, assertive "I"' in the lyric poem, or in society, is left to the man in Venice, or the woman disguised as a man.

In 'Patriarchal Poetry and Women Readers' (1978), Sandra Gilbert discusses the immense power that Milton's *Paradise Lost* has exercised upon women readers and, consequently, women writers. Milton had effectively appropriated the originary archetype of male and female roles and reconstructed this as a literary text. One element of this monolithic influence that Gilbert only touches on is Milton's presentation of a causal relation between gender and genre. Throughout *Paradise Lost*, Eve dutifully obeys the rules that would determine the position of women in the postlapsarian, Western world. Adam functions as her adviser. She is never present during the lengthy dialogues between her partner and the advisory angel, Raphael. The wisdom of these exchanges is transmitted to her, later, by Adam. Her moment of independence, her chance to explore her much-vaunted gift of reason and, more significantly, to test the relation between language and the ultimate truth (that is, what exactly is meant by the rule of obedience?), comes in her exchange with Satan. During this dialogue, she is partly persuaded and partly persuades herself that eating the fruit is part of God's hidden plan. The result of this, as Christianity continually reminds us, is the Fall.

Some years earlier, in *Comus* (*A Mask Presented at Ludlow Castle*), Milton had enacted a very similar exchange between 'the Lady' and the eponymous demon, Comus. And one suspects that the Lady's response to Comus is a thinly disguised sermon to our universal mother and her female descendants. Comus attempts to persuade her to have sex with him and he employs the strategies of wit and metaphoric play that feature in the amatory lyric. The Lady replies:

> I had not thought to have unlocked my lips   (756)
> In this unhallowed air, but that this juggler
> Would think to charm my judgement, as mine eyes,
> Obtruding false rules pranked in reason's garb.
>
> ...
>
> Thou hast nor ear nor soul to apprehend   (784)
> The sublime notion and high mystery
> That must be uttered to unfold the sage
> And serious doctrine of Virginity
>
> ...
>
> Enjoy your dear wit and gay rhetoric   (790)
> That hath so well been taught her dazzling fence;
> Thou art not fit to hear thyself convinced.

Milton, through his character, is the spokesman for the silent (or in Shakespeare's case, silenced) Lady of Renaissance literature. Poetry, Milton concedes, is 'false rules pranked in reason's garb'. It has nothing to do with the disclosure or projection of such sublime notions and high mysteries as the 'serious doctrine of Virginity' (with half an eye on Isabella) – and this passage looks forward to Eve's enthusiastic participation with Satan in an outright festival of reason-twisting and poetic double-dealing, their subject being the will of God and the high mystery of the future of mankind.

There were a number, albeit a small number, of notable women poets of the Renaissance, particularly in the 17th century. They did indeed unlock their lips in that unhallowed air, but having ventured beyond the Lady's self-imposed state of silence, they faced an unwelcoming fabric of conventions. The seemingly unaffiliated lexicon of metrical forms and rhetorical devices was, in truth, shaped according to a masculine role and state of mind. Consider, for example, Katherine Philips' lengthy sequence 'Friendship's Mystery, To My Dearest *Lucasia*'. The scholarly consensus has it that the eponymous Lucasia was based on Philips' friend Anne Owen, while the speaker, carrying the assumed name Orinda, is Philips herself. This biographical resonance is intriguing and unproblematic but irrespective of whether Lucasia and Orinda were precise reflections of their actual counterparts, what becomes most evident throughout the poem is a mood of claustrophobic interiority. Certainly, the speaker, Philips/Orinda, has an impressive command of her medium. She deals adeptly with the complex stanzaic formulae that alter with each thematically governed sequence and her conceits are as inventive yet as unostentatious as those of any of her male peers. However, this mastery of technique is matched by an apparent and unexplained unwillingness to move beyond a single subject, which, it soon becomes apparent, is the self-confining interdependency of the two figures. The following stanza

> I did not live until this time
>   Crown'd my felicity,
> When I could say without a crime,
>   I am not thine, but Thee.

could stand as the mantra for the entire poem. It would be too easy to read the sequence as a tribute to the sublime intimacy of a special friendship, because when one looks closely at its frame of reference one is struck by an unsettling sense of confinement. The two figures have, in effect, become the totality of their respective universes. One is aware that if either were male, then other trajectories of experience and speculation would be explored. But having established their gender, they have also imposed upon themselves, in the poem itself, a range of inhibitions and restrictions comparable to those that obtain for women in the world beyond the text.

Lady Mary Wroth, in her sonnet sequence 'From Pamphilia to Amphilanthus', attempts the very exercise in gender reversal that Philips and indeed all her female peers eschew. The sonnets, characteristically, explore the cornucopia of affections, impulses and obligations that attends the notion of human love. The opportunities to overturn routine expectations are immense, given that the speaker, as technically adept as Philips, is a woman and the listener is a man but what occurs is that the former seems bound by some tacit obligation never to address the latter directly. They become enthralled in a dance of third-person inhibition where 'one' is substituted for the powerful, subjective 'I' and 'He' substituted for such peremptory forms as 'you'. The daring hypothesis of a woman directly, uninterruptedly addressing a man is distilled into a far less presumptuous exchange of asexual abstractions on the general nature of love, desire and commitment.

The figure who most closely resembles Milton's Lady, in her verse, is Margaret Cavendish. Her brief, eight-line piece 'The Claspe' might, at a cursory reading, be taken for a complaint against the rigours and demands of formal poetic design:

> Give *Mee* the *Free*, and *Nobel Stile*,
> Which seems *uncurb'd*, though it be *wild*:
> Though *It* runs wild about, *It* cares not where;
> *It* shewes more *Courage*, then *It* doth of *Feare*,
> Give me a *Stile* that *Nature* frames, not *Art*;
> For *Art* doth seem to take the *Pedants* part.
> And that seemes, *Noble*, which is *Easie*, *Free*,
> Not to be bound with ore-nice *Pedantry*.

But the title sews an ambiguity into such an interpretation. At the time, a Claspe referred both to the ligature that fastened or closed a book – an appropriate image for a complaint against the strictures of poetic writing – and also to an embrace, generally of a woman by a man. The latter seasons the speaker's general deprecations with something far more particular; specifically, the ownership and governance of poetic convention by men and its use as a means of subjugating the woman as the object of poetic discourse.

Cavendish's 'The Common Fate of Books' is an intriguing, complex poem:

> The *worst Fate Bookes* have, when they are once read,
> They're laid aside, forgotten like the *Dead*:
> Under a heap of *dust* they buried lye,
> Within a *vault* of some small *Library*.
>
> But *Spiders* they, for honour of that *Art*
> Of *Spinning*, which by *Nature* they were taught;
> Since *Men* doe spin their *Writings* from the *Braine*,
> Striving to make a lasting *Web* of *Fame*,
> Of *Cobwebs* thin, *high Altars* doe they raise,
> There offer *Flyes*, as sacrifice of *praise*.

The 'Men' of line seven could, of course, refer to all poets, irrespective of gender, but one suspects that Cavendish's sprawling conceit of the cobweb of 'spin', or rhetoric, designed variously to enthral and persuade the listener and promote the self-esteem of the writer, is targeted in much the same way as the Lady's accusation that her seducer 'would charm my judgment ... Obtruding false rules pranked in reason's garb' in Milton's *Comus*.

Cavendish – who was an aristocratic lady, the Duchess of Newcastle-upon-Tyne – elects, unlike her invented counterpart, to enter the male-dominated discourse, and navigates its testing, formal currents with self-evident skill, but she remains, like Philips and Wroth, obliged to observe and meditate upon rather than command her poems.

There is a common thread running through all these encounters between gender and genre, and it confirms the bizarre and paradoxical relation between poetry and the 'real world' reflected and enacted in non-literary discourses. On the one hand, poetry, particularly during the Renaissance, is perceived as standing at the head of the aristocracy of literary and non-literary genres – and its use by Shakespeare as the medium in drama for the conditions of ambition, executive governance and existential responsibility confirms this association of authority with high art. Consequently, poetry, alongside the positions of power and dominance that it supports and mediates, is considered to be an unwomanly activity. On the other hand, poetry is, as Milton suggests, capable of exposing and foregrounding the anarchic relationship between truth and fabrication, capable of showing that the notions of moral, philosophic and religious certainty that underlie social structure are friable constructions of language. This also is an activity thought to be too subversive, too dangerously liberating in its control of the signifier above the signified, to be appropriate to the prescribed roles and activities of women.

During the Restoration and the 18th century, as poetry shifted from a marginal recreation and activity undertaken largely by the gentry to a more public, discursive role, so there was an increase, although still very slight, in the number of women participants. As described above, the Augustan poem, as the equivalent of a versified essay or polemic, involved a far more mechanical and impersonal stylistic register than had obtained during the Renaissance. Despite this, however, women poets continued to struggle against their prescribed status as subject rather than precipitator of the discourse. Hetty Wright, for example, displays a competent enthusiasm for the vituperative resources of the couplet in her 'Wedlock. A Satire' (1725):

> Thou tyrant, whom I will not name,
> Whom heaven and hell alike disclaim;
> Abhorred and shunned, for different ends,
> By angels, Jesuits, beasts and fiends!
> What terms to curse thee shall I find,
> Thou plague peculiar to mankind?
> O may my verse excel in spite
> The wiliest, wittiest imps of night!
> Then lend me for a while your rage,
> You maidens old and matrons sage:
> So may my terms in railing seem
> As vile and hateful as my theme.
> External foe to soft desires,
> Inflamer of forbidden fires,
> Thou source of discord, pain and care,
> Thou sure forerunner of despair,
> Thou scorpion with a double face,
> Thou lawful plague of human race,
> Thou bane of freedom, ease and mirth,
> Thou deep damnation upon earth,
> Thou serpent which the angels fly,
> Thou monster whom the beasts defy,
> Whom wily Jesuits sneer at too;
> And Satan (let him have his due)
> Was never so confirmed a dunce
> To risk damnation more than once.
> That wretch, if such a wretch there be,
> Who hopes for happiness from thee,
> May search successfully as well
> For truth in whores and ease in hell.

It is difficult to judge this as either an unfocused diatribe or an immensely astute example of rhetorical doubling. I would venture that the latter interpretation is just, with the corollary that Wright's guile is an enforced obligation. Ostensibly, the target of her satirical bile is, as her title indicates, the institution of marriage but it is significant that in the poem itself this state is never mentioned. Should we assume that the embodied, male, subject is marriage ('Thou tyrant who I will not name') or is it something more specific; the endemic and loathsome condition of maleness that causes marriage to be unendurable?

Ambiguity of the sort that informed many Renaissance lyrics, in which a sense of indecision or psychological ambivalence vied with the deployment of formal devices, was largely expunged from mainstream Augustan writing. Wright, while maintaining the prevailing stylistic mannerisms of her period, also challenges their ideological underpinnings. Significantly, she turns the piece into an infuriating – for men – interpretative maze, a web of possibilities overseen by herself but designed to entrap or mislead the reader who brings with him orthodox, predominantly masculine, expectations.

Other women poets of the era were indulged as bright intelligences, much like the restless schemers of Restoration comedy, but with the implicit proviso that they decried prevailing custom only according to the conventions designed by those who maintained it. Sarah Fyge Egerton's 'The Emulation' begins:

> Say, tyrant custom, why must we obey
> The impositions of thy haughty sway?
> From the first dawn of life until the grave,
> Poor womankind's in every state a slave,
> The nurse, the mistress, parent and the swain,
> For love she must, there's none escape that pain.
> Then comes the last, the final slavery:
> The husband with insulting tyranny
> Can have ill manner justified by law,
> For men all join to keep the wife in awe.

The litany of complaints is assiduously and competently recorded with man, men, ascribed unambiguously the role of oppressor. At the same time, however, the petition is hollowed by its correctness. Egerton plays the role of the disputatious, indeed talented poetess, and few, if any, would dispute the validity of her case, yet by presenting it in a manner that replicates the style of her male peers, she becomes as much the subject of the poem as its originator, a construct of devices governed by a patriarchy. Egerton represented the standard retinue of 18th-century women poets. The few exceptions, such as Wright, stood out in their ability to at once command and undermine the prevailing conventions of verse. Wright's closest counterpart is Anne Finch, Countess of Winchilsea, probably the best-known woman poet of the late 17th and early 18th centuries. She addresses three male poets:

Happy you three! Happy the Race of Men!
Born to inform or to correct the Pen
To proffitts, pleasures, freedom and command
Whilst we beside you but as Cyphers stand
T'increase your Numbers and to swell th'account
Of your delights which from our charms amount
And sadly are by this distinction taught
That since the Fall (by our seducement wrought)
Ours is the greater losse as ours the greater fault.

This passage operates at two levels. It is an informed, sardonic reflection on the perceived relation between women and writing, and it confirms the argument that style can at once mediate and transform its topic. Finch comments on how women can feature as the subjects but not the producers of poetic discourse, a role established by the original part played by Eve.

Given that it was written in the early 18th century, the manner of the passage is radical and disobedient. The closed couplet, an institution of 18th-century poetic style, is used by Finch as a means of disrupting rather than, in Popeian terms, sustaining and specifying the subject of the piece. The couplets and lines ending as 'Pen' and 'stand' could close their syntactic units, but we are led forward into dependent subclauses: the syntax seems to have completed its specification of sense, yet moves forward to elaborate on the point already made. This sense of ambiguity is paralleled by the constant shifts in the semantic centre of gravity between three themes: the image of wealth and acquisition, the activity of writing and the act of sexual dominance. Each of the principal noun and verb phrases resonates with a semantic trace that unsettles its apparent meaning. In the third line, for example, the word 'proffitts' carries forward a residual sense of the benefits of writing (to profit by informing or correcting the activities of the 'Pen'), a nuance that will be transformed into a pattern of financial images: 'Cyphers', 'Numbers', 'swell th'account', 'amount'. The three conditions of 'pleasures, freedom and command' are similarly dispersed through several subsequent registers of meaning. There are the 'pleasures, freedom and command' of writing about women, the 'Cyphers' (subjects) of poems whose 'Numbers' (a contemporary term denoting measure and syllabic length) will as a consequence 'increase' and 'swell'. Carried along with this pattern are images of sexual pleasure: women are 'Cyphers', child-bearers who increase the dynastic 'Numbers', and they are also the source of more straight-forward sexual 'delights', a noun surrounded by the phallic double entendres of 'increase', 'swell' and 'amount'.

The word that at once synthesizes and disrupts these various layers of form and meaning is 'Pen'. Feminist and non-feminist critics have often remarked, sometimes farcically, upon the drift between the semantic and circumstantial connotations of 'pen' and 'penis', and Finch would indeed seem to have created an intriguing interplay of text and context: it rhymes with men; it features as a vital instrument in the activities of financial gain and poetic endeavour; and its function in the pattern of sexual and procreative images seems clear enough.

Finch's stylistic achievements in this short passage are considerable. She creates a multilayered polyphonic text, reminiscent of the radical interplay of form and signification in Metaphysical verse, combining a method and an effect that ran against the dominant mood of Augustan writing. In an important sense, she set a standard that would be followed by a large number of women writers.

Mary Jacobus (1979, p. 12) claims that in

> the [patriarchal] theoretical scheme, femininity itself – heterogeneity, Otherness – becomes the repressed term by which discourse is made possible. The feminine takes its place with the absence, silence or incoherence that discourse represses.

By 'the repressed term by which discourse is made possible', Jacobus means that the norms, conventions and habits that govern communication effectively appropriate femaleness as a subject. Women are, of course, allowed to participate in conversation, even to write, but since male expectations and perceptions determine the manner and function of speech and writing, the woman becomes rather like a figure in a painting, a participatory element of the overall message but dispossessed of any active role in its formulation. This role emerges clearly enough in the silencing, appropriation and marginalization of the female subject in the above examples from Shakespeare, Milton and Marvell. The Lady, despite her individuality and intelligence, can only counter Comus's discourse with silence. Both he and she know that if she were to enter the discourse, she would become its subject, as did the similarly individualistic Isabella in *Measure for Measure*. Finch escapes these conditions of 'absence, silence and incoherence' not by refusing to participate in the prescriptive codes of poetic discourse but by creating continuous parallels between her own self-conscious exploration of femaleness and her disruptions of the governing conventions of 18th-century poetic form. Finch's achievement is more clearly specified by Hélène Cixous (1981, pp. 249, 258):

> A feminine text cannot fail to be more than subversive. It is volcanic ... If she's a her-she, it's in order to smash everything, to shatter the framework of institutions, to blow up the law, to shatter the 'truth' with laughter.

Jacobus contends that literary writing is complicit with the network of non-literary discourses in reflecting and maintaining the repressed condition of women in society. Cixous argues that the only strategy available to the woman writer is subversion and experiment, an unshackling of the literary code from its more deeply entrenched counterparts in non-literary discourse. A common feature of the work of many of the greatest women writers is a deliberate alteration of the familiar relationship between the two dimensions of the double pattern – those elements of the text which announce its stylistic allegiance to literary writing, and those features which maintain its relationship with non-literary, referential discourse.

Finch's message contains, even in the 18th century, a very familiar complaint against cultural patriarchy, but what distinguishes and strengthens her poetry is her ability to combine this paraphrasable element with a skilful and sardonic reworking of those stylistic conventions that constitute the predominantly male discourse of poetry.

The 19th-century poet Elizabeth Barrett Browning's *Sonnets from the Portuguese* invoke Shakespeare's use of the form as a sequence of staging posts in a meditative fugue in which each sonnet rehearses or offers a new perspective on a related fabric of concerns. Its predominant subject is her relationship with a man, never named but based, one assumes, upon Robert Browning. The most persistent and slightly unnerving feature of this lengthy piece is the subjugation of the speaker's, Barrett Browning's, first person 'I' either to the actual presence of her lover or to the locative elements of a world that she perceives but which seem to be variously reflective of or choreographed by him. This is Sonnet XXIX:

> I think of thee! – my thoughts do twine and bud
> About thee, as wild vines, about a tree,
> Put out broad leaves, and soon there's nought to see
> Except the straggling green which hides the wood.
> Yet, O my palm-tree, be it understood
> I will not have my thoughts instead of thee
> Who are dearer, better! Rather, instantly
> Renew thy presence; as a strong tree should,
> Rustle thy boughs and set thy trunk all bare,
> And let these bands of greenery which insphere thee
> Drop heavily down, – burst, shattered, everywhere!
> Because, in this deep joy to see and hear thee
> And breathe within thy shadow a new air,
> I do not think of thee – I am too near thee.

We will never know if the progress of this figurative image – she as the vines, he the tree – was calculated or directed by unforeseeable spontaneous promptings. It is clear, however, that what appears to be a metaphor dominated by the presence of the woman speaker is suddenly dismantled and treated with apologetic discretion. The initial configuration of herself as the vine and her lover as the tree replicates the conventional allocation of male and female roles; the solid, dependable presence and its dependent, friable attachment. Then, it is almost as if the speaker is allowing her imaginative faculties to transgress convention – her growth appears, literally, to smother him – and feels obliged to curtail the development of this image, to strip away her 'bands of greenery' from his 'boughs'. Indeed, the lines in which she disperses her own presence are hurried, stylistically clumsy:

> And let these bands of greenery which insphere thee
> Drop heavily down, – burst, shattered, everywhere!

It seems inappropriate for something so self-evidently flimsy ('straggling green') to 'Drop *heavily* down', and her description of its contact with the ground as causing it to 'burst, shattered, everywhere!' makes one suspect that the speaker has lost control of the metaphor; the terms seem more appropriate to the dropping of a vase rather than the delicate cascading of vines.

It is difficult to decide how to interpret and, indeed, evaluate this poem. It is almost certain that the effect of impressionistic uncertainty is calculated. One could, perhaps, imagine someone speaking directly to their lover, unrehearsed, or even writing them a letter and finding themselves swamped by unwitting, unforeseen and unwarrantable imaginings and then, hesitantly and almost desperately, altering the nature and character of their address. But we should not forget that Barrett Browning creates, indeed contains, this impression within the manifestly unrehearsed structure of the 14-line sonnet. The double pattern is at work in that she is offering us a meticulously crafted portrait of immediacy and spontaneity. Her self-conscious confinement of improvisation within a strictly regulated, formal structure is perversely, perhaps tragically, appropriate to the predominant mood and theme of the sequence. In every sonnet, she speaks assertively with an unselfconscious sense of her own presence, the 'I', as the controlling feature of the sonnet itself; in short, she orchestrates the purely poetic dimension of the double pattern. Problems seem to arise, however, when she attempts to combine this with a collateral command of the poem's referential function; what it actually says about her relationship and the world in which she and her lover exist. In this, his presence is predominant, to the extent that everything she feels, imagines or rationally scrutinizes is filtered through her compliant relationship with him. She speaks but her identity is absorbed by his; she controls each 14-line structure of iambs and rhymes but seems unable to move beyond it because he and only he is its theme. Sonnet XIV is a typical example:

> If thou must love me, let it be for nought
> Except for love's sake only. Do not say
> 'I love her for her smile – her look – her way
> Of speaking gently, – for a trick of thought
> That falls in well with mine, and certes brought
> A sense of pleasant ease on such a day' –
> For these things in themselves, Belovèd, may
> Be changed, or change for thee, – and love, so wrought,
> May be unwrought so. Neither love me for
> Thine own dear pity's wiping my cheeks dry –
> A creature might forget to weep, who bore
> Thy comfort long, and lose thy love thereby!
> But love me for love's sake, that evermore
> Thou mayst love on, through love's eternity.

She is the speaker, she coordinates the text but in doing so she seems to feel obliged to subordinate her imagined presence to his. She, paradoxically, becomes a function of the poem and despite the fact that she is the poet, she has much in common with Marvell's addressee: the former remains silent, but both become subject to a more powerful figure.

Christina Rossetti's 'An "Immurata" Sister' rehearses a similar acknowledgement of intellectual inertia:

> Life flows down to death; we cannot bind
> > That current that it should not flee:
> Life flows down to death, as rivers find
> > The inevitable sea.
>
> Men work and think, but women feel;
> > And so (for I'm a woman, I)
> > And so I should be glad to die,
> And cease from impotence of zeal,
> And cease from hope, and cease from dread,
> > And cease from yearnings without gain,
> > And cease from all this world of pain,
> And be at peace among the dead.

There is no reason to assume that Rossetti is endorsing this allocation of roles, but the fact that she encrypts it in a structure that she, as a gifted stylistic practitioner, shapes and compels indicates that she accepts it as immutable. The poem bristles with tragic irony. Rossetti, the artist who constructs this magnificently compelling state of subordination and subservience, is also, in life, its vassal.

Modernism, as we have seen, undermined the conventional relationship between the two dimensions of the double pattern, particularly with regard to the status of abstract formal design as a reflection of order and authority. It cannot, therefore, be accidental that a considerable number of women were involved at the gestation and early development of Modernist verse: the speaking presence of the poet was no longer burdened by a predominantly male legacy of conventions. Three women, Hilda Doolittle ('HD'), Harriet Monroe and Amy Lowell, were actively involved in the Imagist rebellion against the entrapment of the lyrical 'I' within the forms and conventions of a male-dominated high culture. The following is Amy Lowell's 'Autumn':

> All day I have watched the purple vine leaves
> Fall into the water.
> And now in the moonlight they still fall,
> But each leaf is fringed with silver.

The contextual frame of reference is predominantly temporal ('All day', 'And now'). The spatial references are directed away from the speaker towards the act of perception and the image perceived. Imagism's emphasis on external objects and linguistic transparency strips the text of the circumstantial and stylistic features that, in traditional verse, enable us to construct an impression of the addresser; and, as the riddle of the surgeon's son shows, we will often carry into this impression predetermined expectations of gender-associated roles and habits. While Finch is obliged to maintain an interplay between the subject of women poets and a demonstration of how she, a woman poet, can unsettle the conventions of the genre, Lowell makes use of a stylistic programme that has freed itself from the locative associations of ordinary language and the patriarchal inheritance of traditional form. Virginia Woolf's use of stream of consciousness as a central feature of narrative structure achieves a similar effect. According to Virginia Blain (1983, p. 119): 'The real bogey handed on to [Woolf] from the nineteenth century ... was the masculine voice of the omniscient narrator.' Woolf, argues Blain (p. 126), set out to 'undermine the very idea of any centralised moral standpoint, any authoritarian idea of omniscience'. The same can be said of the routine association of the speaker in the poem with a figure who both controls the text and predominates in the world engaged with by the text. Women, until Modernism, were unable to do both.

It would, however, be both patronizing and misleading to treat the ideology and aesthetic of Modernism as enabling devices, providential moments in literary history without which women poets would have remained a hapless minority inhibited by prevailing custom. Consider, for example, Charlotte Mew. She was 31 at the turn of the 20th century, very much a scion of orthodox bourgeois prosperity and although her first volume of poems, *The Farmer's Bride*, was published in 1916, most of the pieces had been conceived and composed in an environment that was far more Tennysonian than avant-garde. She was immune from even the earliest stirrings of Modernism yet her early verse is strikingly atypical of the late 19th-century milieu. 'The Forest Road' is a combination of free verse and stream of consciousness. Its speaker drifts eerily between a presence in control of the discourse and a more amorphous figure absorbed by the irregular drift of images and syntax. There is a 'you', sparingly and tentatively referred to who may well be a lover, but whose gender is never established:

> Oh! hidden eyes that plead in sleep
> Against the lonely dark, if I could touch the fear
> And leave it kissed away on quiet lids –
> If I could hush these hands that are half-awake,
> Groping for me in sleep I could go free.
> I wish that God would take them out of mine
> And fold them like the wings of frightened birds
> Shot cruelly down, but fluttering into quietness so soon.
> Broken, forgotten things? there is no grief for them in the green Spring.

The texture of the verse brings to mind Eliot's 'Prufrock' and *The Waste Land*, its conceits overlapping with the minutiae of extrinsic reference, to the effect that metaphors are half-complete and seemingly beyond the control of the speaker. The image of the shot birds gathers its own listless momentum and leaves behind the original notion of fearful eyes and hands. The vocabulary, even many of the composite images, could come from a standard piece of Victorian verse or the diary or letters of someone of Mew's social class but, at the same time, she has elected to assemble these comfortable particulars in a manner that is without precedent. It would, of course, be simplistic and reductive to assert that Mew's gender, plus the fact that she felt especially marginalized by her incipient lesbianism, is the sole raison d'être for the poem's uniqueness, but the question remains as to why it was a woman who would, without the assistance of any collective cultural movement or inspiration, be responsible for producing a poem that dismantles four centuries of accumulated custom and convention.

What, however, are we to make of women poets who are our near contemporaries? The women's movement, along with a sympathetic liberal consensus on equality, gradually, from the 1950s onwards, dismantled the legal status and cultural perception of women as subordinates, but women writers who began to produce poems before the social transformations of the 1960s were already defying the patriarchal legacy of verse; not through creating an alternative to it, as did the early Modernists, but rather by challenging it on its own terms.

In Ruth Fainlight's 'Lilith', the only concession to stylistic innovation is the abnegation of rhyme and metre; in all other respects, the poem rivals Pope or Dryden in its combative lucidity. It is a condensed rewriting of the book of Genesis and indeed of Milton's *Paradise Lost*, with Lilith, a figure from Hebrew scripture, interloping as a dangerous, though ill-defined presence. She unnerves the traditional, male hierarchy of the creation myth and unsettles those women – Eve and 'Good wives' – who buttress the enduring stereotypes. But how exactly she does so remains uncertain; ('She would be/outside', the 'feared', the 'alien'); she informs the texture of the poem as a threatening, unpredictable figure, providing the text with its energy and fascination, but she remains resistant to analysis and, by implication, control. All we know about her is that she is a woman. It is the sort of poem that would resist the overtures of a feminist critic for the simple reason that it requires no assistance in its confident, self-reliant overturning of an entrenched hierarchy. Brilliantly, it infers a conspiratorial alliance between the speaker and the spectral presence of Lilith. We, as readers – and particularly if we are male readers – feel at once provoked and unsettled. The eponymous subject of the poem moves through it in a manner that can only be described as clandestine, leaving some trace of her passing upon the retinue of themes and figures she encounters. But we are never really certain of what she does or who she is. Interpretive closure and the sense of sophisticated assurance that comes from having properly appreciated a poem are invited and foreclosed upon. The commanding presence of the speaker, who knows something of her subject's special qualities and carries us and her through the text, offers an exciting fabric of puzzles. In this respect, the poem is an extraordinary combination of art and polemic. But it resists naturalization not only as an aesthetic gesture but also as a means of maintaining its independence from a field of discourse where accountability, disclosure and clarity of intent are the prevailing ordinances; a discourse that is predominantly male.

A similar effect is achieved, although by different means, in Fleur Adcock's 'Against Coupling', which opens:

> I write in praise of the solitary act:
> of not feeling a trespassing tongue
> forced into one's mouth, one's breath
> smothered, nipples crushed against the
> rib-cage, and that metallic tingling
> in the chin set off by a certain odd nerve:
>
> unpleasure.

In any attempt to naturalize this poem, we must return again and again to the question of what exactly is the 'solitary act', praised by the speaker? The speaker saturates the rest of the poem with images and verbal constructions that connote sexual congress between men and women. We begin with the specifics ('tongue', 'mouth', 'breath', 'nipples'), move towards their less physical, more figurative correlatives ('his gaze/stirs polypal fronds', 'participating in a total experience'), and on to a mildly ironic dismissal of these activities as emotive events transformed into hollow ritualistic habits:

> when
> one feels like the lady in Leeds who
> had seen *The Sound of Music* eighty-six times;
>
> or more, perhaps, like the school drama mistress
> producing *A Midsummer Night's Dream*

The stylistic structure of the piece seems to replicate its frame of reference with the subtle interplay of line structure and syntax generating a mood of control and submission. The major verb phrases either occur at the end of the line and cause us to push forward to a point of syntactic completion, or achieve a similar effect by being cunningly (perhaps coyly) delayed until the beginning of the line ('tongue/forced', for example). But when we attempt to reassemble these stylistic features as a solution to, a completion of, the poem's meaning, our activity is disrupted. The piece is dominated by verbal and adverbial negatives.

Every elaborate reference to sexuality is qualified by a negative ('of not', 'abandoning', 'not participating'), until the closing stanza where the reader is encouraged to 'embrace it':

> No need to set the scene,
> dress up (or undress), make speeches.
> Five minutes of solitude are
> enough – in the bath, or to fill
> that gap between the Sunday papers and lunch.

The 'it', the 'solitary act', is, it seems, a total negation of all activities previously described, but what exactly is 'it'? We will never know for certain, but with Adcock's ingenious coaxing, our gender and predisposition will play a major role in causing us to assume that we do. As a male reader, I confess that my initial, visceral instinct was to interpret 'it' as masturbation. The rest of the poem has, after all, gradually built in my mind the image of a woman preoccupied with sexual congress but searching for an alternative, one that involves satisfaction but without the participation of another. At the same time, however, this figure is as much the product of a subtle, laconic exercise in self-caricature as she is an index to the speaker's genuine state of mind, which, protected as it is by sanguine irony, remains something of a mystery. Adcock's achievement is considerable in that she has created for the reader a potentially embarrassing hall of mirrors, in which the mischievous texture of the poem at once indulges our expectations, based on a gender stereotype, and unsettles them. Considered more impartially, we realize that 'it' might just as plausibly be the savouring of one's own company, undisturbed by the incursions of other people. 'It' might even refer to the act of having bipartite sex without giving too much attention to the efforts or the presence of the man, let alone to the standard cultural and emotional baggage of the act. Adcock's poem resists closure, but not only as an aesthetic gesture. It makes skilful use of the lexicon of orthodox poetic devices – the New Critical and Formalist favourites of paradox, ambiguity and the guileful poetic function are all on display – and in doing so has achieved what Woolf had deemed, for the woman poet, impossible. In *A Room of One's Own*, Woolf (quoted in Eagleton, 1986) reflects on how, when attempting to write,

> a shadow seemed to lie across the page. It was a straight dark bar, a shadow shaped something like the letter 'I'. One began dodging this way and that to catch a glimpse of the landscape behind it.

This is a crisply evocative account of poetic tradition as a double-headed monster, a seemingly impersonal network of conventions whose embodiments in poems themselves were predominantly, almost exclusively male. Adcock and Fainlight, however, disprove Woolf's prognosis that the burdensome, masculine 'I' must oblige the women poet to 'dodge' orthodox writing. They march confidently into a realm that, at least until the early 20th century, was regarded as coterminous with maleness and, without disguising or apologizing for their gender, make just as provocative and efficient use of it as would any of their male peers.

At the other end of the spectrum of modern poetry by women, we encounter those who have kept alight the torch lit by Woolf and Doolittle, Monroe and Moore; the avoidance or deliberate undermining of orthodoxy because of its presumed allegiance to repressive masculinity. Luce Irigaray is a literary theorist who has taken her cue from the work of Jacques Lacan. Lacan's most famous, one might even say infamous, contribution to psychoanalytic and literary theory is his concept of the 'mirror stage' (1949), a confusing and, in truth, confused extension of structuralist and poststructuralist theories of language and identity. Our sense of self, argues Lacan, is attained when we first perceive ourselves as a presence that is separate from the rest of the world, as if we are suddenly seeing ourselves in a mirror functioning independently of everything else. This attainment of identity is, however, not founded upon a prelinguistic act of perception but as a consequence of projecting ourselves into, and believing we can separate ourselves from, language. This belief, contends Lacan, is actually a continual and unresolvable struggle between a desire to secure independence and self-knowledge and an equally powerful, almost fetishistic attachment to the system of signs that enables us to perceive ourselves as we think we are. Irigaray points out that Lacan's model is partial and hidebound, given that, for women, the complex dynamic of attempting to transcend language while depending upon it for a sense of selfhood is complicated by the fact that language is hegemonically male in its functions, conventions and operations. Women, therefore, suffer the double bind of having to deal with the incompatibility and inseparability of sign and referent, plus being consigned to the existential hinterland of the perennial subject; the observed and addressed, rather than the observer and addresser. Irigaray's solution, if this term is apt, is that women should neither connive at nor actively militate against male discourse – both, she argues, would endorse it. They should instead opt for a fluid, evasive brand of autonomy exemplified in a piece of writing of her own called 'When Our Lips Speak Together' (Irigaray, 1974):

> I love you, childhood. I love you, who are not my mother (sorry, mother, I prefer a woman to you) nor sister. Neither daughter nor son. I love you – and there where I love you, the filiations of the fathers and their desire for reflections of men don't matter. And their genealogical institutions – neither husband nor wife. No personality, role or function for their reproductive laws. I love you: your body, there, here, now. I/you touch you/me, it's enough for us to know ourselves alive …
>
> Are we unsatisfied? Yes, if that means we are never finished. If our pleasure is to move ourselves, to be moved, endlessly. Always in movement; openness is not exhausted nor satiated.

The piece has been classified, by consensus, as a prose poem – although Irigaray herself has not commented on its generic status – and its working principle seems to be the continuous undercutting of any reliable interpretation of who the speaker is and the trajectory, even the exact subject, of her(?) speech. The 'I' dissolves into 'I/you' and the addressee, already a somewhat blurred amalgam of a particular individual and a genus ('mother', 'woman', 'daughter' and so on), mutates similarly into 'you/me'. Irigaray concedes by implication that the codes of male sexuality and sociocultural predominance are embedded in even the most seemingly impartial poetic structures; one can assume that her refusal to use lines invokes this ineluctable state of gender governance. While she does not completely eschew all allegiances to the notion of the poetic – the anarchic dispersal of the subject, object and thematic continuity reminds one of a Poundian canto, for example – she seems determined to undermine all attempts by the reader to naturalize the poem. One might indeed assume from this that she perceives naturalization or recontextualization as a procedure that reflects and ratifies an ideology based upon order and control, predominantly masculine axioms.

A more conservative – by which I mean coherent and accessible – variant upon Irigaray's exercise is 'coming out celibate' by Astra:

> so that when i say
> > i am celibate
> smiles of embarrassment appear
> and the subject is quickly changed
>
> i am awarded
> > pity or contempt or simply bewilderment
> that i should not do
> > sexual things with and to
> > another person
> preferably of the other gender

Astra indulges aspects of avant-garde technique – notably the line structures appear to operate as replacements for punctuation and orthodox syntax – but the most significant token of the poem's allegiance to self-conscious feminism is her refusal to shift to the higher case. The 'I' that cast a peremptory shadow over Woolf's page is now subject to a more equitable regime without capital letters, and free also of the burdensome tradition of commas, full stops and the unfair diminution of subordinate clauses. Nor is there room for the practices of irony or paradox, similarly tainted by patriarchal sanction.

All four poems, by Fainlight, Adcock, Irigaray and Astra, address the theme of gender difference, and there are obvious parallels between Adcock's and Astra's preoccupations with relationships and individuality. But a question is raised. Fainlight and Adcock employ techniques that are drawn from the thesaurus of conventional poetry, while Irigaray and Astra contend, by example, that in doing so women poets submit to a repertoire of devices shaped by masculinist perceptions and presumptions. In my opinion, Fainlight, Adcock and many other late 20th-century women poets – Elizabeth Jennings, Anne Stevenson, Denise Levertov, Sylvia Plath, Jenny Joseph, Stevie Smith, Carol Anne Duffy and Jo Shapcott to name but eight – have disproved Woolf's contention that the male 'I' of tradition can only be 'dodged' or looked behind. They and many others have made use of, indeed mastered, the key, definitive characteristic of poetry – essentially the double pattern – without becoming subordinate to it. It is an indisputable fact that until the mid- to late 20th century, all aspects of society and culture in the Western world reflected gender inequality, but does this prove that poetry as a discourse was designed to preclude the expressive potential and active participation of women? To answer this question, consider another: which of the four poems discussed above do you, irrespective of your gender, regard as the more fascinating, demanding and aesthetically pre-eminent?

15

Nation, Race and Place

Poets employ three principal techniques to address the issues of race and nationality:

1 The poem, irrespective of its manner and form, will engage with a memory, an incident or a state of mind. There are, for example, a number of poems by African Caribbean writers that give elegiac accounts of their arrival and first experiences in Britain; Archie Markham's 'Inheritance' and Fred D'Aguiar's 'Home' are notable examples.
2 The poet will make use of a lexicon of conventional devices, largely Anglo-centric in origin, to unsettle the reader's expectations, particularly with regard to stereotypical perceptions of race, nationality or class.
3 Poets will treat conventional poetry, including the orthodoxies of poetic writing and standard English, as a racial and cultural shibboleth, a discourse that appropriates and subjugates its non-English practitioners. As a consequence, they will cause the non-literary vernacular and idiomatic features of their linguistic lineage to dominate the texture of the verse.

This chapter will focus predominantly on the second and third points and we will begin with the tendentious question of what Englishness actually involves.

It is an incontrovertible truth that the political epicentre of what was once the British Empire and is now the loose fabric of Britain and the Commonwealth is England or, more accurately, London, and that England is similarly the focus for British economic activity. Beyond that, however, any attempt to locate a sociocultural or collateral literary unity within England is the equivalent of chasing shadows. Poetry testifies to this because in the majority of poems written by English poets, issues of nationality are either of negligible significance or, as we shall see, bemused curiosity.

The following is from Donald Davie's 'Barnsley and District':

> Judy Sugden! Judy, I made you caper
> With rage when I said that the British Fascist
> Sheet your father sold was a jolly good paper

> And you had agreed and I said, Yes, it holds
> Vinegar, and everyone laughed and imagined
> The feel of the fish and chips warm in its folds

These two stanzas involve an ingenious use of the *contra-rejet*. 'Caper' carries a mildly jovial, perhaps even flirtatious, association until we connect it 'With rage'; 'the British Fascist' conjures up an image of a particular type of person, until it becomes a political newspaper; a paper that holds ... views? Opinions? No, Vinegar. These specifics of place – Barnsley, the surname Sugden (now established for viewers of *Emmerdale* as synonymous with Yorkshire) and, of course, fish and chips – are matched by the informal, conversational nature of the syntax ('And you agreed and I said') to create a feeling that this is a poem as firmly anchored to time and place as a 'northern' novel by John Braine or Stan Barstow. Yet, at the same time, Davie's unselfconscious poetic craftsmanship distances him from these locative images. He plays with and controls the language and its associations with a degree of sophisticated competence that might remind us of Wordsworth's uneasy relationship with the denizens of rural Cumberland and other parts of provincial England: poetic writing can use a place and its associations as a subject, but it can also enable its user to keep their distance.

Tony Harrison, like Davie a Yorkshireman, returns again and again in his poetry to an enduring sense of mild amazement that he, a working-class grammar school boy from Leeds, should have become a major poet, capable of translating the verse of his Greek forebears. In *V*, he meets his alter ego in a Leeds cemetery, a skinhead yob with a taste for violence and spray-can creativity. The 'I' is Harrision:

> 'Listen cunt!' I said, 'before you start your jeering
> the reason why I want this in a book
> 's to give ungrateful cunts like you a hearing!'
> *A book, yer stupid cunt 's not worth a fuck!*
>
> 'The only reason why I write this poem at all
> on yobs like you who do the dirt on death
> 's to give some higher meaning to your scrawl.'
> *Don't fucking bother, cunt! Don't waste your breath!*

All through the poem, Harrison shows how he can move between the cautious, lyrical style of 'the poet' to the idioms of his youth and those of his nasty companion. But this linguistic dexterity is itself contained within a separate language, a language that discloses another less firmly rooted sense of identity: each regional, idiomatic flourish is confidently, almost elegantly, reconciled to the demands of the quatrain. Like Davie, Harrison betrays an uncomfortable sense of poetry as a form of belonging, a way of looking at, of mediating places and experiences, but not of itself part of them.

This raises the question of whether poetry is bound into an elitist, hierarchical system of codes and characteristics; whether the idioms and habits of Yorkshire, the working class and yobbishness are conspicuously separate from poetic discourse.

It is intriguing to compare Harrison's *V* with Blake Morrison's 'The Ballad of the Yorkshire Ripper'. Morrison's speaker's dialect is similar to that of Harrison's acerbic vandal ('Ail teems down like stair-rods/an swells canals an becks', he observes on the rain) but the former is the poem's single speaking presence. He reflects on how many of his male friends share the mass murderer Peter Sutcliffe's view of women as dangerously provocative, and what is striking about the poem is Morrison's reluctance to control or balance the contrasting registers. The metaphors – particularly the images of 'sex', 'like a stormclap/a swellin in thi cells,/when lightning arrers through thi' – are sometimes impressively constructed and vivid and it seems clear that Morrison's intention is to shock the reader into an admission that, yes, we do not expect a figure who speaks like this to have such an astute command of rhetoric. This sense of unease would certainly greet us if we encountered such a person in real life, but our knowledge that he is the invention of the Oxford-educated poet and critic Blake Morrison causes us to suspect that the magnificently poetic seam that runs through the rough Yorkshire idiom is an act of politically correct ventriloquism. The speaker is a grotesque, a figure whose routine, almost violent, mangling of correct syntax and received pronunciation seems somehow appropriate, given his hungry, prurient interest in another act of brutality. One has to wonder, however, about our response if such a vision of savage vulgarity were rendered in an idiom recognizibly African Carribean or even Irish. Attempts to achieve cultural equitability by allowing dialect and idiom to swamp the text can have dire consequences. Harrison avoids such embarrassments by maintaining a distinction between himself, the poet and orchestrator of the text, and his somewhat unnerving alter ego.

Allegedly the poet who most vividly embodies Englishness is Philip Larkin. Larkin's status in this regard is arguable for two reasons; first, the notion of what being English involves is relative and mutable and those who seem most secure in their perception of it are equally united in their hostility; second, Larkin, like Davie and Harrison, is fascinated by the environment in which he was born, grew up and elected to live in, but he certainly does not endorse it as notably worse or better than anywhere else. Instead, he picks out those aspects of it that seem to best suit his somewhat reclusive, saturnine temperament. 'The Whitsun Weddings', one of his best-known, most celebrated poems, is certainly an impression of England, given that it is a record of a railway journey from Hull to London. In an interview with Melvyn Bragg on the *South Bank Show* (16 April 1981), Larkin speaks of how the newly married couples boarding at subsequent stations 'all looked different but they were all doing the same things and sort of feeling the same things!' and recalls that with each stop, it was as though 'fresh emotion climbed aboard'. The previously slow train seemed to have acquired an inexplicable momentum; 'you hurtle on, you felt the whole thing was being aimed like a bullet – at the heart of things you know. All this fresh, open life. Incredible experience. I've never forgotten it.'

His description catches perfectly the beautifully executed change of pace and perspective in the poem itself, and it also replicates an even more significant feature of the verse – studied puzzlement. For much of the piece, Larkin adopts the persona of the genial anthropologist, a poetic Sir David Attenborough, maintaining a balance between sympathetic affinity and objectivity.

'Mr Bleaney' offers another example of Englishness at its most commonplace and lacklustre. Mr Bleaney is looking for lodgings and the landlady's dreary account of the previous occupant of the room is supplemented by its appearance:

> Flowered curtains, thin and frayed,
> Fall to within five inches of the sill,
>
> Whose window shows a strip of building land,
> Tussocky, littered.

The bed inspires no comment, the 'upright' chair is, one assumes, uncomfortable, the 'sixty-watt bulb' – not forty or one hundred, you understand – seems unshaded, the door has no hook and there is no room for 'books'. He adds a dash at the completion of this inventory, indicating the brief moment between impression and decision. 'I'll take it,' he states. Thereafter he settles down to enjoy the ambient misery and reflect upon his occupation of what is not just Mr Bleaney's room but the summation of his drab existence. 'I knew his habits,' he states, particularly regarding the choice between sauce and gravy, summer holidays in Frinton and Christmas with his sister in Stoke,

> But if he stood and watched the frigid wind
> Tousling the clouds, lay on the fusty bed
> Telling himself that this was home, and grinned.
> And shivered, without shaking off the dread
>
> That how we live measures our own nature,
> And at his age having no more to show
> Than one hired box should make him pretty sure
> He warranted no better, I don't know.

In both poems, Larkin blends fascination, perverse affection and distracted apathy, but it is not so much the subjects or mood of the pieces that detain us as his skill as a poet. Yet most critics have treated him as an avatar for a lamentable national condition. Charles Tomlinson (1957) wrote that his

> narrowness suits the English perfectly … They recognise their own abysmal suburban landscapes, skilfully caught … The stepped down version of human possibilities … the joke that hesitates just on this side of nihilism, are national vices.

According to Tom Paulin (1990), Larkin might seem to speak for 'the English male, middle class, professional, outwardly confident, controlled and in control', which Paulin implies is bad enough, but this demeanour marks deeper repressions and complexes. Larkin 'writhes with anxiety inside that sealed bunker which is the English ethic of privacy', a collective mood of loss and failure, the end of Empire.

Both critics base their assessments of Larkin upon an alleged teleological link between his verse – conservative in style, somewhat mordant in tone – and a generalized perception of what Englishness involves. In truth, however, Englishness is a far more amorphous condition, subject to whatever shape the poet is inclined to afford it. John Betjeman is probably the most ostentatious mythologizer of an England that is, by degrees, absurd, beguiling and fantastic. His best-known, much-anthologized, much-quoted poems are littered with the particularities of a country that was sustained, at least in the popular imagination, and for the Americans, by the Ealing comedies and, more recently, by the kinds of figures played by Hugh Grant. Betjeman began writing poetry in the 1930s, a period when the stylistics and mood of Modernism held sway. His sense of place as a correlative for personal and national identity has political resonances and in this respect he is not dissimilar to Yeats or Eliot, but in one respect he is very different. His verse forms are at once traditional, complex, accessible and beautifully correct. One could argue that his enduring popularity and his uneasy relationship with 'serious' (that is, modern, innovative, intellectually challenging) poetry is due to his matching of form and content: his nostalgia for a recognizable form of Englishness is contained within and structured by a particularly old-fashioned type of English form. In 'The Village Inn', Betjeman conducts a dialogue with the 'brewer's P.R.O.', the money-obsessed modernizer and destroyer of that most English of institutions, the pub. One could compare this with Harrison's exchanges with another unpleasant mutilator of monuments. Both poems involve very different voices carrying very different opinions about who we are and how we should live, and both, implicitly, juxtapose these differences with a pattern that will endure, no matter what happens to the village inn or the inner city: the pervasive structure of the poem:

> Ah, where's the inn that once I knew
> With brick and chalky well
> Up which the knobbly pear tree grew
> For fear the place would fall?

> Oh that old pot-house isn't there,
> It wasn't worth our while;
> You'll find we have rebuilt 'The Bear'
> In Early Georgian style.

Betjeman permits himself a degree of self-mockery by reproducing the opinions he detests in the stanzaic form that is, in every respect, his own property.

The four poets discussed so far treat versions of Englishness – regional, temperamental, sociocultural – as extrinsic to the poem itself. Sometimes they set up a contrast between an idiom, and as a consequence a mindset, and the structure that contains it. Each uses their command of poetic form as a lens for the examination and scrutiny of various aspects of England, sometimes affectionately, on other occasions obliquely or satirically. The poem, however, holds itself at a distance, almost a state of immunity, from the state of mind or condition it re-creates. There are numerous versions of Englishness evoked in these pieces, none of which can claim to be endemic or pre-eminent. Larkin is not Mr Bleaney, Harrison's feral acquaintance has wandered into the poem just as he intrudes upon the poet's contemplation of the cemetery, and Morrison's grotesque is something of a Frankenstein creation, uncomfortable with the formal tissue that contains him. In each instance, the poet is in command of the medium, the purely technical devices, the rhythm and temper of the poem itself, but, as a consequence, can we assert that the poem is neutral, unaffiliated to a particular socioethnic inheritance?

Consider a poem by a poet born and brought up in St Lucia, West Indies. Derek Walcott's 'A Country Club Romance' (1962) deliberately invokes, in its jolly quatrains and its specifics of activity and location, Betjeman's 'Joan Hunter Dunn'. Both poems tell of a white, middle-class, athletically attractive woman at her tennis club. Walcott sounds like Betjeman:

> Laburnum bright her hair,
> Her eyes were blue as ponds
> Her thighs, so tanned and bare
> Sounder than government bonds.

For the first four stanzas, the formal and the referential dimensions of the poem fit easily together: the country club, the relaxing middle-class habits of popping in for a game and a drink, the rather naughty reference to 'her breathless bosom', 'As proud as Dunlop balls'; all these seem to belong within the neat but carefree structure of the short-line quatrain. We could be in Aldershot or anywhere else in the home counties, circa the 1950s:

> Until at one tournament, Harris
> Met her, a black Barbadian.

The introduction of Mr Harris sends a shock wave through the fabric of the poem. The first four stanzas orchestrate colouring with objects: she is a 'fresh rose' upon which 'white dew' falls; her hair 'laburnum bright'; her eyes 'blue as ponds'; her thighs are 'tanned'. Mr Harris's blackness transforms these stylistic appropriations of detail into a more uneasy pattern of relations between what your colour makes you and how it circumscribes your activities, particularly regarding sex. At the close, after Miss Gautier and Mr Harris have married, been ostracized, had children and she has prematurely died, the colour/object relations become charged with the grim reality of what actually happens when the home counties meet the Caribbean:

> While the almonds yellow the beeches,
> And the breezes pleat the lake,
> And the blondes pray God to 'teach us
> To profit from her mistake'.

The parallels between Walcott's poem and the style and mood of Betjeman are deliberate and calculated, but by juxtaposing a formal idiom that itself comes close to self-caricature with the theme of racism, he is implying that the former involves a high cultural endorsement of the latter. This is a passage from his lengthy, quasi-epic *Omeros*:

> I felt transported,
> past shops smelling of cod to a place I had lost
> in the open book of the street, and could not find.
> It was another country, whose excitable
> gestures I knew but could not connect with my mind,
> like my mother's amnesia; untranslatable ...
>
> with tongues of a speech I no longer understood,
> but where my flesh did not need to be translated.

His subject is loss, felt doubly since he laments both his absence from the places he shared with his mother in the West Indies – when he wrote the poem, he was based mainly in the US – and the greater, all-encompassing dislocation from a past, presumably in Africa, that was never even recorded.

While attending to no strict formal criteria, the poem is robustly conventional; reflective, unambiguous coherence is underpinned by a hint of rhythmic regularity and a loose but conspicuous rhyme scheme. It is perfectly compatible with the manifesto for postwar British verse devised by Robert Conquest. Poetry – that is, circa 1956 – 'is empirical in its attitude to all that comes. This reverence for the real person or event is, indeed, a part of the general intellectual ambience ... of our time' (Conquest, 1956, p. xiv). Antony Easthope (1996, p. 28) interprets this as not just an *empirical* reliance upon facts but an *empiricist* notion that the real exists unproblematically *'out there'* ... the 'I' that surveys the world with splendid confidence from a position of supposed exteriority, reflects upon it (or mediates), and masters what it sees ... So there it is – the real is English, and Englishness is the real.

According to Easthope's model, the doctrine of empiricism – which formal traditionalism secures as the guarantee of transparency and coherence – is complicit with the cultural hegemony of the English establishment and this, in its turn, involves the preservation of a kind of false consciousness; a belief in truth and facts as secure prelinguistic entities. Experimental poetry, on the other hand, enables us properly to explore our identity not as secure but as a contingent feature of the discourses that variously displace and absorb it. If we take this model seriously, then Walcott has surrendered to the delusionary tactic of self-preservation practised by the white, English cultural elite. But, as we read the above passage from *Omeros*, and indeed the rest of the poem, can we doubt that he has a secure perception of who he is in these crisply transparent lines; of what the 'I', repeated continually, feels and has lost?

Walcott's genus as a postcolonial poet raises an intriguing question, similar to that considered in our discussion of modern women poets. His verse, both in terms of his use of metrical and stanzaic form and his classless, unprepossessing idiom, differs hardly at all from that of his quintessentially English peers who rose to prominence in the 1950s as standard-bearers for empiricism and stylistic conservatism; Robert Conquest, Kingsley Amis, John Wain, Philip Larkin, Elizabeth Jennings and Donald Davie in particular come to mind. Obviously, the subjects of his poems tend to reflect his personal background and experience, and one has to ask if there is something incongruous and inappropriate about a black poet, indeed a man descended from slaves, who makes use of a formal and aesthetic tradition so closely associated with the white British establishment. In an essay entitled 'The Muse of History' (1974, p. 422), Walcott writes that:

New World poets who see the 'classic style' as stasis must see it also as historical degradation, rejecting it as the language, when he limits his memory to the suffering of the victim. Their admirable wish to honour the degraded ancestor limits their language to phonetic pain, the groan of suffering, the curse of revenge. The tone of the past becomes an unbearable burden, for they must abuse the master or hero in his own language, and this implies self-deceit. Their view of Caliban is of the enraged pupil. They cannot separate the rage of Caliban from the beauty of his speech when the speeches of Caliban are equal in their elemental power to those of his tutor. The language of the torturer mastered by the victim. This is viewed as servitude, not as victory.

Walcott himself addresses this in one of his earliest poems, 'A Far Cry from Africa':

> .... how choose
> Between this Africa and the English tongue I love?
> Betray them both, or give back what they give?

He acknowledges his dilemma while disclosing his temperamental affiliation to the 'English tongue'. Later in the essay, he offers a more reflective, measured account of why he has chosen to write in the way that he does (Walcott, 1974, p. 422):

> In time the slave surrendered to amnesia. That amnesia is the true history of the New World. That is our inheritance, but to try and understand why this happened, to condemn or justify is also the method of history, and these explanations are always the same: This happened because of that, this was understandable because, and in days men were such. These recriminations exchanged, the contrition of the master replaces the vengeance of the slave, and here colonial literature is most pietistic, for it can accuse great art of feudalism and excuse poor art as suffering. To radical poets poetry seems the homage of resignation, an essential fatalism. But it is not the pressure of the past which torments great poets but the weight of the present.

Walcott wrote this article four years prior to the publication of Edward Said's *Orientalism* (1978). Said's subject is predominantly the relationship between the West and the Middle East but his concept of 'the other' has been treated as a template for the analysis of all instances of colonialism and cultural tyranny. The 'other' is the reinvention of the colonized subject by the politically predominant culture. Even if the heritage and social fabric of the subordinate nation or race is treated with apparent impartiality, the fact that it is perceived through the discursive prism of the imperious culture causes it to be treated as, at best, a curious antecedent to post-Enlightenment 'civilization', or, more likely, as a form of honourable primitivism. Moreover, a process of cultural naturalization occurs, whereby the character and inclinations of individuals from the subjugated culture are reconstructed according to the expectations of the perceiver. In this respect, Said borrows heavily from Derrida's, and Foucault's, theses that language, or rather a particular cultural discourse, reshapes rather than reflects actuality. Walcott is not a literary/cultural theorist but his article is prescient. As he puts it, to use the conventions of 'the torturer [effectively the coloniser] ... is viewed as servitude'. But consider this: how is it that Walcott, who is clearly as well attuned as Said to the dynamic relationship between the culture of the colonist and that of the colonized, can present himself as having consciously and of his own volition chosen the language – or, to be more accurate, the poetic conventions – that he 'loves', when, according to Said's thesis, this discourse is responsible for the reinvention of the colonized subject according to the expectations of the colonist? The 'other' has become one of the inviolable watchwords of literary theory, yet even before it entered the currency of criticism, Walcott had already raised questions regarding its legitimacy. Indeed, in his use of the Caliban analogy, Walcott both pre-empts and challenges Said's thesis. He concedes that for many to 'abuse the master ... in his own language ... implies self-deceit'. Yet, he contends, those who take this view have blinded themselves to the fact that Caliban's speeches in their 'elemental power' equal those of his tutor. In Walcott's view, the poetic discourse of English, irrespective of its origins and associations, is sufficiently complex and flexible to allow for the innate talent and energy of its user to manifest themselves, irrespective of the latter's status regarding the inequitable forces of history. In Said's model, Caliban and his like become entrapped within a discourse that guarantees their diminutive status; when they speak, they do so as pretenders to a rank they can never attain.

As stated above, there are parallels between the issues raised by postcolonial verse and those involving poetry and gender. Specifically, can those who were once the oppressed, the silenced or the excluded subjects of a discourse come to control it, or must they construct some self-evidently autonomous mode of writing as a token of their independence?

Certainly there are a large number of poets who were born before the 1960s – particularly those who have experienced the transition from empire to a vague postcolonial sense of shared and divergent histories – who have opted for the former, while virtually all of those who chose the latter are presently under 50, but there are sufficient exceptions to this to disprove it as a social and historical guideline. Personal inclination and ideological affiliation are far more reliable indications of cause.

James Berry arrived in London from Jamaica in 1948, and his long poem *Lucy's Letters* is intriguing. It is, as its title indicates, a sequence of letters from Lucy, a Caribbean woman now living in London, to her childhood friend Leela who still lives in their home village. While Leela herself never replies, we feel her presence throughout the poem as the figure whose questions and assumptions, particularly about life in Britain, Lucy feels continually obliged to address. Lucy is, as a consequence, writing about the various states of perplexity and unease that result from being caught between two cultural and racial traditions, but she does so to someone who is a version of a former, perhaps more naive and innocent, self: 'An Leela, darlin', no, I never/meet the Queen in flesh'. Also, this conceit of the poem as a series of letters enables Berry to create a network of contrasts between an idiom that is at once private and culturally marginalized and a broader structure that is affiliated to the literary fabric of white Britain. The non-poetic aspect of the double pattern is an authentic version of the accent and vocabulary of 'ordinary' Caribbeans, while the poem itself, self-evidently the gift of Lucy's creator, Berry, bears allegiance to a monolith of exalted aesthetic conventions. For example:

> Leela, I reely a sponge
> you know, for traffic noise,
> for work noise, for halfway
> intentions, for halfway smiles,
> for clockwatchin' and col' weather.
> I hope you don' think I gone
> too fat when wee meet.
> I booked up to come an' soak
> the children in daylight.

The figure of herself as a 'sponge' is complex and nuanced, in that she is, or at least perceives herself as, a passive recipient of alien impressions ('traffic noises', 'work noise') and ambiguous, perhaps insincere gestures ('halfway/intentions', 'halfway smiles'). It is a skilfully executed, conspicuously poetic metaphor, a persistent but not intrusive counterpoint to the otherwise relaxed conversational style of the 'letter'. Lucy even preserves the final thread of the conceit for the moment, tinged with sentiment and optimism, when she, the 'sponge', will feel more comfortable and expressive in the company of the people she once knew best: 'an soak/the children in daylight'. She will, at last, feel able to show her affections.

It is a credit to Berry's skill that we do not encounter a tension or a grating incongruity between the unpretentious presence of Lucy and the fabric of devices that reshape her as the subject of a poem. The fact that both belong within very different textual and cultural contexts is not something that Berry attempts to conceal or even explain. It is the implicit theme of the text and it returns us to the issue raised in Walcott's essay. Does Berry, by 'mastering' the language of the oppressor, like Caliban, 'indulge' in a form of 'self-deceit'? Although he has never responded to such an enquiry directly, we must assume that he was fully aware of how the sincere but rather unassuming Lucy is as much a device as the beautifully paced lines, where the enjambment

> halfway
>
> intentions

imitates the moment of hesitation prior to the more resigned, 'halfway smiles'. We must assume also that he intends us to leave the poem with an unresolved dilemma: specifically, how can we reconcile our image of Lucy – engaging yet guileless Lucy – with the figure who assembles and patrols the sophisticated architecture of the poem? Perhaps, particularly if we are white, educated and think we are no longer subject to the cosy false consciousness of racial or cultural superiority, Berry is urging us to think again. He has reconciled the two presences and so the problem, it seems, is ours.

Archie Markham's alter ego Lambchops (in *Human Rites*, 1984) differs from Berry's Lucy principally because Markham is the speaking presence of the poem, his subject's observer and narrator. We know enough from contextual clues that Lambchops is of Caribbean descent but his relationship with the poet is uncertain. In his Lambchops' poems – and indeed throughout his other verse – Markham maintains a register of cultured anonymity similar to Walcott's, as, for example, in 'Lambchops' Ally':

> Now is the summer of his disrespect.
> He passes oncoming women on the left
> disdaining a glance at the hopeful strip
>
> of breast – he's been five hours now past
> indignity, and still carries before him
> (like a fireman's ladder at full stretch)
>
> the weight of his first printed poem –
> an arrow in the crowd.

Intriguingly, we are not allowed access to Lambchops' first poem and, of course, we begin to wonder if it bears any resemblance to the stylistic mood and tone of the one he is in. Markham was fully aware that the notion of the poem as an autonomous text floating free of an actual or notional presence with a name and personal history – advocated so fervently both by New Critics and post-structuralists – was an absurdity, particularly now that a modern author's profile and background had become part of the packaging of publication and promotion. To an extent, he exploits this contextual hinterland, and causes the reader, despite ourselves, to enter it when we read the poem. Specifically, he knows that the collection bearing the name of E.A. Markham will automatically be classified as belonging within a subgenre defined not by technique but by authorial race and background; he too is part of the post-*Windrush*, postcolonial generation. The effect of this collision between our contextual knowledge and our impression of the poem is unsettling. The speaker seems to bring to his subject a mixture of affection, condescension and ironic hauteur. Is the opening echo of Shakespeare meant to celebrate Lambchops or mock him? Are we supposed to treat his glance at the 'breast' of his fellow pedestrian as an indication of bravura or, on the reader's part, slight distaste? (And of course, we are then caused to wonder: is the woman white?) Does the speaker urge us to admire his self-perceived elevation from mediocrity (the publication of his poem) or see this as charmingly naive? Markham, brilliantly, sets up outside the poem a fabric of triggers and prejudicial alleyways comparable to those faced by Lambchops himself. We continually have to ask ourselves whether we identify with the, at best, ambivalent or, at worst, calculatedly superior manner of the speaker and then go on to address the question of whether this is, indeed, Markham himself. At the heart of this labyrinth of interpretive problems is the role of the double pattern. The speaker commands it, shows a masterful adroitness as its practitioner: is this Markham, like Caliban, indulging in a brand of 'self-deceit' or Markham the poet moving several paces ahead of his liberal sympathetic, and probably white, interpreters?

Black and Caribbean poets of the post-1950s generation differ from their immediate predecessors in their treatment of or, to be more accurate, their unwillingness to subscribe to orthodox British poetic conventions. Linton Kwesi Johnson's last stanza from 'Inglan Is a Bitch' (1991) could stand as the radical benchmark for this new subgenre:

> Inglan is a bitch
> dere's no escapin it
> Inglan is a bitch fi true
> is whey wi a goh dhu 'bout it?

Noam Chomsky (1957) devised an analytical technique based upon the assumption that everything written or spoken involves a 'surface structure' comprising the relationship between the words themselves, however unconventional or ungrammatical this might be. Each of us, often unwittingly, can make sense of even the most chaotic or impenetrable statement by reducing it to a 'deep structure'; that is, we effectively translate the aberrant verbs, nouns and adjectives of the surface structure into an elemental, coherent model. Crucial to Chomsky's scheme is the presumption that addresser and addressee, writer and reader, come from the same linguistic and social group: a shared, sometimes intuitive, awareness of the normative role of deep structures guarantees within this group an elementary channel of communication between its members. Kwesi Johnson's surface structure resists translation into a deep structure. Certainly the first two lines, once 'naturalized' as standard, non-dialect English, make sense, but thereafter his avoidance of punctuation or structured syntax supplements the already uncooperative vocabulary, to the extent that even the most unbiased, indulgent reader can only, at best, pick out verbs and nouns and some connectives while remaining alienated from the deep structure of the poem. I should, of course, add that such a reader is white, and generally unfamiliar with the linguistic currency from which Kwesi Johnson draws his material. Kwesi Johnson swamps the double pattern with non-poetic registers that are largely exclusive to African Caribbeans and, as a consequence, the poem becomes difficult to interpret or naturalize. As we have seen, naturalization is the procedure by which poems are reconstituted as synoptic, logically structured versions of themselves: in basic terms, the non-poetic dimension of the double pattern is stripped of its poetic counterpart. Kwesi Johnson complicates, even obviates, this process by incorporating non-poetic words and constructions that have no clear equivalents even in standard English. For him, naturalization takes on a literal, politicized meaning: through his poem, he refuses to assimilate to a culture that he regards as hegemonic and predatory.

David Dabydeen's 'Slave Song' involves an even more radical act of calculated culture displacement:

> Black men cover wid estate ash
> E ead haad an dry like a calabash,
> Dut in e nose-hole, in e ear-hole,
> Dut in e soul, in e battie-hole.
>
> All
> day
> sun
> bun
> tongue
> bun
> all
> day
> troat
> cut
> haat
> hut
> wuk na dun, na dun, na dun!
> Hack! Hack! Hack! Hack!
> Cutlass slip an cut me cack!

Poets who employ similar strategies include Michael Smith, Jean Binta Breeze and Oku Onuara (see Breiner, *An Introduction to West Indian Poetry*, 1998). Most share a reluctance to structure their verse according even to the loose syntactic patterns of informal spoken English and few give little more than cursory attention to conventional poetic devices. Instead, their poems take their formal cue from a hybrid blend of indigenous speech patterns and the musical rhythms of reggae – they are known collectively as 'dub' poets.

Jeremy Cronin (1988) finds parallels between the performance-oriented style of 'dub' poetry and the protest poems of apartheid South Africa. He quotes Walter Ong (p. 530) on how the written printed medium secures and ratifies a core tradition of verse and points out that South African spoken or sung poetry is both deliberately marginal and dissentient; it is by its nature impermanent and dynamic, more a testament to the living vibrant presence of the poet than a submission to the impersonal stability of the text. The following is Cronin talking about Mzwakhe and quoting his poem, which, at the time Cronin (1988, pp. 526–7) published his article, was not available anywhere in print:

Mzwakhe is tall and angular … His rhythms are somewhat influenced by the reggae, or dub talking poetry of Linton Kwesi Johnson. He performs at speed, with a heavily syncopated intonation …

Ig-nor-rant
I am ignorant
I am ignorant
I have been fortunate
In the business of ignorancy
I am South African
Without residency
I can read,
I can write,
However ignorant I may be
I know Mandela is in Pollsmoor jail
Though I do not know why.
Oh people of Afrika
Help me before it is too late
Emancipate me
From my ignorancy.

Mzwakhe breaks the rhythm, stops, leans into the microphone, and whispers:

For freedom is getting rusty
On the pavements of oppression.

Sometimes Mzwakhe performs alone. At other times he performs with his group ... Some of the poems are then spoken by one voice, patched over a freedom song that has dropped down to a hum in the remaining three or four voices of the group. The audience will also tend to take up the humming, particularly if it is a well-known freedom song.

Space does not allow for a comprehensive survey of the various dispersals and diasporic hybrids that constitute postcolonial poetry in English, yet it is possible to discern within this sprawling agenda certain indisputable trends. Most significantly, it is notable that the radical characteristics and developments that feature in African Caribbean writing are more the exception than the rule. Consider, for example, the following:

Shropshire shrinks into my mailbox;
my home a neat four by six inches.

I always loved neatness. Now I hold
the half-inch spire of Shrewsbury in my hand.

This is home. And this is the closest
I'll ever be to home. When I return,
the colours won't be so brilliant,

the Severn's waters so clean,
as ultramarine. My love
so overexposed.

The metaphoric excursion provoked by the postcard carries us through the emotional registers of loss and resignation. 'Home', now so distant, has become, like the small photograph on the card, a shrunken yet magical distillation of something apparently irrecoverable. In manner, the poem indicates a mid- to late 20th-century genesis; its use of free verse pays cursory homage to the precedent of Modernism but equally the poised, balanced management of syntax and figurative language, plus a peppering of assonance and off-rhyme, ties it to more conservative trends – a late 20th-century elegiac nod towards Houseman's 'A Shropshire Lad' perhaps. Having established the poem's credentials as an accomplished, unprovocative exercise in lambent Englishness, I should now disclose that its author is Agha Shahid Ali, writing from London of his home in the Indian subcontinent. Its title is 'Postcard from Kashmir' and the only alterations I made to its substance involved the substitution of 'Shropshire' for 'Kashmir', 'spire of Shrewsbury' for 'Himalayas' and 'Severn' for 'Jhelum'.

No such experiment could, for obvious reasons, be conducted on the verse of Kwesi Johnson and Dabydeen or even the more traditional Berry and Markham. For most poets of the Indian subcontinent, writing in English involves becoming aligned with a fabric of conventions maintained within the remnants of a colonial and educational infrastructure inherited from the days of empire, tempered if at all with experience of its more recent counterpart in Britain itself. In India particularly, the distinction between the indigenous language and culture and English is clear and largely inflexible. To write in English might well involve a subject or a state of mind informed by the postcolonial condition, but as I have shown with Ali's piece, the poem's nominal frame of reference is sublimated to its manner and stylistic allegiance.

In an article in the *Hindustan Times* (2004), A.K. Mehrotra provides an intriguing perspective on standard English as the language that both unites the peoples of the subcontinent and displaces them:

English is everyone's language in India; and it is no one's language. Because it is the former, everyone can read the Roman alphabet and knows the meanings of words; because it is also the latter, they can completely miss the tone and emotional charge the words carry, as in poetry words must, always.

Mehrotra's point is that poets of the subcontinent who elect to write in English, even if they have been fluent in the language all their lives, also involve themselves in an uneasy relationship with the Anglo-centric canon. In 'An Introduction', Kamala Das addresses her own experience of this:

　　　… I am Indian, very brown, born in
　　　Malabar, I speak three languages, write in

> Two, dream in one. Don't write in English, they said,
> English is not your mother-tongue. Why not leave
> Me alone, critics, friends, visiting cousins,
> Every one of you? Why not let me speak in
> Any language I like? The language I speak
> Becomes mine, its distortions, its queernesses
> All mine, mine alone. It is half English, half
> Indian, funny perhaps, but it is honest,
> It is human as I am human, don't
> You see?

While Mehrotra claims that English is 'no one's language', its poetry dispossessing Indians of the 'tone and emotional charge' unique to the genre, Das affirms and demonstrates her ownership of this allegedly alien discourse. Her idiom and vocabulary are judiciously correct, and by British standards her grammatical caution is conspicuous, almost archaic; hence her reference to a manner that is 'half English, half/Indian'. Her claim to having made it 'mine' is amply justified in her command of the double pattern. Das sets up a counterpoint between syntax, which is by parts languid and meticulous, and free verse lines, which subtly alter the trajectory of each sentence. 'Why not leave' seems at first a continuation of the paraphrased critique on her use of English but suddenly we encounter Das speaking on her own behalf: 'Me alone'. 'Why not let me speak in' appears to presage a particular affiliation but again as the sentence turns across the line ending, we discover a subclause both evasive and resolute: 'Any language I like'. She has chosen her style and idiolect and, like Walcott, she argues that, in writing poetry, tenacity and competence are more essential than an obligation to anti-colonial ideology.

In a poem called 'A Different History' (1988), Sujata Bhatt asks:

> Which language
> has not been the oppresser's tongue?
> Which language
> truly meant to murder someone?

Her questions are rhetorical. She finds it absurd to attribute to a particular language or culture some form of guilt by association. Bhatt studied in the US and eventually settled in Germany, and her sense of being both at one with herself yet aware of multiple affiliations to different registers and cultures is magnificently realized in 'Shérdi':

> The way I learned
> to eat sugarcane in Sanosara:
> I use my teeth
> to tear the outer hard *chaal*

then, bite off strips
of the white fibrous heart –
suck hard with my teeth, press down
and the juice spills out.

So tonight
when you tell me to use my teeth,
to suck hard, harder,
then, I smell sugarcane grass in your hair
and imagine you'd like to be
the shérdi out in the fields
the stalks away
opening a path before us

The subject, and title, of her poem is not even pronounceable in its original form to English-only speakers, and this sense of a nuance that is intimate, sequestered from the language and manner of the rest of the text gradually dislocates any clear perception of the poem's focus. It seems to be a reminiscence of a world she once knew, exchanged for something, and someone, elsewhere. At a first reading, the passage that opens with 'So tonight' causes us to assume that she is simply taking a meal somewhere far distant from her Indian childhood. But then we begin to wonder if the activity undertaken by the two of them involves something more intense and sensual than a companionable supper. The unusual spacing of the closing four lines imitates the two trajectories of thought that inform the texture of the poem. The word 'shérdi' is present in her mind but at the same time allows itself to be bypassed by a sentence that links her scattered reminiscences with her more immediate sense of a shared experience: 'and imagine you'd like to be/out in the fields/the stalks away/ opening a path before us'. It is an extraordinarily innovative poem, on the one hand invoking the loose, improvisational manner of William Carlos Williams – to an extent avant-garde but thoroughly Western – while on the other evoking a personal register of divided affiliation, present on the margin of the Anglo-centric text and threatening its autonomy. A passage from Bhatt's 'History is a Broken Narrative' could be invoked as the working principle for 'Shérdi':

You take your language where you get it.
Or do you
get your language
where you take it?

In Britain and Ireland, similar nuances of affiliation and dissent obtain. In his 'Broagh', Seamus Heaney, Catholic, Irish, native of Co. Derry, and educated in the very English environment of Queen's University, Belfast, does not tell the (English) reader where or what 'Broagh' is; instead, he sews into the fabric of the text echoes of its phonemic character: 'riverbank', 'broad docken', 'The garden mould/bruised easily', 'the shower gathering' – all carry extended assonated and alliterative resonances of a central core of vowels and consonants. The place is appropriated by the texture of the poem and released sparingly and selectively:

> ... your heelmark
> Was the black *O*
>
> in *Broagh*,
> its low tattoo
> among the windy bourtrees
> and rhubarb-blades
>
> ended almost
> suddenly, like that last
> *gh* the strangers found
> difficult to manage.

'The strangers' are those people who are unfamiliar with the names and dialects of the district, but they (we?) are also those readers who can hear and interpret a familiar pattern of off-rhymes and slightly irregular assonantal and alliterative echoes. The problem for such a reader comes when they attempt to stabilize these subtle shifts against the sound of the central, almost iconic word, 'Broagh'. If we don't know how this word is pronounced, then a ripple of disorientation spreads through our encounters with the rest of the poem. We become, like the 'strangers', lost in an unfamiliar landscape. The frame and structure of the poem belong, or seem to belong, to a predominantly British tradition of the reflective lyric, but within that frame, we encounter continuous moments of subversion and counter-allegiance. In this respect, there are intriguing similarities between Heaney's technique and Bhatt's in 'Shérdi'. It is not Heaney's intention simply to make the poem inaccessible to the complacent English reader – he is too sophisticated a craftsman for that – yet, at the same time, a sense of difference and strangeness informs a text that is in other respects elegantly biddable.

Derek Mahon achieves a comparable effect, although by very different means, in 'A Disused Shed in County Wexford'. The eponymous shed is home to 'a thousand mushrooms', which

> crowd to a keyhole.
> This is the one star in their firmament
> Or frames a star within a star
> What should they do there but desire?

They were abandoned long ago by 'the expropriated mycologist':

> He never came back, and light since then
> Is a keyhole rusting gently after rain.

This image dominates an otherwise impersonal account of a place and a landscape marked by unattended bleakness. Were it not for the locative indicator of
the title, it might be anywhere, but the poem resists the experiment performed
upon Ali's 'Postcard from Kashmir'. The shed, we are told, is in the 'grounds of a
burnt out hotel', an innocuous enough phrase, unless of course one has a
knowledge of the previous half-century of Irish history. Then we are fed other
nuanced clues regarding the question of why the hotel is burnt out and the
reason for the departure of the mycologist:

> They have been waiting for us in a foetor
> Of vegetable sweat since civil war days

We begin to wonder if the abandoned group of mushrooms is the figurative
nexus for a subject that the poem never actually mentions:

> There have been deaths, the pale flesh flaking
> Into the earth that nourished it;
> And nightmares, born of these and the grim
> Dominion of stale air and rank moisture.

Is the anthropomorphic presentation of the mushrooms as a community beset
by tragedies merely a conceit or is Mahon building continuous parallels between
them – imprisoned, cut off from the rest of the world, suffering quiet torments;
'A half century, without visitors, in the dark' – and some aspect of the Irish
condition? If so, does he allude to the notoriously insular nationalism of post-
civil war politics or to the straightened circumstances of the Anglo-Irish, abandoned by a presence to whom they owed their allegiance, even existence?

The poem would delight the Yale deconstructionists in that of the tissue of
questions offered to the reader, none becomes predominant; each demands a
response, all can be addressed but a final conclusion regarding the exclusive
theme of the poem – is it about Ireland or does the image of the mushrooms
incite in the speaker an unspecific mood of desuetude – can never be reached.
Our particular political preconceptions might cause us to believe that we can
reach a conclusion, but in attempting to do so we will have conducted a purblind
reading of a complex, multifaceted poem.

Heaney and Mahon raise a number of significant points with regard to the
unsteady relationship between national identity and the writing of verse in
English. In both of the above poems, Ireland, and more tenuously, its relationship with Britain, is engaged with obliquely, insinuatingly; it exists on the
margins of the poem and the question of whether it should remain there or
become its thematic fulcrum depends largely upon the predisposition of the

reader. Markham, with Lambchops, achieves a comparable effect, a technique that acknowledges the author's regional affiliation or racial identity without allowing either to obscure the quality of the poem as a poem.

This is 'The 6 O'Clock News' from Tom Leonard's *Unrelated Incidents*:

> this is thi
> six a clock
> news thi
> man said n
> thi reason
> a talk wia
> BBC accent
> iz coz yi
> widny wahnt
> mi ti talk
> aboot thi
> trooth wia
> voice lik
> wanna yoo
> scruff. if
> a toktaboot
> thi trooth
> lik wanna yoo
> scruff yi
> widny thingk
> it wuz troo.
> jist wanna yoo
> scruf tokn.
> thirza right
> way ti spell
> ana right way
> ti tok it. this
> is me tokn yir
> right way a
> spellin. this
> is ma trooth.
> yooz doant no
> thi trooth
> yirsellz cawz
> yi canny talk
> right. this is
> the six a clock
> nyooz. belt up.

And in W.N. Herbert's 'Coco-de-Mer', we are asked to 'dinna bathir wi thi braiggil', to 'let gae oan thi dumswaul', told that 'thi luccy-bean tae thi haunds o thi misk' and, even if one is familiar with the modestly diverse dialects south of the border, left to ponder both the sound and the meaning of 'flocth', 'crospunk', 'crullit', 'cothaman', 'brankie' and so on. In fact, only the occasional connective such as 'in' and 'a' – no more than one word in five – will be immediately familiar to the non-Scottish reader. Each is the Scottish counterpart to the African Caribbean genre pioneered by Linton Kwesi Johnson. Both are speech based – eschewing the implicit alliance between print, received pronunciation English and Anglo-centric cultural predominance – and each involves a far more radical reaction against convention than simply the use of an indigenous phonemes, vocabulary and idiom. In Scotland, the latter technique was customized by Hugh MacDiarmid and just as Kwesi Johnson and his peers radicalized the precedent set by the likes of Berry, so Leonard and Herbert went further than MacDiarmid in their use of the speaking voice as a deliverance from the impersonal, Anglicized confines of punctuation and syntactic coherence. Douglas Dunn, Leonard's near contemporary, exemplifies in his verse a very different approach to self-perception and its expressive collateral. In 'The Come On', he asks himself to

> Listen now to the 'professional classes'
> Renewing claims to 'rights'

Unlike Leonard, he does not subscribe to cultural separatism. Instead, he advises

> We will beat them with decorum, with manners,
> As sly as language is.

Significantly, never once is his self-conscious sense of class and status attended by any reference to his nationality. He could as easily be a native of Tony Harrison's Leeds as Renfrewshire. In this respect, the poem is something of a manifesto for the rest of his work, in which Scotland features as a place and a state of mind that he knows intimately but not as something that will determine his breadth and range as a poet.

Twentieth-century poets of Welsh origin – most notably Dylan Thomas, R.S. Thomas, Vernon Watkins, Alun Lewis and Dannie Abse – do on occasion address themselves self-consciously to their land and culture, but there is rarely any sense that Wales, as a place or state of mind, has had a significant effect upon their technique. Consider Watkins's 'Taliesin and the Mockers':

> Before men walked
> I was in these places.
> I was here
> When the mountains were laid.

But for the title we might easily take this evocation of mythology and transcendence as a response to the Lake District. R.S. Thomas is a little more determinate. Figures such as Walter Llywarch, 'well goitred, round in the bum', bred in 'quarries' of 'grey rain' (see 'A Peasant') are endemic to his verse. They are indeed grotesque distorted reflections of Thomas himself, an accomplished poet resigned to a heritage and a landscape that he finds variously fascinating, tragic and appealingly monstrous. Welshness is very often his predominant topic but the character and formal tempo of his verse differs hardly at all from that of his English counterparts.

Dylan Thomas's dense, prodigiously figurative style is sometimes, incorrectly, treated as an Anglicized echo of Welsh-language poetry. Such notions are absurd because the latter incorporates as many exclusive stylistic variations as English; only those who find both Thomas and the verse of his native language equally impenetrable, for different reasons, take the claim seriously.

It is notable that, of the three Celtic nations, only one group of poets, the Scots, have been prompted to create an idiom that militates against standardized English. The reasons for this might well be that, in Wales and Ireland, the distinction between their ancient indigenous linguistic and literary traditions and English has been preserved far more conspicuously and effectively than in Scotland. In Ireland, particularly in the Republic, the Irish language, despite the gradual dissipation of the Gaeltacht, is institutionalized as a standard, often compulsory feature of education, and its Welsh counterpart has an even stronger claim upon residence as a routine medium of exchange and within the media, in schools and universities. In both nations, then, the conspicuous contrast between two utterly dissimilar cultural and linguistic traditions causes there to be less demand for a hybridized alternative to what some regard as the homogenized language of the colonist.

Poets such as Leonard and Kwesi Johnson regard conventional poetic structures and indeed the orthodoxies of standard English as hostages to cultural hegemony. They are, however, in the minority. Davie, Markham, Betjeman, Harrison, Larkin, Berry, Walcott and many others treat verse as a prism for the scrutiny of social, cultural and racial stereotypes. The fact that these figures represent such a diverse range of backgrounds – involving both the culture of the so-called colonists and that of the oppressed – testifies to their perception of poetry as an unaffiliated medium. It can, as they demonstrate, be informed by patterns of reference and association that will prompt in the reader a variety of responses from revulsion to sympathy, but it is demonstrably the case that the poet choreographs such responses. The formal structure of verse, albeit with its antecedent association with Englishness, is, perversely, a blank canvas, a fabric of opportunities against which the poet – irrespective of their colour or national lineage – can test their resources. Each of the poems discussed above engages proactively with issues such as race, region or nationality but to treat the pieces by, say, Walcott, Markham and Heaney as emblematic of their achievement and character is both patronising and misleading. All have written on a vast range of topics whose relevance to their specific racial or cultural legacies is negligible or non-existent. Postcolonial poetry – like the epic or the lyric – is a subgenre that provides an intriguing perspective upon the world outside the text and the nature of poetry itself. However, to classify individuals exclusively as postcolonial poets is to preclude them from the much broader dominion of unaffiliated poetic writing, to perceive them as symptomatic of a condition beyond their control and to blind oneself to their skill and versatility as literary artists. It is in essence a brand of altruistic racism.

16
Evaluation

Each of the critical issues and debates discussed so far carries with it a subtext that is rarely, if ever, acknowledged, let alone canvassed: evaluation. Aside from such involuntary functions as breathing, everything that we encounter causes us to judge it. Look at a building, a landscape, a chair or indeed another human being and somewhere among the spectrum of registers and distractions that attends the experience will feature an elementary, sometimes embarrassing, reflex; whether or not we like it. This could involve all manner of judgements and instincts, from the aesthetic to the visceral, and the same heedless impulsive sensation accompanies our first reading of a poem. For some of us, dissatisfaction, boredom, or perplexity might constitute our conclusive experience of the work, but most will press ahead, read it again and question their initial response. This next, measured stage of scrutiny – perhaps involving a comparison of the poem with others we know – is the doorway between subjective impression and the complex procedure of putting our thoughts into words, talking to others about the poem and the more formal activity of recording our observations on the page. The latter constitutes the activity of literary criticism. In what follows, I want to examine the question of how much of our initial evaluative judgements we leave behind when we pass through that doorway and whether literary criticism, with its various rules and conventions, permits us to make assessments regarding the quality of poetic writing. I shall not promote ill-considered caprice as a substitute for learning and sophisticated scrutiny; rather it will be my intention to consider how the various formal and theoretical ideas covered above might be marshalled as a means of preserving our rudimentary impressions as a prism for discriminatory judgements on the relative value of poems.

When T.S. Eliot's first collection *Prufrock and Other Observations* was published in 1917, the critical reception, at least within conventional literary circles, was largely hostile:

Mr. Eliot is one of those clever young men who find it amusing to pull the leg of a sober reviewer. We can imagine his saying to his friends: 'See me have a lark out of the old fogies who don't know a poem from a pea-shooter. I'll just put down the first thing that comes into my head, and call it "The Love Song of J. Alfred Prufrock." Of course it will be idiotic; but the fogies are sure to praise it, because when they don't understand a thing and yet cannot hold their tongues they find safety in praise.' ... We do not wish to appear patronising, but we are certain that Mr. Eliot could do finer work on traditional lines. With him it seems to be a case of missing the effect by too much cleverness. All beauty has in it an element of strangeness, but here the strangeness overbalances the beauty. (from an anonymous review, *Literary World*, 5 July 1917)

Among other reminiscences which pass through the rhapsodist's mind and which he thinks the public should know about, are 'dust in crevices, smells of chestnuts in the streets, and female smells in shuttered rooms, and cigarettes in corridors, and cocktail smells in bars.'

   The fact that these things occurred to the mind of Mr. Eliot is surely of the very smallest important to any one – even to himself. They certainly have no relation to 'poetry', and we only give an example because some of the pieces, he states, have appeared in a periodical which claims that word as its title. (from an anonymous review, *TLS*, 21 June 1917)

Certainly much of what he writes is unrecognisable as poetry at present ... and it is only fair to say that he does not call these pieces poems. He calls them 'observations' and the description seems exact [because] we do not pretend to follow the drift of 'The Love Song of J. Alfred Prufrock' ... (from an anonymous review, *New Statesman*, 18 August 1917)

Swift, brilliant images break into the field of vision, scatter like rockets, and leave a trail of flying fire behind. But the general impression is momentary; there are moods and emotions, but no steady current of ideas behind them. (Arthur Waugh, *Quarterly Review*, October 1916, reviewing *The New Poetry*, a collection that contained 'The Love Song of J. Alfred Prufrock')

Here we find four members of the critical establishment – sophisticated, well-read, open-minded individuals – treating a collection that we now regard as a classic, a key transitional point in the history of poetry, as self-indulgent and incoherent. Within a decade, however, the consensus had changed and following the publication of *The Waste Land* – a poem even more radical and challenging than his earlier work – Eliot would be celebrated as one of the most important poets of the early 20th century. There are two possible explanations for this:

1 The early, hostile critics were for some reason blind to the intrinsic and enduring qualities of Eliot's work, qualities that would become apparent to those with the time and inclination to properly scrutinize it.
2 The early critics' judgements were accurate and balanced, at least according to the criteria of the time, but in due course collective perceptions of what poetry is and what it should do altered.

The second case, you will note, accords with the model of interpretation proposed by critics such as Fish and Eagleton (see Chapter 10); that we respond not to the enduring, intrinsic features of the text but according to the programmed expectations of our given sociocultural environment. There is some evidence in the reviews themselves that lends credence to this argument. Notably, the *TLS* reviewer contends that Eliot's pieces 'have no relation to poetry' and their *New Statesman* counterpart concurs: 'Certainly much of what he writes is unrecognisable as poetry at present'. These reviewers would no doubt already have encountered examples of Modernist verse. It was in circulation but no one was quite certain of what it was, given that it certainly did not correspond with pre-20th-century definitions of poetry: in general, it eschewed rhyme and regular metre; its use of figurative language was wayward and unfocused; and, as the *Literary World* reviewer put it, it exchanged syntactic coherence for 'the first thing that comes into my head'. Over the next 10–20 years, the poems in Eliot's *Prufrock and Other Observations* collection did not in themselves undergo any changes; what did alter, however, was the rule book regarding what was and what was not acceptable as poetry. According to this explanation, the premise upon which evaluative interpretation is based – that poems possess, or lack, intrinsic qualities that can be discerned by the reader – is an illusion.

By the same reasoning, however, the following hypothesis would be viable: Eliot could have written anything, could indeed have 'pull[ed] the leg of a sober reviewer', perhaps chosen at random a collection of lines from a hundred poems by different poets in an anthology of Serbian verse, had a friend translate them into English, assembled them as a 'poem' and offered it as his contribution to the burgeoning trend in avant-garde verse. If the reception model is valid, then there would be no reason why this piece of creative fraudulence would not have been given similarly indulgent treatment by the new interpretive environment. It might now, therefore, be taught and studied in universities and be the subject of scholarly monographs on the genesis of Modernism. Indeed, this is the very rationale that underpins the exercises undertaken by Fish, Culler, Forrest, Thompson et al.; recontextualize a random series of words or sections of a nonliterary text as a poem, and these will be subjected to the same rigorous patterns of scrutiny as poems that were intended as such and accorded comparable aesthetic status. The implications of this are unnerving. Recognition of quality is reliant upon the identification of the intrinsic defining features of the poem, and if the latter are infinitely mutable constructs of the collective inclinations of a given 'interpretive community', as Fish puts it, then the former too has nothing to do with an abstract criterion for excellence and is instead whatever the fabric of discourses to which the reader belongs decides it to be. For some this might be an acceptable scenario but in my view it is both flawed and pernicious. Consider again the first explanation. There is abundant evidence that when a particular poet or group of poets transgress the consensually agreed formal conventions of writing, commentators have difficulties in reconciling their expectations with their engagement with the text. Milton's *Paradise Lost* was, as we noted in Chapter 3, the first major English poem in blank verse. The prevailing opinion was that without rhyme, the line, the feature that distinguished poetry from everything else, was imperceptible. Therefore many critics throughout the late 17th and 18th centuries found it difficult to read the poem as a poem. Only gradually did it become evident that Milton had built into his work a dynamic relationship between metre, syntax and the unrhymed line that was both unprecedented and served an innately poetic aspect of the double pattern. A comparable, although far more complex contrast between convention and innovation obtained with Modernist poetry and free verse. The standard rules and conventions had been overturned but, crucially, their supplements and replacements were not externally regulated and documented; they were created by the poets themselves and discerned by astute critics. This conjecture buttresses the traditional model of critical interpretation as the discovery and appreciation of inherent and premeditated qualities of the poem, which itself is crucial to the rationale of literary evaluation. To aver that a poem attains a status of stylistic and aesthetic excellence involves the collateral premise that the poet is responsible for this achievement.

Abstract principles such as excellence only become tenable through their exemplification in specific poems, and further verification of prestige will be found when these are contrasted with texts that are demonstrably inadequate. Evaluation therefore entails comparison and in what follows I shall attempt an impartial estimation of the relative qualities of a number of poems. I shall begin with poems by Philip Larkin and William McGonagall. My choice of the latter might seem to question my premise of impartiality, given that his name has become synonymous with laughable incompetence. He is treated with indulgent condescension by everyone within and, indeed, outside the literary establishment and the *Oxford Companion to English Literature* (Drabble, 2000) cursorily refers to him as 'the world's worst poet'. However, it is impossible to locate detailed measured assessments of his work upon which such judgements could be founded. He is, then, ranked by all-comers as an incompetent poet but this, in effect, amounts to condemnation without trial.

There is an intriguing article by Paul Werth, 'Roman Jakobson's Verbal Analysis of Poetry' (1976), which presents Jakobson's methods as embodying the flaws and failed objectives of conventional criticism. Werth claims, correctly, that the application of Jakobson's exhaustive stylistic methodology to a poem by McGonagall discloses levels of complexity and sophistication comparable with those that Jakobson and Jones found in a Shakespeare sonnet. Werth's point is that there is no predictable relationship between 'linguistic evidence and critical instinct' and that it is impossible to prove the general opinion that 'the value of [McGonagall's poem] is ... abysmally low'. It is true that Jakobson does not supplement his analyses with evaluative comments – he leaves that to the reader – but such an omission does not disprove the contention that a knowledge of the primary, formal features of the poem properly enables us to substantiate our judgement of its quality. This is McGonagall's poem 'An Address to the Rev. George Gilfillan':

> All hail to the Rev. George Gilfillan of Dundee,
> He is the greatest preacher I did ever hear or see.
> He is a man of genius bright,
> And in him his congregation does delight,
> Because they find him to be honest and plain,
> Affable in temper, and seldom known to complain.
> He preaches in a plain straightforward way,
> The people flock to hear him night and day
> And hundreds from the doors are often turn'd away,
> Because he is the greatest preacher of the present day.
> He has written the life of Sir Walter Scott,
> And while he lives he will never be forgot,
> Nor when he is dead,
> Because by his admirers it will be often read;
> And fill their minds with wonder and delight,
> And wile away the tedious hours on a cold winter's night.

McGonagall uses irregular rhythm and line lengths, but so did Coleridge in 'Christabel' and Blake and Whitman in their most celebrated work. His rhyme scheme – aa bb cc dd – juxtaposes a note of regularity against an otherwise flexible formal pattern and one might even contend that his piece is a modest forerunner to Modernism, particularly since he eschews metaphor and ostentatious imagery; he could almost be cited as an early quasi-Imagist. So far, then, McGonagall appears to be an engaging innovative writer but his failure as a poet is due to his apparent unwillingness or inability to decide whether he is writing poetry or prose. The rhymes interfere with the progress of the syntax, but not in a way that creates a purposive, let alone elegant, tension between the two dimensions of the double pattern, the poetic and referential registers. The rhymes are found and dumped at line endings as a duty to poetic custom, and syntax is altered only as a concession to this convention. Consequently, we encounter embarrassing sequences of non sequiturs. The line 'He has written the life of Sir Walter Scott' is not in itself clumsy or awkward but one senses that once McGonagall has launched himself into the next one, his desperate search for a rhyme – or perhaps his predecision regarding the rhyme word 'forgot' that he intends to use – blinds him to the ponderous, unintentionally droll character of the resulting couplet. Then we encounter the eye-poppingly inept, laughably incompetent coda:

> Nor when he is dead,

Again one must assume that in his desperate attempts to find matching rhyme words for each unwieldy chunk of syntax, he has lost any cognisance of the terrible effects that can be caused when the two halves of the double pattern are ineptly coordinated.

McGonagall, in his chaotic, mildly endearing way, poses a serious question for evaluative criticism. We may judge him to be a bad poet because his failure to control and command the formal, literary dimension of language compromises his ability to absorb its referential dimension and to offer the reader an unexpected and possibly enlightening perspective on the relation between language and perceived reality. If he had written a prose essay about the activities and characteristics of the Reverend Gilfillan and told us roughly the same as he does in his poem, stylistic evaluation would be suspended. But because he uses a form in which the structural dimensions of the text constantly interfere with its communicative purpose, we begin to ask questions about how, and how well, he deals with this provocative merger of style and function. In effect, naturalization becomes an evaluative rather than a purely practical procedure. McGonagall, by writing a poem, provokes our wish to naturalize the text, only to leave us disappointed. His literary style is an encumbrance, an irritation, rather than a medium that transforms or even constructs the message.

Curiously, there are parallels between McGonagall's bumbling incompetence and the work of a poet judged to be one of the pillars of the English canon, William Wordsworth. Many of the pieces of Wordsworth's, and Coleridge's, debut volume *Lyrical Ballads* replicate the mood and style of the popular magazine ballads of the later 18th century, indulged at the time as a low cultural subgenre. Their perceived status, then, in relation to conventional verse was the equivalent of today's Mills & Boon novels or Westerns compared with 'literary' fiction. Wordsworth conducted an exercise in cultural ventriloquism. He went downmarket in an attempt to invest ordinary, manifestly ill-educated presences with transcendent significance. 'The Thorn' begins:

> There is a thorn; it looks so old,
> In truth you'd find it hard to say,
> How it could ever have been young,
> It looks so old and grey.
> Not higher than a two-year's child,
> It stands erect this aged thorn;
> No leaves it has, no thorny points;
> It is a mass of knotted joints,
> A wretched thing forlorn.
> It stands erect, and like a stone
> With lichens it is overgrown.
>
> Like rock or stone, it is o'ergrown
> With lichens to the very top,
> And hung with heavy tufts of moss
> A melancholy crop:
> Up from the earth these mosses creep,

And this poor thorn they clasp it round
So close, you'd say that they were bent
With plain and manifest intent,
To drag it to the ground;
And all had joined in one endeavour
To bury this poor thorn for ever.

The critical reception of *Lyrical Ballads* was largely unsympathetic and in his piece in the *Critical Review* (1798), Southey indicated the nature of the disdainful consensus, commenting on 'The Thorn':

> The advertisement says that it is not told in the person of the author but in that of some loquacious narrator. The author should have recollected that he who personates tiresome loquacity becomes tiresome himself.

Southey's point is that the speaker is, if not entirely unsuitable for serious poetry, then at least capable of trying the patience of the cultivated reader. In drama or fiction, the presence of a figure whose command of English is as modest as their intellectual acumen is accommodated by the complex architecture of the text: they stand in contrast to others who use language differently and even when they occupy the foreground, they will do so only as a device subordinate to that of the controlling presence of the playwright, narrator or author. In poetry, however, the speaker is coterminous with the boundaries of the text. Wordsworth, in announcing that he is not the speaker of 'The Thorn', pre-empts any criticism of self-evident stylistic incompetence. The speaker is carelessly repetitive, allowing the same word or phrase to appear two or three times in the same stanza and often his lazy, meandering syntax will be shoehorned uncomfortably into the unforgiving framework of metre and rhyme. Clearly, implies Wordsworth, this man has acquainted himself with the basic formulae of the ballad form but lacks the subtlety of touch required in his attempt to marry this structure with his loose digressive habits of speech. He is, like McGonagall, incapable of coordinating the two elements of the double pattern. But there is another aspect of the speaker that rescues the poem from classification as an exercise in sociocultural condescension. His story involves a rumour that the tree of the title marks the grave of a child murdered by its mentally disturbed mother, Martha Ray. Before explicitly telling the story of Martha, the speaker sews small clues on its nature into his ponderous account. Even in the first two stanzas, he lingers curiously on the age and height of the tree, 'Not higher than a two-year's child' and peppers his description of its appearance with rather morbid inferences: 'A melancholy crop', 'this poor thorn they clasp it round', 'To bury this poor thorn for ever'. These signals that the scene carries for the speaker hints of an act too dreadful to properly confront are released involuntarily.

Wordsworth choreographs his creation as an enactment of the primitivist epiphany, a sense of the rawness of existence – in this case the mystery of why a tormented women might kill her own infant – uncluttered by the machinery of learning. The fact that he, the speaker, is demonstrably a bad poet is significant for several reasons. It should be noted that the experiment of *Lyrical Ballads* did not establish a precedent. The glaring incongruity of an unlearned, unpoetic presence in command of a form that demands sophistication was rarely repeated. Thus the rationale for the collection, announced in the advertisement, was exposed as an intriguing contradiction in terms. Poems that attempt to escape the formal legacy that defines verse – to move closer to the transparency of immediate experience – are by their nature unsatisfactory, poorly fashioned pieces of work. This is, I accept, a contentious claim and I make it as an overture to later discussions on the nature of experimental, avant-garde poetry and evaluation. All the major landmarks in the history of poetry since the Renaissance have involved self-conscious revisions of, or shifts away from, established conventions of writing, the most radical of all these being Modernism. Many, although not all, Modernist poets sought to dispense with the mechanisms of style, formal structure, even apparent purpose that had accumulated through the previous four centuries of poetic writing. It would be simplistic to accord an aggregate objective to all writers involved in this but the vast majority shared a belief that the established traditions of poetic form effectively smothered a poet's sense of individuality and hindered innovation and creativity. However, one of the problematic legacies of the Modernist revolution is that the abandonment of the abstract formal conventions carries with it a collateral loss; the means by which we frame or address an assessment of a poet's essential qualities become arbitrary, sometimes non-existent. Some would regard this as a commendably anti-elitist development, the removal of the framing devices that maintain the writing of verse as a recreational preserve of the social and cultural hierarchy. Perhaps, but at the same time, if it is now acceptable for a poem to be treated as a poem simply because its author offers it as such, then how do we discriminate between an assembly of words thrown together without any attendance upon intellectual coherence and the aesthetics of formal structure and those pieces that, while innovative, are also deserving of respect as works of art? In short, once the old rules of the game are abandoned, it becomes difficult to judge the quality of the players. As we have seen, some poets, notably William Carlos Williams, worked outside the confines of abstract structure while, with great subtlety, recreating their own version of the double pattern. Others, as we shall see, exploited the convention-free ethos of poetic writing as an opportunity for self-indulgence. For the time being, however, let us continue with our more general examination of the nature of quality, or its absence, by turning to a poet who a generation after Modernism abjured the easy temptations of experiment.

Despite being loathed by the more sanctimonious among the literary and academic establishment for his alleged personal shortcomings, Philip Larkin, unlike McGonagall, is treated even by his begrudgers as an accomplished poet. Few, if any, have doubted the quality of his 'An Arundel Tomb', but what justifies its ranking as a first-rate poem? The following are the opening and closing stanzas:

Side by side, their faces blurred,
The earl and countess lie in stone,
Their proper habits vaguely shown
As jointed armour, stiffened pleat,
And that faint hint of the absurd –
The little dogs under their feet.

Time has transfigured them into
Untruth. The stone fidelity
They hardly meant has come to be
Their final blazon, and to prove
Our almost-instinct almost true:
What will survive of us is love.

The poem adheres to the complex stanzaic formula of iambic, octosyllabic lines, rhyming abbcac, but the syntax maintains the unforced manner of detail and reflection that one might expect of a private journal. The first three stanzas are dominated by the speaker's description of the details of the tomb and among the diction and syntax is found a light distribution of registers, which are, if not quite anachronistic, self-consciously unusual. 'Proper habits vaguely shown' carries a hint of the naughty ambiguity of the Renaissance lyricist, and the words 'lie in stone' would, if found in a poem three centuries older than this, prompt a suspicion that the verb 'lie' is playing beyond its apparent reference to a recumbent final posture. The poetry that engages most with the brutal contrariness of life as brief, nasty and pointless while pretending to be something else is that of the 17th-century lyricists, the Metaphysicals, and 'An Arundal Tomb' seems to nod sardonically towards that tradition. This suspicion is further encouraged in the final stanza, in which we learn that

Time has transfigured them into
Untruth.

The enjambment is meticulously disingenuous, in that he hesitates but only to delay the acceptance of a grim certainty hinted at throughout the poem. Many commentators on the poem have failed to recognize that its speaker is robustly unpersuaded by everything he apprehends, that the poem is in truth an affirmation of cynical disbelief, both in the significance of love as anything beyond the emblematic and the possibility of there being something after death. Such misreadings testify to the brilliance of Larkin's counterpointing of the respectful deferential manner of the poem against what it actually says. The closing stanza could also make a claim to being a triumphant celebration of what it says. But the deceptively innocuous modifiers 'hardly' and, twice, 'almost' assassinate this optimistic motif; an 'almost true' will always be a lie. Larkin's achievement here is threefold. His orchestration of a demanding stanzaic formula with a relaxed yet shrewd manner is exemplary; the two parts of the double pattern, by their nature incompatible, are elegantly amalgamated. If this were his only accomplishment, then the poem might be classed as a fine example of technical proficiency, but Larkin's meshing of the poetic and referential registers serves as the perfect vehicle for an effect at once beguiling and unimprovable. As we follow the eye and the reflections of the speaker, he appears fascinated yet uncertain about the significance of the tomb, but gradually – particularly when we read the poem two or three times and consider more closely its delicate nuances of meaning – it becomes apparent that the speaker's polite esteem for this tribute to the endurance of love and the spirit is simply that; in truth, he has no illusions regarding anything beyond lived experience. The double pattern frames and orchestrates an interplay between routine and elemental states of mind.

In the non-literary world, there is a consensus on the appropriateness and suitability of idiom or vocabulary. We would not, for example, reply to an email from a boyfriend with 'Your manner of linking the consciousness of deviation to translatability in fact condemns what one wants at least to describe' when 'Are we meeting later, or what?' would do. And nor would we begin a job application or complaint to a council official with a phrase such as 'My dearest Johnny-boy, I wish so much ...'. In general, we have an intuitive alertness to what is required by the context of the statement but in verse this is complicated by the formal architecture of the poem, capable as this is of throwing into bold, incongruous relief phrases or habits of speech that outside the poem might be more cautiously or appropriately situated. Philip Hobsbaum's 'A Lesson in Love' is a brief narrative piece in which an academic tells of how he seduced one of his students, apparently during a tutorial. These are the closing stanzas:

> Which is the truer? I, speaking of Donne,
> Calling the act a means not an end,
> Or at your sweet pudenda, sleeking you down:
> Was there no other way to be your friend?

> None, none. The awkward pauses when we talk,
> The literary phrases, are a lie.
> It was for this your teacher ran amok:
> Truth lies between your legs, and so do I.

Hobsbaum, unlike McGonagall, earned himself a respectable level of esteem within the literary establishment but there is, at least in my view, something about this poem that recalls the former's work. One can observe, without comment, that it comprises irregular pentameter quatrains, is in tone conversational and reflective, with hardly any recourse to figurative language, with the exception of that memorably vivid closing line. Some poems telescope their substance into a brief phrase, which is often recalled or quoted as a condensation of the themes addressed. (Yeats's 'A terrible beauty is born' from 'Easter 1916' is a prime example.) The closing line of 'A Lesson in Love' has a comparable, although lamentable effect. From the first line onwards, one begins to detect an uneasy relationship between the personal idiosyncratic tone of the piece and the dry formality of its structure. If, in a novel, a somewhat condescending, pretentious Lothario were to use the term 'modest Irish miss', and then go on to revel in his recollection of her 'full mouth' and in due course 'legs thrashing', 'stocking tops' and 'tight blue pants bursting to be off', the author might be commended for a grating blend of caricature and candour – especially if that author was male. In a poem as formally painstaking as this, however, the contrast between the locutionary manner and its containing framework seems, to put it lightly, inappropriate. The speaker, who, in a novel or even in the real world, would appear in his own right a blend of the odious and the absurd, is here a constituent controlling element of the text and his presence does considerable damage to the quality of the latter as a work of literature. The dreadful counterpoint between his pompous erudition – 'speaking of Donne' – and his visceral intent, including the prurient phrasing of 'your sweet pudenda, sleeking you down', would in any context cause one to recoil (or if male, perhaps issue an apology on behalf of one's gender). But when framed within the cool exactness of a quatrain, the presence seems anomalous and embarrassing. One even recalls the tragi-comic spectacle of McGonagall as he seeks desperately to cram his unwieldy syntax into a rhyme scheme. Here the execution is more controlled and the effect all the worse for it. Consider the rhymes. They are, in purely technical terms, correctly disposed but the parallelisms of sound point up the grotesque transposition of the speaker's lexicon with his state of mind: 'I knew' – 'your eyes gave me a clue'; 'your tight blue pants' – 'our romance'. The closing line exemplifies the speaker's and, it must said, the poet's blindness to stylistic malapropisms. It is a conceit that defies any attempt to naturalize it but not because of its complexity: critical analysis does not immunize one from unendurable disquiet.

It is not too difficult to identify incompetent writing in regular verse in the sense that a poet's inability to properly reconcile the twin demands of the double pattern will become painfully evident. But with free verse, there are no particular syntactic or metrical rules that the reader might invoke to judge the quality of a poem. As we saw in Chapter 10, Jonathan Culler can turn a prose discourse into a free verse poem by visually foregrounding parts of its syntactic framework, and Stanley Fish claims to have distilled impressive naturalizations from his students in response to a poetically 'shaped' list of surnames on the blackboard (Chapter 10). At the less serious end of the aesthetic spectrum, E.J. Thribb, *Private Eye*'s resident free versifier ('a poet, 17½', although by now probably 57), has produced absurd and amusing examples of 'occasional' free verse. This is 'Erratum' (8 February 1974):

> In my last poem
> 'Lines on the

100th Anniversary
Of the Birth of
W. Somerset
Maugham'

The word 'Yorkshire'
Appeared as
'Workshire'.

Keith's mum
Spotted it
Immediately though
I confess I did
Not when I read
The proofs.

I regret the
Inconvenience this
May have caused to readers.

One mispelt word
Like this can
Completely destroy
A poem.

Thribb has established himself as a comic institution (four of his works feature in Gavin Ewart's *Penguin Book of Light Verse*, 1980) because we, his amused readers, are still uncertain about what the writing and interpretation of free verse actually involve. The cognitive aspect of the above poem makes its context clear enough: an erratum by an unselfconsciously adolescent poet ('Keith's mum spotted it immediately'). As a prose note, this text would function as an engaging, even charming, example of ingenuousness, but it becomes comic because its division into lines projects it into the 'serious' sphere of the poetic. But why do we not find William Carlos Williams' 'This Is Just To Say' (1934) equally laughable?

I have eaten
the plums
that were in
the icebox

and which
you were probably
saving
for breakfast

> Forgive me
> they were delicious
> so sweet
> and so cold.

Jonathan Culler (1975, p. 175) proposes that the only reason we interpret this as a poem is because we have become accustomed to the typographic design of free verse, and that once this signal of high cultural intent registers we bring to it a lexicon of interpretative and evaluative responses:

> Given the opposition between the eating of plums and the social rules which this violates, we may say that the poem as note becomes a mediating force, recognizing the priority of rules by asking forgiveness but also affirming, by the thrust of the last few words, that immediate sensuous experience also has its claims and that the order of personal relations (the relationship between the 'I' and the 'you') must make a place for such experience.

He reprints the poem as if it were a note left on the fridge to demonstrate that the two texts differ only in terms of the reader's programmed response; in short, we would not, if sane, interpret a similar message from whoever else uses our kitchen as a solemn reflection on 'immediate sensuous experience' and the 'order of personal relations'.

One suspects, however, that Culler has allowed the bulldozer of reception theory to crush any nascent, personal register of aesthetic cognisance. His model of interpretation depends upon the assumption that Williams assembled the poem almost at random from a piece of prosaic, raw material; the sentence containing the note on the icebox is the text that he actually 'wrote', while the poetic structure, comprising three free verse paragraphs, is the equivalent of Andy Warhol's famous framing of a soup tin or the positioning of Tracey Emin's unmade bed in an art gallery as an 'installation'. I would contend that when Williams wrote the poem, he was fully alert to how the lines would play the predominant role in the poem's demonstration that the mind can, in no more than 30 words, begin to intuit something subtle and transcendent in the otherwise commonplace. The free verse lines attend to no abstract pattern but they maintain a degree of consistency, never allowing a significant syntactic sequence to overrun their governance of the text. They separate, even mobilize and counterpoint brief noun and verb phrases (which, surely, is evidence more of planning than, as Culler avers, the random redistribution of a pre-existing sentence). This design is immensely effective. The first and the third verse paragraphs are structurally almost identical, yet the latter unfolds the moments of pleasure in such a way that we forget the banality of the opening and are entranced by a speaking presence seemingly preoccupied with his own guilty indulgences. As a poem that marshals the two dimensions of the double pattern to create a portrait of a sentient mind at work, it begs comparison with Larkin's, despite their superficial stylistic differences.

What then of E.J Thribb? Thribb is, of course, the creation of several talented satirists, but his self-evident incompetence, his role as a postmodern McGona-gall, raises significant questions with regard to quality and evaluation. Specifi-cally, if Thribb's creators are capable of making conspicuous stylistic abominations in a free verse poem, then there must, by implication, be ways in which an accomplished poet can create quite the opposite effect. Clearly, Thribb's piece invokes the 20th-century subgenre of the 'found' poem, pioneered by the Imag-ists and exemplified in Williams' 'This Is Just to Say'; a poem whose manner and diction seem to have more in common with casual, unalloyed moments of thought or expression than with the self-conscious stylization of much literary writing. Thribb is guilty of the very compositional bungling of which Culler falsely accused Williams. His poem does indeed, when reprinted as prose, seem as though it was originally intended as an erratum on one of his previous poems. The line breaks point up, give absurd prominence to, domestic banalities:

> Keith's mum
> Spotted it
> Immediately

They also testify to the fact that if the writer of this piece had intended it as a poem and, more significantly, was far more technically proficient than Thribb, he would not first have written it as prose and then redistributed it typographi-cally. He would instead have given attention to the continuous interaction between the line and syntax.

Thribb demonstrates, fortnightly in his appearances in *Private Eye*, the pitfalls and dire consequences of misusing the deceptively simple form of free verse. In 'To A Poor Old Woman' (1934), Williams shows how its potentialities can be handsomely realized:

> munching a plum on
> the street a paper bag
> of them in her hand
>
> They taste good to her
> They taste good
> to her. They taste
> good to her.
>
> You can see it by
> the way she gives herself
> to the one half
> sucked out in her hand
>
> Comforted
> a solace of ripe plums

seeming to fill the air
They taste good to her.

How, then, do I justify my claim that Thribb's and Williams' poems belong at different ends of the aesthetic spectrum?

The subject of Williams' poem is an episode of unadorned unremarkable simplicity – a woman eating plums on the street – yet he invests the moment with vividness by allowing his language to become a mimetic index to an image that, visually, the reader can never apprehend. The movement of the woman's hand from the bag to her mouth and the apparent sense of satisfaction she derives from the experience is telescoped by Williams into his own similar fascination, perhaps even delight, at the shape and texture of the very ordinary phrase, 'They taste good to her'. Just as the woman derives pleasure from 'the way she gives herself/to the one half/sucked out in her hand', so Williams savours the texture of five words, the meaning of which – 'the taste' – is altered slightly with each reshaping.

Let us now consider the procedures involved in evaluating the poems by McGonagall, Larkin, Hobsbaum, Thribb and Williams. Each reading has involved three levels of interpretive engagement, which I list below.

Level 1: Discovery procedures – the identification and recognition of the double pattern
This involves:

1 Those features of the poem that bear principal allegiance to the network of non-literary registers and discourses; at a localized level, the syntactic and referential features the poem shares with other discourses and genres, and, in a general sense, its prevailing theme or topic.
2 Features of the poem that are bound into a patently literary tradition; rhyme, metre, free verse, the persistent or gratuitous use of figurative language, stylistic discontinuities, unprompted or unexplained alterations in tempo, mood or frame of reference.

Our ability to name and particularize these features reflects our literary competence, which is tested more severely at level 2.

Level 2: Reading, analysis and naturalization
In simple terms, this involves making sense of the poem. Level 1 involves the definition of a tension between those elements the poem shares with non-literary discourses and those that are patently literary. We make sense of, or naturalize, a poem by translating it into the terms and conditions of the former: it is effectively destylized. However, this procedure is never, or at least should not be, conclusive. It is the process rather than the potential result or consequence of naturalization that is crucial to the evaluation of poetry. To perceive a poem as containing some immanent message that can be distilled from and

preserved beyond the act of reading is to do a grave injustice to the nature and purpose of poetry. Level 2, then, is a crucial stage in the process of evaluation, in that we involve ourselves in an encounter with the two dimensions of the double pattern:

1   Our rational faculty will, inevitably, involve a form of rewriting of the text itself, an attempt to stabilize the dynamic of reading by finding potential solutions for opaque or stylistically impenetrable passages.
2   At the same time, however, it is possible to adjust our interpretive registers towards a more flexible, non-prescriptive engagement with the text. Instead of attempting to 'translate' the peculiarities, incongruities and gratuitous gestures of the poem into a coherent, explanatory addendum, we allow them to register undisturbed.

Maintaining a balance between these two – and in particular not allowing the former to supersede the latter – is the key to the appreciation and evaluation of poetry. To achieve this might well involve not a single encounter with the text but numerous readings and these will very often be non-linear. We read the text spatially as if it were a map, comparing and considering the relationship between its constituent factors. We become Riffaterre's mythical Superreader (Chapter 9). From this we can venture opinions on the quality of the poem.

Level 3: Judgement
The judgemental criteria proposed here are clear enough. In terms purely of skill and technique, good poets are those who create a fertile contrapuntal relationship between the two dimensions of the double pattern, and in this respect, Larkin and Williams are exemplary. The work of McGonagall, Hobsbaum and Thribb involves clumsy and often embarrassing mismatches between these two dimensions. More significantly, the quality of a poem is concomitant with the poet's success in creating from the double pattern a perspective upon a theme, idea, experience or object that cannot be obtained via non-poetic language. Larkin, without reaching any manifest conclusions, shows how complementary and sometimes competing ratiocinative, emotional and intellectual registers attend an encounter with a sculpted tribute to life beyond death; he does so, moreover, in a manner that belies the normative logic of prose. Williams crystallizes a moment of apparent insignificance as a model of how perception, empathy and language interact, and again he demonstrates how poetry is not merely an autonomous genre but one that is possessed of unique expressive capacities.

   Given that McGonagall and Thribb are patently incapable of orchestrating the two dimensions of the double pattern, the reader is preoccupied almost exclusively with the spectacle of a poet failing to master the fundamentals of his vocation and, as a consequence, any indulgent questions regarding what the poet might be attempting to achieve become immaterial. Hobsbaum is not so much technically inept as guilty of the gauche mismatching of two stylistic registers. The effect is not entirely dissimilar to that caused by Thribb but, since it was unintentional, it is more likely to cause embarrassment than amusement.

It is not my intention to offer these criteria as inflexible and conclusive. Level 3 particularly will probably reflect some aspects of my own sociocultural prejudices. Taste and enjoyment, thankfully, will never quite accord with a predictable consensus. However, I would argue that we need to be reasonably aware of the practice and critical vocabulary of the first two levels to confidently articulate our opinions on the third, the latter involving everything from the specialized polemic of academic criticism, through book reviewing to personal taste, preference and reading habits.

With this in mind, consider Roland Barthes' distinction, expounded at length in *S/Z: An Essay* (1975), between works that are *scriptible* (writerly) and those that are *lisible* (readerly). Roughly summarized, a scriptible text is that which demands the participation of the reader in the production of meaning, while its lisible counterpart involves a straightforward transference of effects to a more passive reader. One could argue that Wordsworth's 'The Idiot Boy' is far more lisible than scriptable, in the sense that we are fully informed of who the characters are, and what they do, and there is an uncomplicated correspondence between these details and the emotive effects of the poem. Eliot's 'Prufrock' is scriptible in that we remain constantly uncertain about the nature of the speaker and the context of their incoherent account, and we are consequently obliged to speculate on how the text works and what it means – in Barthes' terms, we become the co-writers of the text.

One issue rarely addressed in critical debates is this: are lisible poems of higher quality than their scriptible counterparts, or vice versa? It is evident that the two types of writing cannot be treated simply as generic classifications, in the same way that we might distinguish a narrative poem from a lyric. The latter are neutral concepts and it is only when they are embodied in the writing of a poet that we are able to make such judgements as 'this is a fine narrative poem' or 'that is a lyric of abysmally poor quality'. Lisible and scriptible poems are not merely generically distinct types of writing; they have predictably different effects upon the reader and in this regard preference must feature considerably in our response. Many readers, particularly academics, conceal or camouflage such leanings and predilections for the simple reason that a considerable number of lisible and scriptible poems coexist in the canon and the curriculum. It is acceptable to explain and discuss the stylistic differences between the two species of verse and their contrasts as reflections of opposing intellectual and cultural outlooks but not to aver that one is superior to or more significant than the other. To do so would allow the fickle and quixotic aspect of subjective preference to intrude upon measured, learned scrutiny, or the rigours of Critical Theory. It will be my intention in what follows to make use of the three-level model of evaluation as a template for a survey of the relative value and significance of lisible and scriptible poems. The issue is important because virtually all scriptible texts came into being with Modernism, and it is the distinction between Modernist and conventional writing that is by far the most important, both in the history of poetry and at the present time.

The following is the opening stanza of Dylan Thomas's 'When, Like a Running Grave':

> When, like a running grave, time tracks you down,
> Your calm and cuddled is a scythe of hairs,
> Love in her gear is slowly through the house,
> Up naked stairs, a turtle in a hearse,
> Hauled to the dome,

The relative adverb 'When' introduces the complex explanatory clause of the first line, and we are uncertain if the unfolding situation will involve the specific circumstances of when time will track you down like a running grave or whether time will always track you down like a running grave. This uncertainty is not resolved; rather, it is further complicated by a montage of syntactic and semantic discontinuities. What exactly is your 'calm and cuddled'? The semantic pattern of a 'scythe of hairs', 'Love in her gear', 'naked', and 'hearse' suggests perhaps a tension between sensual, physical images and death. The poem extends Eliot's precedent in 'Prufrock', and shifts it beyond any acceptable balance between intrinsic and imposed coherence. Read the rest of the poem and if you can disclose a pattern of syntactic and referential continuity, you are, I believe, deceiving yourself. The potential for self-deceit is provided by a complex and admirably precise formal pattern. Each stanza consists of four roughly iambic decasyllabic lines, followed by a quattrosyllabic coda. These are held together by a system of alliterative/assonantal off-rhymes, binding each stanza into a discernable pattern of a bbb a. Without this concession to regularity, the poem would be meaningless. The reader is literally bounced from one point of metrical and phonic foregrounding to the next and this is the only formal pattern upon which an attempt at naturalization can be based: the conventional has effectively replaced and overridden the cognitive dimension of the double pattern.

We are not dealing with the shambolic utterance of a semi-literate infant or a heroically inept non-native speaker, something that we feel it is our polite duty to 'correct'. Nor are we indulging the stylistic incompetence of a poet such as McGonagall. Thomas's command of both dimensions of the double pattern is self-evident, but he has chosen deliberately to allow the poetic to override the referential features of the poem. On the one hand, Thomas has proved himself to be a versatile craftsman – his abundant provision and dextrous control of the standard lexicon of poetic devices matches that of any Renaissance poet – yet at the same time, he has posed a question for the reader for which there is no simple answer. His poem is as difficult to naturalize as the most radical Modernist or postmodern text, yet in all other respects it is self-consciously conventional. Is he therefore practising a form of self-indulgence, protecting a poem that says very little behind the façade of orthodoxy; or is he challenging the routine expectations of what the double pattern can tell us about the arbitrariness of language? The question is not a matter for impartial scrutiny because it raises a supplementary enquiry. Can we enjoy – by which I mean appreciate both aesthetically and intuitively – what we can never properly understand? Or should we set aside such subjective idiosyncratic inclinations and give attention to overarching intellectual and ideological aspects of poetic writing? If your reply to the former is 'no', then you are more likely to prefer poems that fall into the category of the lisible; and if your response to the latter is 'yes', your favoured territory is most likely scriptable verse.

Within academic criticism, there is a widespread although rarely admitted predilection for the scriptable poem. Since the 1960s, literary theory has been dominated by the premise that language or discourse shapes and determines all brands of belief and experience, so poems that voraciously resist any affiliation to non-literary language – that is, refuse to be naturalized – are sound material for the academic industry. By creating a language that is self-referentially poetic, which hints at coherence and continuity and then forecloses the offer, they point up the arbitrariness of all linguistic systems.

There are only three book-length collections concerned exclusively with the relationship between poetry and theory (Murray, 1989; Easthope and Thompson, 1991; Acheson and Huk, 1996), and in each, more than three-quarters of the essays are concerned with the kind of radical avant-garde verse that lends itself to theory-oriented questions on the nature of signification and the unsteady connection between subjectivity and textuality. Each book indicates that from the perspective of a theory-dominated academic world, scriptible poems are, by their nature, accorded a higher status than their more conservative, accessible counterparts, a consensus that sidelines such questions as authorial skill and craftsmanship in favour of a hierarchy in which the posing of complex intellectual and interpretive questions is the principal criterion. In this regard, J.H. Prynne, one of those who has kept the flame of Poundian Modernism alight, is a particular favourite (he is, for example, accorded an entire chapter in Easthope and Thompson). Peter Ackroyd (1976, p. 130) contends that Prynne's poetry 'does not have any extrinsic reference. There is only a marginal denotative potential since the language aspires towards completeness and self-sufficiency.' Veronica Forrest-Thompson (1978) cites Prynne as an exemplar of what she terms the 'disconnected image complex', which is a concept, a nuance, even a nominative reference to a person or thing, whose thematic frame of reference is distributed almost exclusively through the poem itself, while maintaining no coherent relationship with a fabric of meaning outside the text. Below are two passages from Prynne's 'Of Sanguine Fire', followed by Forrest-Thompson's engagement with it:

> wait for it, Pie
> conceives a whiff of apple, even short crust, wait for
> it, like the bold face too many, pyloric mill

racing; yet Outwash runs on for the cloud –
> *but are always Fresh,*
> *Vigorous and Bright, like the life and*
> *quickness of the Morning, and rejoyce like*
> *the Sun to run their Course –*

and

makes it through zero gravity, he too on the
    verge of deep narcosis. He slides his face
down three stairs, skipping the treads; he merely
    thinks abruptly of a red sexy pudding.

Pie and Outwash inhabit a familiar world of apple-pies, stairwells, taxis, but they are not themselves entirely part of this world. Each of them sums up a complex idea of how the physical world may appear in a poem. Pie stands for the disillusioned imagination facing its own inadequacies while Outwash stresses rather the robust physical world asserting its independence. These two figures are the main image-complexes of the lines. It is difficult to distinguish others since the constant movement from one implied external context to another does not allow consistent development of image-complexes over several lines; they appear momentarily only to disappear again. This disappearing quality in the image-complexes brings the conventional and the thematic levels closer together as the thematic contrast between the angels and the physical world is seen in the contrast between the rhythm of the italicised lines and the rhythm of the long descriptive lines. Yet the very obtrusiveness of the formal differences make these into image-complexes in themselves; each different rhythm has its different theme. (Forrest-Thompson, 1978, p. 142)

Forrest-Thompson also offers her own criteria for evaluation. The most worthy poems are, in her view, those which challenge the routine relationship between the intrinsic features of the text and its extrinsic frame of reference. Such poems create from the poetic dimension of the double pattern a metalanguage and resist what she calls 'bad' naturalization. Such naturalizations are bad because the poem allows the balance of power to shift towards the critic and the normative field of logic and explanation. 'Of Sanguine Fire' incites 'good' naturalization. It 'restores both the resources of lyric and the resources of thinking in poetry'. The key phrase here is 'thinking in poetry', meaning that the best poetry, that which restores good naturalization, obliges, or rather enables, us to suspend our ratiocinative and normative apparatuses, that is, our instinct to 'make sense' of whatever we read or hear. By this, she does not mean that we should aspire to some precognisant quasi-mystical state, but rather to treat the poem's shifts between flickers of extrinsic meaning and internalized patterns of syntax, semantics and image complexes as an incitement to appreciation rather than interpretation. She contends that poetry that aspires to a state of poetic autonomy, unreliant upon the regimen of coherence, order and specificity endemic to all other modes of communication, is accordingly the best. Wallace Stevens' poem 'Anecdote of the Jar' is one of the most well-known, widely discussed poems in English:

> I placed a jar in Tennessee,
> And round it was, upon a hill.
> It made the slovenly wilderness
> Surround that hill.
>
> The wilderness rose up to it,
> And sprawled around, no longer wild.
> The jar was round upon the ground
> And tall and of a port in air
>
> It took dominion everywhere.
> The jar was gray and bare.
> It did not give of bird or bush,
> Like nothing else in Tennessee.

In Forrest-Thompson's view (1978, p. 51), this is a poem meditating on the relation between art and nature, between human and natural reality:

> The process of interpretation involves accepting the world of ordinary experience as given, finding in it various already-known attitudes to the problem of which the poem speaks, and clarifying the poem by relating it to these attitudes. In a sense the interpreters are right: the poem is written in complicity with these assumptions; it demands this type of reading. This is not to say that Stevens is a bad poet; he is not. But he is not an original poet in the sense of questioning what his readers require of him, or the reality they require him to reproduce.

Stevens, then, is a competent but unoriginal poet, producing work that is 'complicit' with the predominantly rationalist and empiricist expectations of non-poetic discourse. Certainly 'Anecdote of the Jar' is far more orthodox than the work of Prynne or indeed much of the verse of Eliot and Pound – all of whom Forrest-Thompson regards as 'original' by her definition of the term – but I would profess that it transcends her strict criteria regarding good and bad naturalizations. It enables us to combine both in a single reading and in doing so presents itself as a far more 'original' and indeed subtle example of poetry at its best. One could indeed argue that it is a meditation 'on the relation between art and nature', but not in the sense that one might expect such reflections to manifest themselves in language. Stevens' syntax achieves what the orthodoxies of language would seem to prohibit, in that he maintains, simultaneously, two registers or nuances of intention, and he does so not simply as a gesture to some aesthetic or philosophical conceit but as a uniquely poetic fulfilment of mimesis. We will never know if the phrase 'And round it was' is a coordinate clause prompted by the feeling of petty omniscience that comes with standing upon a promontory, or if it is an, equally inconclusive, reflection on the jar's roundness. This moment of irresolution informs the remainder of the poem, the sentences reach towards some possible, often intimated conclusion, but always turn back upon themselves, and this beguiling effect of strands of meaning opening, pausing and diversifying is grounded upon the speaker's vacillation as to what exactly is the focus of his thoughts and his discourse: the jar, the hill, the surrounding countryside, the unfixed relationship between all three? Had a comparable effect been discharged via a naturalistic record of hesitant speech, perhaps even the interior monologue, then the speaker and the writer would be disjoined; the latter would be as much the imitative creation of the former as his language. But Stevens achieves both a wonderfully authentic model of extemporization alongside a residue of something more elegant and calculated. The lines move between a relaxed iambic pattern and the abandonment of rhythm, and the competing thematic foci submerge and resurface persistently yet unpredictably in semantic and phonemic echoes: 'round it was', 'Surround that hill', 'sprawled around', 'round upon the ground', 'a port in air', 'everywhere', 'gray and bare'.

The poem can indeed lend itself to a bad naturalization, in that critics have subjected it to abundant projections on Stevens' preoccupations regarding art and nature, intellectualism and primitivism, but this is the fault of the critics, not Stevens. Such naturalizations are, in truth, unappreciative misreadings. 'Anecdote of a Jar' involves 'thinking in poetry', in the sense that its oscillations between up to four predominant foci are too subtle to document precisely. There is never, for example, a single point at which one theme is immune from the nuanced presence of others: the musical equivalent would be counterpoint in which melodic phrases overlap to the extent that their interaction negates any clear perception of their separateness. We are aware, when we read it, that this multilayered effect is occurring but to describe it in terms of, say, degrees of paradox or ambiguity or as a realization of a profound tension between contrary philosophical issues does a grave injustice to the operation of the poem as a work of art. The fact that it provokes such responses in critics testifies to its quality and indeed its superiority to the self-referential poetic work of Prynne and others of his ilk. It catches the reader between a desire to naturalize it – it is, relatively speaking, accessible and coherent – and the responsibility of doing so without ruining its immediate and manifest effects. It is a magnificent example of how level 3, judgement, can become interwoven with the more rational procedures of levels 1 and 2. It is a poem we can enjoy and, at a cursory level, understand, but which, at the same time, confounds our ability to describe precisely how our understanding of it conditions our enjoyment.

Forrest-Thompson was an exceptional and daring critic in that she at least ventured a rationale for the discernment of importance and significance in poems. At the same time, however, the limitations of her technique were depressingly prescient. She was writing in the late 1970s, the beginning of a controversial assault by literary theory upon the redoubt of traditional belle-lettrism, New Criticism. The lexicon, mannerisms and intellectual premises of theory are now endemic features of the critical writing of all but a small number of academics and, as a result, academic criticism is to a large extent immunized from that most contentious, subjective feature of talking and writing about verse: whether or not the poet is possessed of talent. Forrest-Thompson indicated that the fact that Stevens is a good poet – by which she means a skilled literary craftsman – is irrelevant. The reasons for this viewpoint – by now the overwhelming consensus – are various, but most significantly they stem from the perception of the reader and poet as subjects or constructs of specific ideological conditions and discourses, which in turn undermines the notion of being able to recognize aesthetic value or quality as intrinsic features of anything. Talent and refinement have not been completely eliminated from perceptions of a poet's character but their importance is now deemed negligible.

I would aver that the very best poems are not those that make naturalization difficult. That would be to equate significance with some putative intellectual transaction between poet and critic: the latter's training and experience will equip them fully to deal with the poem's refusal to release a seam of intelligibility and to treat this as part of a broader discourse involving matters such as authority, subjectivity, signification. In my opinion, excellence is apparent when naturalization appears unproblematic but where it is equally evident that the skills employed by the poet achieve this apparent state of transparency, and test and sometimes exceed the capacities of the critic to describe how they do so. It is here that critical analysis becomes both symptomatic of the acumen of its practitioner and a diagnostic indicator of true poetic quality. We should work backwards through the three levels of evaluation, beginning with level 3, judgement, and address ourselves to a single straightforward question: What is it about the poem that I most admire or dislike? Then at levels 2 and 1 we engage with our knowledge of the repertoire of devices deployed by the poet in order to pursue a solution to our preliminary question. In doing so, we pay particular attention to how the poet has achieved the effects that prompt our admiration or disdain, and remind ourselves that one of the preconditions for good art is the acceptance by critics that they are witnessing an achievement far beyond their own capacities and indeed those of the vast majority of fellow beholders.

With this in mind, consider the lines from a poem by Andrew Crozier:

> Five quarters duck lofty club-bar rubbish
> With a short but sound composition – secure.
> It's from the oldest opera. As a wise precaution
> Ten cat-men break the laws of pain

> In an old man's stride. As first offenders
> A portly body of nurses is detailed fast
> In a gross Roman style of wrestling. (from 'Coup de Main')

Here, compound images and flickers of continuity are present, but stubbornly resistant to intelligibility. A determination to evade the predatory attention of the interpreter informs the piece and in this respect it belongs in a tradition that began with Pound and has since manifested itself in the work of postmodern writers. Now consider the following poem:

> A dozen boas flailing cheesecake sweet
> And rare. Though spoiled and forward
> Made to last. Not his term – yet.
> If you came to assert they move it slowly
> Use an edge and turn. My mother sat and
> A goitered ream of waltzers all in blue
> Held and clear a Turkish Bath for use.

Depending upon one's cultural and indeed temperamental predisposition, it is possible to be enthralled by both these poems, even perceive them as aesthetic and political refusals to conform. Our incurious and complacent expectations are threatened and we are reminded that art can be thrillingly incitive. Both seem to involve Andrew Crozier's stylistic signature, specifically a tendency to connect resonant noun and verb phrases, such as 'goitered ream of waltzers', 'Roman style of wrestling', 'My mother sat', 'an old man's stride', in a manner that both disrupts any internal thread of continuity and refuses to correspond with any logical sequence in the world outside the poem.

Some might contend that in the first piece Andrew Crozier's breathless disdain for coherence, his creation of a world of signifiers that eludes the normative sphere of order and familiarity is to his credit. Both pieces achieve an extraordinary, almost magical chiascuro of impressions, never allowing the reader to steady themselves even with an intimation of what might happen next.

Others might well feel that poems so consistently impenetrable are little more than prompters to equally abstruse discourses, in prose, on the nature of signification and truth, and that, as works of art, their intrinsic qualities are negligible; they have substituted the traditional responsibility to literary craftsmanship for a role in a much broader discourse – involving critics and theorists – where aesthetics and culture are seen as subdivisions of ideology. At a more elemental level, one might feel that poems that refuse to make sense are both displeasing and predictable.

Both points of view are founded upon subjective predispositions ranging from one's accustomed intellectual outlook to straightforward matters of taste. How do we go about reconciling these variables with a measure of quality that is more objective?

At this point, I should reveal that only the first of these pieces (from 'Coup de Main') is by Crozier. The second poem I put together myself. Would you be able to tell from your own scrutiny which was composed by a respected avant-garde poet and which was put together in roughly 30 minutes by me, Richard Bradford? You might compare your response to each with your engagements with poems that stir a comparable feeling of disorientation. In this respect, you could consider Dylan Thomas as their conventional precursor (in the sense that his use of metre and rhyme is incongruously orthodox) and John Ashbery's 'Sortes Vergilianae' as achieving in narrative verse what these distil into a lyric. Their closest relatives would probably be found within the so-called 'L=A=N=G=U=A=G=E' school of poetry (see Nicholls, 1991), especially in the work of Steve McCaffery. As you subject both 'poems' to the modes of scrutiny described in levels 1–3 above, other questions will arise. Principally, if the dissimilarities between them are so slight, have we not come upon a simple test of quality? A poem whose effects can so easily be reproduced must be of questionable value.

Choose a poem by an anthologized, mid-20th- to early 21st-century poet and adapt the three levels of evaluation listed above to an exercise in imitation. I suggest the use of a piece from recent literary history because it will draw upon our own idioms, vocabulary and accustomed frames of reference; the reproduction of archaisms, involving sufficient background reading, can result in ventriloquism.

First you will need to familiarize yourself with the most telling formal characteristics of the individual poem. Impersonal stylistic features such as the use of a given stanzaic formula, rhyme scheme or metrical pattern are fairly easy to assimilate and reproduce. Less straightforward is the feigning of, say, a preponderance or avoidance of figurative or nuanced language and the original text's level of engagement with an external frame of reference. These exercises correspond with levels 1 and 2 of the evaluative procedure outlined above, but far more difficult than the cataloguing of devices is the re-creation of some aspect of the poem that might on first reading puzzle or intrigue, but which endures thereafter as its most memorable, although often enigmatic feature. This final stage, where you attempt to write not simply 'in the manner of' the poet in question but to capture the quintessence of their achievement, is where the exercise in imitation offers a new perspective on the ways in which we understand and appreciate poetry. To build a poem of any sort requires a thorough knowledge of the mechanics of verse, which are exhaustively listed in this book, and of the range of choices available within the vast but recognizably autonomous zone of the poetic. As a consequence, the re-creation of the formal particulars of your chosen poem will further extend your awareness of what happens in poems per se. It is, however, the shift from stylistic impersonation to the capturing of the poem's uniqueness that involves a collateral move from the mechanics of form to the tendentious issue of excellence. If you are able to re-create, to your own satisfaction, a piece that is identical in its nature, effect and significance to the original poem, then you are either an enormously gifted poet manqué or the chosen poem is of slight importance. If, on the other hand, you are capable of identifying the minutiae of the poet's technique but defeated by the task of achieving a comparable fabric of effects, then you have come upon a vital clue in the search for that feature of verse which is manifest yet difficult to define: inimitable superiority. I have already performed this exercise with Crozier, with self-evident results, and I shall now turn my attention to a short piece by Philip Larkin, 'As Bad as a Mile':

> Watching the shied core
> Striking the basket, skidding across the floor,
> Shows less and less of luck, and more and more
>
> Of failure, spreading back up the arm
> Earlier and earlier, the unraised hand calm,
> The apple unbitten in the palm.

The poem is a brief meditation on a feeling that all of us experience, involving, by degrees, disappointment, pessimism and a sense of failure. No cause or circumstances are attributed to the sensation and indeed any intimation of presence is almost displaced by the image of the thrown apple core. It is an uncomplicated and transparent piece and my synopsis seems in this regard superfluous. However, the striking feature of the poem is the complex yet almost imperceptible interchanges between pictorial images and equally powerful abstractions. In the first two lines, the syntax seems synchronized exactly with the unfolding sequence. The movement of the apple core to the basket and then to the floor is played out in an almost cinematic manner. But at the verb 'Shows', the register shifts suddenly from the visual to the figurative, at least until after 'failure', when we encounter a curious blend of the two. There is a subliminal sense of watching the film played backwards, with the object returned via the basket to the hand, but this is attended by an equally powerful abstraction – 'failure', resignation, the certainty of non-success – which follows the core literally and metaphorically to a point prior to the beginning of the poem, 'the apple unbitten the palm'.

The internal sound pattern is interwoven with shifts between the visual and the abstract. In the first stanza, 's' and 'c' alliterations predominate: 's̲hied', 's̲tri̲king', 'bas̲ket', 'c̲ore', 's̲kidding', 's̲hows', lu̲ck'. It is rare to encounter a sound pattern employed so effectively as a supplement to sense, but here Larkin makes use of alliteration as a coupling device, a means of synchronizing the syntax with the progress of images. Significantly, the last word in this alliterative sequence is 'luck', the point at which the unemotive sequence of objects is exchanged for a concept. Thereafter only two drifting echoes of a previously dense sequence remain – 's̲preading' and 'unrai̲s̲ed' – a magnificently delicate deployment of artifice as mimesis; the sense of acceptance that loss is part of his ineluctable state is accompanied by the speaker's exchange of artifice and design for uncluttered transparency.

My account of how the formal apparatuses of the poem contribute to its
effects is, I think, accurate and insufficient. There are so many delicately nuanced
shifts between the visual and the reflective, the concrete and the abstract,
motion and stillness, observation and rumination – all executed within six short
lines – that it is impossible to document their order or precedence. It speaks
eloquently to the reader who is neither obliged nor inclined to describe its
operations, while for those who attempt to do so, primarily critics, it outpaces
efforts to impose upon it a formula or explanation. It does not, like Thomas,
Prynne or Crozier, create complex images that detach it from the world outside
the text but, at the same time, it makes use of a spectrum of devices and creates
a fabric of impressions that are exclusively poetic. This achievement, in my
estimation, testifies to its exceptional quality and it is for this reason that I shall
not attempt to create a poem of comparable merit. I can catalogue its mechanisms but there is a significant difference between describing what a poet does
and being able to replicate their accomplishment, and this I aver is the most
reliable measure of excellence.

Epilogue
Why Do We Write and Read Poetry?

Aside from the stylistic distinction between poetry and everything else, one other difference stands out. All other discourses are identifiable in terms of their designated function. The philosophical essay, the cookery book and the self-assembly instruction leaflet adopt a particular style and manner in order to best discharge their intention. Even the novel incorporates a version of this interdependent relation between manner and function. Certainly avant-garde fiction offers an approach to mimesis far more radical and transgressive than its conservative counterpart but the two versions of the genre are united in a preoccupation with the processes of representation. There have been numerous attempts to provide a raison d'être for the existence and attractions of poetry and these have been remarkable in their lack of conviction and inconsistency. As we have seen in Chapter 2, Plato was, to say the least, ambivalent on the value of poetry as a means of representation or persuasion. Horace's much-quoted formula that the aim of poetry is 'aut prodesse … aut delectare', to instruct or to delight, is finely ambiguous: entertainment and didacticism are not, generally speaking, compatible activities. The first recorded case of scholarly engagement with poetry involved teams of scrutineers in the Great Library of Alexandria poring over the, dated, 3rd-century BC version of Homer and attempting to intuit the 'real' text beneath what they believed to be the untidy work of previous scribes. Homer's work, indeed poetry per se, was accorded an almost sacred ranking but no one ventured that it might have an obvious purpose. The grounds on which Renaissance critics and poets defended the newly revived classical models of poetry, particularly the epic, were ethical: poetry promoted virtue by representing noble actions in an ostensibly edifying manner. Virgil, Spenser, Rapin and Le Bossu all held that each of the various subgenres of verse made its own contribution to the inculcation of key ideas about human conduct. But by the time the Renaissance began to inspire poetic writing in England in the early 16th century, these didactic formulae were becoming self-evidently obsolete. The period was awash with competing and contradictory models of belief and behaviour, typified by the tension between humanism and religious orthodoxy and the often incompatible versions of Christian doctrine thrown up by the Reformation. One might assume therefore that poetry had an ample amount of material upon which to practise its cautiously rehearsed role as moral arbiter. In fact, however, the birth of modern methods for the distribution of ideas and dogma, predominantly the printing press, ensured that verse would thereafter play no more than a secondary role in public debate.

Within two centuries, from the early 1500s to the mid-1700s, England had exchanged its condition as a feudal, largely agrarian state governed by an auto-cratic monarch and humbly attendant upon a single monotheistic doctrine for an assembly of competing factions, an extended debating chamber in which matters such as governance and religious conviction were open for disputation. Trade, colonial settlement and the incipient growth of urban centres were preparing the ground for the Industrial Revolution. As a consequence, the printed text became the forum for this new multiplicity of issues, causes and perspectives and each of the growing panoply of subgenres had a self-evident purpose and objective. A pamphlet on architecture or animal husbandry was simply what it claimed to be. Poetry, unlimited in its range of subjects, was now beginning to find itself in the invidious position as a redundant supplement to other genres, mostly non-literary, whose existence was guaranteed by their subject and function. Indeed, Milton's Christian epic *Paradise Lost* is a quintes-sential example of the Renaissance poem at the tipping point between relevance and obsolescence. It adapted the grand expectation of its classical predecessors to the post-classical topic of a Christian perception of the Creation and the Fall and much of the debate that it fuelled during the 18th and 19th centuries involved the issue of appropriateness. In short, were such fundamental theo-logical and existential topics suitable for poetry? Few disputed the magnificence of Milton's achievement but equally there was the implicit question of what in the end he was attempting to achieve. If his objective was to reignite theological disputes regarding key biblical issues, then surely a more apposite vehicle would be the prose pamphlet – of which he was an adept practitioner – rather than an elaborate blank verse narrative strewn with grand conceits and monologues reminiscent of Shakespeare.

Consider also the shift in the mood and sense of purpose in poetry after the restoration of the monarchy at the end of the 17th century. For much of the next 100 years, poets endeavoured to compete with prose hacks and pamphlet-eers as commentators on topical contemporary subjects, with a correlative pairing down of the intrinsic, some would say definitive, stylistic extravagances of verse. Poetry, briefly, was attempting to imitate the function and status of prose discourse. To varying degrees it was successful but it could not by its nature achieve anything resembling full equality. Despite their puritanical stylistic restraint, Augustan poems were still indisputably poems. They belonged to a generic family with recognizable characteristics but no clear purpose or role. Poems could indeed address any idea or theme but they could do so only as ostentatious subsidiaries to the work undertaken by prose.

The reaction against Augustanism by the Romantics and the maintenance of various forms of the Romantic ideal during the 19th century further testifies to the collective feelings of unease among poets – a fear that their vocation might be seen as dysfunctional and purposeless. The Augustans had attempted to adapt poetry to the conventions of prose, promoting such notions as order, clarity and logic above imagination or inspiration, while the Romantics, driven by a similar dread of redundancy, took their verse in the opposite direction, attempting to establish for it a special ranking as an autonomous vehicle for existential contemplation, even enlightenment, outside the established routines of conventional religion or philosophy. It can be no accident that the emergence of Romanticism brought with it a collateral programme of writings that sought to justify the independence of poetry according to purely aesthetic principles. The genesis of this can be traced to writers and philosophers of the German Romantic movement. Kant stressed the purity and disinterestedness of the poem as a work of art, Goethe and Schiller emphasized the poem's status as an independent organism, and Schelling averred that poetry involved the unique revelation of the universal. All these beliefs resurfaced in the ex cathedra writings of the English Romantic poets, particularly in the prose of Coleridge, and later in the work of Carlyle and Arnold.

The French Symbolist movement, pioneered by Mallarmé and Verlaine, carries the influence of these Romantic manifestoes and although their verse differs stylistically from that of their German and English predecessors, the notion of the poem as capable of operating independently of all other discourses and creating a unique revelatory fabric of meaning is a key enduring feature of their beliefs. Eliot and Pound, the originators of Modernism in English, drew inspiration in their early work from Arthur Symons' *The Symbolist Movement in Literature* (1899) and what fascinated them most was Symons' concept of the impersonal and objective existence of the poem, a maxim that would, in due course, be disseminated through many of the subcategories of the Modernist aesthetic. A version of this same principle is a key element of New Criticism and Formalism, with critics such as Wimsatt and Beardsley insisting that the poem itself should be the exclusive subject of the reader's scrutiny, and that circumstantial, biographical material should not be allowed to contaminate our awareness of its unique operations.

At the other end of the theoretical spectrum, the Frankfurt School Marxist critics – precursors of the New Historicists and Cultural Materialists – saw poetry as standing at the apex of what they called the 'culture industry', which also incorporated other traditional high arts along with radio, television and film. Poetry, according to the Frankfurt thinkers, feeds a self-perpetuating milieu of docility. It has, they aver, fulfilled the Arnoldian prophecy and become a substitute for religion, or rather a means of avoiding confrontation with the world beyond bourgeois culture. Irrespective of one's opinion on the ideology of this approach, it bears a remarkable resemblance to the consensus that has accompanied poetry on its uneasy journey from classical civilization to the present; it is an activity with no purpose.

It would, of course, be absurd to claim that since the 18th century the idea of the poem as a structure immune from the logic and vagaries of the real world has obtained without challenge. Nonetheless, there persists an enduring, powerful perception of a poem as a cryptogram, a palimpsest, a special form of writing capable of encoding or revealing messages not obtainable elsewhere or by other means. There is, however, a problem with this model. Even if we accept that poems are, by their nature, capable of sustaining within themselves a fugitive, anomalous thread of meaning, how can we describe what this is? As we have seen in our considerations of naturalization and deconstruction, we face, in all our engagements with poetry, a dilemma. The only means by which we can discuss, write about or even privately reflect upon the special characteristics of a poem is by effectively translating it into non-poetic discourse; we can only articulate the operations of the double pattern by entering an alliance with one dimension of it, the referential function. Once we begin to talk or write about poetry, the sense of beguilement that draws us to it, its self-evident aversion to logical reason, is extinguished.

This dilemma is at once irresolvable and a clue to the enduring, addictive power of poetry. We naturalize poems in different ways. Sometimes we clumsily appropriate some element of their fabric as an essential theme and telescope this into an overarching 'interpretation'. On other occasions – more wisely – we accept their skewed logic and devise a response that is respectfully indeterminate. In all respects, however, we are aware that something unusual, indeed unique, is occurring.

We are drawn, simultaneously, in two directions. We attempt to form a paraphrase of the poem, yet the poem, by its very nature, resists us. It is the dynamic between these two trajectories that holds the key to our attraction to poetry. A single sequence of words catches us between opposing states of response, and by this I do not refer to a version of Empson's concept of ambiguity or Brooks' paradox. Rather, poetry involves us in an experience far more fundamental, a dizzying combination of visceral and intellectual questions. Our desire, our elemental need to understand the poem is instinctive, but so is our guilty fascination with a piece of writing that refuses to submit to the standard ordinances of logic, transparency, even intention. We want to tease out its essential meaning, while we are aware that our desire to do so is fed by its enigmatic character, that the latter propitiates the former and thus should remain immune from our interpretive impulse. As Valéry put it, 'the power of [a line of poetry] comes from an *indefinable* harmony between what it *says*, and what it *is*'. This is the double pattern. The poem, being made of language, deceives us into the same state of expectations provoked by all our other encounters with words, yet once this offer is made, all further arrangements are foresworn.

When a stranger asks us the time or the way to the nearest tube station, the process of decoding the message, establishing its intention, is reflexive and unproblematic. We become part of a dialogue or a shared discourse. At a more elevated level, when we listen to a lecture on biochemistry or tackle a work by Wittgenstein, we become similarly attuned to what we perceive as the demands of the message, its context and apparent purpose. In all instances, the participants – writer, speaker, listener, reader – become subject to the conventions and operations of the discourse, accept these as serving a practical purpose. The role of language in all of this is comparable to that of a doorkeeper, the functionary who enables one to pass through the process of interpretation and advance towards what is always the objective, the substantiation of unambiguous truth. This is why we cannot prevent ourselves from operating against the texture of the poem when we attempt to naturalize it. Poetry, however, catches us in a double bind. It plays the doorkeeper and draws us in, yet as it does so, it refuses to stand aside and allow us to continue our search for a determinate meaning. Instead, it takes control of our cognitive registers, lays out perverse spirals of meaning and deploys linguistic devices that have no purposive logic. The essential difference between pre- and post-Saussurian theories turns upon the relationship between language and identity. In the former, we are seen as existing in an autonomous, prelinguistic condition, utilizing language as an instrument, a means of articulating our state. Advocates of the latter hold that consciousness and rudimentary linguistic competence are interdependent; without language, we would have no sense of presence or identity. Poetry oscillates between the two. On the one hand, it is anti-Saussurian, in that it demonstrates that the individual and the discourse can exist independently. The language of poetry – the double pattern – draws upon the language of human beings but it is not the language we use. At the same time, poetry, far more effectively than any poststructuralist, exposes, indeed celebrates, the arbitrary nature of our sign system, exploits the fugitive capabilities of language as material (metre, rhyme, enjambment, shaped poetry and so on) to generate disparate channels of meaning, and demonstrates that language is unfettered by the commands of some prelinguistic substratum of truths and can indeed rewrite the rules of perception and rationalization.

This might seem to give credence to the Frankfurt School model of poetry as a form of erudite escapism, but the opposite is the case. The most controversial statement by a Frankfurt theorist on poetry came from Theodor Adorno in *Prisms* ([1955]1983) – 'to write poetry after Auschwitz is barbaric'. What he means is that since the range of subjects that can be covered by poetry is limitless, this must now include the Holocaust. Therefore, in his opinion, poets face two incontestable prohibitions. They cannot pretend to be ignorant of the Holocaust as an index to the horrible potentialities of humankind. At the same time, there is a ghastly incompatibility between something so transparently horrific and a genre that, by its nature, abjures transparency. Adorno was wrong. Poets have written about the Holocaust and their work is by no means 'barbaric' (and one can assume here that Adorno means that poetry must, by its nature, trivialize its subject). Consider the following extracts from Dannie Abse's 'White Balloon':

> Dear love, Auschwitz made me
> more of a Jew than Moses did
> but the world's not always with us.
> Happiness enters here again tonight
> like an unexpected guest

> ...
> into our night living room
> where, under the lampshade's ciliate,
> an armchair's occupied by a white balloon.
> ...
> But what does it matter now
> as the white balloon is thrown up high?
> Quiet, so quiet, the moon above Masada
> and closed, abandoned for the night,
> the icecream van at Auschwitz.

There is an unsettling disjunction between the statement that opens the poem and the fissiparous, unfixed images of the balloon, the embodied state of 'Happiness' ('with no memory of the future') and the intimate domestic setting shared, we assume, by Abse and his wife. These closing lines return us to Auschwitz, surreally attended at night by an ice-cream van. This is not, in my opinion, 'barbaric'. Abse assumes that, once invoked, the Holocaust requires no elucidation – and in this respect he is in accord with Adorno. It is something that immunizes itself from speculative discourse; it simply exists as a record of gargantuan suffering and systematic inhumanity. For Abse, however, it carries a special resonance. It has 'made me/more of a Jew than Moses did'. He did not, he infers, witness it but at the same time the entire spectrum of his consciousness carries a trace of it. We are tempted by this contextual placement to comb for resonances the curious dreamlike sequence sandwiched between the two specific references to Auschwitz. Is the ghostly embodiment of Happiness symbolic of a sense of resignation and despair? It leads them up the 'lit staircase/ towards the landing's darkness'. Does the whiteness of the balloon indicate unaffiliation, innocence, naivety or any other of the various states of hope that are now foreshadowed by dread: it sits on an armchair 'as if there'd been a party'. Virtually every phrase in the poem is puzzling, pointing to no clear extrinsic fabric of meanings. But having been introduced to the poem's one unambiguous theme, we cannot help but use this as an interpretive key to what would otherwise be a tantalizingly incoherent sequence. This, as I have said, is the effect that attracts us most to poetry: being caught between our desire to interpret and make sense and our equally powerful impulse to submit to illogic and leave the text to its own devices. In this instance, however, the experience goes far beyond an intellectual or aesthetic exercise. We recoil from interpreting the images as symbols of the Holocaust because to do so would be interfering with a very personal, very tragic example of mimesis. Abse is using the unique capacities of verse to simulate a state of mind that is too conflicted and shifting for prose. He is fully, brutally aware of what happened at Auschwitz, it has become part of his life, yet he implicitly raises the question of how he can describe this condition. His answer is 'The White Balloon', a poem that invites us into its web of interpretive possibilities and allows us to go no further. We have a picture of an unsettled consciousness, restlessly, painfully connecting the minutiae of his everyday world – ice-cream vans, armchairs, balloons and so on – with something that is both ever present and inexplicable.

Poetry is something we understand, in the sense that when we read it we appreciate its effects and arbitrary spirals of meaning, yet at the same time it remains uniquely unanswerable. Unlike the enquiry from the man in the street or the opening page of Wittgenstein, we cannot assimilate and translate the message into a shared discourse. We know or at least are fascinated by what happens in the poem, but the key to the magnetism of this experience is twofold. We might claim to feel a similar sense of awe when we encounter a painting by Van Dyck or Pollack, a building by Palladio or Le Corbusier, a piece of music by Beethoven or simply the raw spectacle of an ocean or a mountain. But none of these is assembled from the material that effectively makes us who we are, language. Poetry is about language. It shows us that language is brittle, magical, untrustworthy, arbitrary, but unlike a philosophical essay on such topics, it does not enable us to answer back. It demonstrates that, on the one hand, language creates us, that consciousness and language are coterminous, but also that we can step outside it, contemplate its autonomous operations and peculiarities. Read a poem, or indeed write a poem, and you abscond from the depersonalizing system where language has a specified purpose. At the same time, however, you feel that language and everything else about the unspecified quixotic nature of the human condition are bound together. No other form of writing or expression enables us to simultaneously experience both of these apparently antithetical, exclusive states. This is why we write and read poetry and will continue to do so as long as we exist as a species.

Bibliography

Acheson, J. and Huk, R. (eds) (1996) *Contemporary British Poetry: Essays in Theory and Criticism*, State University of New York Press, New York.

Ackroyd, P. (1976) *Notes for a New Culture*, Vision Press, London.

Adorno, T. ([1955]1983) *Prisms*, MIT Press, Cambridge, MA.

Armitage, S. and Crawford, R. (eds) (1998) *The Penguin Book of Poetry from Britain and Ireland since 1945*, Penguin, Harmondsworth.

Arnold, M. (1865a) 'The Function of Criticism at the Present Time: First Series', in V. Leitch et al. (eds) (2001), *The Norton Anthology of Theory and Criticism*, Norton, New York.

Arnold, M. (1865b) *Essays in Criticism*, in P.J. Keating (ed.) (1970), *Selected Prose*, Penguin, Harmondsworth.

Arnold, M. (1880) 'The Study of Poetry', in P.J. Keating (ed.) (1970), *Selected Prose*, Penguin, Harmondsworth.

Baldick, C. (1983) *The Social Mission of English Criticism 1848–1932*, Clarendon Press, Oxford.

Barthes, R. (1967) *Système de la Mode*, Seuil, Paris.

Barthes, R. (1968) 'The Death of the Author', in V. Leitch (ed.) (2001), *The Norton Anthology of Theory and Criticism*, Norton, New York.

Barthes, R. (1968) *Writing Degree Zero*, Hill & Wang, New York.

Barthes, R. (1975) *S/Z: An Essay*, Cape, London.

Barthes, R. (1987) *Elements of Semiology*, Cape, London.

Bennett, A. and Royle, N. (eds) (1995) *An Introduction to Literature, Criticism and Theory*, Pearson, Edinburgh.

Blain, V. (1983) 'Narrative Voice and the Female Perspective in Virginia Woolf's Early Novels', in P. Clements and I. Grundy (eds), *Virginia Woolf: New Critical Essays*, Vision Press, London.

Blake, W. (1966) *The Complete Writings*, ed. G. Keynes, OUP, London.

Bradford, R. (1994) *Roman Jakobson: Life, Language, Art*, Routledge, London.

Bradford, R. (1997) *Stylistics*, Routledge, London.

Bradford, R. (2002) *Augustan Measures: Restoration and Eighteenth-Century Writings on Prosody and Metre*, Ashgate, Aldershot.

Breiner, L.A. (1998) *An Introduction to West Indian Poetry*, CUP, Cambridge.

Brooks, C. ([1947]1968) *The Well Wrought Urn: Studies in the Structure of Poetry*, Methuen, London.

Brooks, C. and Warren, R.P. ([1938]1960) *Understanding Poetry*, Holt, Rinehart & Winston, New York.

Brown, L. (1985) *Alexander Pope*, Basil Blackwell, Oxford.

Brown, N.O. (1959) 'The Excremental Vision', in *Life Against Death: The Psychoanalytic Meaning of History*, Wesleyan University Press, Hanover.

Caudwell, C. (1937) *Illusion and Reality: A Study of the Sources of Poetry*, extract in D. Lodge (1972), *20th Century Literary Criticism: A Reader*, Longman, London.

Chomsky, N. (1957) *Syntactic Structures*, Mouton, The Hague.

Cixous, H. (1981) 'The Laugh of the Medusa', in E. Marks and I. de Courtivron (eds), *New French Feminism: An Anthology*, Harvester, Brighton.

Coleridge, S.T. (1817) *Biographia Literaria*, ed. G. Watson (1975), Penguin, London.

Conquest, R. (ed.) (1956) *New Lines*, Macmillan, London.

Cronin, J. (1988) '"Even Under the Rine of Terror": Insurgent South African Poetry', in J. Cook (ed.) (2004), *Poetry in Theory: An Anthology 1900–2000*, Blackwell, Oxford.

Culler, J. (1975) *Structuralist Poetics: Structuralism*, Routledge & Kegan Paul, London.

Culler, J. (1983) *On Deconstruction: Theory and Criticism after Structuralism*, Routledge & Kegan Paul, London.

Daniel, S. (1603) *A Defence of Rhyme*,

Davie, D. (1955) *Articulate Energy: An Inquiry in the Syntax of English Poetry*, Routledge & Kegan Paul, London.

De Man, P. (1979) *Allegories of Reading*, Yale University Press, New Haven, CT.

Derrida, J. (1975) 'The Purveyor of Truth', *Yale French Studies*, 52: 31–113.

Derrida, J. (1976) *Of Grammatology*, trans. G. Chakravorty Spivak, Johns Hopkins University Press, Baltimore.

Derrida, J. (1981) *Positions*, trans. A. Bass, University of Chicago Press, Chicago.

Drabble, M. (ed.) (2000) *Oxford Companion to English Literature*, 6th edn, Oxford, OUP.

Dryden, J. (1668) *Essay of Dramatick Poesie*, London, Henry Herringham.

Eagleton, M. (ed.) (1986) *Feminist Literary Theory: A Reader*, Blackwell, Oxford.

Eagleton, T. (1983) *Literary Theory: An Introduction*, Blackwell, Oxford.

Easthope, A. (1983) *Poetry as Discourse*, Routledge, London.

Easthope, A. (1996) 'Donald Davie and the Failure of Englishness', in J. Acheson and R. Huk (eds), *Contemporary British Poetry: Essays in Theory and Criticism*, State University of New York Press, New York.

Eliot, T.S. (1917) 'Reflections on "Verse Libre"', in T.S. Eliot (1965), *To Criticise the Critic*, Faber, London.

Eliot, T.S. (1919) 'Tradition and the Individual Talent', in G. Martin and P.N. Furbank (eds) (1975), *Twentieth Century Poetry*, Open University Press, Milton Keynes.

Eliot, T.S. (1921) 'The Metaphysical Poets', in F. Kermode and J. Hollander (eds) (1973), *Oxford Anthology of English Literature*, vol. III, Oxford University Press, London.

Empson, W. ([1930]1961) *Seven Types of Ambiguity*, Chatto & Windus, London.

Faulkner, P. (ed.) (1986) *A Modernist Reader*, Batsford, London.

Fenollosa, E. (1919) *The Chinese Written Character as a Medium for Poetry*, ed. E. Pound, in K. Shapiro (ed.) (1962), *Prose Keys to Modern Poetry*, Harper & Row, New York.

Fish, S. (1980) 'How To Recognise a Poem When You See One', in S. Fish, *Is There a Text in this Class? The Authority of Interpretive Communities*, Harvard University Press, Cambridge, MA.

Forrest-Thomson, V. (1978) *Poetic Artifice: A Theory of Twentieth Century Poetry*, Manchester University Press, Manchester.

Freud, S. (1900) 'The Interpretation of Dreams', in *Standard Edition* (1953), vols IV and V, Hogarth Press, London.

Freud, S. (1908) 'Creative Writers and Day Dreaming', in *Standard Edition* (1959), vol IX, Hogarth Press, London.

Freud, S. (1920) 'Beyond the Pleasure Principle', in *Standard Edition* (1955), Hogarth Press, London.

Gilbert, S.M. (1978) 'Patriarchal Poetry and Women Readers: Reflections on Milton's Bogey', *PMLA*, 93: 368–82.

Gilbert, S.M. and Gubar, S. (1979) *The Madwoman in the Attic: The Woman Writer and the Nineteenth-century Literary Imagination*, Yale University Press, New Haven, CT.

Gilliland, S.K. (2001) *Milton to Pope – 1650–1720*, Palgrave – now Palgrave Macmillan, Basingstoke.

Greenblatt, S. (1988) *Shakespearean Negotiations: The Circulation of Social Energy in Renaissance England*, Clarendon Press, Oxford.

Griffiths, E. (1989) *The Printed Voice of Victorian Poetry*, Oxford University Press, Oxford.

Groom, B. (1955) *The Diction of Poetry from Spenser to Bridges*, University of Toronto Press, Toronto.

Gross, H. (1964) *Sound and Form in Modern Poetry*, University of Michigan Press, Ann Arbor, MI.

Hartman, G. (1980) *Criticism in the Wilderness: The Study of Literature Today*, Yale University Press, New Haven, CT.

Hartman, G. (1985) 'The Interpreter's Freud', in D. Lodge and N. Wood (eds) (1988), *Modern Criticism and Theory*, Pearson, London.

Hawkes, T. (1972) *Metaphor*, Methuen, London.

Hawkes, T. (1977) *Structuralism and Semiotics,* Methuen, London.

Hill, C. (1946) 'Society and Andrew Marvell', *Modern Quarterly*, no. 5.

Hill, C. (1977) *Milton and the English Revolution*, Faber, London.

Hollander, J. (1975) *Vision and Resonance: Two Senses of Poetic Form,* Oxford University Press, London.

Hulme, T.E. (1908) 'A Lecture on Modern Poetry', in M. Roberts (1938), *T.E. Hulme*, Faber, London.

Irigaray, L. (1974) 'When Our Lips Speak Together', trans. C. Burke, in *Signs: Journal of Women in Culture and Society* (1980), **6**(1): 66–79.

Jacobus, M. (1979) 'The Difference of View', in M. Jacobus (ed.), *Women Writing about Women*, Croom Helm, London.

Jakobson, R. (1960) 'Closing Statement: Linguistics and Poetics', in T. Sebeok (ed.), *Style in Language*, MIT Press, Cambridge, MA. Reprinted in D. Lodge (1988) *Modern Criticism and Theory: A Reader*, Longman, London.

Jakobson, R. ([1939]1971) 'Zur Struktur des Phonems', *Selected Writings I: Phonological Studies*, Mouton, The Hague.

Jakobson, R. ([1959]1971) 'Two Aspects of Language and Two Types of Aphasic Disturbances', *Selected Writings II: Word and Language*, Mouton, The Hague.

Jakobson, R. (1987a) *Language in Literature*, K. Pomorska and S. Rudy (eds), Harvard University Press, Cambridge, MA.

Jakobson, R. (1987b) 'The Dominant', in K. Pomorska and S. Rudy (eds), *Language in Literature*, Harvard University Press, Cambridge, MA.

Jakobson, R. and Halle, M. (1956) *Fundamentals of Language,* Mouton, The Hague.

Johnson, S. (1755) *Dictionary of the English Language*, refs from 2007 edn, D. Crystal (ed.), Penguin Classics, London.

Johnson, S. (1779–81) *The Lives of the Poets*, refs from F. Kermode and J. Hollander (general eds) (1973), *Oxford Anthology of English Literature*, Oxford University Press, London.

Jones, P. (ed.) (1972) *Imagist Poetry*, Penguin, London.

Jordan, J.E. (1976) *Why The Lyrical Ballads?*, University of California Press, Berkeley, CA.

Kenner, H. (1972) *The Pound Era*, Faber & Faber, London.

Kristeva, J, (1986) 'The System and the Speaking Subject', in M. Eagleton (ed.) *Feminist Literary Theory: A Reader*, Blackwell, Oxford.

Lacan, J. (1949) 'The Mirror Stage', trans. A. Sheridan, in *Écrits: A Selection* (1977), W.W. Norton & Co, New York.

Lacan, J. (1953) 'Discourse at Rome', originally 'Fonction et champ de la parole et du langage en psychanalyse', in *Autres écrits*, Seuil, Paris.

Leavis, F.R. (1936) *Revaluation: Tradition and Development in English Poetry*, Chatto & Windus, London.

Leavis, F.R. (1948) *The Great Tradition*, Chatto & Windus, London.

Leavis, F.R. (1952) *The Common Pursuit*, Chatto & Windus, London.

Levin, S. (1962) *Linguistic Structures in Poetry*, Mouton, The Hague.

Levin, S. (1971) 'The Conventions of Poetry', in S. Chatman (ed.), *Literary Style: A Symposium*, Oxford University Press, London.

Lodge, D. (ed.) (1972) *Twentieth Century Literary Criticism: A Reader*, Longman, London.

Lodge, D. (ed.) (1988) *Modern Criticism and Theory: A Reader*, Longman, London.

Lowell, A. (1915) 'Preface to *Some Imagist Poets*', in P. Jones (ed.) (1972), *Imagist Poetry*, Penguin, London.

Lowell, A. (1920) 'Some Musical Analogies in Modern Poetry', *Musical Quarterly*, 6: 127–57.

Lowes, J.L. ([1927]1959) *The Road to Xanadu: A Study in the Ways of the Imagination*, Vintage Books, New York.

Markham, E.A. (1984) *Human Rites: Selected Poetry 1970–1982*, Anvil Press Poetry, London.

Mayo, R. (1954) 'The Contemporaneity of the *Lyrical Ballads*', in A.R. Jones and W. Tydeman (eds) (1972), *Lyrical Ballads: A Selection of Critical Essays*, Macmillan, London.

Mehrotra, A.K. (2004) 'A Legend Springs', *Hindustan Times*, 9 October.

Morrison, B. (1980) *The Movement*, Oxford University Press, London.

Murray, D. (ed.) (1989) *Literary Theory and Poetry: Extending the Canon*, Batsford, London.

Nicholls, P. (1991) 'Difference Spreading: From Gertrude Stein to L-A-N-G-U-A-G-E Poetry', in A. Easthope and J.O. Thompson (eds), *Contemporary Poetry Meets Modern Theory*, University of Toronto Press, Toronto.

Olson, C. (1950) 'Projective Verse', in R. Creeley (ed.), *Selected Writings of Charles Olson*, New Directions, New York.

Pater, W. (1889) 'Style', in *Appreciations*, Macmillan, London.

Paulin, T. (1990) 'Into the Heart of Englishness', *Times Literary Supplement*, 20–26 July, pp. 779–80.

Plato (1888) *The Republic*, trans. B. Jowett, Clarendon Press, Oxford.

Pomorska, K. and Rudy, S. (eds) (1987) *Language in Literature*, Belknap, Cambridge, MA.

Pope, A. (1939–69) *The Twickenham Edition of the Poems of Alexander Pope*, 12 vols, ed. J. Butt, Methuen, London.

Pound, E. (1918) 'A Retrospect', in P. Faulkner (ed.) (1986), *A Modernist Reader*, Batsford, London.

Puttenham, G. (1589) *The Arte of English Poesie*, R. Field, London.

Ransom, J.C. (1937) 'Criticism Inc.', in Lodge, D. (ed.) (1972) *Twentieth Century Literary Criticism: A Reader*, Longman, London.

Rice, J. (1765) *An Introduction to the Art of Reading with Energy and Propriety*, London.

Richards, I.A. ([1924]1966) *Principles of Literary Criticism*, Kegan Paul, London.

Richards, I.A. ([1929]1964) *Practical Criticism*, Kegan Paul, London.

Richards, I.A. (1936) *The Philosophy of Rhetoric*, Oxford University Press, London.

Ricks, C. (1963) *Milton's Grand Style*, Oxford University Press, Oxford.

Riffaterre, M. (1966) 'Describing Poetic Structures: Two Approaches to Baudelaire's "Les Chats"', *Yale French Studies*, **36**(7): 200–42.

Said, E. (1978) *Orientalism*, Vintage Books, New York.

Saussure, de, F. ([1919]1959) *Course in General Linguistics*, trans. W. Baskin, New York, McGraw-Hill.

Shelley, P.B. (1819) *A Defence of Poetry*, in D. Wu (ed.) (1998), *Romanticism: An Anthology*, Blackwell, Oxford.

Sidney, P. (1595) *The Defence of Poesie*, T. Creede for William Ponsonby, London.

Southey, R. (1798) 'Review of William Wordsworth and S. T. Coleridge, '"Lyrical Ballads"', *Critical Review*, October, 24: 197–204.

Sprat, T. ([1667]1908) 'The History of the Royal Society', in J.E. Spingarm (ed.), *Critical Essays of the 17th Century*, Clarendon Press, Oxford.

Stillinger, J. (1971) *The Hoodwinking of Madelaine and Other Essays on Keats's Poems*, University of Illinois Press, Urbana, IL.

Symons, A. (1899) *The Symbolist Movement in Literature*, London.

Tolley, A.T. (1975) *The Poetry of the Thirties*, St Martin's Press, New York.

Tomlinson, C. (1957) 'The Middlebrow Muse', *Essays in Criticism*, 7: 208–17.

Walcott, D. (1974) 'The Muse in History', in J. Cook (ed.) (2004), *Poetry in Theory: An Anthology 1900–2000*, Blackwell, Oxford.

Wellek, R. (1937) 'Correspondence: Literary Criticism and Philosophy', *Scrutiny*, **6**(2): 195–6.

Werth, P. (1976) 'Roman Jakobson's Verbal Analysis of Poetry', *Journal of Linguistics*, 12: 21–73.

Wimsatt, W.K. Jr (1954) *The Verbal Icon: Studies in the Meaning of Poetry*, University of Kentucky Press, Lexington, KY.

Wimsatt, W.K. Jr and Beardsley, M.C. (1946) 'The Intentional Fallacy', in W.K. Wimsatt Jr (1954) *The Verbal Icon: Studies in the Meaning of Poetry*, University of Kentucky Press, Lexington, KY.

Wimsatt, W.K. Jr and Beardsley, M.C. (1949) 'The Affective Fallacy', in W.K. Wimsatt Jr (1954) *The Verbal Icon: Studies in the Meaning of Poetry*, University of Kentucky Press, Lexington, KY.

Wimsatt, W.K. and Brooks, C. (1957) *Romantic Criticism*, Routledge, London.

Wollheim, R. (1980) *Art and its Objects*, Faber, London.

Woodring, C. (1970) *Politics in English Romantic Poetry*, Harvard University Press, Cambridge, MA.

Wordsworth, W. (1974) *The Prose Works*, eds W.J. Owen and J.W. Smyser, Oxford University Press, Oxford.

Index

Abse, Dannie 259–61
Adcock, Fleur 199–200
Adorno, Theodor 259–60
Aldington, Richard 103
Ali, Agha Shahid 218–19
Amis, Kingsley 118
Aristotle 19, 20, 42, 53
Arnold, Matthew 8, 20, 71, 102, 94–8, 100, 125–7, 257
'Astra' 202
Auden, W.H. 12, 20, 78, 79, 115–17
Augustan poetry 67–78

Bakhtin, Mikhail 153
Barthes, Roland 22, 140–2, 148, 244
Beardsley, Monroe 127, 129, 160, 257
Berry, James 213–14, 219, 225, 226
Betjeman, John 208–10, 228
Bhatt, Sujatta 220–2
Blaine, Virginia 197
Blake, William 20, 79, 87–90, 104, 112, 118, 206, 232
Bradford, Richard 12, 15, 18, 65, 70, 139, 155, 156, 252
Breiner, L.A. 217
Brooks, Cleanth 20, 21, 24, 52, 98,100, 128, 129, 132, 145, 258
Brown, Laura 71, 76
Brown, Norman O. 162
Browning, Elizabeth Barrett 194–6
Browning, Robert 11, 57, 92, 97–9, 110, 128
Byron, George Gordon, Lord 83

Caudwell, Christopher 23
Cavendish, Margaret 188–9

Chomsky, Noam 216
Cixous, Hélène 193
Clough, Arthur Hugh 101
Coleridge, Samuel Taylor 9, 18, 20, 79, 81–9, 97, 102, 164–5, 173, 232, 233, 257
Collins, William 76
Conquest, Robert 118
Corman, Cid 109
Cowper, William 11
Creeley, Robert 109
Cronin, J. 217–18
Crozier, Andrew 250–4
Culler, Jonathan 22, 24, 137, 142, 146, 230, 238, 240–1
Cummings, E.E. 109–10, 120

Dabydeen, David 217–18
Das, Kamala 219–20
Davie, Donald 18, 71, 104, 118, 204–6
De Man, Paul 169–70
Derrida, Jacques 150, 165, 167–78
Donne, John 3, 9, 10, 11, 14, 15, 18, 21, 24, 25–31, 33, 35, 37, 38, 42, 56, 57–9, 61, 63, 68, 69, 77, 85, 97, 127, 131, 133, 135, 136, 160, 168, 175, 237, 238
Doolittle, Hilda ('H.D.') 19, 107, 196, 201
Double pattern 25–46
Drabble, Margaret 231
Dryden, John 8, 9, 65, 67, 68, 71, 94, 198
Duncan, Robert 109
Dunn, Douglas 225

Eagleton, Terry 22, 144–6, 230
Easthope, Antony 12, 76, 210, 211, 246
Eliot, T.S. 9, 11–12, 15, 17, 20, 38–9, 57–60, 62, 63, 94, 100, 102, 103, 110–13, 117, 118, 120, 126–7, 130, 131, 185, 198, 208, 228–30, 244, 245, 248, 257
Ellis, John 72–4
Empson, William 21, 128–9, 132, 135, 145, 170–1, 258
Enright, D.J. 118
Evaluation 228–55
Ewart, Gavin 239

Fainlight, Ruth 198–9, 200, 202, 203
Fenollosa, Ernest 104
Finch, Anne, Countess of Winchilsea 19, 191–3
Fish, Stanley 22, 140–5, 230, 238
Flint, F.S. 103, 106
Formalism 133–40
Forrest-Thompson, Veronica 146, 246–50
Freud, Sigmund 158–66
Frye, Northrop 148
Fyge, Sarah Egerton 191–2

Gender 182–204
Gilbert, Sandra and Gubar, Susan 185–6
Gilliland, Robert 75
Goethe 257
Goldsmith, Oliver 9, 76, 113
Gray, Thomas 9, 17, 76
Greenblatt, Stephen 150–3, 157
Gross, Harvey 105

Halle, Morris 134
Hardy, Thomas 92
Harrison, Tony 16, 17, 119, 205–8
Hartman, Geoffrey 165–6, 169–71
Hawkes, Terence 15, 146
Heaney, Seamus 20, 221–3

Herbert, George 56, 59, 60–4, 77, 97
Herbert, W.N. 225–6
Herrick, Robert 56, 62–4
Hill, Christopher 153–4
Hill, Geoffrey 119, 174, 175
Hillis-Miller, J. 169
Hobsbaum, Philip 237–8
Hollander, John 65,
Hopkins, Gerard Manley 92, 101–2, 104
Horace 53
Hulme, T.E. 106–7

Irigaray, Luce 201–2

Jacobus, Mary 193
Jakobson, Roman 18, 21, 43, 133–46, 154–9, 163, 185, 231
Jennings, Elizabeth 203
Johnson, Linton Kwesi 17–18, 216–17, 219, 225, 226
Johnson, Samuel 15, 20, 56–60, 62, 68, 77
Jordon, J.E. 79
Joseph, Jenny 203

Kant, I. 148, 257
Keats, John 7, 10, 15, 20, 83–4, 129–30, 136, 165, 170
Kenner, Hugh 104
Kristeva, Julia 163–6

Lacan, Jacques 23, 162–6, 201
Larkin, Philip 117–19, 206–9, 211, 226, 231, 235–7, 240, 242, 243, 253
Lawrence, D.H. 12, 17
Leavis, F.R. 76–7, 84, 131–2
Leonard, Tom 224–5
Levin, Samuel 137–8, 141
Lowell, Amy 19, 103–4, 196–7
Lowes, John Livingstone 86
Luckács, Georg 153

McCaffery, Steve 252

MacDiarmid, Hugh 17, 225
McGonagall, William 231–5, 238, 241, 242–3, 245
McGuckian, Medbh 4–5
Mahon, Derek 222–4
Mallarmé 257
Markham, Archie 204, 214–16, 219, 224, 226
Marvell, Andrew 56, 60–1, 77, 97, 113, 153–4, 182–5
Marxism 153–5
Mayo, Robert 80
Mehrotra, A.K. 219–20
Metre, style and versification 3–25
Mew, Charlotte 197–8
Milton, John 7, 8, 11, 16, 50, 64–6, 75, 81, 89, 92, 113, 139, 141, 186–9, 193, 198, 231, 256
Modernist poetry 102–23
Monroe, Harriet 19, 103, 196, 201
Moore, Marianne 19, 201
Morrison, Blake 118, 206, 209
Mzwakhe 217–18

New Criticism 125–33
New Historicism 150–8
Nicholls, P. 252

Olson, Charles 109–10, 119

Pater, Walter 97–8
Paulin, Tom 208
Penn Warren, Robert 20–1, 127
Philips, Katherine 187–8
Plath, Sylvia 203
Plato 19, 20, 42, 53
Pope, Alexander 7, 8, 9, 12–13, 20, 35–8, 67, 70, 71, 74, 90, 94, 137–8, 171
Postcolonialism and nationality 204–28
Poststructuralism 140–50
Pound, Ezra 12, 20, 102–8, 114, 117, 130, 146, 202, 246, 248, 251, 257

Propp, Vladimir 133
Prynne, J.H. 119, 246–9, 254
Psychoanalitic criticism 158–67
Puttenham, George 19, 52–3, 152

Quine, W.V. 146

Race 204–28
Ransom, J.C. 127–9, 131
Raine, Craig 5–6, 44, 119, 176–9
Reception theory and reader response criticism 140–50
Reid, Christopher 119, 179–80
Renaissance poetry 49–67
Rice, John 70
Richards, I.A. 13, 107, 112, 126–7, 131–2, 179
Ricks, Christopher 65, 138–40
Riffaterre, Michael 139–40, 243
Rodgers, W.R. 118
Romantic poetry 78–92
Rosetti, Christina 196–7

Said, Edward 212–13
Saussure, Ferdinand de 146–7, 150, 154–5, 157
Schiller 275
Shakespeare, William 7, 8, 9, 21, 49–56, 59, 62, 89, 94, 102, 136–41, 150–7, 185–7, 193, 231–2, 256
Shapcott, Jo 203
Shelley, Percy Bysshe 20, 84–5, 104
Shlovsky, Viktor 133
Sidney, Sir Philip 20, 53, 58, 152
Sitwell, Edith 120
Smith, Stevie 203
Snyder, Gary 109
Southey, Robert 79, 234
Spenser, Edmund 10, 15, 64–5, 255
Sprat, Thomas 68
Stein, Gertrude 19
Stevens, Wallace 248–50
Stevenson, Anne 203
Stillinger, Jack 130–1

Structuralism 133–40
Style (including metre and
    versification) 3–25
Swift, Jonathan 8, 9, 67, 70–1, 160–2
Swinburne, Algernon 92, 101
Symons, Arthur 257

Tate, Allen 127
Tatersal, Robert 71–2
Tennyson, Alfred Lord 8, 10, 18, 57,
    92–4, 197
Thomas, Dylan 13, 117–18, 120,
    225–6, 245–6, 252, 254
Thomas, R.S. 225–6
Thomson, James 11, 75–6, 81
Thribb, E.J. 238–42, 243–4
Tolley, A.T. 117
Tomlinson, Charles 119, 208
Traherne, Thomas 56

Vaughan, Henry 56, 77
Verlaine 257
Victorian poetry 92–102

Wain, John 118
Walcott, Derek 209–14, 215, 220

Watkins, Vernon 225
Wellek, René 132
Werth, Paul 231–2
Williams, Hugo 119
Williams, William Carlos 12, 17,
    32–5, 37, 38, 41, 42, 102, 103, 110,
    120, 144, 146, 175, 221, 235,
    239–43
Wimsatt, W.K. 21, 52, 98, 100, 127,
    129, 160, 257
Wittgenstein, Ludwig 148, 258, 261
Wollheim, Richard 29–32, 40
Woodring, Carl 79
Woolf, Virginia 112, 185–7, 197,
    200–3
Wordsworth, Dorothy 152–3
Wordsworth, William 8, 10, 13,
    17–20, 79–86, 87, 89, 90–1, 92, 97,
    98, 104, 105, 129, 131, 136, 148,
    152–3, 156, 166, 172–3, 179,
    233–4, 244
Wright, Hetty 190–1
Wroth, Lady Mary 188
Yeats, W.B. 18, 78, 115–16, 169, 185,
    208, 237–8